LINCOLN THE PRESIDENT

LAST FULL MEASURE

* * * *

THE LAST PORTRAIT

Taken by Alexander Gardner in Washington on April 10, 1865, the day after Appomattox and four days before the assassination.

Lincoln the President

LAST FULL MEASURE

J. G. Randall
and
Richard N. Current

UNIVERSITY OF ILLINOIS PRESS

URBANA AND CHICAGO

First Illinois paperback edition, 2000
© 1955, 1983 by James G. Thomas and Richard N. Current
Introduction © 1991 by Richard N. Current
Manufactured in the United States of America

Library of Congress Cataloging-in-Publication Data
Randall, J. G. (James Garfield), 1881-1953.
Lincoln the President. Last full measure / J. G. Randall and Richard N. Current ;
with an introduction by Richard N. Current.
p.   cm.
Reprint: Originally published as the 4th v. of the 4 v. work Lincoln the President.
Originally published: 1955.
Includes bibliographical references and index.
ISBN 0-252-01785-4 (cl. : alk. paper)
ISBN 0-252-06872-6 (pbk. : alk. paper)
1. Lincoln, Abraham, 1809-1865.
2. Presidents—United States—Biography.
3. United States—Politics and government—Civil War, 1861-1865.
I. Current, Richard Nelson.
II. Title.
E457.R212   2000
973.7'092—dc21   99-39598
[B]   CIP

1 2 3 4 5 C P 5 4 3 2 1

To Ruth and Rose

INTRODUCTION

AT THE TIME of his death on February 20, 1953, J. G. Randall stood out as the leading authority on the life and times of Abraham Lincoln. He had established his reputation with *Constitutional Problems under Lincoln* (1926; revised edition, 1951), *The Civil War and Reconstruction* (1937), and the first three volumes of a projected four-volume study *Lincoln the President* (1945, 1952). From 1920 to 1950 he had also provided inspiration and guidance for a large number of historians who gained their doctorates from the University of Illinois at Urbana-Champaign.

While at the height of his fame, Randall was beginning to be the target of certain critics, among them Louis M. Hacker, an associate professor of economics at Columbia University and a reformed Marxist. Writing in the July 1947 issue of *Fortune Magazine,* Hacker declared that the only hope for the postwar world, "beset by poverty and threatened by authoritarianism," lay in the "formula of liberty and equality." This formula, he said, was supported by the "great traditions of American history," properly understood. "For this reason," Hacker continued, "it is not an academic matter that a small company of historical scholars—for the most part professors of southern birth or training now teaching in midwestern universities—should seek to undermine the great libertarian tradition of the American Civil War. Following the lead of Professors J. G. Randall, Avery O. Craven, and W. B. Hesseltine (respectively of the Universities of Illinois, Chicago, and Wisconsin), they try to demonstrate that the Civil War—which gave birth to American industrial capitalism—was a tragic mistake."

These scholars, Hacker went on to say, also misrepresented Abraham Lincoln as an "anti-equalitarian" who had been "willing to accept the existence of a slave South." And they were unsympathetic with the Radical Republicans. But the Radicals, according to Hacker, were "equalitarians and economic nationalists" who made possible the rise of the United States as a great industrial power, and Lincoln was in basic agreement with them. Lincoln and the Radicals were the keepers of a tradition that Americans must maintain to assure "America's survival in an increasingly authoritarian world."

Other critics made charges similar to those of Hacker. Arthur M. Schlesinger, Jr., for one, accused Randall and like-minded historians of "historical sentimentalism" in the October 1949 issue of *Partisan Review*. Schlesinger presented what we might call the "logjam theory" of social progress. When a logjam occurs in lumbering, he said, we must blow up the pile with dynamite so as to get rid of the obstruction and enable the logs to move on. In much the same way, we must sometimes use violence to break up social evils or obstacles—such as Nazism in Germany and slavery in the United States—and thus allow society to continue with its moral advance.

There were elements of truth in the criticisms directed against Randall and other "revisionists." Not that he was exactly a man of "southern birth or training." He was born in Indianapolis in 1881 of such devotedly Republican parents that they named him for the "martyr president" who died that year—James Garfield. Still, he received Southern training of a sort when he studied for his doctorate at the University of Chicago under the direction of a Southerner, William E. Dodd. Later he married a Southerner, Ruth Painter, who was quite conscious of her Southern heritage and who assisted him in his writing. He dedicated his book *Lincoln and the South* (1946) to "the Beloved Rebel who abides with me."

Certainly Randall questioned both the inevitability and the desirability of the Civil War. He was (as he wrote in *The Civil War and Reconstruction*) "unprepared to go to the point of denying that the great American tragedy could have been avoided, supposing of course that something more of statesmanship, moderation, and understanding, and something less of professional patrioteering, slogan making, face-saving, political clamoring, and propaganda had existed on both sides." Randall also sympathized more with the Rebels than with the Radicals, and he emphasized the Southern and pro-Southern elements in Lincoln's character.

Similar revisionist attitudes influenced my education at the University of Wisconsin, where I was a student of Southern-born Hesseltine. He introduced me to Randall at the American Historical Convention that met in Washington, D.C., just after Christmas 1939. Randall, a great man in my sight, made an unforgettable impression on me by virtue of his geniality and unpretentiousness in the presence of a stranger who was a young and insignificant college instructor. He had a riddle for Hesseltine and me: Why can't Santa Claus and Mae West get into a telephone booth together? The answer: Because there ain't no Santa Claus. In response to a question about Carl Sandburg's just-published four-volume *Abraham Lincoln: The War Years*, Randall observed that, as a historian, Sandberg made a very good poet.

When my *Old Thad Stevens* appeared in 1942, Randall gave it a quite favorable review, which was to have been expected since the book, my dissertation, reflected the general Randall-Craven-Hesseltine revisionist outlook (not that Randall, Craven, and Hesseltine agreed with one another on every point). I did not have a chance to talk with Randall again, however, until 1946, when I visited the Urbana campus for a job interview and he served as my host. As a Woodrow Wilson admirer, he listened eagerly when I told him of having been present when Wilson stopped at a Colorado Springs railroad station in 1919. Randall introduced me to his wife as a young man who had seen Woodrow Wilson (whom Randall had never beheld).

Not till 1950 did I actually join the Illinois faculty. Randall had just retired, but I was in no sense his replacement. My specialty was to be American diplomatic history, not the Civil War and Reconstruction, which Randall had taught in a seminar and which Fred A. Shannon had been teaching and continued to teach as a lecture course. The Randalls were most hospitable, and I saw them from time to time as they lived on in their Urbana apartment, he working on his biography of Lincoln and she on her biography of Mary Todd Lincoln.

At the Randalls' one evening I happened to comment on Schlesinger's logjam theory. The idea seemed to me, I said, a glorification of violence. It reminded me of something Benito Mussolini's aviator son Bruno had said after a bombing raid on Ethiopian villages during the Italo-Ethiopian war of 1935–36. Bruno Mussolini remarked that once the bombs had exploded, the clouds of dust and debris rising and unfolding took forms as beautiful as flowers. My comment seemed to please Randall. He was strongly opposed to any glorification of war, though he had never been an isolationist (as Hesseltine had been, and so had I).

Afterward I came to believe that this comment of mine, more than anything else, led Randall to think me worthy of completing his Lincoln biography. I was no Lincoln scholar; I had never written a thing about Lincoln. At the time, I had under way a project in recent American diplomacy, a study of the statecraft of Henry L. Stimson. Nevertheless, when Randall died he left a note naming me as his second choice for a co-author to finish the fourth volume of *Lincoln the President.* His first choice was Allan Nevins, who declined the invitation. At the urging of my friend and colleague Frank Freidel, I readily accepted it.

The assignment turned out to be somewhat tougher than I had expected. Randall had written eight chapters, but he had prepared no list of chapters yet to be written and, indeed, no outline of any kind. Nor had he completed the research for the rest of the book, though he had accumulated a tremendous pile of notes on three-by-five cards, many of them the work of graduate students or other research assistants and quite a few lacking in legibility or in proper citation. Apparently he had laid out his chapters as he went along, one at a time, and had supplemented his stock of notes for each of them before going on to the next.

My task was, first, to find out what topics had been covered in the first three volumes and in the first eight chapters of the fourth. This was not easy since a number of themes had been picked up here and there and carried for varying lengths, then dropped. The next step for me was to plan additional chapters to fill out the story. That done, I had to analyze the existing notes and decide what supplementary notes would be needed. Finally, having rounded out the research, I tried to write in as close an imitation as I could of Randall's deliberate and rather ruminative style.

Not all reviewers considered the result an unqualified success. One of them, writing in the *New Yorker,* found evidence of a sad decline from Randall's standards in an embarrasing gaffe on my part. I had given the title of the play at Ford's Theater on that fatal night as *The Country Cousin;* every Lincoln buff in the country knew it was really

Our American Cousin. Still, most of the reviewers were complimentary enough, and the book was awarded the Bancroft Prize in 1956, though this was doubtless a tribute to *Lincoln the President* as a whole, not merely to the concluding volume of it.

In the third of a century that has passed since the book's original publication, historians have altered their view of Lincoln in important respects. Today few scholars would accept without qualification the strictures of such "counter-revisionists" as Hacker and Schlesinger, but still fewer would cling to an out-and-out, unrevised Randall-Craven-Hesseltine interpretation. Probably no one now would see quite so extreme an antagonism between Lincoln and the Radicals as Randall did. His own protégé David Herbert Donald led the way in reinterpreting the relationship between Lincoln and the Radicals. Certainly, if I were writing *Lincoln the President* in the 1990s I would do it in a somewhat different spirit from that of the 1950s. But so would Randall, most likely, if he were still alive. As the author of *The Civil War and Reconstruction*, he said of himself in 1937: "He has tried to avoid being unduly impressed by the mere newness of this or that historical contribution, and, while recognizing—indeed welcoming with keenest pleasure—the work of revisionists, he has at times suspected that some day the revisionists themselves may be revised."

Though *Lincoln the President: Last Full Measure* bears the marks of its time, it may still have much to offer the reader interested in Lincoln and the Civil War period.

PREFACE

AT THE TIME of his death, in early 1953, Professor Randall had finished about half of the manuscript for this, the fourth and final volume of his *Lincoln the President*. He had accumulated notes for most of the rest of the book, and he had made a series of trial lists of topics for the remaining chapters. Anticipating the end of his life, he had also indicated his preferences regarding the selection of an author to complete the work.

This honor having fallen to me, I have tried to carry on in his spirit and with his standards, yet I cannot claim to have succeeded in writing quite as he would have done. His mastery of the Lincoln subject was, of course, unique. Furthermore, he was able to hold in his mind the complex and subtle organization which he worked out for the biography as he went along, and he left on paper no outline for his successor to follow, except for the tentative jottings of chapter subjects. On one point he was explicit. "This biography," he noted, "knows only the living Lincoln." He did not intend to deal with the assassination or with the events following it.

The reader may be assured that the first eight chapters in this volume are "pure Randall." They were written and revised by him, and they stand as he left them, without any textual change. The only liberty I have taken with them has been to re-arrange the order slightly by moving from third to sixth the chapter entitled "Chase Is Willing." The last eight chapters are also in a real sense Professor Randall's, for they were written in the light of his interpretations and with the aid of his research. But I must assume the responsibility for the form they have finally taken.

I am sure that Professor Randall would desire here to thank again those many friends and helpers whom he acknowledged in the prefaces to his first and third volumes. I should like to express my personal indebtedness to several others whose aid and encouragement has been indispensable. I owe a great deal to various friends who happen to be authorities on the Civil War period, to William B. Hesseltine, Fred H. Harrington, T. Harry Williams, and Frank Freidel, and especially to Kenneth M. Stampp, who read and criticized my chapters. I owe a great deal also to Ruth Painter Randall, the foremost student of Mrs. Lincoln and the Lincoln family, who made me the beneficiary of her ripe wisdom; to Wayne C. Temple, who, as Professor Randall's research assistant and then mine, provided continuity for the project and who prepared the bibliography; and to my wife, Rose Bonar Current, who not only did most of my typing but also cheerfully put up with my preoccupation with Lincoln.

R. N. C.

CONTENTS

ILLUSTRATIONS

CHAPTER I

THE STATE OF THE UNION: LINCOLN'S PLAN OF RECONSTRUCTION

IN HIS annual message to Congress in December 1863, in fulfillment of that provision of the Constitution which requires that the President shall "give to the Congress Information of the State of the Union," Lincoln addressed himself to the question of reconstruction. He did not deal in quibbles or generalities, but came up with a plan. Anyone who knew Lincoln would have known that his design for a restored Union would not be hateful and vindictive. It would not rule out the very spirit of reunion. His view had never been narrowly sectional. Born in the Southern state of Kentucky of Virginia-born parents, moving thence to Indiana and Illinois, he was part of that transit of culture by which Southern characteristics, human types, and thought patterns had taken hold in the West and Northwest.

In New Salem, in the legislature at Vandalia, and in Springfield he had remained in touch with men of Southern birth. His marriage into a cultured Kentucky family and his visits to Lexington, his wife's home town, had enabled him to understand the Southern—though here we do not mean the proslavery—viewpoint. (Among the Todd connections had been those who believed in gradual emancipation.) Southern understanding had also been assisted by his political career as a Whig, which greatly exceeded in duration his career as a Republican. His Whig friends had included good Southerners, and his Whig approach had been the opposite of sectional. When political alignments changed with the devil of discord in the 1850's, Lincoln had found no satisfaction in the formation of a sectional party. He obviously disliked being unwhigged. Though he was antislavery and of course antisecession, he was never anti-Southern.

1

I

One can pinpoint the launching of his plan in the month of December 1863, but back of that one must remember that Lincoln's earlier utterances bespoke a preference for conciliatory adjustment. In his Cooper Union speech of February 1860 he had stressed the wrong of slavery and had opposed its extension, but in doing so he had appealed to "the old policy of the fathers" and had strongly emphasized the unwisdom of doing anything "through passion and ill temper." He considered it "exceedingly desirable that all parts of this great Confederacy [the United States] shall be at peace, and in harmony with one another."

He had said in his first inaugural: "Physically we cannot separate," and on various later occasions he had returned to this theme. As he wrote in his annual message of December 1, 1862, to "separate our common country into two nations" was to him intolerable. The people of the greater interior, he urged, "will not ask where a line of separation shall be, but will vow rather that there shall be no such line." The situation as he saw it, in "all its adaptations and aptitudes . . . demands union and abhors separation." It would ere long "force reunion, however much of blood and treasure the separation might cost."

Thus Lincoln's fundamental adherence to an unbroken Union was the point of departure for his reconstruction program. One could find, in the earlier part of his presidency, other indications bearing upon restoration. In an important letter to General G. F. Shepley, military governor of Louisiana (November 21, 1862), he advised strongly against what came to be known as "carpetbagger" policy. He did not want "Federal officers not citizens of Louisiana" to seek election as congressmen from that state. On this his language was emphatic: he considered it "disgusting and outrageous" to "send a parcel of Northern men here as representatives, elected, as it would be understood (and perhaps really so), at the point of the bayonet." [1]

While in this manner disallowing the idea of importing Northern politicians into a Southern state as pseudo-representatives in Congress, he also repudiated the opposite policy of Fernando Wood of

---

[1] *Works*, VIII, 79.

New York which would accept Southerners in Congress prematurely
—that is, before resistance to the United States was ended and loyalty
assured.[2] To mention another point, he had, in considering the formation of the new state of West Virginia, expressed his view that, in
the pattern of the Union, only those who were loyal—i. e., who adhered to the United States—could be regarded as competent voters.

To these points—the indispensable Union, loyalty, and the unwisdom of carpetbaggism—one must add Lincoln's fundamental
policy of emancipation and his non-vindictiveness in the matter of
confiscation. Taking these factors together the historian has, before
December 1863, the ingredients of the President's reunion program.

In announcing that program on December 8, 1863, Lincoln issued
two documents: a Proclamation, and a message to Congress. In his
proclamation, having the force of law, he set forth the conditions of
a general pardon and the terms of restoring a Southern state to the
Union. In his accompanying message he commented upon his plan,
telling more fully what was in his mind and defending his course by
reason and persuasion. The offer of pardon (with stated exceptions)
and restoration of rights (except as to slaves) was given to anyone in
a seceded state who would take and keep a simple oath. Phrased by
the President, this oath constituted a solemn pledge to support the
Constitution of the United States "and the union of the States there-
under." The oath-taker would also swear to abide by and faithfully
support all the acts of Congress and all the proclamations of the President relating to slaves unless repealed, modified, or declared void by
the Supreme Court.[3]

So much for the oath, with pardon and restoration of rights. The
next element in the proclamation was re-establishment of a state government. This again was intended to be simple and practical. Whenever, in a seceded state, a number not less than one-tenth of those
voting in 1860, should re-establish a republican government,[4] such a

---

[2] *Ibid.*, VIII, 142 ff. [3] *Ibid.*, IX, 218–223.

[4] A writer need not be considered facetious if he calls attention to the lower case *r* in
"republican." In all the tremendous efforts of those who disagreed with Lincoln the
partisan motive was a constant factor; with such a man as Thaddeus Stevens, by his own
admission, it was a controlling motive. In insisting that the state government be "republican" Lincoln had in mind that provision of the Constitution (article IV, section 4) which
guaranteed to every state a republican—i. e., a non-monarchical or non-dictatorial—type
of government, and to that end provided Federal protection for the state against invasion
or domestic violence.

government, according to Lincoln's proclamation, would "be recognized as the true government of the State."

Turning from the proclamation to the simultaneous message, we find Lincoln setting forth the reasons and conditions of his policy. In this he addressed himself to various questions that he knew would arise. What about the oath? Why the ten per cent? What about state laws touching freedmen? Why preserve the state as it was? How about state boundaries? Why was the President assuming the power of reconstruction as an executive function? He started with the obvious unwisdom and absurdity of protecting a revived state government constructed from the disloyal element. It was essential to have a test "so as to build only from the sound." He wanted that test to be liberal and to include "sworn recantation of . . . former unsoundness." As for laws and proclamations against slavery, they could not be abandoned. Retaining so far as possible the existing political framework in the state, as Lincoln saw it, would "save labor, and avoid confusion." He did not, of course, mean by this that the system in any state was to be permanently frozen for the future in unchangeable form.

Lincoln gave attention at this point to a practical problem. In some states those ready for resumption of Union status might remain inactive for want of a plan of action. They needed a "rallying point." Potential unionism, or friendly Union sentiment, was not enough; unionist accomplishment must become actual. If a few should agree on a plan they might not know that it would be approved by the Federal government. To state the kind of plan for which acceptance could be assured, was an essential step; it would mean that those ready for restoration would be induced "to act sooner than they otherwise would." [5]

As to the specific formula of ten per cent, he said little; yet his simile of a rallying point held the key. The important object was to get a movement started. Acceptance of an initial electorate of ten per cent did not signify that Lincoln was favoring minority rule. It was not his thought that any minority should usurp the rights of the majority. Within his pattern of loyalty, Union, non-dictatorial government, and emancipation, he was putting the formation of any new state government in the hands of the loyal people of the state.

---

[5] For the message, see *Works*, IX, 224–252.

Government by the people was to him fundamental, but as a practical matter some loyal nucleus was essential; else time would pass, precious time, and nothing would be done.

There was precedent for the setting in motion of a popular government by a minority. That had been done in 1787–88 in the launching of the Constitution in which ratifying delegates had been chosen by a minor fraction of the population. Later Lincoln was to use a figure of speech to explain his meaning—the egg and the fowl.[6] One would sooner have the fowl by hatching the egg than by smashing it. It was as if majority rights were being temporarily administered in trust by a minor portion of the electorate. To administer them in trust was to keep them intact till a loyal majority could take over. The whole situation, of course, was abnormal. All beginnings, or re-beginnings, are difficult, especially rebuilding after or during a war, taking up the shattered pieces of a disrupted social and political order and putting them partly together so that ultimately they could be fully restored. Lincoln was willing to accept informality in order to accomplish the main practical purpose which he considered imperative. He was unwilling to throw away the cause while futilely waiting for perfection. Reconstruction, as he saw it, was a matter of stages. His "ten per cent plan" was easy to criticize. Yet it was the first step. As for those who were thinking up involved theories, looking for some unattainable formula of perfection, it was years before they were to take steps, and the steps they then took were to prove unworkable.

Lincoln would take his first step in the most available manner. A few states could be rebuilt and restored. This was to be done during the war, indeed as an important factor in waging and ending the war. Let people see that Lincoln did not intend an ugly and vindictive policy, and Southerners themselves, the President hoped, would set their own houses in order. Let one or two states do this, they would serve as examples for others as the armies advanced and national authority was extended. In time of war, prepare for peace, was Lincoln's thought. On the other hand, let the months pass, and let the Southern people witness only carpetbaggism, Federal occupation, and a repressive attitude as to the future, and victory itself would lose much of its value. It was Lincoln's intent that policy associated with

---

6 Speech of April 11, 1865, *ibid.*, XI, 91.

victory should envisage willing loyalty while leaving free play for self government.

II

Lincoln's plan of reunion was greeted with a mixed response. The Washington *Chronicle,* regarded as a Lincoln "organ," naturally praised the President's announcement. The editor noted that the President gave out his statement in a setting of military and naval success: our armies victorious, our navy in control of Southern coasts, our cause strengthened by increased friendship of foreign nations. His generous offering of pardon was interpreted by the *Chronicle* as evidence of his kindness and sympathy toward the people of the South. The editor concluded: "Viewing his whole Administration and what he has done . . . we thank God that Abraham Lincoln is President of the United States." [1]

An English gentleman friendly to the United States wrote: "We have just received the news of President Lincoln's message, accompanied with his amnesty; also the message of . . . [Jefferson] Davis. The two documents coming together are doing an immense amount of good for the right cause." [2]

It is doubtful how many readers made the comparison of the two messages, but those who did must have noted a marked difference of tone. In general spirit Lincoln's message of December 8, 1863, was notable for its absence of war-engendered hatred toward the South, ending as it did on the note of "freedom disenthralled." In appealing for reunion the President was holding out the hand for genuine renewal of friendly relations. This attitude, however, was not reciprocated by the Confederate President. Though perhaps the comparison should not be overstressed, one finds quite the opposite note in the message (December 7, 1863) of Jefferson Davis to his Congress. After a depressing account of Confederate military reverses and of discouraging condition in foreign affairs and finance, the Southern Executive threw in bitter denunciations of the "barbarous policy" and "savage ferocity" of "our enemies." At one point he referred to them as "hardened by crime." (There were, of course, those in the

---

[1] Washington *Daily Morning Chronicle,* Dec. 10, 1863, p. 2, cc. 1–2.
[2] Frederick Edge to H. W. Bellows, London, Dec. 22, 1863, Bellows MSS.

North, though not Lincoln, who were saying equally hateful things of the South.) That enemy, wrote Davis, refused "even to listen to proposals . . . [of peace] of recognizing the impassable gulf which divides us." [3] This expression, the orthodox attitude of Confederate officialdom, must be remembered along with Lincoln's other problems. If anyone doubted why the President, in his reconstruction plans and his wariness toward "peace negotiations," realized the hopelessness of expecting high Confederate officials to consider a peaceable restoration of the Union, the reading of this message of Davis would have been enough to dispel such doubt. As was to be expected, this same attitude was reflected in the Congress at Richmond. When Lincoln's restoration plan came up for discussion in that Congress one member referred to "the imbecile and unprincipled usurper who now sits enthroned upon the ruins of constitutional liberty in Washington City," while another speaker suggested that silent contempt was the only treatment for "that miserable and contemptable despot, Lincoln." At about the same time the President's plan was denounced and spurned in the Virginia legislature as "degrading to freemen." [4]

Greeley's *Tribune* was favorable, expressing the view that the President answered the question as to how the "rebels" could "return to loyalty and fidelity"; this would "break the back of the Rebellion." [5] The Washington correspondent of the *Tribune* indulged in superlatives, remarking that "no President's Message since George Washington retired into private life has given such general satisfaction as that sent to Congress by Abraham Lincoln to-day." [6] The New York *Times* remarked apropos of the message that 1863 had become "the most eventful [year] since the Government began." "The process of reconstruction," said the *Times*, "is simple and yet perfectly effective." [7] It was not merely a plan, according to the *Times;* it was a program which "finds us already thoroughly committed to it in every essential particular." It "challenges at once the acquiescence of all truly loyal men." [8] "With regard to the fundamental is-

[3] Journal of the [Confederate] Congress (*Sen. Doc. No. 234* [U.S.], 58 Cong., 2 sess., 435–451, esp. 450–451.

[4] Moore, *Rebellion Record* (Diary), VIII, 21, 24.

[5] New York *Tribune*, Dec. 10, 1863 (editorial), p. 6, c. 2.

[6] *Ibid.*, Dec. 10, 1863, p. 1, c. 2.

[7] New York *Times*, Dec. 10, 1863, p. 6, c. 2.   [8] *Ibid.*, Dec. 11, 1863, p. 4, c. 2.

sues . . . ," writes Ralph R. Fahrney, "the sympathies of Greeley were with Lincoln . . . ." [9]

Some of the newspaper language, however, was stormy and vehement. Radical papers attacked the President and impetus was given to the movement in the Republican party which was already opposing his renomination. Conspicuous among these radical organs in New York were the *Independent* and the *Evening Post*. From an opposite partisan viewpoint the President's message was denounced by such New York papers as the *Journal of Commerce,* the *Daily News,* and the *World*. These papers, rather inconsistently, assailed both Lincoln and the radicals. Friendliness to the South on the part of these journals did not signify support of Lincoln's restoration policy or emancipation. Their attitude was a good deal like that of Vallandigham. In the *World* Lincoln's scheme was held to be "preposterous," without authority, and "the very height of absurdity." [10] The *Herald,* commenting on the ten per cent of the "rebellious" states, did not think there were "that many good men there." According to this widely circulating newspaper of Bennett, "Mr. Lincoln's plan will be a failure." This was the immediate reaction under date of December 9, 1863. Several weeks later, having grown in vituperation, the *Herald,* on January 31, 1864, denounced the plan as pettifogging, flimsy and incoherent.

It was obvious from the start that the President's plan would not have smooth sailing, but on several fronts steps were taken to make it known and put it into operation. Army officers were instructed to take copies of the proclamation and distribute them so as to reach soldiers and inhabitants within Confederate-held territory. Aid and protection was to be extended to those who would declare loyalty. On the occasion of raids into enemy territory a number of men were to be detailed "for the purpose of distributing the proclamation broadcast among rebel soldiers and people, and in the highways and byways." [11]

This matter of the handbills occasioned some correspondence across the lines between Confederate and Union officers. On the

[9] Ralph R. Fahrney, *Horace Greeley and the Tribune in the Civil War,* 175.

[10] Clipping from New York *World,* in Washington *Daily Chronicle,* Dec. 12, 1863, p. 2, c. 6.

[11] R. A. Alger to General Butler, Fort Monroe, Feb. 23, 1864, *Private and Official Correspondence of B. F. Butler,* III, 463–464.

Confederate side Longstreet in eastern Tennessee protested against the handbills, remarking that those who would desert under the promise held out would not be "men of character and standing." The Union cause, he urged, could not gain by the acceptance of such men. A complication in this connection was that going over to the Union side might turn out in some cases to be a mere trick. Union outposts and pickets reported that Confederate officers and men turned up as Union soldiers; in such cases, spying being suspected, the death penalty was enforced.[12]

On the legal or prosecuting front the effect of the pardon policy was explained in an instruction from the office of the attorney general of the United States to district attorneys throughout the country. It was made known that the "President's pardon of a person guilty of . . . rebellion . . . [would] relieve that person for the penalties" of that crime. District attorneys were therefore directed to discontinue proceedings in United States courts whenever the accused should take the oath and comply with the stated conditions.[13]

Such a statement would make it appear that the transition from a kind of rebellious guilt to complete relief from penalty was easy, automatic, and practically instantaneous, but it soon became evident that the matter was not so simple as that. Lincoln found that he had to make a distinction in applying his offer of pardon in return for the oath. What about Confederate soldiers held by Union authorities as prisoners of war? On this point the President issued a later clarifying proclamation, declaring that his pardon did not apply to men in custody or on parole as prisoners of war. It did apply, he explained, to persons yet at large (i. e., free from arrest) who would come forward and take the oath. It was also explained that those excluded from the general amnesty could apply to the President for clemency and their cases would have due consideration.[14]

What it amounted to was that Lincoln himself was generous in the application of his pardon both to soldiers and civilians, and the same was true of the attorney general's office; but army officers were not prepared, in return for the oath, to deliver prisoners nor give up pen-

---

12 Moore, *Rebellion Record* (Doc.), VIII, 296–297.
13 *Ibid.*, (Docs.), VIII, 383–384.
14 Proclamation about amnesty, Mar. 26, 1864, *Works*, X, 58–60.

alties for offences of various sorts, such as violation of rules of war. No one statement applies. Some enemies held as prisoners, on establishing loyalty, were discharged from custody by the President on assurance of good faith by three congressmen.[15] This showed, as in many cases, that Lincoln's general rules were subject to individual exceptions. In numerous instances Lincoln would write out in his own hand a slip of paper similar to the following, which was addressed to the secretary of war on March 15, 1864: "I shall be personally obliged if you will allow Silas H. Highley to take the oath of Dec. 8. and be discharged." [16] Where the President did not wish his pardon of a particular man to be taken as a precedent, he would make that clear. For example, in ordering the discharge (on taking the oath) of a prisoner held at Johnson's Island, he pointed out that this was a special case, not a precedent; the man had voluntarily quitted the enemy service, and was subject to fits.[17]

III

With a scorn of fine-spun theories and an urgent wish to get ahead with the job of reconstruction, the President proceeded, so far as possible, to make restoration a reality wherever, and as soon as, any reasonable opportunity offered in the seceded South. He was notably a patient man, but there was a touch of impatience when dilatoriness, confusion of authority, political intrigue, radical opposition, or mere inertia seemed to obstruct his program or threaten it with failure.

In Lincoln's plan of reconstruction the effort in Louisiana was of vital importance. From the time that New Orleans fell to Union arms on May 1, 1862, the President saw, in terms of Federal occupation, an early opportunity to make reconstruction a wartime reality. Let Louisiana be restored, he thought, let this be done in a reasonable manner with Washington approval, let it be seen that the plan

---

[15] Angle, *New Letters and Papers of Lincoln*, 346.

[16] *Ibid.*, 345. Lincoln collectors have long been familiar with the frequency, in the autograph market, of brief Lincoln originals—notes or endorsements—with the wording: "Let . . . [this man or men] take the oath of Dec. 8, 1863, and be discharged." Hundreds of such autographs—many of them shamefully clipped—i. e., robbed—from war department files, have become the possession of Lincoln collectors; it has been a method of obtaining a Lincoln autograph cheaply.

[17] Angle, *New Letters and Papers*, 350.

would work, and other states would follow. To go into all the details of the Louisiana story, treating its complications month by month, would be a tedious process. These complications were numerous and vexatious: use of military power, attention of the same Union leader to military operations and govermental affairs, civil-and-military conflicts, cliquism, theories as to whether secession had ever really taken the state out of the Union, lack of co-operation between Federal leaders, doubts as to how slavery should be eliminated, transitional labor problems in the shift from bondage to freedom, social differences between the planter class and the common people, need for a promptness that was not forthcoming, constitution re-making in an era of revolution, and the depressing shadow of a great question mark as to what Congress would do or prevent from being done. It will be convenient to reduce this elaborate Louisiana story to four successive phases:

First Phase in Louisiana: Military Rule under Butler and Shepley. The first phase was that of army rule under General B. F. Butler. Immediate adjustments were of course necessary from the moment when New Orleans, largest city of the South, together with a large portion of Louisiana, came under the Union flag. Governmental officials in the occupied region, including merely local functionaries in city or parish, were now under Federal authority—not in terms of any deliberation as to procedure by Congress or the Executive, but simply by the fortunes of war. Where men in local office stood ready to co-operate with the occupying power, they had a good chance of being retained; if unco-operative, they were dismissed. For a time the mayor and council of New Orleans were continued in office subject to General Butler's authority with some relaxation of military pressure, but this situation did not last long. Within a month the mayor was deposed and imprisoned, and George F. Shepley, acting closely with Butler, took over mayoral functions. Then in June 1862 Shepley became military governor of Louisiana; soon afterward he had the rank of brigadier general.

This was military occupation, and of course it was intended only as a temporary condition. It amounted to martial law which has been defined as the will of the military commander; this meant that the sometimes eccentric will of General Butler was paramount. If nothing offered in the form of a re-established and recognized state government, the abnormal and temporary regime would continue. The distinction in the matter of authority between Butler and Shepley seems never to have been adequately worked out. It might have been supposed that army matters belonged to Butler and civil-government affairs to Shepley, but it was not so simple as that. Butler was not only the more famous—"as much a news item as any man except Lincoln" [1]—he was also the more domineering. In power he was ahead of Shepley and he had the military forces at his disposal. Louisiana was in fact under Butler, government and all; it was his regime, and it included such unfortunate acts of capricious severity or *gaucherie* as his "woman order" and his wanton execution of Mumford. [2]

It thus came about that Federal rule in Louisiana, the first step toward what Lincoln regarded as restoration of loyalty and normal conditions, got off to a bad start. [3] The name of "Beast Butler" became a hated by-word in the South, with far-reaching complications in Federal-Confederate relations; [4] it came as a considerable relief when President Lincoln removed him from his Louisiana command on December 16, 1862. His successor, as commander of the military forces stationed in Louisiana and Texas, was Major General Nathaniel P. Banks, with Shepley retaining his position as "military governor of Louisiana."

Under Butler little or nothing had been done toward wartime governmental reconstruction in the state, but this problem, dear to Lincoln's heart, was tackled under the President's urging during the Banks-Shepley regime.

A careful study of these matters reveals a problem as to top executive leadership locally applied—that is, the difficulty of achieving effectiveness in a particular area in terms of policy developed in Washington. Lincoln was President; he was the Chief; he made the appointments and formed decisions; presumably he would choose men to put his policies into operation. Yet so unpredictable were events and so complicated was the situation as to politicians' maneuvers that those who supposedly should have carried out Lincoln's

---

1 Carl Russell Fish, *Dic. of Am. Biog.*, III, 357.   2 *Lincoln the President*, III.

3 Randall, *Constitutional Problems Under Lincoln*, chap. x.

4 These complications were especially bothersome as to threats of retaliation, denial of honorable officer status to Butler, exchange of prisoners, and the like.

purposes promoted their own factional and contrary schemes in such manner as to jeopardize the President's best laid plans.

George F. Shepley was a case in point. He had been a Maine Democrat, an appointee of Pierce and later of Buchanan as district attorney, and a supporter of Douglas in 1860. These factors in his background did not militate against him in Lincoln's view—the President often appointed Democrats—nor should they have been a drawback to successful service in Louisiana's reconstruction. There was, however, the further fact that Shepley became a Butlerite and a radical; remaining after Butler's removal, he played the radical game at a time when it was hoped that a more Lincolnian policy would be inaugurated. Thus Shepley stood as an obstacle to Lincoln's efforts to allay factionalism and to promote speedy and liberal restoration.

Unsatisfactory though this Butler-Shepley period was, Lincoln used it as best he could to push ahead the program of civil reconstruction in Louisiana. "I wish elections for congressmen to take place in Louisiana," he wrote to Shepley on November 21, 1862. He wanted it to be "a movement of the people . . . , and not a movement of our military and quasi-military authorities there." The President recognized that there were difficulties as to state law, but said: "These knots must be cut, the main object being to get an expression of the people." If necessary, Lincoln wanted Shepley to start proceedings. He did not want a day wasted. "Fix a day [he wrote] for an election in all the districts, and have it held in as many places as you can." [5]

Toward the end of the Butler-Shepley period an election was held within the Union lines on December 3, 1862, for members of Congress from Louisiana. Two men of different outlook, were elected: B. F. Flanders from New Hampshire, who was to become an instrument of the radical faction; and Michael Hahn, a citizen of Louisiana born in Bavaria, who was more in tune with Lincoln's purposes. When the question of admitting these gentlemen as members of the House of Representatives was brought before that body (February 9, 1863) a species of dog fight ensued, a forerunner of the rough treatment in store for Lincoln's whole reunion program. Few were ready for frontal attack and sidestepping was more in evidence; the result was confusion, unrelated motions, and postponement. Finally, on

[5] *Works*, VIII, 80–81.

February 17, 1863, the House voted, 92 to 44, to seat Flanders and Hahn.[6] By that time that particular Congress, the Thirty-Seventh, was about to pass out of existence.

Second Phase: Shepley and Durant versus Banks. In the next phase, while Banks was in top command in Louisiana with Shepley as military governor—i. e., governor as to civil affairs under military authority—certain groups in the state got to work, though at cross purposes, to seize control of the process of state remaking. It turned out to be a period of bickering and futility, a time of bitter disappointment to the President. Taking over the rebuilding task and attempting to do it in his own way, Governor Shepley proceeded to make a registry of voters, appointing T. J. Durant, a radical like himself, as commissioner of registration. An oath of allegiance was required (this was before the presidentially prescribed oath of December 8, 1863) and the registration of whites who would take the oath was ordered. It was Durant's idea that ten loyal men in a parish, if no more could be registered, would be a sufficient basis for an election. This was a period when Banks was preoccupied with military command in the Port Hudson and Texas areas, while Shepley was also absent from Louisiana, spending a large part of the summer of 1863 in Washington. Lincoln approved the Shepley-Durant registration and wanted it pushed.

Then, with a kind of fateful contrariness, the reconstruction movement, registry and all, was brought to a standstill. Provoked at the slowness of proceedings, Lincoln wrote to Banks on November 5, 1863. Mentioning the long delay, he said: "This disappoints me bitterly." Lose no time, was the President's injunction. "I wish him [Shepley] . . . to go to work and give me a tangible nucleus which the remainder of the State may rally around as fast as it can . . . . Time is important." Lincoln feared that disloyal men would "preoccupy the ground" and set up a government repudiating emancipation, in which case he could not recognize or sustain their work. He added: "This government in such an attitude would be a house divided against itself." [7]

What Lincoln had in mind was that so-called Louisiana "conserva-

---

[6] *Cong. Globe,* 37 Cong., 3 sess., 1036. The end of the Thirty-Seventh Congress came on March 3, 1863.

[7] *Works,* IX, 200–201.

tives," representing the proslavery planter class, were already organizing with a view to setting in motion the wheels of state government under the old Louisiana constitution of 1853 which recognized slavery and which was in other respects unsatisfactory. Lincoln wanted Union men to "eschew cliquism, and, each yielding something . . . , all work together." "It is a time now," he urged, "for real patriots to rise above all this." [8]

The President was trying to keep himself in the background, to avoid seeming to dictate, and to let things work themselves out as a Louisiana movement. Yet he soon found that a jurisdictional dispute or confusion as to control was spoiling everything. Shepley as military governor and Durant, his appointee, were claiming "that they were exclusively charged with the work of reconstruction in Louisiana," while Banks had "not felt authorized to interfere" with them. In a letter of December 16, 1863, Banks advised the President that he was "only in partial command," adding: "There are not less than *four* distinct governments here claiming . . . independent powers based upon instructions received directly from Washington, and recognizing no other authority than their own."

Judging by the context, the "four . . . governments" were the system of United States courts, the municipal government of New Orleans, the well-knit corps of treasury officials (radical, pro-Chase, and at cross purposes with Lincoln), and the authority of Shepley, who as "military governor" dealt with many matters of civil organization. In addition there was, of course, the army under Banks, but at the time that general was referring to ursurping influences that were working against him. The full story of this confused situation in Louisiana is too elaborate for treatment here, but Lincoln's intense distress because of all this lagging and (as he thought) wrong direction of reconstruction is a factor that cannot be overlooked. [9]

Though this unfortunate situation was due in large part to the activities of radical groups, another factor may have been a bit of inadvertence on the part of the burdened President: he had supposed all the time that Banks was in chief command but had not made that point sufficiently clear. He now wrote a strong letter to Banks

[8] *Ibid.*, IX, 257.

[9] On this point the author has benefited from the generous assistance of Professor Fred H. Harrington, biographer of Banks. For Banks's letter to Lincoln, Dec. 16, 1863, see R. T. L. Coll., 28710–16.

(December 24, 1863) with a fourfold repetition of the main theme: You are master. The President was seriously annoyed at the frustration and delay. Shepley, he wrote, was to "assist" Banks, not to "thwart" him. The desirable object, of course, was to have unity among pro-Union men and leaders, but a serious obstacle to such unity was the attitude of Shepley and his considerable faction. It became increasingly apparent that these radicals were unwilling to co-operate with the man whom Lincoln had placed in chief authority and whom he had plainly designated as "master." Treating delay and factionalism as if things of the past, Lincoln wrote to Banks: "give us a free State reorganization of Louisiana in the shortest possible time." The general was to do this while still conducting his military operation in Texas.[10] For getting ahead with the work, it was Banks's idea that the radicals—the Shepley-Durant element—should be relieved of all functions pertaining to reconstruction.[11]

Third Phase: The Louisiana Constitution of 1864. Under Lincoln's spurring Banks went into action. In January and February of 1864 he issued proclamations for two kinds of elections: an election for governor under the old Louisiana constitution of 1853, and an election of delegates to a convention to make a new state constitution.[12] In his proclamations, copies of which he sent to the President, Banks declared that officials then to be chosen were to govern unless they tried to change Federal statutes as to slavery. Voters were required to take the oath of allegiance to the United States.

Lincoln continued to prod and encourage. On the constructing of a free-state government he considered the words "can and will" exceedingly "precious." Proceed "with all possible dispatch," wrote the President. "Frame orders, and fix times and places for this and that . . . ."[13] Recognition of the death of slavery in Louisiana was causing less difficulty than might have been expected. While the planter class wanted to keep the institution, they were in the minority; the majority of the people were ready to accept emancipation. In doing so they preferred to treat abolition of the institution simply as a *fait accompli*, an unavoidable effect of the war. It was as if many of them wanted simply to look the other way and let the institution

---

[10] *Works*, IX, 273–274.
[11] Harrington, *Fighting Politician: Major General N. P. Banks*, 143.
[12] *Ibid.*, 144.   [13] *Works*, IX, 282–283.

die. Banks reported: "Not a word is heard from any one in favor of a restoration of slavery, and no objection is made to the free state basis upon which the election is based." [14]

Both of the elections were a success from the standpoint of Banks and of Lincoln. Not that Lincoln considered the outcome perfect, but the whole point of Lincoln's policy was that he was not expecting perfection. He wanted steps to be taken, a "free" government set up; modifications and improvements could come later. The vote for state officials was held on February 22, 1864. In a total of 11,411 votes (over a fourth of the normal peacetime vote of Louisiana) Michael Hahn, the moderate Union candidate acceptable to Banks and Lincoln, received 6183 votes and was elected; Flanders, candidate of the anti-Banks radical element, received 2232 votes; J. Q. A. Fellows, nominated by the proslavery conservatives, received the disturbingly large vote of 2996.[15]

Banks was using the psychology of significant dates. The election was on Washington's birthday; the inauguration of Hahn as governor, on March 4, 1864. There were imposing ceremonies for the inauguration which was described as a "magnificent" and enthusiastic demonstration of popular interest; it was reported by Banks that eight thousand public school children participated and that 50,000 people were present.

Amid all this gratification, however, a discordant note was struck. The radicals were organizing solidly to oppose and obstruct the reorganized government, and one of them, T. L. Durant, employed in the treasury department besides being a part of Shepley's machine as already noticed, wrote in dissatisfied mood to Secretary Chase. Casting a sarcastic slur at the "gorgeous pageantry" of the Hahn inauguration, the "stupid starers" and "loud huzzahers" of yesterday, he deplored the whole movement. Those promoting the Banks-Hahn reorganization, he reported, had muzzled the press, intimidated office holders, and debauched the voters.[16] On the same day George S. Denison, an official of the treasury department with important duties as collector in Louisiana, wrote to Chase that both of the defeated

---

14 Banks to Lincoln, New Orleans, Jan. 22, 1864, R. T. L. Coll., 29710–2.

15 Detailed returns of the Louisiana election are found in Reports to Lincoln: R. T. L. Coll., 30770. See also Harrington, 144; Nicolay and Hay, *Lincoln*, VIII, 432.

16 Thomas L. Durant to S. P. Chase, New Orleans, March 5, 1864, Chase MSS., Lib. of Cong.

factions (Flanders of the radicals and Fellows of the "proslavery" element) were forming a "coalition" to oust Hahn.[17]

At this point President Lincoln invested Hahn with the powers of civil government which had been temporarily entrusted to the presidentially appointed Shepley. Since the people had participated in this choice of governor, albeit imperfectly because of war, Lincoln could feel that the republican processes of civil government had been given a considerable impulse.

Next came the problem of constitution remaking. By Bank's proclamation an election was held on March 28, 1864, by which delegates were chosen (not a distinguished lot, but they represented the people rather than officials or politicians) to form a new instrument of government. From April to July the convention labored. Among its main acts was to abolish slavery by a vote of seventy to sixteen. Negro suffrage, then a new question and a difficult one, came harder. After voting it down, the convention reconsidered; it then "empowered" the legislature to grant the vote to colored persons; by the constitution it was provided that a militia be enrolled without distinction of color.[18]

On September 5, 1864, the people of Louisiana voted to ratify the constitution (6836–1566); members of congress were then chosen by popular election, after which the legislature set up under the new constitution chose two senators. If and when these men should be admitted by Congress—a big "if"—reconstruction for Louisiana, so far as essential political structure was concerned, would be complete. In the matter of preliminary steps—shaping up the situation so that Congress could act—the work of the executive branch for this pivotal state was done.

Fourth Phase: Trouble in Congress. Much water was to pass over the mill before one could know what Congress would do as to admitting Louisiana according to Lincoln's plan. The radical clique in Louisiana had opposed the measures taken in 1864 looking toward a new state government. This element made a break with the Lin-

---

[17] Denison to Chase, U.S. Customs House, New Orleans, March 5, 1864, *ibid.*

[18] Among the documents of the time (about March of 1864) is a printed petition of "free colored citizens of Louisiana." They pray that "the right of sufferage may be extended . . . [to Negroes] whether born slave or free . . . , subject only to such qualifications as shall equally affect the white and colored citizens." Andrew MSS., vol. 22, Mass. Hist. Soc.

coln administration, denounced the new constitution as null and void, and proceeded to make their influence felt in Congress. The radical element in Congress was working strongly against Lincoln's program in any case, and it was no surprise that the decision of the solons at Washington concerning Louisiana reorganization was negative. A long period of Federal occupation and troublous abnormality was to ensue. There were a number of uneasy years after Lincoln's death before the state was, one should not say restored, but outfitted with a carpetbag government. After that there was to be further delay—nearly a decade—before that unworkable carpetbag regime collapsed.

CHAPTER II

LINCOLN'S PLAN IN OPERATION:
UNIONISM IN THE SOUTH

I

A S IN Louisiana, so in other regions of the Confederate South, Lincoln did his best to promote reorganization measures so that state governments could supersede Federal military rule, but wartime conditions made for obstruction and progress was slow. In Tennessee, where secession had been strongly resisted and where Union victories came in February and April of 1862, it might have seemed that a choice opportunity was offered for early restoration of civil government under unionist auspices. The pro-Confederate regime in Tennessee was brief; it extended only from May 7, 1861 (legislative ratification of the military league with the Confederacy) to March 3, 1862, when Lincoln appointed Andrew Johnson military governor of the state, a period of ten months. Johnson's attitude had been demonstrated by "violent opposition to slavery and secession" [1] and by retention of his seat in the United States Senate. His unionism was unassailable, but he could only perform the functions of civil government on an emergency basis and Lincoln's hopes for instituting a more permanent and regular regime were repeatedly deferred. There was heavy fighting in 1862 and 1863. Guerrilla warfare, raids by Forrest, agitation among discordant pro-Union elements, puzzlement as to what was "regular" by the old code of the state (nothing could be strictly regular in those war times), lack of popular interest when elections were held, complications as to soldier voting and military influence, divided leadership as between Nash-

---

[1] James W. Patton, *Unionism and Reconstruction in Tennessee,* 1860–1869, 30.

ville and Washington—these were among the factors that caused continual delay.

Not until February 1865 was an election held in Tennessee
which had importance in terms of popular voting for fundamental
state reorganization.[2] After that there loomed, as always, the serious
obstacle of congressional opposition. Tennessee was not to be admitted to the Union until 1866. Yet as early as September 11, 1863,
Lincoln had written to Governor Johnson: "All Tennessee is now
clear of armed insurrectionists." Insisting that "Not a moment should
be lost" in "reinaugurating a loyal State government," the President insisted, as in Louisiana, that prudent steps be taken without delay. Discretion was left with Johnson and "co-operating friends" as
to ways and means, with the presidential injunction that the rein-
auguration should not be allowed to slip into the hands of enemies
of the Union, "driving its friends . . . into political exile." "It
must not be so," wrote Lincoln. "You must have it otherwise." [3] Yet
Lincoln did not feel that specific measures of reorganization should
emanate too much from Washington. Despite the delay Lincoln was
satisfied, by the end of his administration, that Tennessee had been
reconstructed sufficiently for executive recognition. To his mind the
state was free and restored.[4]

In September 1863 Andrew Johnson said to his people: "Here
lies your State; a sick man in his bed, emaciated and exhausted . . .
unable to walk alone. The physician comes. Don't quarrel about antecedents, but administer to his wants . . . as quickly as possible
. . . . This is no . . . metaphysical question. It is a plain, common
sense matter, and there is nothing in the way but obstinacy." [5] Johnson's simile of the sick man and his suggestion as to the ineptness of

---

[2] Local officials in Tennessee counties had been chosen in an election in March 1864.
Ibid., 43–44.

[3] *Works*, IX, 116.

[4] There was delay, confusion, and dispute as to reorganization in Tennessee, but at an
election on February 22, 1865, amendments in the state constitution were ratified by
which slavery was abolished and secession declared null; then an ardent unionist—W. G.
("Parson") Brownlow—was chosen governor. He was inaugurated on April 5, 1865. Thus
Lincoln lived to see the re-establishment of a civil regime which he was willing to recognize as the true government of the state. Patton, *Unionism . . . in Tennessee*, 49–50.
See also E. Merton Coulter, *William G. Brownlow: Fighting Parson of the Southern High-
lands*. In his preface Coulter refers to Brownlow as "one of the most dynamic personalities of his times."

[5] *Ann. Cyc.*, 1863, 828.

those administering to him could have covered a great deal more territory than Tennessee.

II

Events of 1863 and early 1864 in Arkansas proceeded with little difficulty so far as that commonwealth itself was concerned. It was a sparsely settled state, with 435,000 inhabitants in 1860, of whom 111,115 were slaves. Illinois, of comparable area, had nearly four times the population. It was chiefly in the southeastern part, in the plantation area near the Mississippi River, that slaveholding was concentrated. Throughout most of the state there were few slaves, in the northern portion hardly any. People of the Ozark mountain region had little in common with the few cotton-growing magnates. To the vast majority of the people the abolition of slavery would produce no serious reordering of their lives and economy.

The state had avoided secession until swept away by the post-Sumter excitement; when secession was adopted it was done reluctantly. Even after secession, considerable Union sentiment remained. According to a contemporary account, pertaining to the situation in 1863, "Citizens of distinction came forward to advocate the Union cause; among others, Brig.-Gen. E. W. Gantt, of the Confederate army, once held as a prisoner of war." The shift of General Gantt from Confederate to Union allegiance was, as he said, part of a popular movement; Union sentiment, he noted, was "manifesting itself on all sides and by every indication." [1] For many who were of like mind with Gantt the open declaration of loyalty to the Federal government, especially after the Confederate surrender of Vicksburg, came naturally. It was like snapping out of an abnormal situation. Gantt declared in 1863 that "loyalty to Jeff. Davis in Arkansas . . . [did] not extend practically beyond the shadow of his army . . . ." [2] Mass meetings were held, Union regiments were formed, Federal oaths were sworn without solicitation, and measures were set in motion, with less difficulty than in Louisiana and Tennessee, for a reorganization of the state government. Military events provided a considerable impulse toward Union reorganization, especially the Union victories at Vicksburg and Port Hudson, and the

---

[1] *Ann. Cyc.,* 1863, 15.   [2] *Ibid.*

Helena-Little Rock expedition of General Frederick Steele, U. S. A., against Sterling Price, C. S. A., which resulted in Confederate evacuation of Little Rock on September 10, 1863. With this Confederate reverse a large part of the state was brought under Union control.

Lincoln kept in touch with Arkansas affairs, notifying General Steele that he, as in the case of Banks in Louisiana, was "master" of the reorganization process. "Some single mind," wrote the President, "must be master, else there will be no agreement in anything." [3] He had ample reason to realize the truth of this statement.

The pattern of the Arkansas movement reveals much as to Lincoln's plan in practical operation. Sentiment developed in meetings, with Union resolutions, in large parts of the state. Delegates were chosen in such meetings (by no more and no less authority than is usual in such popular movements under the stress of abnormal conditions) for a "convention" designed to make a new regime constitutional and legal. Lincoln encouraged the holding of the convention, welcoming it as a fulfillment of his plan as announced in December 1863. On January 20, 1864, he indicated that the reorganization emanated from citizens of Arkansas petitioning for an election, and directed Steele to "order an election immediately" for March 28, 1864.[4] When, on counting the votes for a Union-minded governor and for changes in the state constitution, the number should reach or exceed 5406 (that being ten per cent of the Arkansas vote of 1860), Lincoln directed that the governor thus chosen should be declared qualified and that he should assume his duties under the modified state constitution. (As a minor detail, when it was found that the Union convention in Arkansas was planning the election for March 14, not March 28, the President quickly acquiesced in the convention plan.)

In the President's mind a milestone had been reached in Arkansas affairs with that election of March 14. By an overwhelming majority (12,179 to 226) the voters, having qualified by taking the Federal oath of allegiance, approved those changes in the state constitution which abolished slavery, declared secession void, and repudiated the Confederate debt. Isaac Murphy, already installed as provisional governor by the convention, was now elected governor by "more than double what the President had required." [5] On April 11 the new state gov-

---

[3] *Works*, X, 11–12. [4] *Ibid.*, IX, 289–291.
[5] Nicolay and Hay, *Lincoln*, VIII, 416–417.

ernment under the modified constitution was inaugurated at Little Rock. The reconstructed legislature chose senators (William M. Fishbach and Elisha Baxter); three members of Congress had already been chosen in the March election.

Obstruction in House and Senate prevented the admission of these representatives and senators, and for long years Arkansas remained outside the pale so far as Congress was concerned. Lincoln's view, however, both as to practical matters and as to his own function in promoting them, was shown in his executive measures to get these important steps taken, and in his advice to Steele (June 29, 1864) that, despite congressional refusal to give these solons their seats at Washington, the new state government should have "the same support and protection that you would [have given] if the members had been admitted, because in no event . . . can this do any harm, while it will be the best you can do toward suppressing the rebellion." [6] The President knew that admission of solons in Washington was only part of the process of reconstruction, that the setting up of a reorganized state government was indispensable, that Federal protection for such reorganization was essential, and that much of the value of such reorganization would be lost if matters were allowed indefinitely to drift.

III

A different type of situation presented itself in Florida, where the reconstruction effort was of a minor sort. Military accomplishment, so evident in Louisiana, Tennessee, and Arkansas, was lacking in this detached area, which was off the main line of strategy and unpromising as a field in which to commit any considerable body of troops. Aside from holding a few coastal points and maintaining the blockade, the United States paid little attention to the region of the St. John's, the St. Mary's, and the Suwannee. The war was to be decided elsewhere; and the fate of Florida, smallest in population of all the Southern states, would follow as a corollary of that decision. The only sizable engagement in the state during the war was the ill-starred "battle of Olustee," in the northeast corner, a short distance inward from Jacksonville, where a minor Union force under General Tru-

---

[6] *Works*, X, 139–140.

man Seymour, U. S. A., was defeated by somewhat superior numbers, with advantage of defensive position, under General Joseph Finegan, C. S. A. This engagement, February 20, 1864, was the futile anticlimax of an army-navy expedition of Seymour, a subordinate of General Quincy A. Gillmore who was in command of the "Department of the South" with headquarters at Hilton Head, S.C. Such was the sorry result that Gillmore put the blame upon Seymour, while at Washington Halleck disclaimed all responsibility for the operation.

Under these circumstances, though Union sentiment was held to be widespread in the state, the small-scale efforts to restore Florida were subject to the taunt that their motive was to give a plausible basis for sending pro-Lincoln delegates to the coming Republican convention; even the Seymour expedition was derided as a feature of the political campaign of 1864.

From Lincoln's standpoint the approach to reconstruction in Florida was like that in other Southern areas. On January 13, 1864, he wrote Gillmore advising that the general was to be "master" if differences should arise; in this letter the President urged that restoration be pushed "in the most speedy way possible," and that it be done within the range of the December proclamation. To handle some of the details John Hay was sent to Florida "with some blank-books [for recording oaths] and other blanks, to aid in the reconstruction." [1] This trip of Hay (February–March 1864) was not a brilliant success and the sum-total of the Florida gesture for reconstruction was far from impressive. Hay, now a major, wrote: "I am very sure that we cannot now get the President's 10th & that to alter the suffrage law for a bare tithe would not give us the moral force we want. The people of the interior would be indignant against such a snap judgment taken by incomers & would be jealous & sullen." [2] Hay also wrote of his own mission: "The special duties assigned him occupied little time; there were few loyal citizens to enroll; the most of his service was as an ordinary staff officer to General Gillmore, and there need be no further mention of him, except to say that the movement to restore a legal State government for Florida at that time failed for lack of material." [3] Florida's "delegates," chosen by a few in Jacksonville, did turn up at the Republican convention in June, 1864, but not until after the war

---

[1] *Ibid.*, IX, 283–284.   [2] Dennett, ed., . . . *Diaries* . . . *of John Hay*, 165.
[3] Nicolay and Hay, *Lincoln*, VIII, 283.

did the commonwealth proceed to the making of a new state constitution within the range of the Union; readmission to the Union—i. e., inauguration of carpetbag government—occurred in 1868; restoration of home rule—the throwing off of radical Republican control—was deferred to 1877. It should be added that Lincoln never considered Floridan reconstruction complete according to his design and proclamation.

Small though it was, there was more in the Union effort in Florida than at first met the eye. One could treat the Seymour, or Gillmore-Seymour, expedition of 1864 as a sorry military enterprise, or as a disappointing phase of Lincoln's reconstruction plan, but in a realistic study one needs to enlarge the scope of inquiry. The episode must also be viewed in its relation to such subjects as the use of Negro troops (in which there was creditable performance), maneuvers in the pro-Chase sense, the opening of trade, and what has been called "carpetbag imperialism." In a detailed study George Winston Smith has pointed out that grandiose schemes or experiments were conjured up in connection with the Florida effort. There was, for example, the "extravagant plan" of Eli Thayer of Kansas emigrant fame—a well-intentioned plan to set up "soldier-colonists" and create model communities on the most approved New England pattern. The plan reached "only the blueprint stage," but it reveals much as to Yankee enterprise in the deep South. There was also injected into the wartime Florida scene the "machinations" of Lyman K. Stickney, "the most notorious of the early Florida carpetbaggers," who operated under Secretary Chase in the enforcement of a congressional act for collecting the Federal direct tax in the South. This law, writes Smith, was a "move to confiscate the real property of southern landholders" and was so administered as to become "an instrument of predatory corruption in Florida." [4]

These factors need to be borne in mind in judging Lincoln's approach to reconstruction. It was a complicated problem of many facets, with idealistic motives combined with profit-seeking greed. Lincoln tried to keep restoration on the main track and keep it unmarred, but it was part of the history of the time—the prelude to the "Gilded Age" —that debased and uninspiring maneuvers would creep in. Florida

---

[4] George Winston Smith, "Carpetbag Imperialism in Florida 1862–1868," *Fla. Hist. Quar.*, XXVII, 99–130, 260–299 (1948–49).

was only an example. When one remembers such influences, he can realize with fuller force the significance of Lincoln's rejection of the whole drive and tendency toward carpetbaggism.

IV

In Lincoln's planning for a restored Union he kept his eye constantly on a highly important factor, that of unionism in the South. Of course it could have been said by critics that Lincoln was not bothering with the opposition, that he was requiring an oath of Union allegiance as a prerequisite for the right to vote on any state reorganization, and that he was thus stacking the cards in his favor, working only with friends of the Union. This seemed the more striking because of his willingness to depend on a Union-minded minimum of ten per cent (of 1860 voters) for the initial steps of reconstruction.

Yet on closer study it will be seen that success for any reunion movement was dependent upon popular support in the state. Always at some point there had to be an election, a popular choice of a constitutional convention to remake the state constitution, and a vote for state officials and members of Congress. People who voted in these initial elections had to take the Union oath; but no one was to be coerced into taking it, and if the number of oath-takers was too insignificant, the plan would not get very far. Lincoln was starting with a loyal minority, but the quality and extent of that minority was never unimportant. Furthermore, the President was planning for peace, for the long years ahead after the war ended. This would involve withdrawing Federal forces and allowing Southerners to take over their state administrations. This was what Lincoln was looking forward to as the normal situation. The ten per cent "rallying point" was to be only a prelude to that restoration.

At all times the President felt assured that his plan would work for the whole South. He could hardly have proceeded with such confidence unless he genuinely believed that unionists in the South were, for the long run and for normal times, in the majority. In fact the validity of Lincoln's basic political philosophy depended upon self rule by the people. To impose a government upon an unwilling state —even a benevolent government—would have been contrary to this fundamental philosophy. There was a risk involved in Lincoln's scheme but it was a calculated risk. When there would come the hazard of an election, that would not merely mean that people should vote because of having sworn allegiance. It meant that such allegiance was expected to prove justified in the type of government set up, the working out of labor adjustment, the choice of well-disposed officials, the installing of honest government, and the like. If these things went wrong even after the initial steps had been taken in compliance with the President's plan, the broad policy would fail. Lincoln's feeling of assurance that it would not fail must have been based on more than wishful thinking. It is therefore of importance to look into the matter and find the basis for this assurance—in other words, to discover some of the evidences of unionism in the South which were known to the President. To give the whole body of such evidence is obviously impracticable, but a few items may be mentioned with the understanding that they were typical of a large and impressive total.

There was the element of war-weariness in the South; people were sick and tired of the continued slaughter. A captured Union general, the famous Neal Dow, wrote to Lincoln from Libby Prison, Richmond, on November 12, 1863: ". . . I have seen much of Rebeldom, behind the curtain, and have talked with a great many soldiers, conscripts, deserters, officers, and citizens. The result of all is, to my mind, that . . . the masses are heartily . . . anxious for its [the war's] close on any terms . . . ." He went on to mention numerous Confederate desertions, soldier infirmities, general debility, the worthlessness of conscripts, depreciation of the currency, flour at $125.00 a barrel, and "everything in the provision line . . . [bearing] a corresponding price." [1]

In Virginia the attitude of intelligent and patriotic unionists was typified by Alexander H. H. Stuart. Though not active against secession during the war, he had been fundamentally opposed to it as inexpedient, and stood ready to support early measures of reunion. Stuart defined his wartime attitudes as follows:

"During the war, I abstained from all participation in public affairs, except on two or three occasions when I was called to address public meetings to urge contributions for the relief of the suffering soldiers and the prisoners going to as well as returning from the North.

---

[1] Neal Dow, Brig. Genl. U. S. V., to Lincoln, Libby Prison, Richmond, Virginia, Nov. 12, 1863, R. T. L. Coll., 27980.

"My age relieved me from the obligation to render military service, and all the assistance I gave to the Confederate cause was by feeding the hungry and clothing the naked and nursing the sick Confederate soldiers, and making myself and urging others to make liberal donations for their relief." [2]

Another prominent Virginia unionist was the distinguished lawyer John Minor Botts. He had strongly opposed Southern Democratic disunionists, and, though disapproving also of abolitionists, had given support to the efforts of John Quincy Adams in the matter of antislavery petitions presented to Congress. When Lincoln was a Whig member of Congress from Illinois, Botts was a Whig member from Virginia (1847–49); indeed many of his views were similar to Lincoln's. Both in 1850 and in 1860 he was an earnest opponent of secession, his opposition to Jefferson Davis and to Governor Henry Wise of Virginia being especially marked. He greatly regretted the secession of his state in 1860, which he had tried to prevent. During the war he was so far out of sympathy with the Confederate government that he was arrested and confined for some months in jail. For the most part, however, he spent the war years in retirement. The collapse of the Whigs in the 1850's had left him without any adequate party outlet. Though not fully approving of Lincoln, he stood ready to assist in the reconstruction of his state. When elected United States senator by the "restored" Virginia legislature at Alexandria (the legislature of the Pierpoint government), he declined to serve, but he did not want this declination to be taken as evidence of any anti-Union attitude. It was rather that in his opinion the Alexandria regime lacked validity. On January 22, 1864, he wrote a long letter in which he gave consent to the publication of a certain letter he had previously written—i. e., the letter declining the senatorship but without prejudice to the cause of restoration. He wrote: "I think its publication would materially strengthen the Union cause with all Union men in the South, and especially in this state . . . ." [3] His later career showed the steadfastness of his Union loyalty.

2 Alexander F. Robertson, *Alexander Hugh Holmes Stuart 1807–1891: A Biography*, 241.

3 John Minor Botts to J. B. Fry, "Private and confidential," Auburn, Culpepper County, Jan. 22, 1864, R. T. L. Coll., 29714–27. (On April 12, 1864, Fry wrote to Lincoln enclosing the Botts letter.) In the crisis of 1861 Botts had been deeply disappointed by the failure of men like himself to hold Virginia in the Union. He differed with J. B. Baldwin, another

The fact that certain Southern areas had never left the Union was, of course, significant. That was true of Kentucky. It was remarked that the mountainous districts of that border state were "with very few exceptions . . . thoroughly union." The same observer noted derisively that in the central part of the state "most of the large slave holders, . . . the gamblers . . . all the decayed chivalry . . . all the fast & fashionable ones & nearly all the original Breckinridge Democrats are bitter to secessionists." [4]

From Little Rock, Arkansas, in March 1864 came a choice letter urging that members of Congress elected in the South be required to travel in the North and vice versa; "they would meet together at Washington in a better spirit." [5]

E. W. Gantt of Arkansas, whose wartime shift from Confederate to Union allegiance has been noted, issued a twenty-four page pamphlet (October 7, 1863) which belongs in any case study of unionism in the South. Much of his statement was a blistering denunciation of Jefferson Davis. With the whole cotton crop at his disposal, wrote Gantt, the Confederate President's foreign policy had been "a stupid failure," while at home he was "weak, mean . . . and supremely ambitious." Though supporting weak generals—such as Pemberton, Hindman, and Holmes—he had waged personal feuds against Joseph Johnston, Price, Pike, Beauregard, and even Stonewall Jackson. "We are whipped—fairly beaten," wrote Gantt. "Our armies are melting and ruin approaches us." Slavery, he said, was "doomed." Urging prompt steps for reunion—this was after severe military reverses in the southwest—he wanted no doubt to remain "that our people are loyal"; "let bygones be forgotten," he added, "and let us all unite to bring about peace . . . ." [6]

In the same month there appeared, in a printed broadside, the proceedings of a mass meeting of "Unconditional Union Men" of western Arkansas at Fort Smith, expressing a willingness to co-operate for re-establishing law and order and for promoting success to Union

---

unionist, in some of his statements, but the record of that time showed the sincerity, as well as the bitter frustration, of those who hoped for an understanding that would have averted secession in Virginia.

[4] W. Hamilton Stockwell to John P. Usher, Boyle Co., Ky., Aug. 28, 1863, R. T. L. Coll., 25903–04.

[5] C. C. Andrews to Lincoln ("Private"), Little Rock, Ark., Mar. 9, 1864, *ibid.*, 31396–97.

[6] Printed pamphlet by E. W. Gantt, Little Rock, Oct. 7, 1863, R. T. L. Coll., 27012–23.

arms.[7] And again from a citizen in Little Rock came the suggestion, months before the thing was done, that the President call upon the people "by proclamation of amnesty . . . to return to their allegiance," Federal protection being offered in return. "Do this," the President was assured, " and I venture to promise, that Arkansas, ere long, will be numbered among the loyal States of the Federal Union." [8]

V

Unionist voices were audible throughout the unhappy South. A clear sign of the times in Louisiana was the editorial of the *True Delta* of New Orleans (February 5, 1864) praising Lincoln, comparing him to Washington and Jackson, and favoring his re-election.[1] In Mississippi a local judge wrote: "I have *first, last and all the time*, been a Union man." Secession, he reported, had been put over without the people understanding what was involved.[2] In another report from Mississippi it was indicated that there were "thousands . . . who desire most ardently the restoration of the United States." [3]

In North Carolina peace movements were rife and it was reported early in 1864 that troops from the Old North State were deserting rapidly and extensively from the Confederate service.[4] In the previous year a group of North Carolina citizens had presented a petition to the President, asking him to "order an election day for this district for the purpose of electing a representative for the next Congress." These petitioners represented themselves as "loyal to the Constitution of our country anxious that it should be perpetuated." [5]

As to Alabama it was predicted that if the question of returning to the Union were submitted to a vote, the people would "vote aye,

[7] Printed broadside, *ibid.,* 27599.

[8] C. P. Bartrand to Lincoln, Little Rock, Ark., Oct. 19, 1863, *ibid.,* 27322–25.

[1] New Orleans *True Delta,* Feb. 5, 1864, clipping in R. T. L. Coll., 30185. For a similar clipping, see no. 30057.

[2] L. S. Houghton to Lincoln, Vicksburg. Miss., Aug. 29, 1863, *ibid.,* 25910 ff.

[3] A. Burwell to Lincoln, St. Louis, Aug. 28, 1863, *ibid.,* 25884–85. The writer sent the letter after returning from Vicksburg. He expressed the view that there were *"more unconditionally Loyal or Union men in that state [Mississippi], in proportion to population, than in . . . Ohio or New York."*

[4] Col. R. A. Alger to Nicolay, Washington, Feb. 9, 1864, *ibid.,* 30343–44. (One should not argue too much, of course, from the factor of army desertion; there were huge numbers of deserters on both sides. See Ella Lonn, *Desertion during the Civil War.*)

[5] Petition signed by twenty-two names, Sept. 30, 1863, R. T. L. Coll., 26757.

five to *one.*" The President was given the following assurance· "Could you know how deep and universal is the returning love for the union among the people of Ala & Geo you would discharge your great responsibilities with a hymn of joy in your heart." [6]

These evidences, and more of the same, were available to Lincoln. Since his day further material has come to light tending to reveal the extent of Union sentiment in seceded states. There is a wealth of information on the subject in Federal archives. One is not speaking here of the "amnesty papers"—that large body of written testimony emanating from numerous Southerners who sought special pardon under President Johnson and who in doing so reported their previous position as to secession and Confederate rule. Those papers, though still extant, have been closed to investigators. but there are similar letters outside the "amnesty papers" in various manuscript collections. A notable example was a letter of Alexander H. Stephens to President Johnson, written during the Georgian's brief imprisonment in Fort Warren: ". . . I clearly saw that the great objects in view by me . . . [in accepting Confederate office] were not likely to be obtained even by the success of the Confederate Arms . . . ." Stephens added that the war was inaugurated against his judgment and that he accepted its results.[7]

Of similar importance are the records of Federal agencies such as the United States Court of Claims and the Southern Claims Commission.[8] Since various claims, as for restoration of property, were brought before the Court of Claims, and since proof of loyalty was held to be essential, that court became the tribunal for judging the facts as to the conduct of thousands of professed unionists.[9] In the voluminous testimony which the court examined the historian of Civil War loyalists will find material rich in human interest and close to authentic cases. Naturally, men and women of Union sympathies in the South found existing conditions difficult for any expression of loyalty in active, organized form. Yet their restricted attitude was significant

---

[6] Edmund Fowler, M. D., to Lincoln, New York, Oct. 27, 1863, *ibid.*, 27529–30. The writer was a citizen of Montgomery, Alabama; he had served as surgeon to Union prisoners.

[7] A. H. Stephens to President Johnson, Ft. Warren, June 9, 1865, Johnson MSS., Lib. of Cong.

[8] Frank Wysor Klingberg, "The Southern Claims Commission: A Postwar Agency in Operation," *Miss. Vall. Hist. Rev.*, XXXII, 195–214 (1945).

[9] Randall, *Constitutional Problems Under Lincoln*, 335–338.

as they maintained a kind of passive resistance, avoided voluntary measures against the government at Washington, opposed the Confederate draft, carried provisions and medicines to Union soldiers, contributed money for the welfare of blue-coats, attended boys in hospitals, and performed other friendly acts for Federal troops. Such acts incurred persecution, and the Southern unionist moved often in an atmosphere of scorn and hostility not unaccompanied by threats and acts of personal violence. Of course, in various respects he was compelled to act against his will when it was a matter of serving as conscript, subscribing to a Confederate loan, contributing cotton, paying taxes, or performing labor. Since Southern wartime history has been largely remembered and recorded in Confederate terms, these details are still somewhat obscure; at least their full force is not generally recognized.

No history of Lincoln, however, can ignore them. His reports from the South were a vital element in policy making. When he made his broad appeal in December 1863, offering pardon, prescribing his simple oath, and opening the way for new state governments by genuine Southern effort looking toward peace with freedom and union, he had reason to know, at least in large part, the kind of support and fulfillment upon which he could count. His sense of his own function as leader was strengthened by his realization that Southern unionism did not signify willingness to accept the program and regime of congressional radicals. On the contrary, such union-mindedness was oriented in Lincolnian terms. In taking on the responsibility of launching and promoting reconstruction, Lincoln saw an opportunity which needed to be seized while its most fruitful results were yet possible. He was mindful of the fact that he had a Southern following, a support south of the line which was both actual and potential, and which needed to become more vocal and assertive. With that following in view, and with the interest of the whole nation at heart, he was making pledges and commitments. It would only have been a lesser man, or a do-nothing President, who would have held back and avoided such commitments.

CHAPTER III

PUBLIC RELATIONS

I

LINCOLN'S remark that he was "environed with difficulties" [1] could have related to a variety of vexations. He could have had in mind an unco-operative Congress, bickering among generals, factions in his own party, misguided peace efforts, unsought advice as to his cabinet, innumerable petty demands, patronage seekers, or perchance a muddled condition in Missouri.

Or it might have been newspaper trouble. In journalism it was the heyday of the "special" writer and the ubiquitous reporter. It was at once a time of remarkably active newspaper enterprise and of lax governmental control over the press. "No war," it has been said, "was ever before so waged in the world's eye." [2] Metropolitan dailies spent huge sums on their "war departments," half a million being spent by the *Herald* alone. Correspondents were seemingly on every march and at all fronts. They were accorded special privileges, eating at officers' mess, using army transportation for their baggage, enjoying the confidence of admirals and generals, unrestrained as they overheard camp talk or picked up snatches of military information. Usually they had army passes and sometimes they even carried military messages or orders. Though gestures were made toward governmental censorship, there was little effective curbing of reporters. Steps were taken early in the war to control the issue of telegraph news from Washington, and at the time of the *Trent* affair an effort was made to impose silence as to correspondence between Seward and Lord Lyons, but a committee of the House of Representatives raised charges of undue interference and the idea of a government censor, known

[1] *Collected Works*, V, 438 (reply to serenade Sept. 24, 1862).
[2] *Harper's Pictorial History of the Civil War*, I, 122.

as such, was found impracticable. It is true that during the war the telegraph system was under government control by congressional authorization and a special officer was set up with the title of assistant secretary of war and general manager of military telegraphs. This offered some chance for a sifting of news, while at the same time the government had taken over the railroads, so that an offending journal could be denied facilities for transporting papers by train.

Yet the mind of the American people was firmly conditioned against restrictions on the press, and efforts to protect the government proved to be no more than half-way measures. At no time were news channels fully or effectively closed. The mails were open to reporters, messengers could convey material to the home office, "leaks" from a general's headquarters were not uncommon, and confidential communications held up in Washington could be released from other points.

Generals differed in their treatments of journalists. Those ambitious for publicity petted and favored the reporters; if this was not done an offended journalist might vent his spite by misrepresenting a general or sending untrue reports of army conditions. The least effective generals were made to bask in newspaper glory, while abler commanders such as the laconic Grant or the peppery Sherman were basely abused. A Cincinnati editor, questioned as to the dissemination of the newspaper canard that Sherman was "insane," remarked that it was a news item of the day and that he had to keep up with the times. For this and many other reasons Sherman became probably the most severe of Union generals in his attitude toward reporters and editors. He despised the papers, declaring that they had "killed" able generals, incited jealousies, given notice of unexpected military movements, functioned as the "world's gossips," distorted their stories, and injected the names of generals into the political controversies of the day.[3]

Special coloration of certain newspapers in this and other countries is familiar to historians, though perhaps its full effect has not been measured. Francis Lieber, who knew much of European military politics, wrote: "I happen to think of what Joseph Bonaparte once said to me. I had mentioned the saying of Frederic II, that he who

---

[3] J. G. Randall, "The Newspaper Problem during the Civil War," *Amer. Hist. Rev.*, XXIII, 303–323 (Jan. 1918).

has the last shilling remains the master of the field. Joseph Bonaparte replied: Yes, but not because he can pay the last grenadier as Frederic believed, but because he can pay the last newspaper, within and without the country." [4]

In the newspaper world of the time there were great names— Greeley, Bowles, Bennett, Bryant, Raymond, Dana, Forney, and men of like caliber. Lesser men who nevertheless had potent influence included Whitelaw Reid of the Cincinnati *Gazette;* George Wilkes, interested in jockeying and sporting news, whose *Wilkes's Spirit of the Times* combined sports with political comments (seldom pro-Lincoln); George Alfred Townsend, a vigorous correspondent and prolific special writer with a flair for depicting personalities; the picturesque Ben: Perley Poore, notable for wide experience, travel, voluminous compilations, and descriptive column writing; and George William Curtis, influential in his Harper's "Easy Chair."

II

It could hardly be disputed that most of the newspapers were against Lincoln. Among the more partisanly virulent were the Chicago *Times,* the Columbus (Ohio) *Crisis,* the Baltimore *Exchange,* the New York *World,* and the New York *Daily News,* to mention but a few. The *World* characterized Lincoln's emancipation policy as "miserable balderdash"; the Chicago *Times* described his second inaugural as "slipshod," "loose-jointed," and "puerile." [1] Such journals as the Chicago *Times* and the New York *World* were Democratic sheets, but it was also true that Lincoln had a "bad press" among well known Republican publications such as the *Tribune,* and *Post,* and the *Independent* of New York. Bryant of the *Post,* angered by what he considered the monopoly of patronage by the Seward-Weed faction, wrote: "I am so utterly disgusted with Lincoln's behavior that I cannot muster respectful terms in which to write him." [2] Theodore Tilton was anti-Lincoln though pro-Republican. The Chicago *Tribune* was known as one of the stanch Republican papers, but John Hay wrote as follows of its editor: "I found among my letters here

[4] Francis Lieber to Gen. H. W. Halleck, New York, March 4, 1863, Lieber MSS., Huntington Lib.
[1] New York *World,* Feb. 7, 1863; Chicago *Times,* Mar. 6, 1865.
[2] Forbes, *Letters and Recollections,* II, 101.

. . . one from Joe Medill, inconceivably impudent, in which he informs me that on the fourth of next March [1865], thanks to Mr. Lincoln's blunders & follies, we will be kicked out of the White House." [3]

If to these few instances there were added a full coverage of newspaper opposition to Lincoln and his administration, one would find provocation for punitive and suppressive measures on the part of the government. Yet in general it was Lincoln's policy to avoid suppression and to endure abuse as the price, often a high price, of press freedom. To understand this statement one must remember that it is a generalization, and that in such a vast arena as the American Civil War, with its hundreds of newspapers and its array of generals and judges advocate, there could be enough exceptions to make a considerable list and yet the generalization would still hold good. In other words, after one has fully listed all the instances of governmental action against journals and editors, even though the list seems impressive in itself, the number untouched and unmolested would still constitute an overwhelming majority of the immense total.

The government was not lacking in potential methods of discipline. Newspaper men who moved with the armies were within military jurisdiction and were subject to the 57th Article of War which prescribed court-martial trial, with death or other punishment, for anyone "giving intelligence" to the enemy. It would, however, be hard to find any application of this part of the military code. Other possible methods of discipline were military arrest of editors, exclusion of offending correspondents from the bounds of a general's command, and the requiring of passes fortified by regulations for their issuance. As an ultimate punishment there remained the severe expedient of dealing with reporters as spies. It was Secretary of War Stanton who was responsible for one of the rare uses of this stern device. On February 10, 1862, he ordered that a Washington representative of the New York *Herald* "calling himself Dr. Ives" (Dr. Malcom Ives) be "arrested and held in close custody . . . as a spy." [4] The offending writer, according to Stanton, had "intruded" himself into a war department conference and Stanton ordered that no news gatherer could thus "spy out official acts." Ives was released after four months, his case not having been prosecuted in any regular manner; his con-

---

[3] Dennett, ed., . . . *Diaries . . . of John Hay,* 211–212.   [4] *Ann. Cyc.,* 1862, 509.

nection with the *Herald* was broken.[5]

On the question of whether newsmen could be considered spies there was one Union general who had no doubts. Sherman so pronounced them, and it was true that Confederate leaders perused Northern papers for the military information which they constantly supplied. Yet aside from the somewhat eccentric action of Stanton this form of punishment does not appear to have been enforced. To have done so properly would have required proof in each case that the offender was in the actual employ of the enemy.

If a newspaper was "suppressed," that usually meant that its publication was suspended for a period. In addition to the famous cases of the Chicago *Times,* the New York *World,* and the New York *Journal of Commerce,* which have already been treated, there were less known cases of "suppression," such as those of the Dayton (Ohio) *Empire,* the *South* of Baltimore, the *Maryland News* sheet of Baltimore, the Baltimore *Bulletin,* the Louisville *True Presbyterian.* Sometimes a single edition of a paper would be seized without the paper being suppressed, or the distribution of the paper would be checked.

A controversy arose as to whether offensive newspapers could be denied the use of the mails. Postmaster-General Blair, who had refused postal distribution for certain papers judicially condemned as disloyal, defended his legal right to do so. He disclaimed, however, any intent to strike against legitimate freedom of the press and he sharply denied a charge in the New York *World* that his department conducted a regular espionage against newspapers. The charge, he wrote, was "false in every particular." His department did not open papers to discover their contents, yet where evidence was clear he felt justified in excluding matters designed to stir up insurrection.[6]

There were cases of editors being put under military arrest as "prisoners of state," but where this was done there was a reasonable claim or suspicion of disloyalty against the editors, who were usually released after brief confinement. A notable case of such imprisonment was that of F. Key Howard, editor of the Baltimore *Exchange,* who was confined in Fort Lafayette. Immediately after the Howard arrest

---

[5] Robert S. Harper, *Lincoln and the Press,* 132–133.

[6] *Constitutional Problems Under Lincoln,* 501–502; Montgomery Blair to A. Wakeman, Aug. 2, 1864, Gist Blair MSS., Lib. of Cong.

the *Exchange*, which continued to appear, burst out with a denunciation of the Lincoln government, whereupon its publisher W. W.
Glenn, was also put under military arrest.[7] In like fashion another
Baltimore editor, Thomas W. Hall of the *South,* was consigned to
Fort McHenry. Baltimore was indeed a kind of hotbed of anti-Lincoln
journalism. It has been stated by Robert S. Harper that no newspaper
other than the Baltimore *American* "made even a pretense of ad-
vocating the Union cause." [8] (Incidentally there is a bit of irony in the
fact that this hostile city was the one in which the convention was
held which renominated Lincoln for the presidency.) The net result in Baltimore, in view of the widely published denunciations of
high handed military action, was unfavorable to the government, and
Howard was released after confinement for several months.

Lincoln himself was no suppressor of journalistic freedom. It has
been seen that he promptly revoked the Burnside order against the
Chicago *Times,* and when General M. S. Hascall attempted a military policy of newspaper suppression in Indiana in 1863, word came
from Washington of the President's disapproval of indiscreet assumption of "military powers not essential to the preservation of the public peace." Because of the harm done by an officer "issuing military
proclamations and engaging in newspaper controversies upon questions that agitate the public mind" General Hascall was relieved of
his provocative Indiana command.[9] Military arrest of editors belongs to the vast problem of arbitrary arrests and political prisoners,
but the President's attitude stood out clearly. When the editor of the
Missouri Democrat was arrested the President regretted the act. He
wrote to General J. M. Schofield: "Please spare me the trouble this
is likely to bring." [10]

In the matter of a dramatic "scoop" Lincoln stepped in to prevent
severe action by Stanton against a news writer. A *Tribune* correspondent, Henry E. Wing, with great difficulty labored his way through to
Grant at the time when the country and the government at Washington were without news of what was happening to the Commander
and his great army at the time of the fighting in the Wilderness. Having achieved the notable feat of reaching and talking with the gen-

---

[7] Harper, *Lincoln and the Press,* 160.   [8] *Ibid.,* 159.

[9] *Midstream,* 235–236; *Offic. Rec.,* 2 ser. V, 723–724, 759.

[10] *Collected Works,* VI, 326 (July 13, 1863).

eral, Wing made his painful way back, partly walking and running and partly by railroad handcar, and managed to send a wire to Charles A. Dana, assistant secretary of war, whom he knew and with whom he negotiated: if permitted to send one hundred words to the *Tribune,* he would tell the war department what he had so laboriously learned. Stanton threatened the writer with arrest, but the President, so goes the account, approved the transmission of Wing's despatch (New York *Tribune,* May 7, 1864), talked with him on arrival in Washington, and (uncharacteristically for Lincoln) rewarded him with a kiss on the forehead.[11]

When a *Herald* writer, Thomas W. Knox, was excluded from Grant's military command, Lincoln intervened in the newsman's favor. Being advised that the offense was "technical, rather than wilfully wrong," the President revoked the court-martial sentence of exclusion, though with the proviso that Knox's reinstatement would depend upon Grant's "express assent." [12] This seems to have been a matter of difficult relations among generals. The correspondent was acceptable to McClernand but unacceptable to Grant. Lincoln's maneuver was designed to placate both generals while undoing a measure of army discipline against a journalist.

III

While Lincoln found that it was best for him to avoid influencing the press by any of the coarser methods such as dictating editorial policy or imposing censorship, he could not ignore the effect of newspaper publicity. It has been remarked that it was "not uncommon" in the period "to place journalists in important military and political positions whence they could write for the papers with a view to directing public opinion." [1] It has been stated that "Lincoln seems to have chosen more newspaper men for official positions than any of his predecessors." [2] A Baltimore paper declared at the outset of the Lincoln administration: "Editors seem to be in very great favor with the party in power—a larger number of the fraternity having received

---

11 F. Lauriston Bullard, *Famous War Correspondents,* 406–408; Welles, *Diary,* II, 25 (May 7, 1864).

12 *Collected Works,* VI, 142–143 (Mar. 20, 1863).

1 Dennett, ed., . . . *Diaries . . . of John Hay,* 56 n.

2 Carman and Luthin, *Lincoln and the Patronage,* 125.

appointments . . . than probably under any previous Administration." [3]

John Bigelow, who had been connected with the New York *Evening Post,* was appointed consul general at Paris, which enabled him to exert influence upon European newspapers. Irish-born Charles G. Halpine, colorful and adventurous author-journalist with a varied record of service with the *Herald* and the *Times,* had military appointment leading up to that of brevet brigadier general. While with the army, on General Hunter's staff, he used his facile and poetic pen to influence sentiment; his pieces under the name of "Miles O'Reilly," fictitious Irish-American private, were popular and influential. John W. Forney, who supported the Lincoln administration with his Philadelphia *Press* and his Washington *Chronicle,* was close to the President. He had been a Pierce Democrat but his support of Douglas in 1860, which involved bitter antagonism to Buchanan, had deepened the split in the Democratic party, thus helping to promote Republican victory in Pennsylvania. Lincoln showed a marked friendliness to Forney and used presidential influence to have him chosen secretary of the Senate. When the editor dedicated his new printing establishment in Washington with a "blow-out" as Hay termed it, the President was in attendance.[4] Having spent an evening at Forney's in December 1863 with "political people," Hay reported that Forney "talked a great deal about the President," emphasizing the "unconditional confidence and the loyalty to his person that is felt throughout this land." [5] It would not be amiss to speak of the *Chronicle* as a pro-Lincoln organ. In one of its issues (December 7, 1864) the paper published an article written in full by the President. (For this purpose Lincoln used the good offices of his friend Noah Brooks who assisted in seeing that the article was printed.) The President's contribution pertained to certain wives' requests that their husbands, held in the North as prisoners of war, be released on the ground that each husband was "a religious man." The President gave his idea of a religion that sets men to fight against their Government in order to benefit by the "sweat of other men's faces." [6]

Among others in the newspaper profession who had governmental

[3] Baltimore *Evening Patriot,* Mar. 30, 1861, quoted in Carman and Luthin, 128.
[4] Dennett, ed., . . . *Diaries . . . of John Hay,* 74.   [5] *Ibid.,* 146.
[6] Harper, *Lincoln and the Press,* 181–182; *Daily Washington Chronicle,* Dec. 7, 1864; Brooks, *Washington in Lincoln's Time,* 299.

appointments were Scripps of the Chicago *Tribune* who became postmaster in Chicago (though Lincoln came to dislike his methods); Charles A. Dana of the New York *Tribune* (later of the *Sun*) who served as assistant secretary of war; and John D. Defrees, an Indianapolis editor who took a keen interest in pro-Lincoln politics and who became government printer by Lincoln's appointment.[7] There were also George Fogg of New Hampshire (minister to Switzerland), James S. Pike of the New York *Tribune* (minister to Holland), Bayard Taylor of the *Tribune* (secretary of legation at St. Petersburg), and James C. Welling of the Washington *National Intelligencer* (assistant clerk of the United States court of claims). But this brief enumeration gives no adequate impression of the great number of appointments given to journalists; the full number of such men is too long to be listed here.[8] Referring to a certain newspaper, Lincoln once wrote of the possible withdrawal of "the patronage it is enjoying at my hand." [9] The power of bestowal or withdrawal was his to be used at discretion; that power was not capriciously applied, but it was natural that one of the firms singled out for printing contracts was that of Forney, whose profits from this source were not inconsiderable.[10]

IV

The case of James Gordon Bennett the elder posed a special problem as to Lincoln's press relations. Though a thorn in the flesh to the President, it was felt that Bennett could possibly be won over. The *Herald* editor, born in 1795, was pre-eminent in Civil War journalism but stood apart in a class by himself. His complex personality and shifting positions cannot be defined in a word. His newspaper, known for its spicy journalism, was outstanding in success as judged by its circulation, estimated at about 77,000. The rising importance of this one journal was a kind of phenomenon, though earnest souls were often angered by its content. During the sectional crisis and the war the *Herald* shifted about, so that a chart of its attitude toward Lincoln and the government at Washington

---

7 Bates, *Diary*, 37 n. 8 Carman and Luthin, *Lincoln and the Patronage*, 125–128.
9 *Collected Works*, VI, 188 (Apr. 27, 1863).
10 Carman and Luthin, *Lincoln and the Patronage*, 120–121.

would show sharp peaks and deep troughs. In the crisis before Sumter the paper was pro-Southern (or pro-secessionist); then, as a diarist remarked, its "conversion . . . [was] complete" after the April firing started.[1] On May 22, 1863, Lincoln was represented as a strong candidate for the presidency in 1864. On May 28 the word was: "Give us Abraham Lincoln for the next Presidency." There followed suggestions that the President should "at once cut loose from his cabinet (June 6, 1863); on November 3 the verdict was that Lincoln was "master of the situation."

The tone then changed. On December 16, 1863, the *Herald* pronounced that Lincoln's administration had "proved a failure"; on December 18 the country had had "quite enough of a civilian Commander-in-Chief"; on December 21 Old Abe was "hopeless"; and on February 19, 1864, the acme of denunciation was reached in a long and stinging editorial in which the President was contemptuously mocked as this or that kind of joke; a "sorry joke," a "ridiculous joke," a "standing joke," a "broad joke," and a "solemn joke." The Bennett daily then took up for Grant for President in '64, overlooking the patent fact that Grant's indispensable function was that of military commander in the field.[2]

The idea of enlisting Bennett for the Lincoln cause had formed expression at an early date. A curious letter on the subject was written to Lincoln by Joseph Medill of the Chicago *Tribune* on June 19, 1860, who intended to sound out Bennett whom he considered susceptible to a "dicker." "Terms moderate," wrote Medill, "and 'no cure no pay.'" It was suggested that Medill or Ray of the Chicago *Tribune* go to New York taking Norman Judd along. Desiring an interview with his "Satanic Majesty" the Chicago editor reasoned that his "affirmative help" was not important, but he was "powerful for mischief." The journalistic giant did not want money. "Social position is what he wants. He wants to be in a position to be invited with his wife and son to dinner or tea at the White House and to be 'made of' by the big men of the party. . . . He has a vast corps of writers . . . at home and abroad and universal circulation North, South, East, West, Europe, Asia, Africa, and the Isles of the Sea."

---

[1] Allan Nevins and Milton Halsey Thomas, eds., *The Diary of George Templeton Strong*, III, 122 (Apr. 16, 1861).

[2] For instance, the *Herald* on January 6, 1864, carried an editorial entitled: "Why Grant is the Best Candidate for the Presidency."

This 1860 gesture came to nothing, but the President (who once wrote: "It is important to humor the Herald") [3] persisted in his efforts to enlist the support of the famous editor. As an intermediary he used Weed who is said to have remarked that "Mr. Lincoln deemed it more important to secure the *Herald's* support than to obtain a victory in the field." [4] That Bennett desired favors was shown when he offered the government his fine sailing yacht, the *Henrietta*. The offer was accepted and Bennett's son, at the father's request, was given a lieutenant's commission in the revenue cutter service under the treasury department. [5]

After many shifts the *Herald* support was belatedly given to Lincoln in 1864 and it has been supposed that this result was related to Lincoln's offer to appoint Bennett as United States minister to France. Lincoln's letter extending the offer was dated February 20, 1865. [6] Under date of March 6, 1865 Bennett wrote the President declining the offer but taking special pains to show his "highest consideration" of the President's attitude in "proposing so distinguished an honor." [7] Secretary Welles disapproved of the proffered appointment, referring to Bennett as "an editor . . . whose whims are often wickedly and atrociously leveled against the best men and the best causes . . . ."

Though Lincoln's offer was not written until February of 1865, it was the opinion of A. K. McClure that the President's tender of the French mission to Bennett was one of the "shrewdest of Lincoln's . . . political schemes." [8] This, together with the fact of Bennett's delayed support of the Lincoln ticket, implies that the prospect of the appointment was made known to the editor during the 1864 political campaign. It is known that the idea of such a presidential favor was pending in the pre-election period. Senator Harlan suggested that "it would pay to offer him a foreign mission." John Hay wrote on September 23, 1864, that Forney "had a man talking to the cannie Scot [Bennett] who asked plumply, 'Will I be a welcome visitor at the White House if I support Mr. Lincoln?' " [9] Bennett's biogra-

---

3 R. T. L. Coll., 22036 (Feb. 28 [?], 1863).

4 Autobiography of Thurlow Weed, 615–616; Carman and Luthin, *Lincoln and the Patronage,* 123.

5 Don C. Seitz, *The James Gordon Bennetts,* 181–182; Carman and Luthin, *Lincoln and the Patronage,* 123–124.

6 Draft in Lincoln's hand, R. T. L. Coll., 40843–44.   7 R. T. L. Coll., 41070–1.

8 A. K. McClure, *Abraham Lincoln and Men of War Times,* 90.

9 Dennett, ed., . . . *Diaries* . . . *of John Hay,* 215.

pher, Don C. Seitz, quotes Thurlow Weed as saying that "two well-meaning friends" were responsible for the affair of the French offer. Seitz adds: "The surmise left open is that 'the two well-meaning friends' may have conveyed some word of the President's intention to honor the editor during the campaign and so brought about the switch in the *Herald's* attitude . . . ." [10]

V

Changing habits of the presidency have brought elaborate modern processes of "White House publicity," but it was quite a different matter under Lincoln. There were no "press conferences," no "White House spokesman," no speech writers, and but few speeches by the President. In 1864 he remarked: "It is not very becoming for one in my position to make speeches at great length." [1] His annual messages, though distinguished by eloquent passages, were not delivered to Congress in person, and throughout his presidency his principal speeches were his two inaugurals, his immortal Gettysburg address, and his last speech (April 11, 1865) pertaining to reconstruction. Showmanship was not congenial to Lincoln's temperament and there was little fanfare associated with the person or even the public duties of the Chief Executive.

This, of course, does not signify that the more important uses of presidential publicity were altogether ignored. Thought was given to public pronouncements and to their timing. When, after Gettysburg and Vicksburg, the fall of Port Hudson was expected, thus opening the entire Mississippi River, Halleck wrote to Grant: "The Prest will then issue a genl order congratulating the armies of the east & west on their recent victories. This consideration has prevented me from issueing [*sic*] one myself for your army. I prefer that it should come from the Prest." [2]

Such was the Halleck idea, but Lincoln did it in his own way. On July 13, 1863, he wrote a friendly personal letter to Grant expressing "grateful acknowledgment for the almost inestimable service you have done the country." Then on July 15 he issued, not a military "order," but a proclamation to the nation setting aside a special day

---

[10] Don C. Seitz, *The James Gordon Bennetts*, 194–195.

[1] *Collected Works*, VII, 302 (Apr. 18, 1864).

[2] Halleck to Grant, Hq. of Army, Washington, July 11, 1863, MS. Ill. State Hist. Lib.

of thanksgiving for "victories . . . so signal and so effective as to furnish grounds for augmented confidence that the union of these States will be maintained . . . and their peace and prosperity permanently restored." On July 4 he had announced the news from Gettysburg as promising "a great success to the cause of the Union." It has already been seen (*Midstream*) that Lincoln made reluctant but effective use of serenades which were thrust upon him.[3]

The work of the Sanitary Commission—the Civil War counterpart of the Red Cross—made a special appeal to Lincoln's mind and he was called upon to speak at Sanitary Fairs held to raise money. At such a fair in Washington on March 18, 1864, he admitted that he was "not accustomed to the . . . language of eulogy," but added that "if all that has been said . . . in praise of woman were applied to the women of America, it would not do them justice for their conduct during this war." His speech at the Sanitary Fair in Baltimore on April 18, 1864, was somewhat of a major effort. He spoke of slavery, of the meaning of liberty, and of the knotty problem of wartime retaliation which he characterized as a "mistake." At the Sanitary Fair in Philadelphia on June 16, 1864, he made a moderately long speech, praising the Sanitary Commission and the Christian Commission for their "benevolent labors" and giving a word of encouragement for all voluntary activities to contribute to soldier comfort or relief of sick and wounded. He used the occasion for a morale-building word as to war aims. The conflict had taken three years for "restoring the national authority." So far as he was able to speak, he said "we are going through on this line if it takes three years more." For this he asked a "pouring forth of men and assistance." [4]

One technique of publicity was peculiarly characteristic of Lincoln: he made notable use of the occasional open letter, or the fine art of correspondence with a public purpose. Where an important matter needed to be presented to the people, in lieu of a speech, he would often write a careful letter to the appropriate person or group, intending it for the nation's ear. To Greeley on August 22, 1862, he wrote of his "paramount object . . . to save the Union." To Erastus

---

[3] *Lincoln the President*, III, 11–12.

[4] For these speeches, before Sanitary Fairs, see *Collected Works*, VII, 253–254, 301–303, 394–396.

Corning and others (June 12, 1863) he sent an extended argument concerning wartime executive measures which were being assailed as unconstitutional. To James C. Conkling he sent a public speech to be read at the elaborate Springfield rally of September 3, 1863. For a committee from the Workingmen's Association of New York (March 21, 1864) he wrote an important address on the fundamental relations of capital and labor. Recognizing that "Capital has its rights," he declared that "Labor is the superior of capital." He went on to show that the "strongest bond of human sympathy, outside of the family relation, should be one uniting all working people, of all nations, and tongues, and kindreds." To A. G. Hodges, of Kentucky (April 4, 1864) he wrote of his antislavery views, his official acts concerning slavery, his arming of the Negroes, and his challenge to those who doubted his policy. He did not claim credit for himself, but ended on the note "If God . . . wills." In general, it is in these occasional letters that one finds some of Lincoln's best turned passages of eloquent but unprovocative appeal to public sentiment.[5]

VI

To study Lincoln's letters of consolation is to find a blending of sentiment, uplift, and delicate, unaffected sympathy. When Colonel Elmer E. Ellsworth of the "Ellsworth Zouaves," a personal friend of the Lincolns, was killed at Alexandria in May 1861, the President's exquisite letter to the young warrior's parents, though innocent of effusiveness, came from the heart. Pointing out to the parents that "our affliction here, is scarcely less than your own," he wrote of the young man's indomitable yet modest qualities and his promise of usefulness to his country. It was not for him to remove the grief, but he could give assurance that both the pain and the appreciation of the son's gallant service were shared by the nation. He concluded: "In the hope that it may be no intrusion upon the sacredness of your sorrow, I have ventured to address you this tribute to the memory of my young friend, and your brave and early fallen child. May God give you that consolation which is beyond earthly power." The final

---

[5] For these occasional letters, see *Collected Works*, V, 388 (Greeley), VI, 260–269 (Corning); VI, 406–411 (Conkling); VII, 259–260 and V, 52 (Reply to Workingmen); VII, 282 (Hodges).

touch was in the subscribing of his name: "Sincerely your friend in a common affliction, A. Lincoln." [1]

It was characteristic that a Lincoln letter would be fitted to the case. In his words of sympathy to Fanny, daughter of Colonel Mc-Cullough of Bloomington, Illinois (December 23, 1862), Lincoln's old-time friend, the man in the White House talked as if face to face with the "young heart" that was suffering "beyond what is common in such cases." Sorrow comes to all, he wrote, but "to the young, it comes with bitterest agony, because it takes them unawares." Yet he told the girl, as if seeking to enter her inmost mind: "You are sure to be happy again . . . . The memory of your dear Father, instead of an agony, will yet be a sad sweet feeling in your heart, of a purer, and holier sort than you have known before." [2]

The most famous of Lincoln's letters of consolation was to Mrs. Bixby of Boston; it has taken a pre-eminent place as a Lincoln gem and a classic in the language. The letter reads as follows:

> Executive Mansion,
> Washington, Nov. 21, 1864.
>
> Dear Madam,—I have been shown in the files of the War Department a statement of the Adjutant General of Massachusetts, that you are the mother of five sons who have died gloriously on the field of battle.
>
> I feel how weak and fruitless must be any words of mine which should attempt to beguile you from the grief of a loss so overwhelming. But I cannot refrain from tendering to you the consolation that may be found in the thanks of the Republic they died to save.
>
> I pray that our Heavenly Father may assuage the anguish of your bereavement, and leave you only the cherished memory of the loved and lost, and the solemn pride that must be yours, to have laid so costly a sacrifice upon the altar of Freedom.
>
> Yours very sincerely and respectfully,
> A. Lincoln. [3]

It is futile to paint the lily and it is always a question of how far one needs to comment on a literary classic. In the case of the Bixby letter the literature is tremendous. The subject is clouded by controversies, a deal of mythology has been thrown in, and commercialism has invaded the field. As a result the main significance of Lincoln's phrases has been obscured by irrelevant or unhistorical de-

---

[1] *Collected Works*, IV, 385–386 (May 25, 1861).   [2] *Ibid.*, VI, 16–17.
[3] *Ibid.*, VIII, 116–117.

THE BLAIR FAMILY

Upper: Francis P. Blair, Sr., once a member of Jackson's "Kitchen Cabinet," afterwards a self-appointed adviser to President Lincoln.

Lower left: Francis P. Blair, Jr., Army officer and Congressman, administration leader in the House of Representatives.

Lower right: Montgomery Blair, Postmaster-General, 1861–1864.

Executive Mansion,

Washington, September 4. 1864.

Eliza P. Gurney.

My esteemed friend.

I have not forgotten— probably never shall forget — the very impressive occasion when yourself and friends visited me on a Sabbath forenoon two years ago. Nor has your kind letter, written nearly a year later, ever been forgotten. In all, it has been your purpose to strengthen my reliance on God. I am much indebted to the good Christian people of the country for their constant prayers and consolations; and to no one of them more than to yourself. The purposes of the Almighty are perfect, and must prevail, though we erring mortals may fail to accurately perceive them in advance. We hoped for a happy termination of this terrible war long before this; but God knows best, and has ruled otherwise. We shall yet acknowledge His wisdom, and our own error therein. Meanwhile we must work earnestly in the best lights He gives us, trusting that so

LINCOLN REVISES HIS LETTER—

working still conduces to the great
ends, the ordains— Surely He intends some
great good to follow this mighty con=
vulsion, which no mortal could
make, and no mortal could stay=

Your people— the Friends— have
had, and are having, a very great
trial. On principles, and faith, opposed to both
war and oppression, they can
only practically oppose oppression by war.
In this hard dilemma some have chosen
one horn and some the other. For
those appealing to me on conscientious
grounds, I have done, and shall do,
the best I could, and can, in my own conscience,
under my oath to the law. That
you believe this, I doubt not; and believe=
ing it, I shall still receive, for our
country and myself, your earnest prayers
to our Father in Heaven.

Your sincere friend,

A. Lincoln

—TO MRS. GURNEY, SEPT. 4, 1864

PROFESSIONALS AND POLITICOS

Upper: Grant and Sherman, professional soldiers, in 1865.
Lower: B. F. Butler (standing) and N. P. Banks, political generals. The differences in pose and costume are revealing.

tails. If one reads the letter and appreciates its noble meaning and distinguished form, that after all is the prime consideration. For our present study, emphasizing Lincoln, a brief statement must suffice.

Amid the hundreds of thousands of casualties the Bixby boys were singled out in the following manner. William Schouler, state adjutant general of Massachusetts, gave a statement concerning the alleged death in battle of the five sons of Mrs. Lydia Bixby of Boston to Governor Andrew; the governor added his endorsement; the record came up to the war department in Washington; and the statement was communicated to Lincoln. It was on this evidence that Lincoln's letter of consolation was based.

The records themselves are confused. The report of five sons killed was erroneous; [4] Mrs. Bixby was an obscure person who frequently changed her residence; furthermore, there is evidence that her character was not that of respectability.[5] It must be added that the records clearly show two sons killed, this being truly enough a "costly . . . sacrifice."

Most troublesome of all has been the contention that it was not Lincoln, but John Hay, who composed the letter. If this could be proved to be true it would have to be accepted, but in so famous an instance readers on Lincoln will wish to know how the matter stands. The Hay-authorship theory depends not on clear evidence but on

---

[4] Two sons, according to reliable records, were killed in action: Sergeant Charles N. Bixby at Fredericksburg, May 3, 1863, and Private Oliver C. Bixby near Petersburg, July 30, 1864. Corporal Henry C. Bixby was captured at Gettysburg, held prisoner, and honorably discharged. (Also reported, less reliably, as "missing at Gettysburg" and "killed at Gettysburg.") In the case of Private George A. Way Bixby the records seem conflicting. According to one record he was captured, held prisoner, and died as a captive; he was also said to have been killed at Petersburg; by a third record (statement of Col. F. C. Ainsworth, U. S. Record and Pension Office, December 8, 1863) he was captured in July 1864, confined in Southern prisons, and "Deserted to the enemy." As to the youngest boy, Private (Arthur) Edward Bixby, William E. Barton has concluded that he was a deserter, and that he lived on until 1909. The summary by F. L. Bullard (33–34) reads: ". . . two . . . were killed in action, one was honorably discharged . . . , one may or may not have been a deserter and may or may not have died a prisoner . . . , and the youngest deserted . . . but apparently not 'to the enemy.'" On this subject the writer has studied, along with other material, the elaborate notebook of Dr. Barton in the University of Chicago Library, also the archives of the adjutant general's office of Massachusetts at Boston; in this office at Boston the author was ably assisted by Fred W. Cross.

[5] For a highly unfavorable account, reporting that Mrs. Bixby kept a house of ill fame, see L. Vernon Briggs, *History and Genealogy of the Cabot Family* (statement of Mrs. Andrew C. Wheelwright, formerly Sarah Cabot), I, 300–301.

an indirect and delayed transmission of reminiscence. One gets it from Nicholas Murray Butler, who wrote: "John Hay told Morley that he had himself written the Bixby letter . . . ." [6] This was not to be disclosed until after Hay's death. Morley, having talked with Hay in 1904, reported the matter to Butler in 1912, when again there was a pledge of secrecy; nothing was to be said of the matter until after Morley's death.

Some have accepted the Butler-Morley-Hay transmission (reading backward) and have bolstered it with supposed evidence that Hay was an imitator of Lincoln's style, of his handwriting, and of his signature. Butler makes the incredibly erroneous statement: "Abraham Lincoln wrote very few letters that bore his signature. John G. Nicolay wrote almost all of those which were official, while John Hay wrote almost all of those which were personal." [7]

With such flimsy statements as these and with various conjectures that Hay himself would never have approved, the subject has become artificially complex and hard to follow. A reader who wants a reliable analysis will do well to read the admirably thorough and fair minded study of the whole subject by F. Lauriston Bullard.[8] The notion that Lincoln wrote very few letters is a serious error. He wrote hundreds in his own hand while President. The statement that Nicolay wrote "almost all" the official ones and Hay the personal ones is demonstrably and astonishingly false. As for Hay imitating Lincoln's handwriting as stated by Butler, it has been shown by Bullard that no actual case of such an imitation can be found. "Nobody has brought forward any definite and convincing confirmation" of this claim,[9] to say nothing of the doubtful propriety of such an imitation on the part of a private secretary. Why should he have imitated Lincoln's handwriting and signature?

Hay did not compose Lincoln's personal letters though there may be found a few letters written for Lincoln in Hay's hand—that is, "routine run-of-the-mine documents" [10] which Lincoln signed though

6 Nicholas Murray Butler, *Across the Busy Years*, II, 390–393.   7 *Ibid.*, II, 390.

8 F. Lauriston Bullard, *Lincoln and the Widow Bixby*. For the argument supporting the Hay-authorship theory see the following pamphlets by Sherman D. Wakefield: *Abraham Lincoln and the Widow Bixby*, and *Abraham Lincoln and the Bixby Letter*. See also "Mr. Bullard's Reply to Mr. Wakefield," *Lincoln Herald*, Vol. 49, 45–46 (June, 1947); "Mr. Wakefield's Reply to Mr. Bullard," *ibid.*, Vol. 49, 27–29 (Dec., 1947).

9 Bullard, 79, 95.   10 *Ibid.*, 82, 86.

they were not holograph letters, and which did not require the special touch of Lincoln's personality. There is a considerable contrast in style between the writing of the young Hay and that of the President. Sometimes a Lincoln letter, if rather long, would be rewritten by a scribe to save labor for the President, but such a letter would be none the less Lincoln's own, probably being based on a draft or working copy in Lincoln's hand.

One of the factors on which careful historians are agreed is that reminiscence is not enough, and it must be repeated that the idea of Hay's authorship rests upon indirectly reported conversations.[11] Memories of honorable men are "fallible," as Bullard shows, and in the case of Hay it is a matter of record that when he talked to Morley in 1904 (eight years before Morley is reported to have talked to Butler), the former secretary of Lincoln was "heavily burdened with grief" from the death of his brother. Hay's own diary account reads: "I talked with him [Morley] hardly knowing what I was saying." [12] It should be added that in this contemporary diary record there is no mention by Hay of having chatted with Morley concerning the Bixby letter; what is more to the point is that one can trace no direct statement by Hay himself that he ever claimed Bixby-letter authorship.

The letter to Lydia Bixby is a genuine Lincoln document printed in the newspapers about the time of its delivery in person to the bereaved mother [13] in Boston and authenticated by inclusion in the *Complete Works of Abraham Lincoln* edited by Nicolay and Hay. On January 19, 1904, the very year of the statement later quoted to Morley, Hay wrote to W. D. Chandler: "The letter of Mr. Lincoln to Mrs. Bixby is genuine . . . ." [14] It must at once be added, however, that the familiar "facsimile" of the letter, or rather several differing facsimiles which have often been used for commercial advertising and for sale, are fakes. Lincoln scholars do not believe that the maker, or fabricator, of any "facsimile" had the actual handwritten letter of Lincoln before him. By comparison with genuine Lincoln letters of the late 1864 period one can see that the "facsimile"

11 *Ibid.,* 112.   12 *Ibid.,* 117.

13 Lincoln's letter was printed in the Boston *Transcript,* Nov. 25, 1864 (where it was reported as received "this morning"); in the Boston *Daily Advertiser,* Nov. 26, 1864; and in the *Army and Navy Journal,* II, 228 (Dec. 3, 1864).

14 Bullard, 122 ff.

lacks the easy flow and the vital quality of letters penned by Lincoln's hand. The writing is a labored and artificial, though superficially plausible, imitation of the President's handwriting. If any one of the facsimile makers had been in possession of the Lincoln original, or of an authentic photographic copy of it, the original would now in all probability be known to collectors, for the process of Lincoln collecting had gone far by the time these "facsimiles" were made. Yet the fact is that the original of this priceless letter has simply been lost,[15] and being a popular topic, it has been a likely subject of forgery. It must be emphasized, however, that it is the *facsimile* purporting to reproduce Lincoln's handwriting which is forged; the Lincoln letter, though long lost, is authentic and its printed form can be trusted as the recognized text.[16]

It is unnecessary to go fully into the mythology of the subject, but it may be briefly remarked that the original manuscript was never at Oxford University (Brasenose College), that it was never in the J. P. Morgan Collection, and that various and sundry "discoveries" of the "original" letter have proved erroneous. Mrs. Bixby did not preserve the letter nor did her family; what happened to it after she received it is unknown.

The vignette-like beauty of the letter, the tender reference to "a loss so overwhelming," the thanks of the Republic to the mother, are given with deep feeling and fitting expression as coming from the spokesman of the whole nation to a parent who stood in a representative capacity for all similarly afflicted parents. Then follows the lofty religious sentiment, the prayer to "our heavenly Father" to assuage the anguish, and the final complimentary mention of "solemn pride" in "so costly a sacrifice." The letter is sincere and heart-to-heart. It is a fine example of Lincoln's personal tact. It stands with the Gettysburg address as a masterpiece in the English language.

---

[15] "Since the day of its delivery neither the original letter nor an undoubted facsimile of it has been seen, and yet it is perhaps the most sought-after letter in the world." Sherman Day Wakefield, *Abraham Lincoln and the Bixby Letter,* (pamphlet), 4.

[16] For further treatment of the Bixby subject, see *Abr. Lincoln Quar.* III, 313 and IV, 35–39; Kendall Banning, "The Case of Lydia Bixby," *Bookman,* vol. 54, 516–520 (1922); William E. Barton, *A Beautiful Blunder;* Elmer Gertz, "Mrs. Bixby Gets a Letter," *Lincoln Herald,* Dec. 1942; Sherman D. Wakefield, in *Hobbies,* Feb. 1941. Numerous other titles are to be found in newspapers and magazines.

CHAPTER IV

LINCOLN'S GOOD NEIGHBOR
POLICY: FRANCE, RUSSIA, MEXICO

IT WOULD make an interesting study to consider American leaders side by side with foreign contemporaries: John Adams with Talleyrand, Jefferson with Napoleon, John Quincy Adams with Metternich, and so on. Such a view presents divergences between the old world and the new which seem at times grotesque. Without laboring the point nor overplaying the superiority of new-world politics, one finds the contrast especially striking in the period when Abraham Lincoln stood forth in a world whose luminaries included a Son of Heaven, a Romanoff, a Hohenzollern, a Hapsburg, sultans and sheiks, daimios and rajahs, throned monarchs and dictators, a Napoleon, a Bismarck, a Garibaldi and a less dashing Cavour, a phantom-crowned Maximilian and an avenging Juárez.

Of some of these foreign elements little needs to be said except that they were contemporaneous; as to others their bearing upon America was vital. A President who had grown up in quiet and remote surroundings, and whose familiarity with foreign things was very slight, was thrown into a series of confused and delicate international situations which presented a constant demand for astute statesmanship. Toward Canada and Mexico, Britain and France, the importance of favorable relations was imperative; in any of these quarters a false step would have been disastrous. Any interruption of traditionally friendly relations with Russia would also have been deeply unfortunate. In dealing with Japan the oppositeness of East and West was startlingly revealed, though this seemed at the time a minor problem, while in the case of China the role of good neighbor in the days of Burlingame presented a challenge to the best and highest in American diplomacy. It was perhaps in the cases of Britain, France, Mexico, and China that the neighborly attitude of the Lincoln government stood out most noticeably; in these important areas especially, and in others also, the good will and foresight of Lincoln, Seward, and Company were weighed and found not wanting.

I

In considering the relation of France to the government of Lincoln one is dealing with an unnatural and abnormal situation. Genuine French opinion, as the documents amply reveal,[1] leaned heavily to the Union side. Accustomed to a unitary government and a concept of national solidarity, the people of France saw no fundamental wisdom in secession, while they were also powerfully influenced by their equalitarian views, their abhorrence of human slavery, and their remembrance of the traditional friendship between the lands of Lafayette and Washington. In contrast, however, to this natural harmony between the two nations was the fact that France was not herself under the Second Empire. The flamboyant dictatorship of Napoleon III, though unable completely to ignore public opinion, was under no specific democratic control, especially in those superficial attitudes that caused false ideas to arise. In following the tortuous diplomacy of the Tuileries one has a sense of unreality. In all the Empire's international dealing one notices an inconsistency between propaganda and fact, façade and main structure, promise and performance. While the war was yet raging violently the Confederacy suffered a collapse of gilded hopes as to French support, while on the other hand the cause of Lincoln and Seward, discouraged as it was by many a portent of French interference, came through with success in virtually every point at issue.

In France, as in Britain, the most serious difficulty was focused on the problem of mediation, with its menacing possibilities for an armistice, recognition of the Confederacy, and European intervention. Superficially a proffer of good offices might be phrased in terms of friendship for both sides, but the eagerness with which the government at Richmond hailed any foreign suggestion for a cessation of

---

[1] Lynn M. Case, *French Opinion on the United States and Mexico, 1860–1867* (contains a mass of official documents reflective of public sentiment); Owsley, *King Cotton Diplomacy,* 564.

the war in terms that envisaged an enduring Confederacy may be taken as sufficient evidence of the harm that such a plan would have brought to the Union cause. It was therefore an ominous fact that in the autumn of 1862 the French Emperor presented a proposal for joint mediation, asking the governments of Britain and Russia to join him in proposing to the American belligerents an armistice of six months. The proposal was understood (certainly by the Confederates) to imply the French imperial wish not only for "mediation," but also for recognition of the Confederacy.[2]

There had been a good deal of secret questioning as to the French proposal at St. Petersburg and London. On previous occasions Napoleon III had created the impression in Confederate minds that France was about to extend recognition. When, after considerable mulling in preliminary conversations, the French proposal for joint mediation came on November 10, 1862, it was published in the newspapers, and the matter was quickly brought to a head by the refusal of Russia and Britain to identify themselves with it. In a British cabinet meeting all present except Gladstone "proceeded to pick it to pieces." [3] In Russia the reaction, official and unofficial, was decisively unfavorable.

These were not snap judgments. Palmerston's cabinet gave the matter careful examination, remembering Adam's reminders of American hostility to the idea, while in Russia Prince Gorchakov [4] was given similar assurances. Seward's dispatches made it clear that "mediation," implying success of disunion (for otherwise no settlement would even have had a hearing by Confederate officials), was regarded at Washington as an alarming and unfriendly proposal.

In all these discussions nothing was more obvious than the propensity of those who favored mediation to misunderstand both American sides. The idea that the Lincoln government could make peace with an independent Southern Confederacy was but one aspect of this misreading of the American situation. Another aspect was seen in the Paris *Constitutionnel* of June 9, 1862, which misinterpreted a speech delivered the previous November in London by W. L. Yancey as a suggestion that the Confederacy might be willing to give

---

[2] *Offic. Rec.* (Nav.), 2 ser., III, 601, 610–611.

[3] E. D. Adams, *Great Britain and the American Civil War,* II, 63–64.

[4] Vice chancellor and minister of foreign affairs of the Russian government. In contemporary American diplomatic correspondence the spelling is Gortchacow.

up slavery in order to gain foreign support for peace. The Con
federacy made no such abolition move until the last phase of the
war, and the inaccuracy of this French interpretation was shown by
the Confederate diplomatic agent A. Dudley Mann who wrote: "The
'care of our honor' peremptorily forbade such a commitment . . . ." [5]

That "peace" by mediation, armistice, or any process that envisaged an undefeated Confederacy was equivalent to utter defeat of
the Union cause must have been evident to an informed observer.
Such a proposal necessarily implied normal continuing existence of
two separate nations in America through an indefinite future. At
no point did the representatives of the Richmond government leave
any doubt as to their refusal to treat for the only kind of peace that
the Lincoln government would consider—i. e., re-establishment of the
American Union. A Frenchman who had visited the United States
and had seen Seward, later conversed with Slidell in Paris, showing
that he envisaged such a restoration of the Union as would allow
"conditions and guarantees" favorable to the South, but Slidell resented his suggestion as pro-Northern and bluntly told him: "if Mr.
Lincoln were to present us a blank sheet of paper on which we were
to write our own . . . guaranties, we would never consent to live
with the men from whom we had . . . forever separated." [6]

Despite the complete failure of joint mediation the government
of Napoleon III made a strictly French move in isolated diplomacy
in January 1863, when his foreign minister sent a dispatch to Washington, deeply deploring a "war, worse than civil," and extending
a proffer of "good offices" in order to "shorten" the hostilities. If
there was any doubt of Washington's attitude, that doubt was dissi-
pated by Seward's emphatic answer (Feb. 6, 1863) and by a stinging
resolution adopted by Congress (March 3, 1863). Though paying
respect to the motive of friendship which, as he said, inspired the offer,
Seward made it unquestionably clear that the government of Lincoln had "only one purpose— . . . to preserve the integrity of the
country." [7] In sharper terms, for Seward kept the amenities of international intercourse, both houses of the American Congress on March
3, 1863, passed a concurrent resolution which did not require Lin-

---

5 *Offic. Rec.* (Nav.), 2 ser, III, 443.   6 *Ibid.,* 519.
7 McPherson, *Hist. of the Rebellion,* 345.

coln's signature, denouncing "foreign interference" as "unreasonable and inadmissible," and declaring that any further step in this direction would be regarded as "an unfriendly act." [8]

There was evidence that French statesmen were sensitive to the lack of European support for their mediation proposal. Expressing the official attitude, the *Moniteur* declared on April 1, 1864: "if it had obtained the concurrence of . . . St. Petersburg and London, the idea of France might not have been either so fruitless or so badly received at Washington, as it was by remaining in the state of an isolated initiative." [9]

II

Dealings of Napoleon III's government with Confederate officials are suggestive of a kind of a pipe-dream diplomacy. Whether it was a financial deal, a bid for warships, or a quest for recognition, Confederate success seemed often to beckon, but substantial aid was an ever receding mirage. A loan was arranged with the French firm of Erlanger, but Confederate negotiators had to allow an unflattering discount, a one-sided deal as to the price of cotton on which the bonds were based, and enormous profits to the takers of the loan. Functionaries of Napoleon's government, openly sympathetic to the Confederacy, had built up Southern hopes; they had even served as Confederate propagandists. Certain ironclads were actually built, but they were never delivered; the Confederacy got no warships from France.

In receiving Confederate agents the French government had gone much further than the British government. Slidell was accorded the honor of personal interviews with the Emperor, as on July 16, 1862, when, by Slidell's account, the news of Union reverses near Richmond "appeared to give him [Napoleon] much satisfaction." [1] Napoleon might give a favorable gesture toward the South, as in the ludicrous episode of Lindsay-Roebuck diplomacy,[2] but such a move was

---

[8] *Cong. Globe*, 37 Cong., 3 sess., 1497–1498, 1541.

[9] The article in the *Moniteur* was a conspicuous reprint of an editorial published in the *Courrier des États Unis*. It was enclosed in a despatch of William L. Dayton to Seward on April 4, 1864, in which Dayton referred to the *Moniteur* as "exclusively an official paper." *House Exec. Doc. No. 1*, 38 Cong., 2 sess., pt. 3, 61–64.

[1] *Offic. Rec.* (Nav.), 2 ser., III, 482. For Napoleon's interviews with Slidell see *ibid.*, 481–487, 574–578, 808, 812–814, 1218–1219.

[2] See *Lincoln the President*, III, 350–353.

more likely to do the Confederacy harm than good. This episode [3] signified to the Confederate envoy Mason that Napoleon's "professions" had been reduced "to a mere shadow," and that the French monarch "held one language" to Roebuck and Lindsay and "a different language to his ambassador in London." [4]

Putting together the comments of Mason, Slidell, Mann, and Benjamin, one concludes that the Confederates themselves were not far misled by Napoleonic blandishment. Mann wrote in May 1863 that his side had "nothing whatever to expect . . . from . . . the Emperor of the French." [5] Hotze, Confederate propagandist, wrote in October 1863 that "the heart of France [beats] for our enemies." [6] After being shifted from one prospect to another, Secretary Benjamin had learned midway in the war to count on nothing as assured, remarking that European conduct was "so different from what was anticipated . . . that we no longer seek to divine their probable course of action." [7]

III

In the case of no other country did the United States under Lincoln enjoy such a marked demonstration of friendliness as in the case of Russia. It becomes necessary here, of course, to recall to mind the Russian-American situation of the nineteenth century. Seward wrote midway in the war: "In regard to Russia, the case is a plain one. She has our friendship, in every case, in preference to any other European power, simply because she always wishes us well, and leaves us to conduct our affairs as we think best." [1] That this good feeling was reciprocated at St. Petersburg was shown by Prince Gorchakov, Russian foreign minister, when the United States chargé d'affaires, Bayard Taylor, presented a friendly letter from Lincoln to Tsar Alexander II in October 1862. Gorchakov said: "We desire

---

[3] For Lindsay's interviews with Napoleon, see *Offic. Rec.* (Nav.), 2 ser. III, 392 ff.; Owsley, *King Cotton Diplomacy,* 298 ff.

[4] *Offic. Rec.* (Nav.), 2 ser., III, 825.

[5] *Ibid.,* 758. He had expressed the same sentiment before (*ibid.,* 516).

[6] Hotze was pointing out what he regarded as the antithesis between public opinion in Britain and in France. He wrote: ". . . the heart of England beats for us and the heart of France for our enemies." In noting Hotze's misreading of British public opinion it must be remembered that he was probably thinking of those Englishmen—such as James Spence—with whom he had been associating and working. *Ibid.,* 946.

[7] *Ibid.,* 656.   [1] *House Exec. Doc., No. 1,* 38 Cong., 1 sess., pt. 2, 851.

above all things the maintenance of the American Union, as one indivisible nation. . . . We have no hostility to the southern people. . . . There will be proposals for intervention. We believe that intervention could do no good at present. Proposals will be made to Russia to join in some plan of interference. She will refuse any invitation of the kind." [2]

A combination of circumstances joined to produce this friendly attitude. In the troubled diplomacy of nineteenth-century Europe France and Britain had been antagonistic to Russia, and in the Crimean War, 1854–1856, there had been armed hostility and bitter resentment. In that war the United States was, of course, neutral, but in feeling many Americans tended toward sympathy with Russia. This sympathy was shown by outspoken comments in the press and by efforts toward mediation on the part of distinguished Americans such as Sumner, Mason, and Fish, as well as by tentative official gestures.[3] The whole effect of the Civil War was to draw Washington and St. Petersburg "even closer together." [4]

This friendship was no less sincere because of being linked with Russian self-interest. The Russian minister at Washington, Edouard de Stoeckl, might fail to understand the Americans among whom he sojourned.[5] Yet distrust of Palmerston's Britain and Napoleon's France naturally strengthened the Russian wish to find, or keep, a friend in the New World. Early in the war it became obvious that Confederate diplomatic success, or even reception, at St. Petersburg was impossible, and it was promptly recognized that "a strong, united

---

[2] *Ibid.*, 840.

[3] "Numerous Russian well-wishers in Congress, among them Sumner, Mason, Clayton, Clingman, and Fish, introduced resolutions or sponsored petitions requesting the President to tender his good offices to end the war. . . . Marcy himself [secretary of state] informed Stoeckl [Russian minister at Washington] that mediation had been discussed in the cabinet . . . ." Benjamin P. Thomas, *Russo-American Relations, 1815–1867,* (*Johns Hopkins Studies,* ser. XLVIII, No. 2), 115. After noting the conciliatory efforts of Elihu Burritt, tireless crusader for international peace, Roy Franklin Nichols writes: "[President] Pierce did not take the steps to further the cause of arbitration [in the Crimean War] which Burritt had hoped, but he and his cabinet had ambitions to act as peacemakers." Nichols, *Franklin Pierce,* 346.

[4] Benjamin P. Thomas as above cited, 120.

[5] It appears that Stoeckl misjudged the American conflict, thought the war would be over soon, considered the old Union gone, and regarded the breach between North and South as irreparable. Lincoln seemed to him to have no far-sighted plan, and he had little respect for American leaders, or, in fact, for republican government. All this is revealed in Frank A. Golder, "The American Civil War through the Eyes of a Russian Diplomat," *Am. Hist. Rev.,* XXVI, 454–463 (Apr., 1921).

American state was an axiom of Russian foreign policy." [6]

For an understanding of these matters one must consider two principal episodes: Russian conduct in the drive toward European "intervention," and the visit of Russian fleets to American waters. Knowing that mediation was resented at Washington, the Russian government, despite its keen wish for a termination of hostilities, turned a cold shoulder toward those suggestions for negotiation which were actively promoted in late '62 and early '63. Especially did the Russian government throw a damper upon mediatory proposals emanating from Paris. Gorchakov besought Bayard Taylor to impress upon his government the feeling of Russia that permanent separation of the American sections would be a great misfortune. One separation, he feared, would be followed by another; the great American nation would break into fragments. He left no doubt in Taylor's mind as to the genuineness of Russian sympathy with the Lincoln government and the meticulous care of his government to maintain a strictly correct attitude in its dealings with Washington.[7] When by May 1863 American prospects abroad were seen to be "decidedly improving," [8] and when the tension as to mediation had noticeably relaxed, it was obvious that the Russian situation had much to do with this improvement.

The sending of the Russian fleets is a complex problem whose ramifications cannot be explored here. Because of a crisis in the perennial Polish question it seemed probable in 1863 that war might again break out between Russia on the one side and Britain and France on the other. Conferences dealing with this possibility were held in the Russian capital which involved anxious deliberation as to how Russia's naval forces could be best disposed. Not all the motives and complications in these conferences can be reconstructed,[9] nor can one say how much stress should be laid on the safety of the

---

6 Thomas, 127.   7 *House Exec. Doc. No. 1,* 38 Cong., 1 sess., pt. 2, 839–841.

8 "Our prospects are decidedly improving. The English antagonism has passed its climax, and I don't think intervention will again be hinted at." Bayard Taylor to Simon Cameron, St. Petersburg, May 12, 1863, Cameron MSS., Lib. of Cong.

9 To set forth these complications is impossible here. Among the factors were the oft-expressed American interest in Polish claims, criticism of the Tsar's Polish policy by American newspapers (as far back as Jackson's administration), difficulties as to Russian America, refusal by the United States to adhere to the international abolition of privateering, the Federal blockade, and the privateering activities of the Confederacy. Thomas, *passim* (esp. 88, 92 ff., 108 ff.).

fleet or the chance of a problematical attack upon enemy colonies, but what the fleets did is a matter of history. One of them appeared in New York harbor under Admiral Lesovsky (Lisovskii) in September 1863; another turned up at San Francisco next month under Admiral Popov. The whole international situation made it seem advisable for Russia, in view of her own interests, to choose American ports for friendly visits, and from the Russian standpoint the episode can be sufficiently explained without supposing that the giving of specific aid to the Union side was the primary purpose. Nevertheless the arrival of the fleets, which amounted to an international sensation, was enthusiastically cheered by American citizens, newspapers, and officials. Russian officers were given elaborate high-society parties; the roster of gentlemen who constituted the committee on arrangements for the ball in New York City in honor of the Russian Naval officers reads like a social blue book.[10] While at New York the fleet enjoyed through Secretary Welles the facilities of the Brooklyn Navy Yard.

As Seward remarked, the American welcome to the Russians required no official prompting. It was "as universal as it was spontaneous." [11] When in December the fleet of Lesovsky sailed into the Chesapeake and up the Potomac Seward himself entertained the admiral and his associates, together with department heads and a large party of American naval officers at his home. This was but an incident of a series of social and official functions at Washington in which the courtesies of the United States were strengthened by the participation of foreign legations.[12]

While Popov's fleet was at San Francisco its assistance was given in extinguishing a fire. Furthermore, the fleet was ready, "simply in the name of humanity, but not of politics, to exercise . . . influence for the prevention of harm." [13] Some may have thought that this brought

---

[10] A printed list is found among the Tilden MSS. in the New York Public Library. Among the names that appear are W. H. Aspinwall, John J. Astor, Jr., Henry W. Brevoort, Hiram Barney, H. W. Bellows, George Bancroft, S. L. M. Barlow, August Belmont, Frederick E. Church, John A. Dix, Franklin H. Delano, Frederick De Peyster, William M. Evarts, Hamilton Fish, Cyrus W. Field, Moses H. Grinnell, Abram S. Hewitt, Francis Lieber, Robert Dale Owen, George Opdyke (Mayor), Edwards Pierrepont, Theodore Roosevelt, A. T. Stewart, John Austin Stevens, A. V. H. Stuyvesant, Samuel J. Tilden, and Alexander Van Rensselaer.

[11] *House Exec. Doc. No. 1,* 38 Cong., 2 sess., pt. 3, p. 279.   [12] Welles, *Diary,* I, 481.

[13] The words of Stoeckl as quoted by E. A. Adamov in *Jour. of Mod. Hist.,* II, 600 (Dec. 1930).

Russia "very near [to] becoming our active ally." [14] Whether this is true may be doubted, for anything like specific assistance to the Union cause would have been interpreted as intervention. It was felt, however, that the presence of the fleet would have checked European warlike impulses against the United States had they existed in any serious degree, and such presence, in London and Paris no less than in Washington and St. Petersburg, was regarded as a gesture of Russian-American amity. After the naval squadrons returned home there occurred a renewed outpouring of Russian gratitude "for the hearty welcome and magnificent hospitality" which the fleet had enjoyed while in America.[15]

The "tradition" which accepted the motive of the Russian naval visit as a token of Russian-American friendship has been considerably tossed about in learned historical articles. Certain writers have shown (a) that in fact the Russians had other motives in terms of their own European situation, and (b) that these other motives—e. g., to avoid being bottled up in case war in Europe should break out—were sufficiently recognized at the time by the American people and press.[16] In a recent study, however, by Thomas A. Bailey [17] it is shown that there was real basis for the familiar tradition, and that in contemporary editorials the "most popular surmise . . . was the one relating to friendship, alliance, and succor." It is Dr. Bailey's conclusion that a "majority of interested citizens at the time—and certainly an overwhelming majority later—appear to have accepted the

14 F. A. Golder, "The Russian Fleet and the Civil War," *Am. Hist. Rev.*, XX, 809 (July 1915).

15 C. M. Clay to Seward, Oct. 12, 1864, *House Exec. Doc. No. 1*, 38 Cong., 2 sess., pt. 3, 290 ff.

16 The following articles by Earl S. Pomeroy are helpful: "The Visit of the Russian Fleet in 1863," *New York History*, XXIV, 512–517 (Oct. 1943), and "The Myth After the Russian Fleet, 1863," *ibid.*, XXXI, 169–176 (Apr., 1950). In the latter article Mr. Pomeroy points out that contemporary American newspapers were aware of Russia's own strategic reasons for the naval visit.

17 Thomas A. Bailey, "The Russian Fleet Myth Re-examined," *Miss. Vall. Hist. Rev.*, XXXVIII, 81–90 (June, 1951). Dr. Bailey takes note of the treatment by William E. Nagengast ("The Visit of the Russian Fleet to the United States: Were Americans Deceived?" *Russian Review*, VIII, 46–55 [Jan., 1949]), which emphasizes America's prompt and acute grasp of the true explanation of Russia's demonstration—e. g., that Russia's motives were to avoid the possibility of having the fleet "bottled up," and to enable the fleet to be used for commerce destruction. On the basis of a "wider coverage of the American newspaper press," Bailey finds less American attention to the Russian fleet than might have been expected; his careful research tends to reinstate the interpretation that "the friendship-alliance hypothesis was the one that took root" (p. 87).

visit of the fleets as primarily a gesture of friendship . . . ." [18]

Another element in promoting Russian-American community of feeling was the factor of slavery. On the one hand Confederate objections were raised to the prohibition of the international slave trade in any future treaty with the Richmond government (should its independence be recognized) on the ground that this was a problem belonging to the states.[19] On the other hand sympathy for Lincoln came naturally to a Tsar (Alexander II) who made a great point of social reform, of the breakdown of caste, and especially of his own notable emancipation of the Russian serfs. Whatever may have been the diversities of customs and institutions, it was felt by statesmen of this period that solidarity of peoples would find expression. In the words of a modern writer this solidarity was not "darkened because of the irreconcilable contradiction of the forms of the governmental order then existing in Russia and in the United States." [20]

IV

In relation to Mexico Lincoln's good neighbor policy moved unhurriedly toward its goal against alien forces that offered the utmost threat to the integrity of that important nation in its hour of revolution and hopeful change. When the United States of America was facing its own fiery ordeal the Mexican Republic was struggling with the greatest menace to its independence since the extinction of Spanish rule in 1821. That menace took the form of a full blown intrigue toward French imperial domination by way of conquest and the imposition of a foreign monarch upon an unwilling people.

If Spanish control in the land of Montezuma had brought civilization and enlightenment, it had also produced absolutism, peonage, and exploitation. With a grasping aristocracy and an avaricious clergy

---

[18] *Ibid.*, 85, 90.

[19] L. Q. C. Lamar, serving in March 1863 as Confederate emissary at St. Petersburg, indicated that, despite the strong insistence of European powers upon the suppression of the slave trade, no such arrangements should be inserted in a treaty with the Confederacy, since this function was not included within the treaty-making power. Bayard Taylor to Seward, St. Petersburg, March 3, 1863, *House Exec. Doc. No. 1*, 38 Cong., 1 sess., pt. 2, 861 ff. In Britain also there was Confederate objection to a treaty stipulation against the slave trade. Not that the British Government was contemplating any treaty at all; the matter was mentioned in conversation between Mason and Lord Donoughmore, cabinet member under the former Derby administration. *Offic. Rec.* (Nav.), 2 ser. III, 598.

[20] Adamov, in *Jour. of Mod. Hist.*, II, 602.

the Spanish system had permitted, among other things, enormous land holdings by the church. Clerical privileges were jealously guarded and numerous fees were exacted from the peasants. Around this powerful influence clustered a political group known as the Church party which stood firm in opposition to nineteenth-century liberalism and in protection of agelong abuses. Not even the boon of governmental stability had been produced by this aristocratic domination. It was characteristic of Mexican politics since the days of liberation that every election tended to become a revolution.

In the period of the American conflict—some years in advance of it—a condition of civil war had existed in Mexico in which the reactionary Church party had contended unsuccessfully with the Liberal party, headed by the popular leader, Benito Pablo Juárez. Coming into power by hard won military success as the constitutionally elected President of Mexico, Juárez proclaimed a series of reforms including religious toleration, confiscation of church property and civil marriage. His government was formally recognized by the United States. Not all went smoothly, of course; hasty measures were unavoidable in the turbulence of the time; blunders were naturally committed by a country suddenly thrown upon its own resources without adequate political experience; adjustments in a radical change of regime were by no means easy. In addition to all these difficulties there was a deplorable weakness in Mexican finances.

Under these circumstances the Mexican Congress under Juárez suspended payment of obligations to foreign financiers for a period of time; this supplied the incident, if one were needed, for foreign intervention. On the side of Juárez it may be said that Mexico was not an opulent nation and that the obligations were considered fraudulent. For a joint enforcement of these outside financial claims a treaty was made between France, Spain, and Britain in October 1861. The United States was invited to join but declined, at the same time offering to guarantee the interest on Mexico's foreign debt if intervention were dropped. Seward did not let the episode pass without expressing his country's strong disapproval of any foreign acquisition of territory in a neighboring republic.

By January 1862 the three powers had put 10,000 troops into Mexico. The Juárez government proved reasonable to deal with, and by May 1862 Britain and Spain, concluding separate agreements in which they had obtained satisfaction from the Republic of Mexico, had withdrawn their forces and dissociated themselves from the joint armed intervention.

Contemporary sources reveal that Napoleon in this phase of his policy had grandiloquent ideas of race pride, religious domination, and what would later have been called *Geopolitik*. The vision of a powerful French monarchy in the New World originated as a kind of dream, then unfolded as an ambitious, flamboyant policy. Such a scheme was natural to a monarch who remembered the achievements and forgot the colossal failures of his spectacular uncle, and whose foreign policy ran easily to unsound foreign adventures. Forgetting the Monroe Doctrine, the Emperor's advisers conceived of a program in which they saw promise of commercial advantage and imperial greatness.

In this episode of power politics nothing is more clear than the contrast between British and French purposes. In a detailed study of the tripartite treaty of October 1861 between England, France, and Spain concerning Mexico, William Spence Robertson has shown that the joint intervention was intended as a means of obtaining satisfaction of financial claims and that British statesmen repeatedly insisted that there be no "forcible interference in the internal affairs of an independent nation." To this disclaimer the French minister for foreign affairs, Thouvenel, agreed, but with "mental reservations," while Napoleon III had secret designs toward a French-dominated monarchy before the treaty was signed. When French designs became unmistakably clear Britain was done with the violated treaty for good and all, while the Spanish government considered that the convention was only suspended. In the discussions pertaining to the whole transaction the Monroe Doctrine was of conscious influence.[1]

Thus after Spanish and British withdrawal in the spring of 1862 the Mexican enterprise was a French affair, evolving as a project in Napoleonic imperialism. More and more French troops were sent; hard campaigns were pushed against stealthy Mexican guerrilla resistance; Puebla yielded to siege in May 1863 after more than a year of fighting; Mexico City was entered by a French army in the following month. In the following year Maximilian of the Austrian house of

---

1 W. S. Robertson, "The Tripartite Treaty of London," *Hispanic American Hist. Rev.*, XX, 167–189 (May, 1940).

Hapsburg, more unsuspecting victim than designing conspirator, was installed as "Emperor of Mexico." In May 1864 Maximilian and his wife Charlotte landed at Vera Cruz and proceeded to the capital city where they were greeted by a synthetic ovation and crowned amid an artificial demonstration. A superficial legal form was contrived to make it appear that the crown was "offered" as the "gift of the Mexican people," but Juárez and his followers fought stubbornly on and it was obvious that the important rulers, however well disposed they might be personally, could not last a day without the protection of the French army.

Ignorant of Mexican affairs, isolated from true Mexican contacts, and utterly at odds with New-World trends, the ill-fated monarch soon found his Austrian associates becoming sullen toward the French, while the "pacification" of the country, to say nothing of the attitude of the United States, proved an insurmountable difficulty. Gradually he found also that Napoleon's glittering promises were not kept. Juárez, at war with both France and Maximilian but still recognized by the United States, suffered serious military setbacks. At the beginning of 1865 his visible support was so slight that his movement seemed about to collapse; yet he persisted in his claim as constitutional President of the Republic, and the authority of the French-sponsored monarchy was never completely recognized in the unhappy country. When in October 1865 an imperial "black decree" consigned all supporters of the Republic to sentence of death by court martial, so fierce a resentment was stirred up that reconciliation became impossible.[2]

V

In shaping American policy toward the Mexican affair the Lincoln administration took a course which may be described as moderate but firm. Having maneuvered France into a disavowal of any intention to establish permanent sway in Mexico, Seward blandly repeated his assurances of American confidence in this disavowal. Thus within the language of friendly diplomacy he contrived to give the most convincing expression of the American point of view as if it were both axiomatic and in harmony with the policy of France. In a

[2] On the Mexican question, see Count E. C. Corti, *Maximilian and Charlotte of Mexico;* Dexter Perkins, *The Monroe Doctrine, 1826–1867;* J. Fred Rippy, *The United States and Mexico.*

strong despatch to Dayton, American minister at Paris, under date of September 26, 1863, Seward summarized the American position, stressing Mexican preference for republican government free from European interference, predicting the sure failure of any foreign attempt to control American civilization, and emphasizing the sympathy of the United States for the Mexican people in their determination to control their own affairs. Referring to rumors of incidents that might produce collision between France and the United States, he said: "The President . . . does not allow himself to be disturbed by suspicions so unjust to France . . . ; but . . . he knows . . . that it is out of such suspicions that the fatal web of national animosity is . . . woven." He made it clear that the United States would be ready for action if necessary (conveying this impression in non-aggressive phraseology), but added that assurances of the French Emperor's intentions were entirely satisfactory to the government at Washington.[1]

There is hardly room in these pages to treat the relation of the Confederacy to the Mexican venture. Leaders and agents of the Richmond government wanted the United States to get into foreign war. Forgetting the Monroe Doctrine, they recognized Maximilian as Emperor. They also showed a readiness to form an alliance with France, thus disregarding Jefferson's historic disapproval of "entangling alliances." [2] Just how a French imperial government in Mexico could have worked to the advantage of the Confederacy, supposing Southern independence to have been achieved, is hard to understand, but for its immediate effect in weakening the Washington government such a foreign embroilment would have been welcome.

In a situation of great delicacy the government of Lincoln continued its recognition of the Republic of Mexico, whose representative, Señor Matias Romero, was made welcome at Washington.[3]

---

[1] *House Exec. Doc. No. 1,* 38 Cong., I sess., pt. 2, pp. 781–783.

[2] Confederate recognition of the Maximilian government was indicated in the fact that President Jefferson Davis appointed William Preston of Kentucky "envoy extraordinary and minister plenipotentiary" to "His Imperial Majesty, Maximilian." (Preston's mission was a failure, as were also certain Confederate efforts to deal with the Juárez government.) As to the idea of an alliance with France, the Confederate agent A. Dudley Mann wrote on August 15, 1863, that he would "gladly see [his] Government entering into an offensive and defensive treaty with the Emperor of the French." F. L. Owsley, *King Cotton Diplomacy,* 541; *Offic. Rec.* (Nav.), 2 ser., III, 155, 871.

[3] In an official despatch dated at Washington, March 12, 1864, Seward referred to "Don

In these trying years Thomas Corwin of Ohio, an elder statesman whom Lincoln had appointed United States minister to the Mexican Republic, gave dignified evidence that friendship between the two countries was unbroken. This was especially significant in view of the notable scarcity of ranking diplomats in Mexico during the French occupation.[4] Not only did the United States decline to send or receive envoys to or from Maximilian, thus denying him international recognition; the American minister to France was instructed on the occasion of the Archduke Maximilian's appearance in Paris to "entirely refrain from intercourse with him." [5]

While the establishment of completely normal relations with Mexico was deferred, the correctness of the American attitude (looking forward to Mexican independence) was carefully watched. In the summer of 1863, with the French army installed in Mexico City, the question arose whether United States minister Corwin should move to San Luis Potosi, temporary seat of the government under Juárez. When Corwin decided not to move, this decision was approved at Washington (August 8, 1863), and at the same time permission was given for Corwin to take a leave of absence. For a time after this, Corwin remained in Mexico City, though accredited only to the government of the Republic; but in the spring of 1864 he left for New York, after which for some years the legation at the Mexican capital was maintained on a reduced basis, with no representative of full rank—i. e., minister—present. This was the situation until in July 1867 Marcus Otterbourg became United States minister at Mexico City. French intervention had by that time terminated and Juárez was back in the capital.

A memorandum of the department of state under date of July 17, 1865, gives significant indication of the attitude of the Lincoln-Johnson administration toward the Maximilian regime. On that date Secretary Seward refused to receive a special agent bearing a letter addressed by Maximilian to the President of the United States. Returning the letter, Seward informed the Marquis de Montholon, French minister at Washington, "that the United States are in friendly communication now as heretofore with the Republican Government

---

Matias Romero, the minister plenipotentiary of the Mexican republic residing at this capital." *House Exec. Doc. No. 1*, 38 Cong., 2 sess., pt. 3, p. 201.

[4] *House Exec. Doc. No. 1*, 38 Cong., 1 sess., pt. 2, 1229–1256 *passim*.

[5] Seward to Dayton, Feb. 27, 1864, *House Exec. Doc. No. 1*, 38 Cong., 2 sess., pt. 3, p. 45.

in Mexico and therefore cannot depart from the course of proceeding it has heretofore pursued towards that country . . . ." The minister was informed that the President declined to receive the letter or to hold intercourse with the agent of Maximilian.[6]

There were, of course, complicating elements in the situation: Yankees camped on the Texan border, Russia keeping a watchful eye and assuring the Union of its friendship, supplies given by Americans to Mexican guerrillas, rumors that Juárez would take refuge in Texas, repeated governmental difficulties within Mexico, the insertion of planks on the Monroe Doctrine in the National Union platform of 1864.[7]

It would have been far from the truth to suppose that the American people were detached or indifferent with reference to the Mexican question. In previous decades they had shown great concern for far-off nations such as Greece and Hungary; naturally the Latin-American world was of even greater concern. Here was a difficulty on the very border and newspapers in the United States kept the Napoleonic menace under constant discussion. A society at New Orleans known as "Defenders of the Monroe Doctrine" kept up its half-understood efforts. Ultimately, after the close of the Civil War, a military force of the United States appeared at the border. Meanwhile, on April 4, 1864, a resolution unanimously passed by the House of Representatives (109–0) declared opposition to "a monarchical government, erected on the ruins of any republican government in America, under the auspices of any European power." [8] It was not until after the war that the matter was cleared up under pressure from the United States by the ultimate withdrawal of French troops and the reinstatement of Juárez as president of Mexico.

In arriving at the complete achievement of United States objectives, Seward did not alienate the French. In a threatening and difficult situation the United States had maintained neutrality as between the French imperials and the Mexican armies; there was no American intervention, this being unnecessary; the Napoleonic Mexican project was allowed to collapse of its own top-heavy weight. It is true that the collapse came after Lincoln's death, but it came while

---

[6] Matters in this paragraph are based on records in the department of state; for a summary the author is indebted to Marcus W. Price and Carl L. Lokke of the National Archives.

[7] *Ann. Cyc.* 1864, 788.   [8] *Cong. Globe,* 38 Cong., 1 sess., 1408.

American procedures remained as the Lincoln-Seward government had shaped them. The American position was upheld none the less effectively because the method of that upholding was non-violent. The episode stands as an impressive testimonial that the Monroe Doctrine does not in practice necessitate the actual hostile use of American armies; the Doctrine is a force for peace, not for embroil-ment.

CHAPTER V

TYCOON, DAIMIOS, AND MIKADO

HE Lincoln government, of course, had business with the whole world. The administration had formal contact with the Sultan of Turkey and with that Ottoman functionary known as the "Sheik-ul-Islam," whose office was something like a combination of lord high chancellor and archbishop of Canterbury.[1] There were dealings, by no means unimportant, between the President of the United States and His Majesty the Sultan of Morocco, so that when complaints arose as to the treatment of Israelites in the Moroccan Empire, American influence was exerted in the direction of civilized amelioration.[2] On the Latin-American side (in addition to Mexican troubles) the Lincoln administration had to consider the Spanish-Cuban situation, "inter-oceanic transit through Nicaragua," troubles in Chile and Peru, and diplomatic relations with Colombia.[3]

As to Canada there were problems touching the St. Lawrence River at one geographical extreme and the Hudson's Bay Company at the other, and there was always the need of adjustment in the matter of trade. Irish groups, bent on involving America in their bitter anti-British movements, were a continuing embarrassment. The Fenian Society had conspiratorial projects involving designs upon Canada and would have welcomed American involvement in their schemes. Later in the war Confederate use of Canadian territory for anti-United-States intrigue seemed at certain stages to offer serious disturbances in Canadian-American relations. Canada has always had a double orientation, looking toward Britain, yet finding its policies and needs "largely determined by conditions indigenous to the Amer-

---

[1] *House Exec. Doc. No. 1*, 38 Cong., 2 sess., pt. 4, p. 375.   [2] *Ibid.*, 425 ff.
[3] *Works*, IX, 225–227 (annual message to Congress, Dec. 8, 1863).

ican continent." [4] Through all these problems and difficulties the enduring factor was the continuance of peace on the "unguarded frontier" and the growing recognition that common and mutual interests were overwhelmingly more valid than temporary, local, or merely private matters of dispute and rivalry.[5]

Among the Japanese in this period the problems of contact with the western world produced one long continued crisis. Strains and stresses in that far-off realm were peculiarly difficult for occidentals to understand. There were times when a solution seemed impossible: Europe would not let Japan alone once Perry had broken the exclusion of centuries, while anything like a secure international adjustment seemed always to recede into the oriental mysteries of Yedo or Kyoto. In a period when Japanese foreign policy was in the making amid violent internal agitation it seemed to Europeans that the island empire of the East had no arbiter of its affairs, no single group or ruler who could speak with authority. At Yedo (Tokyo) there resided the Shogun or Tycoon, a kind of practical executive head of the government (if such a head existed); at Kyoto, in a kind of inaccessible mist, there existed the Mikado, awesome spiritual head, hereditary Emperor, supreme symbol, Son of Heaven. It was not sufficient to say that the Tycoon managed things while the Mikado lived in secluded grandeur surrounded by his impressive court. By rallying round the Mikado, certain aristocratic feudal lords (daimios) might threaten to undo the work of the Tycoon and even to conspire against his somewhat insecure official position. These daimios dreaded foreigners with their commercial exploitation and modern ways; they suspected the Tycoon's government of seeking to monopolize the benefits of foreign trade; they held to their feudal privileges; they felt constrained by no duty to obey orders issued by what foreigners considered the "government" of Japan. Rather they were little, or rather sizable, powers in themselves. If occidental diplomats reached an agreement after protracted negotiation, they might have need for all

---

[4] Edgar W. McInnis, *The Unguarded Frontier: A History of American-Canadian Relations,* 180.

[5] The book by McInnis (see preceding note) gives an excellent survey of relations between the United States and its northern neighbor. The author emphasizes the value of "broad vision and a comprehensive good will on both sides" rather than divergent tendencies on one side and economic nationalism on the other (p. 370). He shows that many Canadians enlisted in the Union army, and that "On the whole there was little positive support for the South in Canada" (p. 222).

their patience to obtain ratification and to know that something had been nailed down which would have effect within Japan.

That nailing down, or attainment of a workable understanding, was what westerners typically wanted, while to the oriental mind, in an age when concessions to the West were nothing less than startling, there was always a further barrier, if only a ceremony, which had to be surmounted before a commitment had been reached. The ceremony might not be the essence of the thing, yet it could not be ignored. A protracted chapter of diplomacy might come to naught for lack of it. And who could finally say that those who controlled ceremony and adulation were less effective or influential than those who tended the government machine? Any threat to the private interests of the princes might cause them to assert their will in the name of the Mikado.

In a day when it was doubted whether the Tycoon could maintain his throne, this was a serious matter. Under the impact of foreign penetration the nation of Japan was experiencing so serious a transition that its very government, as well as its international policy, was insecure and unpredictable. In the midst of assassinations, burnings, attacks on foreigners, interruptions of intercourse, and incidents of private war, pending international questions—rights of residence, opening of ports, promotion of trade, and protection of occidentals—were held in abeyance.

I

To draw together all these complicated factors of the Japanese situation is impracticable in these pages. The subject is unfamiliar to most American readers who seldom think of Japan at all in connection with Lincoln's foreign problems. To treat the Shogun (Tycoon) as practical head of state, or prime minister, seemed the reasonable course from the western point of view, but it was doubtful whether the Mikado's function could be considered merely nominal, for that would be to overlook the powerful position of the barons (daimios). These barons did not like the admission of foreigners to their land. The Emperor to them was an indispensable institution, an enduring conservative tradition, a source of power, and even a tool. With private armies at the disposal of rebellious lords, the Shogunate—the institution with which westerners were dealing—was under formidable attack. These cross currents within Japan were a constant difficulty, but equally disturbing were the differences among the western powers. Britain, France, and Russia were truculent and excessive in their demands, while the United States maintained an attitude of marked friendliness toward the Japanese people.

For this friendly attitude the credit lies largely with two New Yorkers—Townsend Harris, envoy until April 1862, then Robert H. Pruyn, his successor in that post. It has been said (by a British writer) that Harris's services were not "exceeded by any in the entire history of the international relations of the world." [1] Pruyn's conduct may be judged by the statement: "If Perry opened the gates of Japan, and Harris threw them open wide, then Robert H. Pruyn is entitled to no little credit for preventing their being closed again." [2]

In their policy of conciliation and peaceable adjustment, Harris and Pruyn labored amid hazardous conditions, buffeted as they were and almost overwhelmed by the explosive forces within the Empire. A bare enumeration of some of the leading international events in Japan, though inadequate as interpretative history, will at least convey an idea of the turbulent situation.

April 25, 1862: Pruyn, United States minister arrived in Japan. He was well received. *June 26, 1862:* A Japanese assassin killed two British sentries and then committed suicide.[3] The British legation (July 15) retired to Yokohama. Pruyn found himself the only foreign envoy remaining at Yedo. He seemed to be making progress with his demands for opening further treaty ports and did not consider that an unfortunate incident (in which guards of the British legation may have been partly to blame) should be magnified into an international disaster.

September 14, 1862: Another serious incident now occurred. A small party of British subjects was attacked on a road near Kanagawa, and one of them, C. L. Richardson, was murdered, apparently because the party had got into the way of a retinue of a Japanese noble.[4] To the Japanese mind they had committed a deliberate insult and an unforgivable offense against etiquette.

---

[1] J. H. Longford, *The Story of Old Japan*, 302.
[2] Payson J. Treat, *Diplomatic Relations Between the United States and Japan*, I, 131.
[3] *Ibid.*, I, 135.   [4] *Ibid.*, I, 137.

February 1, 1863: The British legation was burned.[5] After these unfortunate events Pruyn still relied on the Shogun for adjustment (the Shogun himself being greatly distressed by these outrages), but other foreign influences were pushing for the most severe measures. The British ultimatum for the Richardson affair (delivered at Yedo on April 6) demanded an indemnity or penalty of £100,000 from the Japanese government and £25,000 from the offending daimio. This led to further demonstrations.[6]

May 24, 1863: The United States legation was burned.[7] Though accepting the explanation that the fire was accidental, Pruyn reluctantly retired to Yokohama (June 1); it was two years before the legation was re-established in Yedo. There was now an interval in which the Shogun, summoned to the presence of the Mikado, agreed to the expulsion of foreigners. It was characteristic of the insecure situation that the agreement was not regarded as final or conclusive. The British demand for an indemnity was complied with.

June 26, 1863: Chosiu, a powerful daimio, strongly anti-Shogun, moved by an intense wish to expel the foreigners, now acted on his own by firing upon a small American merchant vessel, the *Pembroke*. This was followed by retaliatory bombardment by the U. S. S. *Wyoming*.[8] Matters had reached a serious pass. Could open war be averted?

In this critical situation the prestige of the Shogun took a temporary upward turn; he avoided enforcement of the expulsion decree (to which he had given only nominal consent); rebellious barons fell into disrepute; it now appeared that matters could be peaceably adjusted. Such, however, appears not to have been the intent of Sir Rutherford Alcock, British minister, who had the idea "to make war for the sake of forestalling war." [9]

August 28–29, 1864: There now occurred a joint expedition of the western powers (British, Dutch, French, American) resulting in a battle between the ships and shore batteries at Shimonoseki. This "punitive expedition" was not regarded as war, nor was it an attack upon the government of Japan. It was rather a punishing of Chosiu, the daimio of that region.[10] Chosiu quickly capitulated, the straits

---

5 *Ibid.,* I, 155.   6 *Ibid.,* 157–162.

7 Incendiarism was suspected, though the burning was "not an unusual incident . . . where houses are built of light wood and paper." *Ibid.,* I, 172.

8 *Ibid.,* I, 184 ff.   9 *Ibid.,* I, 212.   10 *Ibid.,* I, 233.

were opened, and an indemnity was agreed to.

In Lincoln's annual message to Congress of December 1863 the Far Eastern situation was thus reported: "In common with other western powers, our relations with Japan have been brought into serious jeopardy, through the perverse opposition of the hereditary aristocracy of the empire, to the enlightened and liberal policy of the Tycoon designed to bring the country into the society of nations. It is hoped, although not with entire confidence, that these difficulties may be peacefully overcome."

II

Through all the intrigue, violence, and official evasions in the far eastern Empire the key to American policy was forbearance, avoidance of war, patient attention to the oriental point of view, and cultivation of friendly relations.

At length matters became easier as the Emperor, now becoming more of a power, agreed to the ratification of the international treaties which had been the subject of such long negotiation. As the Lincoln administration ended in 1865 the signs pointed to the success of American policy. This was evident in the abandonment of isolation by Japan (though this came hard) and the establishment of more normal economic and political relations between Yedo and Washington. Authorities writing of the situation as of 1865 have regularly commented on the subsidence of anti-foreign agitation within the Mikado's realm and the improvement in understanding and good will.[1] In the course of the years Lincoln was to become the subject of numerous Japanese books and to take an honored place in the island Empire's gallery of heroes and great men.[2]

Doings of the Lincoln government were important also in relation to China, whose pagodas and art treasures had long been familiar to Yankee mariners and shipowners. When the Emperor of China sent an autograph letter to the President of the United States,[3] or

[1] In addition to the important study by Treat, already cited, the following works should be consulted for an understanding of the Japanese question under Lincoln: Tyler Dennett, *Americans in Eastern Asia; House Exec. Doc. No. 1,* 38 Cong., 2 sess., pt. 3, 445 ff.; Paul H. Clyde, *A History of the Modern and Contemporary Far East.*

[2] For Japanese books on Lincoln, with illustrations, see Jay Monaghan, *Lincoln Bibliography, 1839–1939,* II, 405 ff., plates iii, iv, vi.

[3] *House Exec. Doc. No. 1,* 38 Cong., 1 sess., pt. 2, p. 961.

when Chinese-American treaty provisions required negotiation and ratification, such matters called for studiously correct attention in diplomatic intercourse. While the relation of the United States to Japan in the Lincoln era was somewhat special—different from that of other nations—such a statement could have been made with equal significance as to China, where the American diplomat, Anson Burlingame, bore the high title of envoy extraordinary and minister plenipotentiary at Peking. In the days when the relations of China to the maritime powers called for great delicacy, and when the Chinese mind was decidedly apprehensive of the designs of foreign nations, the fruits of American oriental diplomacy were evident in those unusual marks of respect which that nation bestowed upon Mr. Burlingame. In the period of Lincoln's successor, so great was the confidence of the Chinese government in Mr. Burlingame that, on returning from the Orient, he was appointed by the Chinese government as its own envoy to the United States and other nations. Burlingame has been called "the most successful diplomat America has ever sent to Eastern lands." [4] In view of this high praise it is worth remembering that Burlingame went as Lincoln's envoy and that his influence was exerted not only toward China itself but also toward other powers, in the promotion of enlightened treaty relations and in opposition to Chinese dismemberment.

III

Relations with the Papacy at Rome, and with the newly welded Italian nation at Turin, may be omitted for lack of space to treat such subjects adequately, but there is one Italian episode that requires attention: an American offer of military command to Garibaldi in 1861. Such an offer emanated from Seward and involved considerable discussion. It led to no actual appointment for the distinguished Italian liberator, but it does form at least a curious minor chapter in Italian-American relations.

Briefly, the facts are as follows. Suggestions having been made in American newspapers that Garibaldi's services could be enlisted in the Union army, the American consul at Antwerp, J. W. Quiggle, presented the matter in a letter to Garibaldi himself, who replied in-

---

[4] L. M. Sears, *A History of American Foreign Relations*, 337.

dicating a "great desire" to serve the American cause. After the rude shock of Union defeat at Bull Run (July 21, 1861) Seward, possibly with an eye to incompetence in the Union army, wrote to Henry B. Sanford, United States minister at Brussels, instructing him to "proceed at once and enter into communication with the distinguished Soldier of Freedom." "Tell him [wrote Seward] that he will have the grade of major-general in the army of the United States, . . . with the cordial approval of the whole American People." [1]

There was more to the story, with letters passing between Garibaldi and his Italian friends on the one side and various American diplomats on the other. Not only was Quiggle involved, but also George P. Marsh, accredited to the new Kingdom of Italy at Turin, and Theodore Canisius, United States consul at Vienna, a German-American editor from Illinois.[2] Of Seward's assurance that Garibaldi might have a major generalship in the Union army, one of many, there is no doubt, and the illustrious foreign patriot seems to have been told, correctly enough, that he was being offered "a commission of the highest rank in the power of the President to bestow." [3] This of course meant that no army rank above that of major general lay at that time within the power of the President's appointment. Charles Francis Adams, however, was under the impression that Quiggle had led Garibaldi to believe that he would be invited "to *take the supreme command* in America," which, if true, would have been an egregious bit of bungling on Quiggle's part.[4]

From start to finish it was a queer business and one which illustrates how the same episode, or the same set of words, may produce one impression in foreign minds and another in American. In 1861 Garibaldi was a shining name; he had an immense world reputation as Italian liberator; he had lived in America; he had referred to himself inaccurately as an "adoptive citizen" of the United States. He considered his first allegiance due to Italy, but his services were not

1 Seward to Sanford, July 27, 1861, MS. (Dep. of State), National Archives.

2 In May 1859, with a view to the German vote, Lincoln had made a contract with Canisius for the publication of a German-language Republican newspaper at Springfield. *Lincoln the President*, I, 130–131.

3 Sanford to Seward, Sep. 12, 1861, MS. (Dep. of State: Belgium Despatches), National Archives.

4 *Proceedings*, Mass. Hist. Soc., 3rd series, I, 321 (1907–08).

being sought at home for further strokes toward nationhood and unification. He was in retirement, and his relations with the royal house and government of Sardinia were such that he may not have been unwilling to use an American offer as a kind of pressure upon his king, while at the same time being interested in the offer for its own sake. Sanford wrote an account of an interview which he had with Garibaldi in which the general said that "the only way he could render service . . . to the . . . United States, was as Commander-in-chief of its forces" and that he would also wish authority to emancipate the slaves. In treating this episode C. C. Tansill assumes that if Garibaldi had come it would have been as "head of one of the armies of the North," and indeed it would have seemed unreasonable to expect so distinguished a leader to accept a lesser role. Professor Tansill goes on to say (and this is no more than a doubtful conjecture) that Garibaldi "would at least have spared the Union cause the vacillating incompetence of McClellan, the costly blunders of Pope, and the pitiful collapse of Hooker." [5]

It is not likely, however, that historians will find it advisable to rewrite the history of the war on the basis of assumptions as to what would have happened "if" the highest Union command had been assigned to the Italian leader. The whole discussion as to what Garibaldi would have done is mere speculation: certainly it would have seemed strange for the Army of the Potomac to serve under a foreign general, no matter how illustrious. There is no evidence that this army would have welcomed Garibaldi as a substitute for the highly popular McClellan. It is not easy to transplant a celebrity or hero. Garibaldi's career had been in terms of the Italian milieu and environment. Transferred to America he might have suffered something of an anticlimax. If the documents were not before us, the offer from Seward, and in fact the whole episode, might seem hard to believe. [6]

[5] Charles C. Tansill, "A Secret Chapter in Civil War History," *Thought,* Fordham Univ. Quar., XV, 215–225 (June 1940).

[6] In addition to the items by Charles Francis Adams and by Tansill cited above, the Garibaldi episode is treated by H. Nelson Gay in *Century Magazine,* LXXV (new ser. XIII), 63–74 (Nov. 1907); by Carey Shaw, Jr., in *New York Times Magazine,* (Jan. 11, 1942); and by Howard R. Marraro in *Jour.,* Ill. St. Hist. Soc., XXXVI, 237–270 (Sep. 1943). Documents in the case are found among the manuscripts of the Department of State in the National Archives at Washington.

IV

Matters treated in this and preceding chapters lead naturally to the question: What of Lincoln himself in international matters? Did incidents and controversies merely occur during his administration, or did the man who was President put his stamp upon events and adjustments? In pondering this question one notes first that Lincoln had comparatively little to do with international affairs. In this respect the contrast with Woodrow Wilson is striking. Wilson was in large part his own secretary of state. Throughout his notable administration the course and pattern of international dealings was shaped by the President. Sometimes when a note was signed by Bryan or Lansing it was written by Wilson. Lincoln, however, left the foreign field to Seward. It is true that diplomatic dispatches emanating from Seward's office made frequent, almost constant, mention of the President. The reader of these despatches would be informed that the secretary of state had submitted a matter to the President or that he was conveying the President's wishes, reporting the President's concern, or expressing the President's satisfaction. He would be told that "the President thinks" this or that, that the President had engaged for a certain thing to be done, or that the secretary was doing a particular thing on the President's behalf. Such phrases, however, were so much a matter of mere form and usage that even if the matter involved had in fact been taken up in consultation with the President, the mention of such consultation in a Seward dispatch would not be adequate evidence that Lincoln's judgment had been sought.

With a prairie-lawyer President projected against a complicated world scene, two things were evident: the Chief was aware of his international limitations; and foreigners, both diplomats and citizens, did not at first expect much of the Illinois President. When his friend, John W. Forney, intending to visit foreign parts, asked for notes of introduction, Lincoln wrote in July 1864: "I have no European personal acquaintances, or I would gladly give you letters." [1] In addition to having not one personal acquaintance among Europeans, Lincoln admitted his lack of familiarity with the law of nations. In April 1861, when the President issued his first proclamation of blockade shortly

---

[1] Lincoln to John W. Forney, July 28, 1864, photostat, A. Lincoln Assoc.

after the firing on Fort Sumter, Thaddeus Stevens "packed up and went to Washington, to lecture the president on international law," urging that a blockade, bringing the conflict within the purview of regular international relations, was no way to deal with a domestic insurrection. According to Stevens's report of the interview Lincoln did not seek to defend his own official conduct. Instead, he admitted knowing nothing about the law of nations, remarking that his experience had been that of a "good enough lawyer in a western law court" where international law was not practiced. Seward, he thought, knew all about it; in any case, he said, the thing had been done, it could not be helped, and we must now "get along as well as we can." [2]

Nor did Lincoln claim any fullness of knowledge of the history of other countries. As the war neared its end in February 1865, in a peace conference at Hampton Roads, the question came up of a government entering into an agreement with persons in arms against constituted authority, and one of the Confederate Commissioners, R. M. T. Hunter, "referred to repeated instances of this character between Charles I . . . and the people in arms against him." Lincoln, as quoted, said in reply: "I do not profess to be posted in history. On all such matters I will turn you over to Seward. All I distinctly recollect about the case of Charles I, is, that he lost his head in the end." [3]

At the time of the 1860 nomination Lord Lyons commented with surprise on the Republican convention throwing out Seward and choosing "a man almost unknown." [4] After Lincoln's election Lyons showed distrust of both Lincoln and Seward: he thought "they would think it a safe game to bully us in words." [5] The war came and still the British minister had little confidence in Lincoln's ability; he thought the new leader had not shown "any natural talents to compensate for his ignorance of everything but Illinois village politics." [6]

On April 21, 1861, Archibald, British consul at New York, wrote unfavorably of the government's "vacillating and . . . objectless policy" and of the "ambiguity" of the President's inaugural address.[7]

---

2 Richard N. Current, *Old Thad Stevens, A Story of Ambition*, 146–147.

3 Alexander H. Stephens, *Constitutional View of the War Between the States*, II, 613.

4 Lyons to Lord John Russell, May 22, 1860, Russell Papers, Public Record Office, London, G. D., 22/34.

5 Lord Lyons to Lord Russell, November 12, 1860, Russell Papers, G. D., 22/34.

6 Lord Lyons to Lord Russell, April 9, 1861, Russell Papers, G. D., 22/35.

7 Archibald to Foreign Office, April 24, 1861, F. O., 5/778.

Richard Cobden considered Lincoln's serenity in the midst of war "really quite Pickwickian" and regarded his first regular annual message to Congress as "a quaint, droll affair." [8]

As time passed, however, Lyons, Cobden, and others developed increasing respect for the soundness of Lincoln's judgment in the actual business of foreign intercourse. In October 1863 Cobden was satisfied that Lincoln was determined to avoid a rupture with England or France and to steer clear of any meddling with Mexican politics. In all this he felt that the homely President's "strong common sense" was "much to be commended." [9] A year later Cobden's favorable view was confirmed. Lincoln, he thought, had "honesty, self-control, & common sense, in an eminent degree." [10] British appreciation of Lincoln's merits in international matters came with no less force because little had been expected. In the tense month of December 1862 it was reported from London that the "tone of the President's message in treating of the foreign relations is regarded with more favor, for the reason that something of a different kind had been anticipated in quarters where it was hoped an interpretation might be made of it to our disadvantage." [11]

Contemporary comments differ as to the character and manner of Lyons. To Edward Bates in September 1860 he seemed "unattractive and cold, with a countenance disturbed and uneasy, and an expression very like a suppressed sneer." [12] On the other hand William Howard Russell referred to the minister's discreet reticence, adding that when he did speak, he expressed "sentiments becoming the representative of Great Britain at the court of a friendly Power." [13] About to depart for England on sick leave in June 1863, Lyons had an "affectionate parting" with Lincoln. The two men talked face to face, and they must have conversed rather informally, because, according to Lyons, the President told "a number of stories more or less decorous." Then, coming to more serious matters, Lincoln said: "I suppose my position makes people in England think a great deal more

---

[8] Cobden to William Hargreaves, Midhurst, Dec. 18, 1862, Cobden MSS., British Museum, Add. MSS., 43655, pt. 4.

[9] Cobden to Bright, Oct. 12, 1863, Cobden MSS., Add. MSS. 43651, pt. 3.

[10] Cobden to Bright, Oct. 4, 1864, Cobden MSS., Add. MSS. 43650.

[11] C. F. Adams to Seward, London, Dec. 18, 1862. *House Exec. Doc. No. 1*, 38 Cong., 1 sess., pt. 1, p. 20.

[12] Bates, *Diary*, 148.   [13] W. H. Russell. *My Diary North and South*, 388.

of me than I deserve, pray tell 'em that I mean 'em no harm." Lyons went on to say: "He does not pay much attention to foreign affairs, and I suppose did not like to talk about them without Mr. Seward." [14]

V

Unfortunately Charles Francis Adams seems to have had a low opinion of the President's competence in the international field. Benjamin Moran wrote in his diary on November 19, 1862: "After business hours to-day Mr. Adams had a long talk with me about Lincoln. He thinks the recent political defeats [in the congressional election] a natural result of his management. His whole course from the beginning has been unstatesmanlike, and nothing in his Presidential career was more stupid than the selection of his Cabinet. He appointed Mr. Welles without knowing anything about him, and took the others in an equally hap-hazard way. The conversation satisfied me that Mr. Adams regards Lincoln as a vulgar man, unfitted both by education and nature for the post of President, and one whose administration will not be much praised in future." [1] One can also quote Moran's own view as to Lincoln's bad management. Referring to the 1862 election of Seymour of New York, he wrote: "This strikes me as a piece of bad luck. It is one of the consequences of the wretchedly bad management by Lincoln of this war . . . ." [2]

The question of Lincoln's qualities became the subject of sharp controversy when, after Seward's death, Adams delivered (at Albany on April 18, 1873) a panegyric on the secretary of state. It was fitting that Adams should praise Seward, for that was the specific purpose of this speech delivered at the invitation of the New York legislature; but, to quote Welles, "it was not anticipated that the occasion would be used to elevate the reputation of the deceased statesman . . . by depreciating or underrating the abilities of the President under whom he served." [3]

Welles was correct in his view that Seward's eulogist was less than

[14] Lord Lyons to Lord Russell, June 13, 1862, Russell Papers, G. D., 22/36.

[1] Sarah Agnes Wallace and Frances Elma Gillespie, eds., *The Journal of Benjamin Moran, 1857–1865*, II, 1092.

[2] *Ibid.*, II, 1091 (Nov. 17, 1862).

[3] Welles, *Lincoln and Seward: Remarks Upon the Memorial Address of Chas. Francis Adams, on the Late Wm. H. Seward*, iii–iv (preface).

just toward Lincoln. In his address Adams referred to "the . . . appalling . . . fact that we were about to have, for our guide through this perilous strife, a person selected partly on account of the absence of positive qualities . . . and absolutely without the advantage of any experience in national affairs" beyond a brief congressional term. Warming to his theme, he said: "I must, then, affirm without hesitation that, in the history of our Government down to this hour, no experiment so rash has ever been made as that of elevating to the head of affairs a man with so little previous preparation for his task as Mr. Lincoln. If this be true of him in regard to the course of domestic administration, with which he might be supposed partially familiar, it is eminently so in respect to the foreign relations, of which he knew absolutely nothing. Furthermore, he was quite deficient in his acquaintance with the character and qualities of public men, or their aptitude for the positions to which he assigned them. Indeed, he seldom selected them solely by that standard." [4]

With a good deal of outraged feeling Welles answered the Adams address at length in a book published in 1874. The former secretary of the navy wrote: "A greater error could scarcely be committed than to represent that Mr. Lincoln 'had to deal with a superior intelectual [*sic*] power' when he came in contact with Mr. Seward. The reverse was the fact." [5] The more sensible view is to disparage neither Lincoln nor Seward. Their diplomacy was the responsibility of both, with Seward in practical charge, and it is worth while to recognize the ability of the secretary of state, despite quirks which Adams seems to have overlooked, and in doing so to give due credit to the President who appointed him, and who, amid fearful complications gave him co-operation without meddling and constant support without embarassing interference.

This presidential support was no slight factor. Lincoln knew what it meant to operate with his secretary of state while that important official was under repeated sniping, especially by senators. The crisis of December 1862 was but one example of this kind of trouble. While responsibility for foreign affairs was vested in the President, and while the Senate had its proper function in this respect, yet these

----

[4] Charles Francis Adams, *An Address on . . . William Henry Seward . . . at Albany, April 18, 1873*, 47, 49.

[5] Welles, *Lincoln and Seward*, 7.

attacks, in the manner in which they came, placed pitfalls in Lincoln's path. Some of his most skillful steering had to do with persistent efforts to get rid of Seward. Lincoln knew how to work with his Senate, but if he had given in to this kind of pressure, the result would have been an unfortunate sense of cabinet insecurity and a disturbing interruption of international dealings. In terms of enduring historical appraisal the President was justified in the continued confidence he gave to his foreign minister.

One may admit Seward's merits while remembering also those of Lincoln, the more so since the President was needlessly belittled. The editorial comment of Charles A. Dana is worth noting here. At the time of Adams's eulogy of Seward, Dana wrote: "There are several things in this oration which are likely to excite dissent, and there is one especially which seems to require immediate correction. Having been absent from the country during . . . President Lincoln's administration, and never having enjoyed the advantage of personal intimacy with that remarkable man, Mr. Adams falls into the rather natural error of attributing to Mr. Seward a degree of influence with Mr. Lincoln and of control over his actions which he did not possess or exercise."

Dana continued: "No doubt the Secretary of State had his full share in the transactions of that time. He was much consulted by the President, who was fond of his conversation and his society; but the truth is—and this we say . . . from personal knowledge—no man was ever more entirely the master of his own affairs . . . than President Lincoln of the executive power of this Government. He was on friendly terms with all the members of his Cabinet, and gave them due latitude in the discharge of their proper duties; but when any one had to yield his opinion it was the Secretary and not the President . . . . This we say not to lessen the just glory of Mr. Seward or any of his colleagues, but to state the exact truth and do justice to Abraham Lincoln." [6]

Despite his small acquaintance with Europe and with international law, Lincoln came through his stormy presidency with painful crises averted and international matters wisely handled. Shrewdness, common sense (a phrase that often recurs), and the tact that goes with calmness and good will were elements that made up for lack of speci-

---

[6] Editorial, New York *Sun*, April 19, 1873.

fic experience in formal diplomacy. The picture of Lincoln's ineptness and of Seward's bluntness is after all superficial. In essential dealings the Lincoln-Seward team performed well; it is a pity that so much cannot be said of the Lincoln-Stanton team. In most matters Lincoln and Seward worked smoothly together. Differences between them appear never to have led to serious friction. Not always did Lincoln follow Seward's advice, but instances of clashes of will were exceedingly few. Other members of the cabinet resented the influence of the secretary of state over the President, as when Welles complained in August 1863 that Seward was yielding too much to the wishes of Lord Lyons.[7] In this there was the implication that both the President and his foreign secretary were easy going, which in a way was true. Bates felt much the same about it when he mentioned that the usual procedure was for "knotty cases" to be passed by without reaching a conclusion.[8]

Yet of course there were international decisions made by the Lincoln government, as preceding pages amply reveal, and while "concessions" were made to Britain, properly enough, equal or greater concessions were made to us by the British. Moreover, American concessions themselves were fruitful of results in international good will and in solid benefit. A stroke of international policy might amount to a "concession" and yet might constitute an actual advantage. Seward's tact in dealing with Lyons was as often associated with an American diplomatic victory as with a setback. When in 1861 the United States revoked the exequatur of Robert Bunch, British consul at Charleston, for his diplomatic negotiations with the Confederacy, the secretary of state, while fully upholding the American position, lost nothing in the process by coupling his victory with a compliment to Lyons.[9]

Lincoln's international contribution cannot be lightly dismissed. A President who appointed Charles Francis Adams to the mission at London, who put the tactful quietus on his secretary of state at the time of his April 1 aberration in 1861, who added touches of masterful revision to Seward's dispatch of May 21, 1861,[10] and whose mind turned to arbitration rather than truculent blustering in the *Trent* affair, was a President whose influence in foreign

---

[7] Welles, *Diary*, I, 409.
[8] Bates, *Diary*, 266.
[9] Bancroft, *Seward*, II, 201.
[10] *Lincoln the President*, II, 35–37.

matters was exerted in the direction of sanity and peace. The reply to the workingmen of Manchester was an example of the manner in which the democratic-minded President could speak to the millions in England. The overwhelming response of those millions to the head of the government at Washington was under no misguidance. The confidence of the liberal minded Bright was not misplaced. The friendliness of Bright and the appeals of British labor, though associated with politics at home, were not without significance as tributes to Lincoln's humanity.

In the matter of America's larger responsibility Lincoln held views that were not dissimilar to those of Woodrow Wilson. Each thought that democracy in the world, with peace and order, was at stake in the struggle. When Lincoln said that the issue embraced "more than the fate of these United States," [11] when he urged that we must demonstrate to the world that ballots are better than bullets, his thought was that to do so would be "a great lesson of peace." [12] With no grudge against the people of the South, he nevertheless felt that the "insurrection" constituted "a war upon the first principle of popular government." [13] In blue books and diplomatic dispatches Lincoln's role in international affairs is somewhat hidden, but the subject is not to be studied in these sources alone.[14] To deal fundamentally with Lincoln's significance in the larger world scene it is necessary to remember the man's whole confession of faith, his concept of democracy, his concern for growing economic opportunities for laboring people, and his deep sense of the enduring value of popular institutions.

---

[11] Nicolay and Hay, *Works,* VI, 304 (message to Congress, July 4, 1861).

[12] *Ibid.,* VI, 322.   [13] *Ibid.,* VII, 56.

[14] For a comprehensive and vividly written account of international relations under Lincoln, see Jay Monaghan, *Diplomat in Carpet Slippers: Abraham Lincoln Deals With Foreign Affairs.*

CHAPTER VI

CHASE IS WILLING

A S THE nation faced the presidential election of 1864 the political outlook was confused and the prevailing temper was
that of disharmony. The "envenomed . . . spirit of party"[1]
was rampant, whether the label was "Democrat," "Republican," or
"Union" which being interpreted meant "Republican." Neither of
the major parties was what conscientious Americans would have
wished—that is, a consistent grouping of voters for a civic purpose.
So strong was the tendency toward factionalism that adhesion within
any major party remained less a matter of like-minded opinion than
of organization pressure for winning elections and seizing or retaining governmental office. If party factions closed ranks for 1864, that
would mean that there was political self-interest in victory under the
party label and for the organization. It would not necessarily mean,
for instance, that after the election the winning candidate could
count on the support of those whose party name he shared.

I

The "next election" was, of course, on everyone's lips. The Republican party, a newcomer in politics, was torn by bitter internal
dissension between the Chase-Butler-Frémont faction and the Seward-
Blair-Welles-Bates faction, Lincoln being identified with the latter
of these groups. It was not that the President was encouraging factionalism. He wished to avoid it, but the radical opposition to him
was so intense and its drive for power so determined that anti-Lincoln
maneuvers within the party were sure to arise. Against these maneuvers it was certain that support of Lincoln would also be expressed

---

[1] Welles, *Diary*, I, 211.

and organized.[1] If on Lincoln's part there was a wish for a kind of presidential neutrality between factions, the success of that attitude would depend on how it was taken or treated; it would have to be watched lest it be interpreted as surrender to the "radicals."

Political preferences determined the manner in which men of varying opinions read the signs. The 1863 elections, which were many and important, were regarded as notably favorable to the existing administration (as in the rousing defeat of Vallandigham),[2] but as the winds seemed to be taking a Republican turn the moves of this or that group to seize control of the party became intensified. There was disagreement as to the full meaning of those elections in which, though Lincoln was upheld, Henry Winter Davis was favored and Montgomery Blair was "repudiated." [3] It was not merely a question of Republican success in '64, but of how that success, once achieved, should be used.

The *pros* and *cons* of particular leaders were elaborately debated in the press. The New York *Herald,* in its issue of February 19, sounded off on the theme that "President Lincoln is a joke incarnated." His election, said the *Herald,* was a "ridiculous joke"; his secret manner of entering Washington "a practical joke"; his debut in Washington society and his inaugural address were "jokes"; his cabinet a "standing joke"; his military letters "cruel jokes," his reconstruction "another joke," and so. The climax of this devastating enumeration was reached with the statement that his hopes for renomination and reelection were "the most laughable jokes of all." Since the President had "nothing but jokes to recommend him" it was suggested that he ought "to make the most of them." Returning to the theme on March 7, the *Herald* came through with another scurrilous jibe at the President. After mentioning various factions in the Republican party (followers of Frémont, Chase, and Wendell Phillips), it added: "fourth, there are the smutty republicans, who go for Lincoln, the joker."

---

1 Lincoln's secretary-biographers assert that "from the opening of . . . 1864 the feeling in favor of the renomination of Lincoln grew so ardent and so restless that it was almost impossible . . . to hold the manifestations of the popular preference in check." Nicolay and Hay, *Lincoln,* VIII, 323. If this was an overstatement, it is nevertheless true that the Lincoln papers, open to scholars since July 1947, are full of enthusiastic letters expressing support for the President.

2 *Lincoln the President,* III, 239–291.   3 *Ibid.,* III, 287–288.

The whole tune of the *Herald* was that Lincoln was a failure and would "imperil our republican institutions if, by any chance, he should happen to be re-elected." The people were "tired of incapacity, tired of partisanship, tired of corruption . . . ." "The age of small politicians like Lincoln, Chase, Seward, Welles, Stanton, Weed, the Blairs or the Buncombes, is past and gone." [4] "Give us . . . a practical military man." [5] With the idea of getting clear of existing parties, the *Herald* offered its solution: "the independent ticket" of Grant and Dix with the understanding that General McClellan would be identified with this ticket and would be "our future General-in-Chief." [6]

Quite different was the policy voiced by Greeley's *Tribune*. This distinguished newspaper did not go "all out" against Lincoln. It admitted (February 23) that the President had "well discharged the responsibilities of his exalted station," and noted that he was "the first choice . . . of a large majority of those who have . . . supported the Administration and the War." Yet in the *Tribune's* reasoning it did not follow "that Gov. Chase, Gen. Frémont, Gen. Butler, or Gen. Grant, cannot do as well."

In a careful study of Greeley's wartime attitude, Ralph R. Fahrney shows how the famous editor persisted in his opposition to a second term for Lincoln. He "lost faith in the ability of Lincoln to weather the crisis," sought repeatedly to postpone the 1864 Republican national convention (an anti-Lincoln move), gave support to Chase and repelled attacks upon that statesman, discouraged the formation of Lincoln clubs, advocated "the good old Harry Clay 'One Term' principle," and, on the collapse of the Chase boom, turned with other radicals to Frémont.[7]

II

Lincoln's strait-laced secretary of the treasury and presidential rival had not been lacking in courage and forthrightness. Not only did he appreciate with a burning earnestness the moral importance of the antislavery cause; he had held this moral principle to be of

---

[4] New York *Herald*, Mar. 2, 1864, p. 4, c. 3.   [5] *Ibid.*, Mar. 5, 1864, p. 4, cc. 2-3.
[6] *Ibid.*, Feb. 22, 1864, p. 4, cc. 2-3.
[7] Ralph Ray Fahrney, *Horace Greeley and the Tribune in the Civil War*, 139-140, 184-185, 187.

more validity than party adherence. Though formerly a Whig, he was prominent in the 1840's as a zealous leader in the Liberty and Free Soil parties. Then, convinced that a party could not live on antislavery alone, he operated with the unrealistic hope of capturing the Democratic party for the antislavery cause. It was partly with the help of Democratic votes in the Ohio state legislature that he was elected United States senator in 1849. When later he joined the "anti-Nebraska" (Republican) party, that was because of its free-soil stand. Having made the shift, he was genuinely pained, as were Giddings and others, when it seemed at times that his adopted party was slipping in its adherence to principle. In the disunion crisis he had not been inflexible against the right of secession. For a time he favored letting the erring sisters go in peace.[1] He considered this preferable to a compromise that would have sacrificed principle; he also seems to have held it preferable to war.

Lincoln did not satisfy him. As of 1860 the Ohioan was a man of more prominence, with a longer record in public office and in party leadership, than the Springfield lawyer. He had been governor of his state and senator at Washington. Disappointed in his efforts for the presidential nomination in 1860, he had worked for Lincoln, and his appointment to the cabinet was not only natural; it was a matter on which Lincoln's mind was clearly made up as it had not been, for example, in the case of Cameron. Lincoln felt that he simply had to have Chase in the cabinet, as, for a balancing reason, he also had to have Seward. In the opposition of these two men and their followers—beginning at the very outset of Lincoln's administration in 1861—the long-standing cleavage within the Lincoln team had its inception.

Chase had always been uncomfortable in the Lincoln cabinet and people wondered how two men of such different temperament and outlook could wear the same yoke. Often he expressed dissatisfaction with "the whole state of things" along with regret that he could do so little outside his own department.[2] He was pained at what he saw: "irregularity, assumptions beyond law, deference to Generals and reactionists. . . . ."[3] He visualized himself as alone in his high-

---

[1] *Lincoln the President,* I, 320–321.

[2] Chase to Murat Halstead, Washington, May 24, 1862, copy in Chase MSS., Pa. Hist. Soc.

[3] Chase to Greeley, May 21, 1862, copy in *ibid.*

minded motives. Referring to the attitude of "the old laborers for freedom" who complained that Chase had not done more, he wrote: "They forget that I am but one member of the administration, and the only one who has any special sympathy with them." [4] Considering the President's methods slipshod, he referred scornfully to the "so-called cabinet," whose meetings he deemed "useless." He "chafed" under Seward's management and resented the New Yorker's patronizing and superior manner. According to Welles, Lincoln felt that both of these men were serviceable. "He is friendly to both. He is fond of Seward, who is affable; he respects Chase, who is clumsy. Seward comforts him; Chase he deems a necessity." [5] The tense situation led to repeated efforts (or gestures) on Chase's part toward resignation, the most striking of which was in the "cabinet crisis" of mid-December 1862. This had been a time of senatorial attack upon the secretary of state and of deep distress to the President, but Lincoln's self control and shrewd tact had overmatched the clamorous pressure against him, so that he succeeded in keeping in his cabinet not only the target of senatorial displeasure (Seward), but also the embarrassed member (Chase) who had become a center of anti-Lincoln intrigue.[6]

Cabinet methods were "all wrong," thought Chase; he was "mortified that things were so conducted." [7] This attitude was genuine. Chase honestly believed that Lincoln was wanting in energy, inefficient in military leadership, unsystematic in method, needlessly willing to compromise, and in general inadequate to the fearful demands of the emergency. Being a vigorous man and tremendously in earnest for the cause as he saw it, the secretary of the treasury, more than any colleague in the cabinet other than Seward, often took a hand in the management of affairs. He took up for particular generals such as Frémont and Hooker, visited Hooker's headquarters, and assumed a kind of direction of Hooker's future.[8] He told Butler what to do at New Orleans.[9] He sought frequently to exert influence in military matters. "Please let me hear from you . . . frequently," he wrote to General N. B. Buford. "Give me all the facts . . . es-

4 Chase to Thomas Heaton, June 21, 1862, copy in *ibid.*   5 Welles, *Diary*, I, 205.
6 *Lincoln the President*, II, chap. XXV.
7 Chase to Greeley, Sep. 7, 1862, Greeley MSS., New York Pub. Lib.
8 Welles, *Diary*, I, 335–336, 349.
9 Diary and Letter Book of S. P. Chase, Lib. of Cong., May 16, 1862.

sential to forming a correct judgment. . . . Tell me who are your
best officers old and young, and in all ranks . . . ." [10] He had a way
of writing as to what he would do if he "were in the field." [11] He
had not only joined with a cabinet clique to have McClellan dismissed but had been opposed to the President's action in reinstating
the general in the critical pre-Antietam phase.[12] When Frémont and
Hunter seemed prematurely to be taking emancipation policy into
their own military hands, out of the hands of the President, Chase
sympathized with the generals and was supposed to have encouraged
them. He opposed Lincoln's revocation of the Hunter order.[13] At
times, though it need not be supposed that this was beyond his
duty, he told the President what to do. For example, he earnestly
regretted the removal of Rosecrans from command in the Chattanooga area.[14] Welles remarked that he made himself "as busy in the
management of the army as the Treasury." [15]

III

The more Chase thought of presidential matters the more did
his distrust of Lincoln color his views. As an example one could note
his changing attitude toward Cameron. In 1860–61 he had opposed
the Pennsylvanian's entry into the cabinet, but after Cameron became associated with anti-Lincoln groups Chase wrote favorably of
him. The other side of the same coin was that Chase disliked men,
such as Frank Blair, Jr., who were championing the President. The
one cabinet member toward whom Chase's feeling gravitated was
Stanton. Men who wrote statements friendly to Lincoln were not
likely to couple them with praise of Chase. Those two thoughts did
not go together. An Ohioan in December 1862 wrote: "It is a comfort . . . to know that there is one honest man in the Administration. . . . That man is Abraham Lincoln himself." This state-

---

10 Chase to N. B. Buford, Oct. 11, 1862, copy in Chase MSS., Pa. Hist. Soc.

11 "If I were in the field I would let every man understand that no man loyal to the
Union could be a slave. We must come to this." Chase to John Pope, Aug. 1, 1862, copy in
ibid.

12 Welles, *Diary*, I, 93 ff.; *Lincoln the President*, II, 112.

13 Chase to Greeley, May 2, 1862, copy in Chase MSS., Pa. Hist. Soc.; Diary and Letter
Book of S. P. Chase, Lib. of Cong., May 16, 1862.

14 Chase to Lincoln, Oct. 31, 1863, R. T. L. Coll., 27610.

15 Welles, *Diary*, I, 108 (Sep. 3, 1862).

ment was significantly joined with strong denunciation of Chase: Ohio owed him nothing, it was said; there were worthier men in the state; the weakest thing Lincoln had done was to call such rivals into his cabinet.[1]

It may be footless to speculate as to the bounds or dimensions of Chase's self esteem. When a man is prominently mentioned for the presidency he naturally has some concept of himself in relation to that position. Chase appears to have believed that, in the existing circumstances, his availability for the high office had to be taken into account. Believing that Lincoln was falling short while the nation's interests were in gravest peril, he had definite views as to broad policies, presidential techniques, and specific measures. Not only was he regarded as one of the outstanding leaders of the Republican party; in the eyes of his admirers he was its principal leader. He had ability, experience, and a knack for administration. Many in the party who could see no compelling reason to renominate Lincoln in 1864 were urging upon Chase that he was the man. Bates wrote in 1863: "I'm afraid Mr. Chase's head is turned by his eagerness in pursuit of the presidency." [2] Wade's comment, as quoted by Hay, was: Chase "thinks there is a fourth person in the Trinity." It was also noted that Chase desired to injure the Lincoln administration.[3] The secretary "wished others to believe him omniscient," wrote Welles; he "lamented the President's want of energy"; anti-administration remarks in the Senate had "their origin in the Treasury Department." He had, continued Welles, "inordinate ambition, intense selfishness for official distinction and power to do for the country, and considerable vanity." Welles thought that these traits impaired his moral courage; "they make him a sycophant with the truly great; and sometimes arrogant towards the humble." [4]

It was significant that in February 1864 the treasury head was writing long "autobiographical letters" to J. T. Trowbridge who in that election year, obeying the vogue for self-made heroes, brought out a campaign biography with the Alger-like title, *The Ferry Boy*

[1] Editorial by Lyman W. Hall, *Portage County Democrat:* undated clipping, Chase MSS., Lib. of Cong., no. 9302.

[2] Bates, *Diary*, 310 (Oct. 17, 1863).

[3] Dennett, ed., . . . *Diaries . . . of John Hay*, 53, 231.

[4] Welles, *Diary*, I, 494, 520, 525; II, 121.

and the Financier.[5] In the treasury department, with Jay Cooke's support, the unprecedented expenses of war were met, though the high interest rate bespoke a none-too-high credit for the government, while much of the financing was a matter of forced bank-borrowing, suspension of specie payments, and greenback issues. Yet the treasury was holding up and superficially its management bespoke great administrative skill. Chase himself wrote: "I am astonished at my own success, financially. The public credit is now established." Again he wrote: "Would you believe it? In spite of all embarrassments, I yet raise a million a day!" [6]

Naturally Chase's attitude was influenced by incoming letters in which his name was featured for the presidency. "All things considered," wrote one correspondent, "my opinion is that you ought to be our next President. . . . The country demands that our best and only our best, men should be placed in nomination . . . ." [7] As he read his mail Chase found a Wisconsin man urging that pro-Chase "wires" be laid; [8] an Ohio man declaring: "You are head and shoulders above any other statesman in America." [9] His papers show that he was getting a stream of such letters.

To set a date for the beginning of Chase's 1864 aspirations for the presidency is not easy. A competent scholar has written: "It would . . . be difficult to say at just what point Chase began to think seriously of himself as a rival to Lincoln for the Republican-Union nomination of 1864, but certain it is that by September, 1863, he was actively doing just that." [10] What might be called a specific "boom" for Chase was launched—or an organization for launching

---

[5] The Trowbridge letters are among the Chase MSS. in the Pa. Hist. Soc. One of Chase's admirers wrote: "Every body—friend and foe, ascribe all the good work of the administration to you & all its weak doings where they belong. You may never be our president, but you may well be content with the honor of having the people everywhere feel that you deserve to be. The children are learning this . . . from the 'Ferry Boy.' A delightful book. We have enjoyed it exceedingly," H. B. Walbridge to Chase, Toledo, May 16, 1864, Chase MSS., Lib. of Cong.

[6] Chase to E. D. Mansfield, May 31, 1862, and to James Watson Webb, Oct. 21, 1862, copies in Chase MSS., Hist. Soc. of Pa.

[7] J. R. Freese to S. P. Chase, *State Gazette* office, Trenton, N.J., Dec. 18, 1863, Chase MSS., Lib. of Cong.

[8] E. A. Spencer to Chase, Madison, Wis., Dec. 8, 1863, Chase MSS., Lib. of Cong.

[9] M. F. Conway to Chase, Atchison, Kan., Dec. 8, 1863, *ibid.*

[10] George Winston Smith, "Carpetbag Imperialism in Florida, 1862–1868." *Florida Hist. Quar.*, XXVII, 275 (Jan. 1949).

it was mapped out—at a meeting in Washington on December 9, 1863, significantly the day immediately following Lincoln's message outlining his restoration program. The conference then held was designated as "a meeting of the friends of Freedom and the Union," and a set of "committees," Central and State, or Local, was "appointed." It is not certain what this appointing meant, but one can look down the list of names and find those Republicans who were—or were understood to be—uncommitted to Lincoln and friendly to Chase. The list included General Schenck and Congressman Rufus P. Spaulding of Ohio; Roscoe Conkling and John Austin Stevens of New York; Andrew Johnson and W. G. Brownlow of Tennessee; Henry Wilson and Governor Andrew of Massachusetts; Hannibal Hamlin of Maine; "Gov. Pierpont" of "E. Va."; John Wentworth of Illinois; David Wilmot, A. H. Reeder, and Jay Cooke of Pennsylvania; O. P. Morton of Indiana; Charles D. Drake of Missouri; Samuel R. Curtis and Governor Samuel Kirkwood of Iowa; and Charles Durkee of Wisconsin. There were other names. The list was tentative as indicated by question marks attached to the names of Conkling, Wilmot, Henry Wilson, Reeder, and others; certainly Andrew Johnson and "Parson" Brownlow had not consented to inclusion in the enumeration. For some states—Rhode Island, New Jersey, Kansas, Minnesota, and Michigan—no one was named. The idea was to set down a list of men who could, conceivably, as it was supposed, become part of an organized Chase movement. The endorsement on the memorandum of proceedings read: "Organization to make S. P. Chase President: Dec. 9, 1863: Important." The advisory committee consisted of Schenck, Spaulding, Conness of California, Henry Wilson, L. E. Chittenden, Whitelaw Reid, and D. Taylor. The letter-head was that of D. Taylor, "Paymaster, U. S. A." [11]

That the Chase effort was not confined to managers at Washington was indicated by a statement (quoting Doolittle of Wisconsin) in Welles's diary for December 28, 1863: ". . . there is an active, zealous, and somewhat formidable movement for Chase." He added: "Chase clubs are being organized in all the cities to control the nominating convention."

---

[11] The manuscript report of this Chase organization meeting is in the Library of Congress.

As with all such movements politicians got out their pencils to figure prospects, not so much in terms of popular support, but in the hard currency of delegates at the coming Republican national convention. In one such prediction, arrived at in January 1864, the one who made the calculation placed New York, Pennsylvania, Indiana, Illinois, and a scattering of others in the Lincoln column, while in the Chase column he included all of New England along with Ohio, Missouri, Wisconsin, Michigan, Iowa, and other commonwealths. The final conjectural result came out as almost a tie: 119 delegates for Lincoln, 118 for Chase. Some of those set down for Lincoln were mentioned as doubtful.[12]

To study the reports of willing workers for Chase would be to learn much, if not of the way Presidents are chosen, at least of the manner in which presidential bees are encouraged. "Under all . . . circumstances, I desire to see you the next President of the United States," wrote a gentleman from New York: "Try me, assign me any part in securing your nomination, and see how well I will perform it." [13] On February 18 an editorial leader in the New York *Independent* indicated that the Tilton publication, with more than 50,000 subscribers, was working for Chase. The editorial did not proclaim any candidate by name, but declared oracularly that the nominee's credentials should be "a sublime allegiance to God, Liberty, and Human Rights." Reprinting the editorial the New York *Tribune* explained: ". . . it *means* Mr. Chase; it describes him without mentioning his name." It was known that Theodore Tilton, ardent antislavery editor of the *Independent,* did not prefer Lincoln. The proprietor, Henry Chandler Bowen, wrote calling attention to the leader which he hoped would please Chase. "You see," he wrote, "that our article . . . contemplates a change in Presidents . . . ." [14] A newspaper publisher in a small Ohio town wrote: "You ought to have the nomination, because you have done more, in the management of our fiscal affairs, to carry on the war than Lin-

12 S. H. Boyd to S. P. Chase, Washington, D.C., Jan. 16, 1864, Chase MSS., Lib. of Cong. The endorsement reads: "Hon S. H. Boyd . . . His calculation as to complexion of Rep. Nat. Convention."

13 W. C. Cooke to S. P. Chase, "Strictly Confidential," Feb. 19, 1864, Chase MSS., Lib. of Cong.

14 Henry C. Bowen to S. P. Chase, *Independent* office, New York, Feb. 17, 1864, Chase MSS., Lib. of Cong.

coln and all the Generals in the field." [15] Another laborer in the cause, whose motto should have been that newspapers are not what they seem, proposed to start a journal to run with "gratuitous circulation" from February to November 1864. It could advocate whatever cause Chase might direct, "while the real object of the paper would be attained without any ostensible effort to that end being made." The writer of the letter, who seems to have supposed that Chase would be the next President, added that he made the offer "with the earnest . . . desire of serving you, and, of course, collaterally of serving myself." [16]

IV

In the month of February 1864 the Chase drive for the Republican nomination came quickly to a head with the "Pomeroy Circular," a printed letter put out over the name of Senator S. C. Pomeroy of Kansas. This senator, originally from Massachusetts, had come up through the turbulent years of jayhawkers and ruffians—and, it should be added, of normal pioneers—in Kansas Territory. He had been active in free-state efforts and was chosen senator when the state was admitted to the Union. Accusations in connection with his political activities led to various investigations; as a result, his record could hardly have been described as stainless.[1] His position as senator was that of a "Jacobin" or anti-Lincoln radical. After opposing colonization as the solution of the emancipation problem, he became a promoter of a scheme to set up a colony of Negroes in Central America (Chiriqui); a fellow-radical admitted that the project "was simply an organization for land-stealing and plunder." [2]

Pomeroy's colleague in the Senate, vigorous and military-minded James H. Lane, was the opposite of Pomeroy.[3] Yet Lane was such a fiery individual, so involved in Kansas feuding, that the President was sorely tried by both these senators. On May 12, 1864, Lincoln

---

[15] W. H. P. Denny to Chase, Circleville, Ohio, Jan. 29, 1864, Chase MSS., Lib. of Cong.

[16] From J. F. Brennan, Fort Monroe, Va., *ibid.*, Jan. 18, 1864. This correspondent, in the quartermaster department, seems to have been close to the influence of B. F. Butler.

[1] *Dic. of Amer. Biog.*, XV, 54.

[2] George W. Julian, *Political Recollections*, 226–227. See also Browning, *Diary*, I, 577; *Lincoln the President*, II, 139 n.

[3] "The feud between Pomeroy and Lane centered, in the last analysis, around the question of Lincoln's renomination for a second term. While Lane was satisfied with Lincoln, Pomeroy was not." H. J. Carman and R. H. Luthin, *Lincoln and the Patronage*, 229.

wrote to Pomeroy: "I wish you and Lane would make a sincere effort to get out of the mood you are in. It does neither of you any good. It gives you the means of tormenting my life out of me, and nothing else." [4]

The Pomeroy Circular was a movement of Chase's friends (Lincoln's opponents) to rally their forces and create a nation-wide organization to promote the nomination of their favorite. It was printed, issued from Washington, marked "Private," and signed by S. C. Pomeroy, "Chairman, National Executive Committee." It read in part: "The movements recently made throughout the country, to secure the renomination of President Lincoln, render necessary some counter-action on the part of those unconditional friends of the Union, who differ from the policy of his administration." It was then stated that those who demanded "a change" had "no choice but to appeal at once to the people, before it shall be too late . . . ."

Point by point the argument was elaborated. Re-election of Lincoln was "practically impossible." If re-elected, "temporary expedients" would become stronger and the war might "continue to languish during the whole administration." Government patronage had become so enormous and "so loosely placed" as "to render the 'one-term principle' absolutely essential to the certain safety of our Republican Institutions." Salmon P. Chase possessed "more of the qualities needed in a President" than any other available candidate. Finally, it was asserted that Chase's developing popularity was "unexpected even to his warmest admirers." For these reasons a "Central organization" had been effected with connections in all the states in order "most effectually to promote his elevation to the Presidency." All who wished to further this object, and thus "make our American nationality the fairest example for imitation which human progress has ever achieved" were therefore urged to join in the work of organization in their sections of the country and to apply to the Chairman for "receiving or imparting information." [5]

---

[4] *Works*, X, 98.

[5] Copies of the circular appear in various manuscript collections—e. g., as enclosure in letter from Jesse Dubois of Springfield, Illinois, to Lincoln, Feb. 25, 1864, R. T. L. Coll., 30936. Philip Speed of the U. S. internal revenue collector's office, Louisville, Ky., also sent the President a copy he had received; it bore the frank of Henry T. Blow of Missouri. The Anna E. Dickinson MSS., and the Simon Cameron MSS., both in the Lib. of Cong., also contain the document.

In some quarters the famous circular was treated as a kind of anti-Lincoln conspiracy. To others it seemed that, since Lincoln's friends were organizing in his favor, some such move was but natural on the part of politicians who preferred another candidate. The *Tribune*, while disapproving the "invidious comparisons" between Lincoln and Chase, declared that the latter's friends had "a perfect right to present his name" which was entitled "at least to respectful and generous consideration." [6]

Lincoln's attitude toward the Chase movement was that of a patient but also a shrewd though unprovocative leader. His friends wrote numerous letters showing their resentment and reporting their observations as to activities in the Chase camp. From Springfield the President's old friend Jesse Dubois sent the document with the suggestion that Chase would "have his head in the basket if he does not take heed . . . ." J. P. Usher, Lincoln's secretary of the interior, thought that Chase had knowledge of the Circular. He added: "It contains reflections upon the President of such an offensive character that there will have to be explanations and will I think cause a rupture in the cabinet. There is much caballing & plotting going on here all dangerous to the government . . . ." As to the President's attitude, Usher observed: "Lincoln says but little finds fault with none & judging from his deportment you would suppose he was as little concerned as any about the result." [7]

Welles wrote: "It will be more dangerous in its recoil than its projectile. That is, it will damage Chase more than Lincoln. . . . Were I to advise Chase, it would be not to aspire for the position, especially not as a competitor with the man who has given him his confidence . . . ." [8]

Correspondence between Chase and Lincoln, though revealing embarrassment, showed that matters were carefully watched in order to avoid, at that time, a break in official relations. Chase explained that he had no previous "knowledge of the existence" of the communication from Pomeroy until he saw it (Feb. 20) in the *Constitutional Union*. He maintained that friends had urged the use of his name

---

6 New York *Tribune*, Feb. 24, 1864, p. 4, c. 3.

7 These comments are found in two manuscript letters of J. F. Usher to R. W. Thompson both from Washington: Feb. 17, 1864, MSS., Lincoln Nat. Life Foundation, Ft. Wayne, Ind.

8 Welles, *Diary*, I, 529.

in connection with the approaching election, that there were "several interviews," but that he told them he "could render . . . no help, except . . . from the faithful discharge of public duties." He asked them to withdraw his name whenever the "public interest" would require it. After more of the same, he declared: "I do not wish to administer the Treasury Department one day without your entire confidence." [9]

The letter in itself, while not stating the whole truth, showed dignity, correctness of attitude, and "affection" despite differences.

After some delay Lincoln answered the secretary, though admitting that he found "very little to say." He had been aware of the "existence" of the Pomeroy Circular but had not read it. He had known as "little of these things" as his friends had allowed him to know. "They bring the documents to me, but I do not read them; they tell me what they think fit to tell me, but I do not inquire for more." Whether Chase should remain at the head of the treasury department, he wrote, "is a question which I will not allow myself to consider from any standpoint other than my judgment of the public service." He perceived no "occasion for a change." [10] Later (March 4) the President wrote that he had no wish for the publication of the correspondence between himself and Chase in regard to the Pomeroy Circular.[11]

Chase had noted a certain omission in the correspondence: "there was no response in his letter to the sentiments of respect & esteem which mine contained." [12] Such a sentiment would not have been inappropriate in Lincoln's letter. Perhaps the President, from his relations with the stiffly dignified secretary, did not realize that the omission of affectionate or appreciative comment would have been noticed. He was thinking rather of the public interest and the official relationship. He was, of course, not a man to dissemble or express an attitude he did not feel, yet his personal relations were regularly characterized by unusual, often exquisite, tact and personal friendliness. The correspondence was published and the Washington *Chronicle* (March 8, 1864) remarked: "nothing in them [the Chase and Lincoln letters] shows the slightest abatement of mutual respect and confidence." So Chase remained in the cabinet.

9 Warden, *Chase*, 573–574.
10 Lincoln to Chase, Washington, Feb. 29, 1864, *Works*, X, 25–26.
11 Lincoln to Chase, Mar. 4, 1864, *ibid.*, X, 29–30.
12 Chase to Greeley, Washington, Mar. 4, 1864, typed copy, Chase MSS., Lib. of Cong.

Welles had been right. The Chase boom hurt the secretary more than Lincoln. Chase's biographer, J. W. Shuckers, noted that the movement "fell . . . into bad hands; it was badly officered and . . . badly managed. . . . With a surprising want of tact and sense, this circular was marked 'confidential' and was sent to perhaps a hundred persons. . . . If at any previous time the 'Chase movement' had been attended by the least likelihood of success, that likelihood was promptly and utterly extinguished by the appearance of the 'Pomeroy Circular.' " [18]

V

The vigorous and explosive Frank Blair Jr. now played his part by delivering severe attacks upon the secretary of the treasury in the House of Representatives (February 5 and February 27, 1864), and the resulting outcry became an angry tempest of feuding within the President's official family. Blair spoke of the "odium" attaching to the ideas of Lincoln's rivals. He defended the President's policy of amnesty and restoration and asserted that the whole anti-Lincoln business, especially in Missouri and Maryland (Blair territory), had been "concocted for purpose of defeating the renomination of Mr. Lincoln." He sarcastically asked whether the radical discontents who were needling the President had either a valid grievance or a reason for gratitude to Chase.

These speeches of Frank Blair occurred at the time when the short-lived Chase "boom" was at its peak. Thus, in addition to all the other subjects of angry difference, the provocative incident entered into the intraparty warfare that was raging not only for the presidency but for basic policy. Part of the trouble was that Blair, a major general, was alternating between army service, commanding a corps in the Chattanooga area, and membership from Missouri in the House of Representatives. Lincoln needed all the help that could be mustered in Congress and after the close of the Chattanooga campaign it was agreed by Lincoln and Stanton that Blair should temporarily resign his army commission in order to assist in the important business of organizing Congress in view of the highly significant work of implementing the President's program of restoring the Union.

---

[18] Shuckers, *Chase*, 476.

Only the most extreme doctrine of isolating the President from the vital work of Congress would have militated against some executive effort to find a spokesman in the national legislature. This is not to imply that Blair, or any general, was the most suitable agent for the President's purpose, but it is fundamental in Lincoln's whole administration to remember that he was poorly supplied with instruments for promoting that executive-legislative co-operation which is always essential and was especially so in these critical times. There had been a promise that, after a period of congressional service, Blair could go back into the army; but when this was actually put into effect after the broadsides against Chase, the secretary's friends bitterly resented it, feeling that the President was rewarding the fiery Missourian, thus becoming himself a party to what was considered undeserved abuse of a highly placed cabinet member.[1]

A friend of Chase wrote: "A deep seated feeling of indignation . . . is manifested every where, at the attack on the Secretary by that pup, Blair;—and the course pursued toward him by Mr. Lincoln,—after that attack." It was mentioned that Blair was helping Jeff Davis. The writer continued: "You can judge, then, of the indignation . . . against Blair, for the dastardly course he has pursued; and . . . it is even more bitter against Lincoln, because it is unmanly in him thus to endorse what he dare not do in person." It was also charged that the appointment of Blair without the action of the Senate was "a high handed measure" and "the first dawning of a Dictatorship." [2]

The flare-up became quite a tempest and there was considerable speculation as to whether Chase's resignation would follow. President Lincoln, however, explicitly "disavowed . . . all connection with, or responsibility for, Blair's assault, and expressed his decided disapproval of it." Chase hoped that his "every friend" would denounce "these vile calumnies" and express their honest resentment "by voice, pen, and press." [3] A. G. Riddle, who left a full account of the episode, showed how excessive was the abuse of the President at the time. Explaining that "it was impossible that the President could have been a party to Blair's assault," Riddle took a hand in reassuring Chase and inducing him not to resign. "There really was," wrote

---

[1] *Works*, X, 83–84; 87–89.
[2] Letter of John Wilson, Chicago, May 2, 1864, Chase MSS., Lib. of Cong.
[3] Warden, *Chase*, 584.

Riddle, "a very unpleasant state of feeling among thoughtful men of both parties, the old abolitionists generally were in a rage." [4] The whole unfortunate imbroglio showed how the President was misrepresented within his own party (so far as it was a party), being equally embarrassed by the barbs of his opponents and the awkward maneuvers of his friends.

VI

What may be called the Chase "machine" for 1864 was found in the wide-flung personnel of the treasury department with its collectors, assessors, customs officials, assistants, clerks, and agents scattered over the land. A New Jersey gentleman wished to be appointed a revenue collector in his district in the place of the incumbent who was a "warm supporter of Mr. Lincoln for the next nomination." Pointing out that he could still run his paper while serving as collector, this office seeker wrote: "I could so arrange the appointment of my subordinates as to make the influence available for *our* candidate at the proper time. Besides, the duties of the position would give me reason & *excuse* [italic in the original] for visiting all parts of the District, and State, during which time I could use my personal exertions (in connection with my Journal) to forward your wishes." [1]

From friends over the country Lincoln had word of the workings of the Chase machine. An assessor in Indiana wrote the President that overtures had been made to him by a revenue agent to organize a Chase movement in Indiana. This friend, favoring Lincoln, wanted the President's protection if the treasury department should make trouble for him. [2]

A rather wretched but widespread practice of the time was the issuing of permits to profit-seeking individuals wishing to trade across enemy lines. When permits were applied for, so it was reported, an agent close to Chase would question the applicant as to his presidential preference. If the applicant favored Chase, full privileges would be readily granted; if not, there would be reservations and curtailed advantages. [3] Samuel Galloway of Ohio, well known friend

[4] Riddle, *Recollections of War Times*, 267 ff.

[1] Jacob R. Freese, of the *State Gazette & Republican,* to Chase, Trenton, N.J., Jan. 23, 1864, Chase MSS., Lib. of Cong.

[2] William A. Bradshaw, Feb. 22, 1864, R. T. L. Coll., 30725–26.

[3] John Donnally, Louisville, Nov. 26, 1863, *ibid.,* 28237–8.

of Lincoln, wrote: "The fact is notorious that the officials of the Treasury Dept are using every false and foul effort to suppress the voice . . . of the people." Noting that the people desired Lincoln's renomination and re-election, Galloway explained: ". . . these minions of a madly ambitious aspirant have been laboring with all their wicked zeal to prevent utterance of the popular voice." [4]

Dr. A. G. Henry, old-time intimate friend of the Lincolns, wrote from Washington Territory that the "whole influence of the Treasury Department" was used against Lincoln and for Chase.[5] William Pickering, governor of Washington Territory wrote on the same date giving similar information.[6] Thus Lincoln was kept informed of maneuvers which were by no means intended for his knowledge.

It was in Louisiana that the activity and intrigue of the Chase "machine" was most strikingly exemplified. Under Federal occupation, that state was serving as proving ground for testing the plan of reconstruction which Lincoln had earnestly favored and which the radicals were stoutly and angrily opposing. There was yet another factor: because of wartime laws concerning captured property and the like the state was covered with an expanded army of treasury agents. Without going into all the details of this widespread Chase instrument, one may note that Shepley, Flanders, and Durant were working for him. Shepley was military governor; Flanders and Durant were officials of the treasury department who devoted much of their time to politics. The Chase forces gained control of the New Orleans *Times* and it became their organ. The tone of this newspaper appears from the following statement of March 11, 1864: "We turn with sorrow from the contemplation of the evils that are to result from Mr. Lincoln's friends bringing him out for the second contest." [7] Following the pattern of Chase argument, the *Times* praised the secretary, criticized Frank Blair,[8] expressed fear that Lincoln's powers would be "despotic," deplored the prospect that the party would be "Tylerized"—e. g., seized for un-Republican purposes as under Tyler for un-Whig purposes—and sarcastically referred to the amnesty proclamation of the President as a kind of

4 Samuel Galloway in a letter of stinging indignation to Lincoln, Columbus, Ohio, Feb. 25, 1864, *ibid.*, 30938.

5 A. G. Henry, Olympia, W. T., to Benj. F. James, Feb. 20, 1864, R. T. L. Coll., 30699.

6 R. T. L. Coll., 30706-8.   7 New Orleans *Times*, Mar. 11, 1864.

8 *Ibid.*, Feb. 25, 1864.

trick to get the Southern states back into the Union "in time for the June convention . . . [and] recruit votes for Uncle Abraham in that body." [9]

Lincoln, of course, also had some strength in Louisiana. Michael Hahn was an earnest supporter, Cuthbert Bullitt served as president of the "Lincoln club," General Banks worked for the Lincoln type of state reorganization, and the New Orleans *True Delta* came "out for Lincoln." When Hahn, purchaser of the *True Delta*, was elected governor in the first "free-state election" the event, coinciding in time with the Chase boom, indicated that, for the time, the pro-Lincoln forces had popular support and were moving, but the sulking attitude of the radical element among the Republican leaders in the state gave warning of trouble ahead.

It became increasingly evident that people were taking sides—pro-Chase or pro-Lincoln. Greeley's feeling for the secretary was, whether rightly or not, attributed to "selfish motives." [10] The attitude of the Cincinnati *Gazette* and particularly of Whitelaw Reid, was resented, and John Hay took steps to have Reid removed from his assignment as correspondent of the Western Associated Press because he was "so outrageously unfair to the President and so servilely devoted to Mr. Chase." [11] The feeling that Lincoln was but going halfway in support of emancipation was a big factor in causing distrust. In Dubuque, Iowa, a German-American editor, favoring Chase for President, noted that he had lost the support of Lincoln men; he expected Chase to offer "compensation for said loss." [12] The situation seemed to be getting so far out of hand that some of Chase's friends cautioned him against getting out on a limb. James Freeman Clarke sounded a warning: ". . . your friends who are bringing you forward for the Presidency . . . are not doing you any service." [13] Justice Swayne of Ohio wrote to his friend Samuel Tilden that the "current is altogether in favor of honest and glorious Old Abe." [14] David Tod, ex-governor of Ohio, wrote that he favored Lincoln and

9 *Ibid.*, Feb. 27, 1864.

10 James M. Scovel to Lincoln, London, Dec. 30, 1863, R. T. L. Coll., 29007–08.

11 Dennett, . . . *Diaries* . . . *of John Hay*, 138.

12 Gustavus Grahl, publisher and editor of the Dubuque *Staatszeitung*, to Chase, Mar. 7, 1864, Chase MSS., Lib. of Cong.

13 James Freeman Clarke to Chase, Boston, Feb. 26, 1864, Chase MSS., Lib. of Cong.

14 Justice Noah H. Swayne of the United States Supreme Court to Samuel J. Tilden, Washington, Feb. 19, 1864, Tilden MSS., New York Pub. Lib.

was mortified to be set down as a Chase man.[15] The radicals themselves did not all favor Chase, some of them going for Frémont or Butler or Grant, while some who would otherwise have been inclined toward Chase felt that he did not "remember his friends" and had not bestowed sufficient favors.[16]

VII

When all was said the Chase "boom" was remarkable for its short life. On March 5, 1864, about two weeks after the opening of the drive for the presidency first became a matter of formal publicity in the newspapers, Chase wrote a letter asking that "no further consideration be given to my name." [1] The letter was addressed to James C. Hall of Toledo, to whom the presidential aspirant had written on January 18 explaining in typical Chasian phraseology that, while he had no objection to the use of his name by a committee for the chief magistry, "whenever any consideration, either by them or by the friends of the cause, thought entitled to weight, should indicate the expediency of any other course, no consideration of personal delicacy should be allowed to prevent its being taken." [2]

Chase's announced withdrawal may have been largely motivated by embarrassment arising from the boom itself and especially by the action of the party caucus of the Ohio general assembly, which on February 25 voted in favor of the President's renomination. Similar resolutions were issued elsewhere in the country, which showed that the effect of the clumsy Pomeroy Circular had been to bring out formal and open declaration of support for Lincoln. At the moment of withdrawal it was obvious that Chase was giving up something he did not have. In such papers as the New York *Tribune* and the Washington *Chronicle* the withdrawal was coupled with praise of the secretary's distinguished service and appreciation of "the honorable disinterestedness which has prompted this noble letter." [3] This disinterested pose ran through Chase's own correspondence, as

---

[15] David Tod to Lincoln, Youngstown, Ohio, Feb. 24, 1864, R. T. L. Coll., 30902–3.

[16] S. M. Booth to Chase, Milwaukee, Mar. 7, 1864, Chase MSS., Lib. of Cong.

[1] Chase to James C. Hall of Toledo, Mar. 5, 1864, in Shuckers, *Chase*, 497, 502–503; New York *Tribune*, Mar. 11, 1864, p. 4, c. 3; *Daily Washington Chronicle*, Mar. 11, 1864, p. 2, c. 1; R. T. L. Coll., 31306.

[2] Shuckers, 497.   [3] *Daily Washington Chronicle*, Mar. 11, 1864.

when he wrote to Hiram Barney, prominent but uncomfortable collector of the port of New York: "I no longer have any political side save that of my country; and there are multitudes who like me care little for men but everything for measures." [4]

After years had passed and Chase had died (1873) there came further light on the "boom," the Circular, its actual authorship, and the imperfectly understood relation of the secretary of the treasury to the movement. One finds a revealing now-it-can-be-told story on this subject in the New York *Times* of September 15, 1874, which carried a letter to the editor by J. M. Winchell of Hyde Park, New York, dated September 14. Having read the *Times* extract from Shucker's life of the secretary, Winchell felt compelled to refute the biographer's statement that Chase had been "ignorant of the preparation of this circular, and was as much surprised at its appearance as anyone, and regretted it as deeply . . . ."

Shuckers was "quite mistaken," wrote Winchell. He explained: "Before the preparation of the circular the committee had spent a good deal of effort in trying to give the 'movement' some coherency and life. Mr. Chase had manifested no reluctance whatever to be a candidate against Mr. Lincoln, whom he honestly believed to be totally unfit to the crisis; his only reluctance was to be connected with a failure. . . . His most earnest friends were greatly depressed by the general timidity of the politicians in opposing the President, ... Mr. Chase was himself vacillating to a painful degree; moved alternately by aspirations and fears. Finally, . . . the writer hereof [Winchell], who was acting as Secretary of the committee during the period of suspense, conceived that it would be better to take some action *which would determine Mr. Chase's pluck and popularity,* and either place him at once before the country as a candidate, or withdraw him definitely from the attitude of rivalry which the President, as well as all Washington politicians, knew him to hold."

Winchell concluded: "To this end I wrote this circular . . . . *Mr. Chase was informed of this proposed action and approved it fully.* He told me himself that the arraignment of the Administration made in the circular was one which he thoroughly indorsed and would sustain. The circular was, therefore, sent out. No one expected it long to remain a secret."

---

[4] Chase to Hiram Barney, May 24, 1864, Chase MSS., Pa. Hist. Soc.

At the time of the brief pre-convention excitement there had been knowing persons all along who had refused to take Chase's withdrawal very seriously and who doubted that it was real or final. Attorney General Bates remarked: "This forced declention of Mr. Chase is really, not worth much. It proves only that the *present* prospects of Mr. Lincoln are too good to be openly resisted . . . . The extreme men who urged Chase . . . will only act more guardedly . . . with the hope of bringing in Mr. C, at least, as a compromise candidate." Bates thought that in the meantime these men would try "to commit Mr. L. to . . . their extreme measures." [5]

Just before the withdrawal letter to Hall, the secretary had conferred with Mr. Winchell. On that occasion (March 4, 1864), though regretting the withdrawal, Winchell indicated that it "may . . . enable you to give your friends aid which you cannot now bestow." [6] This probably meant that stepping out of the race would relieve Chase of embarrassment, give him a kind of independent position, keep the question open while radicals searched, and allow an option by which the secretary might later head a presidential movement or not as circumstances should suggest. It was indicated editorially in the *Herald* that Chase's declination was a feint; open electioneering would have required his withdrawal from the cabinet; though he "allegedly" did not want his candidacy, the people still desired it.[7] At any rate Chase's friends still hoped he would somehow remain available. Governor Andrew of Massachusetts regretted the Ohioan's "supposed purpose" of withdrawing from the cabinet though perceiving the "discomfort" of his official position in view of "being in a sense complicated with the policy and non-policy of the administration touching many grave . . . affairs which you would gladly influence to the better." [8] The confidential comment of David Davis, political-minded regular, to Thurlow Weed on March 14, 1864, showed that this expectation of Chase's friends was held also by his opponents. Davis wrote: "Mr. Chase's declension is a mere sham, and very *ungracefully* done. The plan is to get up a great opposition to Lincoln through Frémont and others, and represent when the convention meets, the necessity of united effort and that anybody can unite, ex-

[5] Bates, *Diary*, 345 (Mar. 9, 1864).

[6] J. M. Winchell to Chase, Washington, Mar. 4, 1864, Chase MSS., Lib. of Cong.

[7] New York *Herald*, editorial, Mar. 12, 1864, p. 4, c. 3.

[8] John A. Andrew to Chase, May 2, 1864, Andrew MSS., Mass. Hist. Soc.

cept Lincoln, and then, to present Chase again." With a quip about Micawber hoping for something to "turn up" Davis added that his informant on this matter was Henry D. Cooke. Davis concluded his letter with the remark that Lincoln must have been "obstinately pacific." [9] The President, of course, had his methods. He was not blundering into any explosion. For his own reasons he was keeping Chase in the cabinet, though it could not be denied that relations were undergoing severe strain.

[9] David Davis to Weed, confidential, Mar. 14 [1864]. Thurlow Weed MSS., Univ. of Rochester Lib. If Henry D. Cooke, brother and partner of Jay Cooke of the Philadelphia banking firm, was Davis's informant, he was getting his information, or interpretation, from a source which involved confidential relations with Chase.

CHAPTER VII

THE RENOMINATION OF LINCOLN

AFTER the collapse of the Chase movement events on the 1864 political front moved through a series of changing phases. There was the pre-nomination period with threats of angry radical opposition to the President, the launching of an independent party headed by Frémont, and in early June (many thought, too early) the Republican convention in which Lincoln's renomination was neatly and easily achieved. Then followed a long discouraging summer of defeatism and discontent in which many men of Lincoln's party despaired of his re-election. After three years of war the atmosphere was darkened by military operations which were at the same time shocking in human cost and deeply disappointing as to result. It was not until September and October that the auguries brightened for the Union cause; with these changing currents the withdrawal of Frémont registered a concession of Lincoln's strength on the part of his bitter opponents; finally, in November came the decision of the people to sustain the President for another four years. Some of these political difficulties of Lincoln were like bumps or ruts in the highway; others were serious road blocks. The most serious road block of all would come not so much in the problem of votes for the presidency, but in the process of obtaining congressional support for carrying out the basic programs which Lincoln favored and for which, in all sincerity and reason, his candidacy was significant.

I

The expressions of dissatisfaction with Lincoln constituted a medley of radical displeasure, uncertainty among friends who desired patronage changes, misgivings as to what men would "control" him, and doubts as to how in each state the national cause could be co-ordinated with that of local office holders or seekers. Such a thing as the unpopularity of certain Federal appointments and the dread of having incumbents continue in office might cause hesitation or might defer commitment on the part of Lincoln's friends. It was not merely a matter of supporting Lincoln but of seeing which men in a particular state would get "credit" for such support and would consequently wield what politicians called "influence." In such a situation one Republican faction might seek to gain superior control by accusing leaders of another Republican faction of being the President's enemy.

The period prior to the meeting of the Republican national convention was not the most propitious for inspiring confidence in national leadership. The sickening disappointment in the slow progress of Union arms under Grant, the cumulative load of war weariness, and the constant talk of peace efforts, combined to set the stage for a presidential campaign that became unique for dark foreboding and open disunity. A book could be made up of letters expressing distrust of the President. Mark Howard of Hartford, Connecticut, had been a follower of Lincoln. "But now [he wrote] I am unable to see our way out of our National troubles through the drifting, conciliatory and temporizing policy of Mr. Lincoln, but believe its continuance would ruin us." [1] From a more unfriendly source came the complaint that if Lincoln's policy did not change, "there are a very large class of earnest men who will feel very little interest in this contest." The writer continued: "It makes me sick to think what we have lost & the prospect of having nearly five years more of this thing." [2] Another observer, who referred to the President's policy as "muddy," wrote: "I pray God we may have a change, as anything positive can hardly be worse." [3] "Mr. Lincoln may mean well," wrote another, "but he has far greater faculty for perpetuating evil than good, he is a politician never a statesman, he lives, breathes, and has his being in the brief hour that fortune—ever blind—has allotted to him. . . . Vacillating in policy, undecided in action, weak in intellectual grasp, he writhes in contortions of dissimulation that

[1] Mark Howard to Gideon Welles, Hartford, May 30, 1864, Welles MSS., Lib. of Cong.

[2] John A. Hiestand to Thaddeus Stevens, Lancaster, Pa., May 29, 1864, T. Stevens MSS., Lib. of Cong.

[3] A. Wattles to Horace Greeley, Washington, D.C., Feb. 6, 1864, Greeley MSS., New York Pub. Lib.

would do Blondin honor." [4] Striking the same note of gloom, the wife of General Butler wrote her husband: "I think the country is doomed if Lincoln is again elected." [5]

II

In the effort to find a focus for all this scattered opposition, the names of political rivals, or supposed rivals, of Lincoln were put forward. Most prominent among these was Chase whose name was still on the radical horizon though temporarily in the background. To take the next step and inquire as to who besides Chase were to be seriously regarded as available presidential timber is to reveal the poverty of high-power leadership in the radical camp. To answer that question is to mention Frémont and Butler and then to take the somewhat preposterous step of naming Grant, though this was hard to believe, as the man to supplant Lincoln. It was in Missouri, on fire with radical agitation, that actual moves in the party sense took definite shape in terms of offering a substitute in the drive to prevent a second term for Lincoln.

By May 1864 it was known that the plan to put Frémont forward had reached the stage where a nominating convention was scheduled to be held in Cleveland. Frémont was out of the military picture, being no longer an active general. In the summer of 1862 he had resigned and for the rest of the war he remained on the shelf. His friends, always ready to magnify a grievance, put the blame for this lack of command upon Lincoln's unfriendliness or upon West Point influence. In reality the actual factors were Frémont's military failure in the campaign against Stonewall Jackson, his refusal to serve under Pope whom he detested, his declination of offers which Lincoln would have given, and his well known tendency toward insubordination. The army question, however, was but one factor in the confused situation. In the background was the old Frémont-Blair feud, the complex Missouri imbroglio, and, especially the whole radical attitude of discontent because Lincoln did not favor the proce-

---

[4] S. Wolf to Rev. Dr. McMurdy, Washington, D.C., Mar. 7, 1864, *Private and Official Correspondence of Gen. Benjamin F. Butler*, III, 497. (Blondin performed the amazing feat of walking a tight-rope across Niagara Falls, varying his technique with theatrical and incredible handicaps and contortions.)

[5] Mrs. Butler to Gen. Butler, Fort Monroe, June 11, 1864, *ibid.*, IV, 342.

dures which the extremists were demanding. They favored not only abolition of slavery but wholesale immediate abolition by processes which Lincoln deemed unconstitutional; they also favored confiscating in sweeping fashion all the lands of Southern "rebels," and they advocated a drastic policy of reconstruction which was the opposite of Lincoln's and which in his view would have perpetuated a condition of disunion after the conclusion of a war whose object was to restore the Union.

The Chase people favored the Frémont drive, not so much for approval of the general as for disapproval of Lincoln. The "Missouri radicals" gave their support, and the Germans of the Middle West (from a strong antislavery motive and a feeling that Lincoln was dragging his feet as to emancipation) were drawn into the movement. Many German papers of Illinois and Missouri had hoisted Frémont's name as early as March 1864. Medill of the Chicago *Tribune* wrote: "There is no use in concealing the fact that the Germans are deeply offended [by the "treatment" of Frémont and Sigel] and feel very bitter towards Lincoln and we cannot afford to have them alienated from our party." As a remedy, better army commands for Sigel, Schurz, and Osterhaus were suggested, climaxed by Frémont to the West Virginia department.[1]

In addition, many ardent abolitionists of New England were denouncing Lincoln as they had been for years and demanding Frémont for President. Apropos of a meeting for woman's rights, W. L. Garrison expected that its leaders would "turn their meeting into a Frémont conclave, showing no mercy to Lincoln or his administration." [2]

With obvious lack of political experience but with a quick impulse to get their man nominated before the meeting of the Republican national convention, the representatives of what was called the "radical Democracy"—a Republican offshoot—met at Cleveland, listened to oratorical and epistolary outbursts, set up an extreme platform, and adopted their ticket for 1864: Frémont for President, John Cochrane for Vice President. Cochrane was in that year attorney general of New York. The turns and shifts in his career serve as a kind of

[1] Joseph Medill to E. B. Washburne, Chicago, Feb. 12, 1864, Washburne MSS., Lib. of Cong.

[2] W. L. Garrison to Oliver Johnson, May 5, 1864, Garrison MSS., Boston Pub. Lib.

mirror of the stresses of America in the mid-century. Though a Democrat friendly to Southern attitudes, he favored neither slavery nor secession. His support of the Union was demonstrated by his raising a regiment and his service as colonel and later as brigadier general until his retirement because of ill health in February 1863. He was not as vociferous and impulsive as Frémont, but it was enough that in May 1864 he was at odds with Lincoln's policy. His very unlikeness to Frémont, together with the hope that he could garner disparate votes including those of Democrats, may have been factors in his selection for second place on a ticket that was never taken too seriously even by its promoters. (Since both Frémont and Cochrane were residents of New York, they could not have been legally chosen President and Vice President. The Constitution provides that these two officials may not come from the same state.)

The Frémont convention, like the drive for Chase, showed the ineptitude of the anti-Lincoln radicals when it came to political action. With the nominees openly in the field, people speculated with some confusion as to their real intentions. Did this radical enterprise have a definite program, or was it a catch-all for diverse elements of discontent? How would a practiced politician expect to draw dividends from such a movement? How far could it be expected even to rally the radicals? It was observed that Greeley was not present and that the *Tribune* had no reporter to cover the Cleveland convention.[3] According to one report there were no more than two hundred men in the hall at any time, and no crowds in streets or hotels.[4] The proceedings were cut and dried, Frémont being nominated by acclamation and Cochrane with only three opposing votes. People questioned whether the Cleveland affair was oriented to the Baltimore (Republican) convention or the Chicago (Democratic) convention. To the *Herald* it seemed that nineteen-twentieths of the gathering were planning with a view to the Democratic convention.[5] The *Herald* writer may have had in mind that Frémont men, looking far ahead, contemplated joining with Democrats to nominate Grant. This should be regarded as meaningless in terms of realities as to Grant; it was rather a kind of wishful thought as to how the Frémont drive

---

[3] Cincinnati *Daily Gazette,* June 1, 1864, p. 3, cc. 4–5, (special dispatch dated Cleveland, May 31).
[4] *Ibid.*
[5] New York *Herald,* June 2, 1864, p. 5, c. 3 (a dispatch dated Cleveland, June 1).

could work mischief for the Lincoln cause, especially at a time when the renomination of the President seemed virtually certain, so that his defeat would depend on Democrats. Out of all these puzzled speculations the only clear conclusion seemed to be that the object of the Cleveland convention was not the election of Frémont, but the defeat of Lincoln on the alleged ground that he had "proved false to the cause of 'human freedom' " and that "a new President . . . [was] essential to the salvation of the country." [6]

Welles found it hard to understand Cochrane's part in the scheme. "A Democrat, a Barnburner, a conservative, an Abolitionist, an Anti-abolitionist, a Democratic Republican, and now a radical Republican. . . . It will not surprise me if he should change his position before the close of the . . . campaign, and support the nominees of the Baltimore Convention." Welles believed that "weak and wicked" men in the party "would jeopard and hazard the Republican and Union cause," and that "many of them would defeat it and give success to the Copperheads [he meant Democrats] to gratify their causeless spite against the President." [7]

In its platform the Cleveland group took a stand for limiting the President to one term, electing President and Vice President by direct vote of the people, and intrusting the question of reconstruction to Congress but "not to the Executive." Finally, there was a declaration in favor of "confiscation of the lands of the rebels, and their distribution among the soldiers and actual settlers." [8]

One of the incidents of the convention was a long letter from Wendell Phillips expressing the hope that if Lincoln was renominated, "we shall fling our candidate's name . . . to the breeze"; otherwise, he hoped that "some plan" could be arranged so that all could unite on a "common basis." The Phillips letter was full of denunciation of Lincoln and especially of his plan of reconstruction. With many of the elements of a sincere liberal and with the commendable motive of elevating the Negro, Phillips favored only that type of restoration which would "admit the black to citizenship and the ballot." For this reason he favored "quick and thorough reorganization of States on a democratic basis" but not in acceptance of

---

[6] Editorial, New York *Herald*, June 2, 1864, p. 4, c. 3.

[7] Welles, *Diary*, II, 43 (June 1, 1864). Welles's surmise was correct; as it turned out, Cochrane did support the Republican candidates.

[8] McPherson, *Hist. of the Rebellion*, 413.

Lincoln's plan. "If Mr. Lincoln is re-elected," he wrote, "I do not expect to see the Union reconstructed in my day, unless on terms more disastrous to liberty than even disunion would be." [9] Though Phillips thus earnestly advocated Negro suffrage, which Lincoln himself was coming to accept in part, the Cleveland platform made no reference specifically to the subject, though broadly demanding that the Constitution should "secure to all men absolute equality before the law." There was a declaration for an amendment to abolish slavery, but that abolition was also to be favored both by the President and the Republican national convention.

In his letter of acceptance General Frémont defended himself against "the reproach of creating a schism in the party with which I have been identified." No schism would have resulted, he said, if Lincoln had "remained faithful to the principles he was elected to defend." The general laid it on heavily in denouncing the Lincoln administration for military abuse, disregard of constitutional rights, feebleness, incapacity, alienating true friends, and making "humiliating concessions." The principles of the platform had the general's "cordial approbation," yet he could not concur in all the measures proposed. Confiscation of the property of all "rebels" he did not consider either practicable or sound policy; at the beginning of the war he could understand it, "but not as a final measure of reconstruction." As to the intent of his candidacy, Frémont declared that if the Baltimore convention should put up a man favorable to what he called "our cardinal principles," he would support him (which meant withdrawal), but if Lincoln should be nominated, it would be "fatal to the country" to give him renewed power and there would be "no other alternative but to organize against him . . . with the view to prevent the misfortune of his re-election." [10]

III

Republicans of the anti-Lincoln drift looked to the party's convention with doubt and discontent. With wearisome sameness the familiar complaints were repeated. Lincoln was slow, weak, not sufficiently decisive and active against slavery, too friendly to Seward and the Blairs, incompetent, unsatisfactory as to patronage, influenced

[9] *Ibid.*, 412.   [10] *Ibid.*, 413–414.

or controlled by "dishonest" men, and far too lenient in plans for reconstruction. To some he was a coarse joker, an imbecile, susceptible to the advice of "that arch criminal" (Seward), guilty of "damnable blunders," and "too angelic for this devilish rebellion." He lacked backbone, it was said, encouraged corruption, squandered millions, failed in the military task, and was using Southern delegates, set up under his reconstruction scheme, to insure his own renomination. It was stated in April 1864 that overwhelming majorities of both houses of Congress were opposed to the President's re-election.[1] Horace Greeley felt "a very strong desire to see some man besides Old Abe nominated for President." [2] Greeley's *Tribune* declared: ". . . we are known not to favor his [Lincoln's] renomination . . . ." [3] Even when conceding Lincoln's good points, the *Tribune* would go on to oppose him.

The call having gone out in February for the Republican national convention to meet at Baltimore on June 7,[4] there were loud and urgent demands for postponement. The desire was for "a suspension of judgment until this question of renominating Mr. Lincoln is first fully discredited." [5] In nearly every case the insistence on a later date came from anti-Lincoln men. Better not act in June, they urged. Wait till September. Give the disaffected time to defeat the administration. If the convention were postponed, it was argued, Lincoln would not be nominated. Chase called it a "Blair-Lincoln Convention." [6] Joseph Medill of the Chicago *Tribune* wrote: "I don't care much if the Convention is put off till August. . . . If Lincoln loses the nomination thereby he will have nobody but himself to blame. . . . I am free to say . . . that if it shall be known to be his intention to continue his present cabinet I don't believe we could elect him if nominated." The points of dissatisfaction on which Medill focused were Lincoln's attachment to the three Blairs, "old granny Bates," and Halleck; also his giving the "cold shoulder" to the Missouri radicals. The Chicago editor continued: "Lincoln has some

---

[1] Editorial, New York *Herald*, Apr. 2, 1864, p. 4, c. 2.

[2] Greeley to Brockway, New York, Apr. 9, 1864, Greeley MSS., Lib. of Cong., misdated 1861.

[3] New York Semi Weekly *Tribune*, Apr. 29, 1864, p. 4, c. 1.

[4] McPherson, *Rebellion*, 403.

[5] James W. White to Horace Greeley, Albany, Jan. 15, 1864, Greeley MSS., New York Pub. Lib.

[6] Chase to Brough, May 19, 1864, Warden, *Chase*, 593.

very weak and foolish traits of character." [7]

Eminent men in New York, including W. C. Bryant and George Opdyke, joined in a published statement (March 25, 1864) objecting to the seventh of June as the date of the coming national convention. These men—an impressive list—argued that unity for a single candidate was important but that such unity could not be reached at the early date named. Events in the spring and summer should be awaited, for upon them would "depend the wish of the people to continue in power their present leaders, or to change them for those from whom they may expect . . . more satisfactory results." [8] It was suggested by the Washington correspondent of the Cincinnati *Gazette* that to make Lincoln the Union candidate would be "most perilous, if not suicidal." If there were defeat in the field, it was urged, the President's popularity would vanish. If the seat of government were in any large city, the imbecility of the Administration would provoke a revolution in thirty days. (This was a strange suggestion—the idea that a revolution to overthrow the government could be started by the populace of a large American city.) It was also reported that prominent leaders were considering the propriety of demanding Lincoln's resignation as the only means of saving the government.[9] Charles Sumner, though cautiously non-committal as to candidates, opposed the June date. He wrote: "I regret very much that the Baltimore Convention is to be at so early a day. I see nothing but disaster from mixing our politics with battle and blood." [10]

IV

Despite strong protest the Republican national executive committee headed by Edwin D. Morgan of New York went ahead with its plan for opening the Baltimore session on June 7, and in the months prior to that date the friends of the President saw many encouraging signs. The radical effort was brushed off as a minor factor. "The great majority," wrote a party worker, "are in favor of the reelection of Mr. Lincoln . . . . [He] can get more votes than any

---

[7] Joseph Medill to E. B. Washburne, Chicago, Apr. 12, 1864, Washburne MSS., Lib. of Cong.

[8] *Ann. Cyc.*, 1864, 785.   [9] Cincinnati *Daily Gazette*, Apr. 13, 1864, p. 3, c. 8.

[10] Charles Sumner to Charles Eliot Norton (private), Senate Chamber, May 2, 1864, *Proceedings, Mass. Hist. Soc.*, LVIII, 135 (1925).

other man." [1] There were numerous similar comments, running true to what was considered a prevailing pro-Lincoln pattern. From Illinois came the report, "*A. Lincoln* is the first choice of the great body of the people." [2] From Concord, New Hampshire: ". . . I think Mr. Lincoln is the strongest man we can take and the *best* man." [3] From New York: "My business calls me among a great many people . . . in all parts of the country . . . and a large majority are for you [Lincoln] for the next four years." [4] From Kentucky: "If Old Abe is nominated for re-election I am strongly inclined to the belief that he can carry this State against any named man . . . ." [5] From Cincinnati: "I intend to go to the State Convention and see to it that Lincoln is endorsed. . . . He is the only man." [6] From Philadelphia: "The masses have an abiding faith in his honesty and ability." [7]

Granted this popular support, it was also true that much of Lincoln's strength was in party organization. Each state had its Republican party; that party had its conventions, officials, and committees; dissident groups could be overridden by the sheer power of political machinery. The men who operated that machinery had executive party positions; they had much to do in controlling the choice of paymasters, collectors, postmasters, and the like; they took a hand in obtaining government contracts; finally, through state or district conventions they managed the choice of delegates to the national nominating convention. These politicians foresaw Lincoln's renomination and wanted to keep their influence in the party. Thus it happened that while radicals freely expressed their discontent, the party "regulars" or managers somehow saw to it that pro-Lincoln resolutions were passed by state legislatures or conventions, setting in motion the process by which men were pledged to support the President.

This practical process of actually committing official groups to support of the President was evident as early as January of 1864. In

---

[1] J. D. Defrees to R. W. Thompson, Washington, Feb. 2, 1864, MS., Lincoln National Life Foundation, Fort Wayne, Ind.

[2] Thomas Gregg to E. B. Washburne, Hamilton, Ill., Dec. 23, 1863, Washburne MSS., Lib. of Cong.

[3] B. F. Prescott to Anna E. Dickinson, Concord, N.H., Mar. 13, 1864, Anna E. Dickinson MSS., Lib. of Cong.

[4] C. M. Smith to Lincoln, New York, Feb. 7, 1864, R. T. L. Coll., 30277-8.

[5] John Jay Anderson to H. C. Adams, Side View, Ky., Jan. 24, 1864, R. T. L. Coll., 29805.

[6] Will Cumback [to Nicolay], Cincinnati, Feb. 11, 1864, R. T. L. Coll., 30449-50.

[7] J. W. Stokes to Isaac Newton, Philadelphia, Feb. 10, 1864, R. T. L. Coll., 30427-28.

New Hampshire the state Republican convention took early action, the movement for Lincoln was off to an early start, and on January 6 the state convention of the Granite State registered its support for the President's renomination.[8]

From Pennsylvania came a like wave of Lincoln endorsement. In the legislature of the Keystone State a paper was passed around on January 6, addressed to the President and urging him to accept another term as President. Within a few days the full Republican strength in the legislature had been mustered and every member of both houses had signed the paper. It was pointed out in this address that a change of national administration would be most undesirable and that support of Lincoln was needed in order to crush the rebellion. On January 14, 1864, Simon Cameron wrote the President: "You are now fairly launched on your second voyage, and of its success I am . . . confident . . . ." [9]

Thus even before the February call for the convention there were actual pledges for Lincoln, but especially from February on through May the process of building up votes for him was evident throughout the North. The call itself, of course, could have been interpreted as a pro-Lincoln maneuver, since, as has been seen, those who preferred another candidate were solidly opposed to so early a date. February declarations for Lincoln—by Republican members of the legislature or by state party convention—occurred in New Jersey, Indiana, Maryland, Colorado, and California. As the weeks passed, the movement, thus aided by an early start, steadily gained momentum. In March Rhode Island was added to the Lincoln column, and in the same month a pro-Lincoln declaration of Republicans in Ohio signalized the end of the Chase boom, for a candidate who could not "carry" the party men of his own state would have a hopeless prospect as national leader. This decisive action came when in early March a large majority (90 out of 107) of Republican legislators in Ohio passed a resolution favoring Lincoln's renomination.[10] Prior to this, in late February, a caucus of Republican members had declared for Lincoln. It was not until May, however, that the state convention in Ohio took similar action.[11]

---

[8] Nicolay and Hay, *Lincoln*, IX, 52–53; New York *Times*, Jan. 7, 1864, p. 4, c. 6.

[9] Nicolay and Hay, *Lincoln*, IX, 53.   [10] New York *Herald*, Mar. 9, 1864, p. 5, c. 2.

[11] Cincinnati *Daily Gazette*, May 26, 1864, p. 3, c. 4; Eugene H. Roseboom, *The Civil War Era 1850–1873 (Hist. of the State of Ohio*, IV), 430.

Kansas also made an early pro-Lincoln commitment. Its legislature by concurrent resolution on February 2 called for the nomination of Abraham Lincoln and Andrew Johnson "by general acclamation, without the formality of a National Convention." [12] Confirming this attitude, the Kansas state convention meeting at Topeka in April unanimously instructed its delegates to support Lincoln.[13] Another April state in which pro-Lincoln action was unanimous, was Wisconsin.[14]

Thus the ball rolled on. States that had not acted by May were influenced by the commitments of those which had done so. Men who belonged to the managing wing of the party, even if not enthusiastic for the President, were swept along with the Lincoln tide. In Maine the renomination of the President was given party endorsement on May 5,[15] while similar action was taken in Vermont on May 17 and in Massachusetts (at the state convention in Boston) on May 19.[16]

To elaborate the detailed methods by which these results were achieved in the state conventions would be to reveal in some cases the strategy—some would have said the questionable tricks—by which the opposition was overridden. Such a complaint was made as to the procedure in Indiana. Throughout that state it could not have been said that in February the party was united for Lincoln. Dissatisfaction with the President and support for Chase were by no means lacking. For this reason it was likely that if the matter had been presented for debate and deliberation, the State Republican convention at Indianapolis would have resolved in favor of sending an uninstructed delegation to Baltimore. Among Republican workers there was more ardent support for Governor Morton than for Lincoln, the more so since the movement to renominate the governor had been sedulously nurtured among local and district groups. Morton himself was somewhat cool toward Lincoln and favored an uninstructed delegation, which would have been entirely satisfactory to Lincoln's opponents. With eleven districts in the state, only five of the district

---

12 Kansas *Concurrent Resolution No. 2,* Topeka, Feb. 2, 1864, R. T. L. Coll., 30121–2.
13 Editorial, Washington *Daily Morning Chronicle,* Apr. 26, 1864, p. 2, c. 1.
14 *Ibid.,* Apr. 2, 1864, p. 2, c. 3.
15 Cincinnati *Daily Gazette,* May 7, 1864, p. 1, c. 5 (special dispatch from Bangor, Me., May 5).
16 Washington *Daily Morning Chronicle,* May 20, 1864, p. 2, c. 6.

conventions had acted as to any declaration on the subject of a presidential nomination, and these had voted for uninstructed delegations.

Under such circumstances a quick maneuver was employed by which the Indiana convention, in the manner of a popular mass meeting, was swept off its feet. A delegate from Knox County, friend of Lincoln and bitter opponent of Morton, stepped on the stage at the outset of the meeting before the chairman was seated, and read resolutions to an audience of thousands who were prepared to cheer every allusion to the Union cause. The first resolution praised Lincoln and declared that the convention "instruct the delegates" (yet to be appointed) to vote for his nomination. By the second resolution Governor Morton, who was sure to be supported in any case, was then and there declared the candidate for re-election as governor. In a burst of enthusiastic cheers and without debate, both resolutions were passed by a shouting affirmative. By this scheme the gathering was committed before it had time to catch its breath and the convention was put on record. Naturally the Chase men were disgusted. Renomination of Morton was unopposed, yet there was no such agreement on the presidency or on debatable public issues. Endorsement of Lincoln was tied to the sure-fire endorsement of the governor and the whole thing was done by a mass-meeting proceeding in which discussion was impossible.[17] It was reported that the German element especially was stirred up by the maneuver.

In New York, despite political cross currents and intraparty feuds, the strength of organized Republican support was decisively added to the Lincoln cause. Though the *Tribune,* the *Independent,* and the *Post* worked against Lincoln in the prenomination phase, and though a huge meeting was held in favor of Grant, such men as Henry J. Raymond, Edwin D. Morgan, and Thurlow Weed held the Republican forces together for the President, and the state convention of the party, meeting at Syracuse on May 24, resolved by acclamation to approve the Lincoln administration and to favor his renomination.[18]

In Lincoln's own state there were ample evidences of difference within the Republican party, but anti-Lincoln efforts were more a

17 Indianapolis *Daily Journal,* Feb. 24, 1864, p. 2, c. 2; H. B. Carrington to Chase, Indianapolis, Feb. 27, 1864, Chase MSS., Lib. of Cong.

18 Sidney D. Brummer, *Political History of New York during the . . . Civil War,* 379.

matter of agitation than of management; dominance and political guidance were held by supporters of the President. It is true that the strength of the radicals could not be brushed off, and the Chicago *Tribune* showed an attitude of caution and a tendency to accompany its endorsement of Lincoln with insistence upon the need for recognizing the radicals. Germans in Illinois were strongly moved by radical doctrine, which meant displeasure with the President, and when the state convention met at Springfield on May 25 it was far from a harmonious body. A radical effort was made in opposition to an endorsement of Lincoln, but this movement failed; for one thing, there was no satisfactory alternative to Lincoln on the score of availability. When action was taken on the question of a presidential candidate, it was done by including a rather mild pro-Lincoln declaration in a long series of resolutions passed by the convention. By this method the Illinois Republican delegates were "instructed to use all honorable means to secure his [Lincoln's] renomination." The unusually late date of party action in Illinois (May 25) was but one indication of the difficulty of uniting the party solidly behind the President.[19]

In addition to regular party conclaves various agencies or citizen organizations worked for the President. This was true of the Union Lincoln Association of New York, the Union Leagues in many states, and the New England Publication Society. Of the widely influential newspapers that came out for Lincoln's renomination one should mention the New York *Times,* the Washington *Chronicle,* the Philadelphia *Press,* and the Springfield (Mass.) *Republican.* It was remarked by A. K. McClure that the *Times* was "the only prominent New York journal that heartily supported Lincoln." [20] His renomination was not favored by such powerful New York papers as the *Tribune,* the *Post,* the *Independent,* the *Herald,* and the *World.* In that important publicity organ, the Loyal Publication Society, sentiment among the leading managers was divided. Charles Eliot Norton favored Lincoln's renomination but such men as John A. Andrew and John Murray Forbes agreed with the radicals in opposing the

---

19 The attitude of Illinois Republicans toward the renomination of Lincoln is treated in A. C. Cole, *Era of The Civil War,* esp. 315–317, with full citations of newspapers and other material, and in Paul G. Hubbard, "The Lincoln-McClellan Presidential Election in Illinois," doctoral dissertation, 1949, Univ. of Ill.

20 McClure, *Abraham Lincoln and Men of War-Times,* 121; see also Francis Brown, *Raymond of the Times,* 218 ff.

President and urging a postponement of the convention. The Society, however, did not swing to their anti-Lincoln point of view.[21]

V

The gathering which in 1864 performed the important and uniquely American quadrennial function of nominating a President and Vice President consisted of somewhat more than five hundred delegates, not counting alternates, assembled in the Front Street Theater at Baltimore on the seventh of June. The scene was enlivened by a "splendid band," "graced by the presence of many ladies," and honored by the attendance of distinguished guests including the commanding general of the department, Lew Wallace.[1] There was excitement because of the crowds and the interest which a presidential nomination always produces, but there was virtually no contest as to the head of the ticket and the occasion presented no such dramatic situation as that in Chicago in 1860. The whole emphasis was pro-Lincoln, in spite of the New York *Herald* which declared on June 4 that if nominated Lincoln would not be elected. J. W. Forney is said to have remarked that the convention had no candidate to choose; the choice had already been made.[2]

For two days these delegates talked, raised points of order, considered and reconsidered, offered and withdrew motions, called the roll, and, in the result, managed somehow to get ahead with their appointed business. Some of the proceedings were confusing and hard to follow. Members would at times be in doubt as to the rules under which they were operating and uncertain as to what motion or amendment was before the house. A rule or motion would be "adopted," and some would immediately ask what the action meant and where they stood. Amid the five hundred, most of whom might as well have been nameless, it devolved upon a few men to steer the course and evoke order out of what looked at first like unorganized chaos. Thaddeus Stevens spoke authoritatively as an expert on procedure, but a more important function was performed with special

---

[21] George Winston Smith, "Broadsides for Freedom: Civil War Propaganda in New England," *New England Quarterly*, XXI, 305–307 (Sep. 1948).

[1] *Proceedings of the First Three Republican National Conventions of 1856, 1860 and 1864*, 176.

[2] Nicolay and Hay, *Lincoln*, IX, 63.

skill, yet unobtrusively, by Henry J. Raymond, who remarked that the gathering began as nothing more than a mass meeting, and that the problem was to organize that mass meeting and convert it into a convention of authorized delegates.[3] It was no easy job for the permanent presiding officer, William Dennison of Ohio (chosen after considerable delay) to focus the action of the meeting amid a maze of conflicting motions, personal explanations, parliamentary sparring, and "out of order" rulings. At one of the awkward moments the distinguished and honored Robert J. Breckinridge, having been told that, under the rule, he could not speak on the pending question, declared: "I wish to say a single sentence . . . . I do not wish to be gagged." [4] (Breckinridge persisted and managed to have his say.)

After the preliminaries the report of the committee on credentials was presented and this started the only ripple of dissent in the matter of the nomination. Missouri had sent two delegations—one pro-Lincoln, the other radical and anti-Lincoln. The committee on credentials recommended seating the radical group; those who were steering the convention were opposed in sentiment to this group so far as the presidency was concerned, but to recognize and admit them was a concession that could well be afforded. This Missouri question, the most controversial of all the convention's problems, had produced earnest and animated debate in which George William Curtis wanted it to "ring out" over that land "that we recognize the radicals of Missouri," while Robert J. Breckinridge objected that the convention, in so doing, would be refusing seats to "a delegation from a party in Missouri, whose main business . . . has been to support . . . the President of the United States, whom we are about to nominate by acclamation." By such action, added Breckinridge, the convention would "come as nigh to playing the devil as any set of gentlemen ever did with their eyes blindfolded." [5]

There was a confusing proposal to admit both delegations: the idea was that where they agreed they should cast the Missouri vote, but if they disagreed the vote of the state should be lost. This proposal, which would have pleased neither side, was rejected, and the convention voted to follow the lead of the credentials committee and admit the Missouri radicals as official state delegates.

[3] *Proceedings . . . Republican National Conventions*, 185, 210.
[4] *Ibid.*, 215.   [5] *Ibid.*, 213–216.

Questions then arose as to other delegations—those of Tennessee, Louisiana, Arkansas, Virginia, Florida, and South Carolina. It was complained that the presence of some of these state groups at Baltimore was too closely related to the President's controversial reconstruction scheme and was therefore distasteful to the radicals. The controversy involved degrees of recognition: some thought that certain delegations should be given "seats" but without the right to vote. As to three important states—Tennessee, Louisiana, and Arkansas (all pro-Lincoln)—the decision was to admit them with the voting right. (This was not accomplished without opposition; there were negative votes in considerable number from Massachusetts, Pennsylvania, Kentucky, and Michigan.) In the case of Virginia and Florida, where the restoration process was clouded and incomplete, the delegates were admitted without the right to vote; in the case of South Carolina the delegates were rejected. These troublesome matters were handled smoothly and in such a manner as to allow dissenting opinions to be expressed, yet to keep explosive factors in the background.

VI

For this efficient yet unprovocative handling of the convention's business a considerable share of credit should attach to Henry J. Raymond of the New York *Times*. In addition to being fully steeped in the politics of New York and specially gifted for political journalism, Raymond was also known as a champion of the President. His *History of the Administration of President Lincoln*,[1] an elaborate volume crowded with speeches, messages, and other documents, was completed in manuscript in May 1864 and was "designed wholly and frankly to promote his [Lincoln's] nomination and reelection." [2] Throughout the war Raymond had regularly defended Lincoln and his policies, though showing his concept of press freedom by occasional blame and criticism where this was considered appropriate. His arguments on reconstruction showed fundamental agreement with Lincoln and his support of the President for another term had been indicated in the *Times* at the beginning of 1864.

---

[1] A similar but longer book by Raymond appeared in 1865 under the title *The Life and Public Services of Abraham Lincoln . . . Including his Speeches . . . [etc.] and the Closing Scenes Connected With His Life and Death."*

[2] Francis Brown, *Raymond of the Times*, 249.

With its tendency to slip off the track the convention needed guidance and at awkward times it was Raymond who offered the steadying touch, though in no sense taking over or seeming to dominate the proceedings. At an early stage when Cameron moved to call for a roll of the states so that some one from each state should present a list of its delegates (before any committee of credentials was even appointed), the Pennsylvanian's motion became "so tangled in amendments, withdrawal of amendments, votes of approval and disapproval, motions and counter-motions, that the bewildered Breckinridge confessed that he had no idea where matters stood." [3] In this well nigh impossible situation it was Raymond who offered the clarifying word and sensible procedure which enabled the convention to "organize" and get ahead with its task.

With this background it can be understood why Raymond became the "natural choice to draft the platform" of the convention.[4] Without clashing with anti-Lincoln radicals he managed to keep the resolutions comparatively harmless. This part of the business gave the convention no trouble. In fact, after being read, the resolutions were adopted "by acclamation" without debate; one of the members remarked that they were "their own argument." [5] In Raymond's hand the platform was so framed as to elicit sure-fire applause while sidestepping or ignoring some of the burning controversies which agitated the nation and on which the Republicans were far from united. For example, though broadly pledging the party to prosecute the war and punish the "rebels," the platform contained no formula or plan for reconstruction, whether the moderate and practical plan of Lincoln or the vindictive program of the radicals. Thus the keenest political question of the day was avoided.

There had been vigorous pressure for a radical platform, the more so as the radicals were unable to prevent the renomination of the President. If they swallowed Lincoln, they insisted that the platform should suit them, while from the standpoint of pro-Lincoln men the

---

[3] *Ibid.*, 253. Breckinridge's bewilderment becomes easy to understand when one reads the confused proceedings on the Cameron proposal. Progress to a reasonable result seemed impossible in the parliamentary maze until Raymond straightened out the tangle.

[4] *Ibid., Raymond of the Times*, 254.

[5] *Proceedings . . . Republican National Conventions*, 227.

acceptance of such a platform was regarded as a maneuver to check the Frémont movement.[6] In the result it may be said that the 1864 resolutions had a radical tone and emphasis but were free from any specific or clear-cut radical plank. The soldiers were thanked in glowing terms and paragraphs were included favoring an antislavery amendment to the Constitution, a railroad to the Pacific, and full national faith for the redemption of the debt. The tariff was not even mentioned, nor the national banking system, nor the use of paper money on which the government was largely relying. Some of the declarations, while phrased in a generalized wording, were intended, among those who knew, to have a specific and partly hidden application. This could have been said of the sixth resolution which indicated that none could be trusted except "those who cordially endorse the principles proclaimed in these resolutions." This was announced as being essential to "harmony," but it could have been interpreted somewhat in the sense of a "purge"; instead of giving the Republican blessing to differing shades of opinion, the declaration signified that moderates were not "worthy of public confidence" and that radicals were to take over. This specific meaning was not spelled out, for lack of clarity is often the fashion in party platforms, but those who knew the cross currents of the time understood well enough what was the intent and meaning. In particular, this part of the platform, called the "denunciatory" clause was "aimed . . . at the Blairs, primarily, though Welles and Bates were included." [7] There were many who understood that the declaration as to those who could and could not be trusted was directed also against Seward.

The striking and distressing fact was that the men who were thus denounced as unworthy, and as if they should have no support from the party, were moderates who on essential points agreed with the President. The sixth resolution really implied, if its purpose were to have been put into effect, that pro-Lincoln moderates should get out of the government and the party; yet all this was set forth in the supposed cause of "harmony." As part of this clamor for alleged harmony there was a lively demand in the convention, though it was not expressed in the proceedings, to get rid of Seward. In frustration

---

[6] Cincinnati *Daily Gazette,* June 6, 1864, p. 3, c. 6.
[7] William E. Smith, *The Francis Preston Blair Family in Politics,* II, 267.

of this effort "the managers, under the contrivance of Raymond, . . . so shaped the resolution as to leave it pointless," [8] as to any particular cabinet member.

When the states were polled in the balloting for the presidential nomination, every delegation cast its full total for Lincoln except that of Missouri whose radical vote, under instruction, was given to Grant. Mr. J. F. Hume, however, speaking for the Missouri radical delegation, carefully explained that they were with the Union party, would assist in carrying its banner to victory, and would support its nominees. He further explained that in voting for "the head of the fighting Radicals of the Nation, Ulysses S. Grant" the Missouri delegates were bound by instructions from their state convention and could not do otherwise than obey that instruction on the first balloting.[9] On the roll call Lincoln thus received 484 votes and Grant 22 (all from Missouri), after which, on motion by Hume of Missouri, the nomination of Lincoln was made unanimous. When one considers all the factors of opposition to the President and all the maneuvers to block his nomination, this result, so easily achieved, stands out as an impressive demonstration of Lincoln's popularity and of the practical force of party organization and steering.

VII

In terms of unforeseen history one of the most important functions of the Baltimore convention was the nomination of a candidate for Vice President. Numerous names were suggested for this post, including Hannibal Hamlin, Simon Cameron, Andrew Johnson of Tennessee, Joseph Holt of Kentucky, B. F. Butler, Daniel S. Dickinson of New York, Schuyler Colfax of Indiana, and even Horatio Seymour of New York.[1]

In the actual balloting for the vice-presidential nomination there was no Butler movement and support for him was minor, yet he received 28 votes: they included twenty from the Missouri faction and eight from New England, thus indicating the radical flavor of his following. Only three names were prominent in this voting: John-

---

[8] Welles, *Diary*, II, 174.

[9] *Proceedings . . . National Republican Conventions*, 232–233.

[1] Alfred Churchill to Richard Yates, Kanesville, Kane Co., Mo., June 11, 1863, Yates MSS., Ill. State Hist. Lib.

son who received 200 votes on the first roll call, Hamlin with 150 votes, and Dickinson with 108. When the trend toward Johnson became clearly evident several delegations changed their votes, and when the first and only ballot was finally recorded Johnson had 494 votes, Dickinson 17, and Hamlin 9. A highly important part of the convention's work was thus smoothly concluded. Of the winning candidate for second place the Washington *Chronicle,* which was understood to be in sympathy with Lincoln wrote: "Of this noble Unionist, who has been selected as a Union candidate for Vice President, we cannot speak in terms of sufficient commendation. A son of poverty and obscurity, he has won his way, by dint of energy and superior ability, to the highest offices in the gift of his adopted State [legislator, congressman, governor, senator]." [2] There were, of course, Republicans who had no love for Johnson. That was true of Thaddeus Stevens, but then he had no love for Lincoln either.

On the floor of the convention the choice of Andrew Johnson was rather quickly accomplished, but the nomination was to become the theme of lively speculation and controversy, particularly as to the part said to have been played in Johnson's favor by the President. There had been considerable feeling that it would be appropriate to renominate the incumbent, Hannibal Hamlin of Maine, but the friends of Hamlin were "safe"; they could be counted on to support the ticket in any case, and convention support for him, though substantial, decreased as attention focused on sturdy Andrew Johnson of Tennessee. The main argument for Johnson was that by his nomination the party would be reaching out for "War Democrats." (Hamlin had formerly been a Democrat but had joined the Republican party in 1856. In contrast, Johnson was a Southern Democrat of 1860, though differing strongly from Democratic colleagues of the South who favored secession.) Openly and on the surface Lincoln avoided interference with the work of the convention on the vice-presidency and otherwise [3] and the statement has been made that he did not favor Johnson.[4] On the other hand, Ward H. Lamon, old friend of Lincoln, stated in reminiscence that Lincoln "was decidedly in favor of a Southern man for Vice-President" and that "his preference, as he expressed

---

[2] Editorial, Washington *Daily Morning Chronicle,* June 9, 1864, p. 2, c. 1.
[3] See below, p. 133, note 7.
[4] Noah Brooks, *Washington in Lincoln's Time,* 152, 160.

himself to prudent friends, was for Andrew Johnson." [5] Those who in later years thus reported that the President favored Johnson the Tennessean explained that he did not wish this preference to become public; it was a delicate question, and, according to Lamon, Lincoln did not want to give offense to Hamlin's New England constituency.

The acrimonious dispute as to Lincoln's vice-presidential preference was revived in postwar years. After Hamlin's death in 1891 the Philadelphia *Times* stated that Lincoln had favored Johnson's nomination. This statement was contradicted by J. G. Nicolay, who asserted that Lincoln's "personal feelings" were for Hamlin's renomination but that he carefully avoided any move to influence the action of the convention. This Nicolay statement was in turn emphatically contradicted by A. K. McClure who criticized Nicolay for his "ignorance" and for presuming to speak for Abraham Lincoln. McClure commented that "Nicolay was dress-parading at Baltimore and knew nothing of the President's purposes." "He [Nicolay] saw and knew President Lincoln [wrote McClure]; the man Abraham Lincoln he never saw and never knew." As the newspaper controversy went on it became ugly and vituperative. Nicolay referred to McClure's "personal abuse" and his "rage and wounded vanity at being exposed in a gross historical misstatement." He quoted Lincoln's written statement at the time of the convention: "Wish not to interfere about V. P. Cannot interfere about platform. Convention must judge for itself." This exceedingly brief jotting by Lincoln, a June 6 endorsement on a letter which Nicolay wrote to Hay from Baltimore on June 5,[6] was no more than a bit of advice as to the President's official attitude or open position. It would hardly be accepted by critical writers as a full statement of the whole truth as to behind-the-scenes comments. Lincoln knew that a statement given through his private secretary would have somewhat the character of an official statement by the President himself. In rejoinder to Nicolay, McClure declared that Nicolay did not know fully what was going on in June 1864, that some of his statements were "flagrantly . . . false," and that Mr. Hay "refused to sustain" Nicolay's interpretation of the President's brief non-committal note. Without dwelling further on the unseemly

---

[5] A. K. McClure, *Abraham Lincoln and Men of War-Times*, 477.

[6] Nicolay and Hay, Lincoln, IX, 73; Works, X, 115 (endorsement dated June 6, 1864); Helen Nicolay, *Lincoln's Secretary*, 323.

controversy it is sufficient to observe that in the nature of the case Lincoln's confidential understandings were not revealed in his public declarations. He talked with politicians without making all his thoughts known to his secretaries.[7] McClure was a knowledgeable politician, and his account of Lincoln's unpublicized preference deserves historical attention, especially since it has confirmation from other sources.[8] That Lincoln managed the matter so as not to offend Hamlin and his followers was another example of the President's handling of human relations. On this point McClure praised the President's "curiously characteristic diplomacy." [9]

In a careful study focused on Ward Lamon, Clint Clay Tilton confirms the report that Lincoln favored Andrew Johnson as having greater appeal at the polls than Hamlin. Leonard Swett and A. K. McClure, according to Tilton, personally favored Hamlin but yielded to Lincoln's insistence that they should work for the defeat of the incumbent Vice President in favor of Johnson. These "master politicians" apparently worked to promote Joseph Holt of Kentucky, but this was only a "smoke screen" behind which the maneuver for Johnson was successfully managed. Tilton states that Ward Lamon was present when McClure and Swett conferred with Lincoln at the White House, and that the President gave a letter to Lamon embodying his views. The letter, however, (as Tilton states), was not used "and later was returned to the writer at his request." So far as the convention was concerned, Lincoln's confidential attitude was not revealed.[10]

Much of the discussion on this subject was colored in later years by fierce radical hatred of Johnson in reconstruction days, but on that aspect of the subject it is sufficient to say that Johnson's restoration policy was essentially the same as Lincoln's and that, in the considered

---

[7] Nicolay's side of the controversy is supported by his daughter, Helen Nicolay. She repeats that Lincoln gave a personal word favoring Hamlin and that the President at the time of the convention wrote that he wished "not to interfere about V. P." She treats McClure's postwar statements in disagreement with Nicolay as untrue, but in general her account leaves the controversy about where it stood in the Philadelphia *Times* correspondence between Nicolay and McClure in 1891. Helen Nicolay, *Lincoln's Secretary: A Biography of John G. Nicolay*, 207–208, 322–325.

[8] For the documents on the Nicolay-McClure controversy, with material also from Lamon, see A. K. McClure, *Lincoln and Men of War-Times*, appendix, 457 ff.

[9] *Ibid.*, 16, 119 ff.

[10] Clint Clay Tilton, "Lincoln and Lamon: Partners and Friends," *Transactions* Ill. State Hist. Soc., 1931, 212.

opinion of contemporary leaders and of historians the same type of postwar radical opposition and bitter congressional obstruction would have confronted Lincoln if he had lived and had adhered to his policies as stated during his presidency and on down to the time of his last speech on April 11, 1865.[11]

VIII

Of all the aspects of the 1864 vice-presidential candidacy the most sensational (in its possible implications) was the effort to put Benjamin F. Butler in second place. The details are given in the recollections of A. K. McClure and in an article by Louis Taylor Merrill. McClure recounts how "Lincoln's first selection for Vice-President was General Butler," how in March 1864 he explained this purpose to Simon Cameron, and how he made Cameron his messenger to Fort Monroe to "confer confidentially with Butler."[1] Despite all the heated antagonism attaching to his personality and career, Butler was a real political force. This was demonstrated by the enthusiastic ovation that greeted him (after his removal from the New Orleans command) when he spoke in his home town of Lowell, Massachusetts, while similar popular approval was also shown at a speech in Boston's Faneuil Hall and in a reception in New York. He was spoken of as a presidential prospect, also as a cabinet officer, "especially Stanton's place."[2] The man evoked emotional acclaim; he inspired headlines; he had unusual publicity value; he was one of the most prominent of those men around whom it was believed the radicals could rally. There was a persistent effort on his part, though without success, to enhance his military importance; he was one of the most "political" of the Union generals.

To resume the story of this reported 1864 offer, when Cameron turned up at Butler's headquarters at Fort Monroe the general decisively rejected the opportunity. It is stated that the President

---

[11] The biographer of Henry J. Raymond gives that New York journalist and Republican leader considerable credit for the nomination of Johnson. It is known that Raymond was acting in Lincoln's interest. Francis Brown, *Raymond of the Times*, 255.

[1] McClure, *Abraham Lincoln and Men of War-Times*, 118 ff.

[2] Louis Taylor Merrill, "General Benjamin F. Butler in the Presidential Campaign of 1864," *Miss. Vall. Hist. Rev.*, XXXIII, 541 (Mar. 1947).

planned to visit Fort Monroe with Mrs. Lincoln to confer with Butler, but the plan was never carried out and about this time the President's mind was directed favorably toward Andrew Johnson as his
running mate.

This account of the Butler offer through Cameron—a rather unlikely go-between for Lincoln—has not been verified on the Lincoln
side, and as it stands the story has features which are undocumented
and other features which are of the tongue-in-cheek quality. Yet it
should be added that Butler himself confirmed the story in later
years. In an article published in 1885 he wrote that "a gentleman
who stood very high in Mr. Lincoln's confidence" came to see him at
Fort Monroe to convey the message from Lincoln that the President
desired Butler to serve as candidate for Vice President. At this point
Butler reported a bit of misplaced humor on his part. "Please say to
Mr. Lincoln that . . . I must decline. Tell him . . . I would not
quit the field to be Vice-President, even with himself as President,
unless he will give me a bond with sureties, in the full sum of his four
years' salary, that he will die or resign within three months after his
inauguration. Ask him what he thinks I have done to deserve the
punishment . . . of being made to sit as presiding officer over the
Senate . . . [etc.]." [3]

It is known that Butler's real interest in 1864 was in the first, not
the second, place. The Cameron visit was reported as having been
made at a time in the spring of 1864 when Republican maneuvering
for the presidency was highly active; people who knew the radical
anti-Lincoln game at that time and who knew Butler's ambition,
would hardly have expected him to make an advance commitment
which would have kept him out as presidential candidate and at the
same time have placed him in support of Lincoln.

There has been speculation as to Butler's possible thoughts when
further pages of history were unfolded and he heard of Lincoln's
assassination. As Dr. Merrill puts it, " 'bold Ben' Butler had muffed
the highest prize." [4] There were, however, matters of greater importance than Butler's feelings, and the historian may well ponder the

---

[3] B. F. Butler, "Vice-Presidential Politics in '64," *North Amer. Rev.* CXLI, 333 (Oct. 1885).
[4] Merrill, as above cited, 570.

possible situation that would have resulted if the explosive, unpredictable, flamboyant, and radically vindictive Butler, of all Union generals the most hated in the South, had been the executive head of the nation in the confused and viciously partisan days of so-called "reconstruction."

IX

As a sequel to the convention Lincoln received committees and delegates, addressing them with brief responses. On June 9, the day after his nomination, he spoke to a committee of notification. In a sentence that was characteristically Lincolnian (in its attitude of caution as to a pledge or commitment) the President stated that perhaps he "should not declare definitely before reading and considering what is called the platform." He made it clear, however, that he approved the anti-slavery amendment to the Constitution as "a fitting and necessary conclusion to the final success of the Union cause." [1] Eighteen days later Lincoln issued a more formal acceptance indicating that the platform was "heartily approved." He did, however, offer one qualifying statement. The plank upholding the Monroe Doctrine and denouncing any effort to overthrow republican government on the western continent could have been interpreted, by reading between the lines, as a rebuke of Seward as secretary of state. Consequently Lincoln, while concurring in the declaration, took occasion to announce that "the position of the government . . . as assumed through the State Department" would be "faithfully maintained." [2]

Reactions to the results of the Baltimore convention varied. The Union Leagues loudly approved of the convention's work, though radical rumblings in those leagues had not been lacking. Some dissent and dissatisfaction was expressed shortly after the convention, but most of it was withheld. Later in the summer it would become abundantly evident. There were, it should be added, withdrawals, resignations, and replacements, but these will be discussed at a later period. One member of the cabinet, Attorney General Bates, wrote on June 10: "The Baltimore Convention . . . has surprised and mortified me greatly." Many of the delegates, he remarked, though they were

---

[1] *Works*, X, 116–117 (June 9, 1864).   [2] *Ibid.*, X, 136–137 (June 27, 1864).

instructed to vote for Lincoln, "hated to do it." He added: "I shall tell the Prest. in all frankness, that his best nomination is not that at Baltimore, but . . . by the People, by which the convention was constrained to name him." [3]

---

[3] Bates, *Diary*, 374–375 (June 10, 1864).

CHAPTER VIII

WAR FRONT AND PEACE TALK

AS THE armies renewed their fighting with fierce intensity in the spring of 1864, a new situation presented itself. In three years of indecisive warfare a certain repetitive pattern had become familiar: advance by one or the other side (usually the Federal), concentration on a one- or two-day battle, "victory" by one side or the other (usually the Confederate), Union withdrawal, change of Union commanders, then considerable delay for each side, neither being really defeated, to reorganize for the next concentrated push and sanguinary though indecisive engagement. Seemingly, the war could have gone on indefinitely in such fashion. Now, however, came a kind of struggle that was different as to broad strategy, as to method in the field, and as to pace. These changes coincided with the shifting of Grant from the field of his western triumphs to the main area of operations against Lee in Virginia; moreover, the shift involved the placing of general command of the Union armies in Grant's determined hand. The strategy was now for co-ordinated forward drives, continued assaults though producing no immediate advantage, killing and wounding at a thousand a day, emphasis on fighting and slaughter rather than on this or that battle—in a word, a "war of attrition."

As the doubtful spring gave way to a summer of deepest gloom, the Union cause appeared to be in a hopeless stalemate, while the mounting casualties produced a wave of shock and indignation in the North. The "political" result of all this was a rising tide of anti-Lincoln sentiment in the President's own party, while at the same time the nation's attention was continually focused on unofficial and misguided "peace" maneuvers which the President could not ignore, though they offered no tangible hope for genuine peace.

I

On February 29, 1864, Lincoln signed an act of Congress reviving the grade of lieutenant general, a rank so high that it had been used only for Washington and (as brevet) for Winfield Scott. It was understood that this high rank was to be conferred upon U. S. Grant, who arrived in unspectacular fashion in Washington to become the sensational center of interest and the cynosure of social eyes at a White House reception remarkable for the presence of the nation's notables (May 8). There was an unusually large attendance in expectation of Grant's presence and a considerable "stir and buzz" (as Welles recorded) when the "short, brown, dark-haired man" appeared. As the general passed into the East Room escorted by Seward, there was clapping and "a cheer or two"; to Welles it "seemed rowdy and unseemly." [1]

Next day, March 9, there occurred a formal ceremony of military investiture at the White House. As Lincoln and Grant had met for the first time on the evening of the reception, the President, with tactful thoughtfulness toward the diffident hero, explained the nature of the coming occasion, giving him a copy of his (the President's) speech and adding a friendly suggestion that a brief response would be in order. In the presence of the cabinet, specially summoned for the purpose, the military notables gathered (Grant and his staff with Stanton and Halleck) and Lincoln presented the unusual commission. It was remarked that the general was "somewhat embarrassed" as he gave his response.[2] On March 10 the President and Mrs. Lincoln invited Grant and Meade to dinner at the White House. Lincoln was omitting nothing that could improve the social and personal as well as the official recognition of the officer who was now regarded as the man of the hour.

For this dinner there was a special courtesy in the inclusion of General Meade; if either Meade or Grant had been of smaller stature, the new situation might have developed into an awkward rivalry of the kind so common among Civil War generals, or at least a sense of hurt feelings. It was not merely that Grant was elevated to supreme military "rank." He was at the same time "assigned to the

---

[1] Welles, *Diary*, I, 538–539 (Mar. 9, 1864).   [2] *Ibid.*, I, 539.

command of the Armies of the United States." Though in a sense this high general command had been held by Scott, McClellan, and Halleck, yet it had been exercised with so little effectiveness that the investiture in the case of Grant came with all the force of something new and untried. Lincoln had found Halleck unsatisfactory in the role of general in chief and his dissatisfaction on that score was well known. Halleck, with the best of motives, now offered his resignation, not for the first time, but the President, as previously, made it clear that "Old Brains" was to remain at his post.

To appreciate the extent of the change now instituted it must be remembered that general direction of the armies was to be no longer in the hands of a lofty desk commander in Washington. If Grant had so chosen he might have continued the old system, but the "new" general from the West, now the main leader in the East but with authority for all the fronts, promptly decided that his headquarters would not be in Washington, but with the Army of the Potomac, with himself as leader of that army in the field. Yet he never became its appointed commander; that office was retained by Meade. It augured well for the Union cause, and it revealed much as to the personalities of these generals, that they could stand in this unusual and potentially difficult relation to each other—the one the official commander, the other the effective leader of the main army—without personal friction and without detriment to efficiency.

If lesser personalities had been involved the feuding might have disrupted the team as in the case of Hooker and Slocum in the fall of 1863. Or another possible result might have been that any successes would have been credited to Grant, who was wearing an aura of military triumph, while failures would have been Meade's. As explained, however, by Meade's chief staff officer, Colonel Theodore Lyman: "In point of reality the whole is Grant's: he directs all, and his subordinates are only . . . executive officers having more or less unimportant functions." [3] Lyman also wrote: "he [Grant] is a man who does everything with a specific reason; he is eminently a *wise* man." The colonel added: "He knows very well Meade's precise capacity and strong points. For example, if Meade says a certain movement . . . should be made, Grant makes it, almost as a matter of course,

---

[3] George R. Agassiz, ed., *Meade's Headquarters, 1863–1865: Letters of Colonel Theodore Lyman from the Wilderness to Appomattox*, 224.

because he is so wise as to know that there is one of Meade's strong points." [4] This statement only partly covers the subject. Fully to understand the unusual relationship which was nevertheless made workable, one must remember Grant's statement of his own feeling: "Meade's position . . . proved embarrassing to me if not to him. . . . All other general officers occupying similar positions were independent in their commands so far as any one present with them was concerned. I tried to make General Meade's position as nearly as possible what it would have been if I had been in Washington or any other place away from his command. I therefore gave all orders for the movements of the Army of the Potomac to Meade to have them executed." [5]

In person and temperament, Grant was "different." He lacked style, made an undistinguished appearance, showed carelessness of dress, and appeared bored by unusual attention. Describing him at the time of his arrival in Washington, Ben: Perley Poore wrote: "He wore a plain, undress uniform and a felt hat of the regulation pattern, the sides . . . crushed together. He generally stood or walked with his left hand in his trousers pocket, and had in his mouth an unlighted cigar, the end of which he chewed restlessly." From these externals Poore proceeded to points of personality and character. "His square-cut features, when at rest, appeared as if carved from mahogany, and his firmly set under-jaw indicated the unyielding tenacity of a bull-dog, while the kind glances of his gray eyes showed that he possessed the softer traits." It also seemed to Poore that the general "seemed always preoccupied." He "would gaze at any one who approached him with an inquiring air, followed by a glance of recollection and a grave nod of recognition." [6]

An observer wrote: "He is rather under middle height, of a spare, strong build; light-brown hair, and short, light-brown beard. His eyes of a clear blue; forehead high; nose aquiline; jaw squarely set, but not sensual. His face has three expressions: deep thought; extreme determination; and great simplicity and calmness." [7] Other details have

---

[4] *Ibid.,* 359.

[5] Grant, *Memoirs,* II, 117–118. More than two weeks after the White House ceremony putting Grant in full command, Bates wrote in his diary (March 27, 1864): "Day before yesterday, Lt. Genl. Grant went to the front—Hd. Qrs. A. P. It seems not known whether he will supersede Genl. Meade, or only supervise him, as all the rest."

[6] Poore, *Perley's Reminiscences,* II, 150.   [7] Agassiz, ed., *Meade's Headquarters,* 80.

been added to the portrait. "He is a man of a natural, severe simplicity, in all things—the very way he wears his high-crowned felt hat shows this: he neither puts it on behind his ears, nor draws it over his eyes; much less does he cock it on one side, but sets it straight and very hard on his head. His riding is the same: without the slightest 'air' . . . he sits firmly in the saddle and looks straight ahead, as if only intent on getting to some particular point." [8] Again we have the following: "He is an odd combination; there is one good thing, at any rate—he is the concentration of all that is American. He talks bad grammar, but talks it naturally, as much as to say, 'I was so brought up and, if I try fine phrases, I shall only appear silly.' " [9]

II

The military planning for 1864 soon unfolded itself in terms of a grand scheme by which the Union armies on all major fronts would be co-ordinated in a series of encircling or squeezing operations. By simultaneous movements on several fronts Federal numerical superiority would be brought into play while the resulting Confederate necessity of manning a number of distant points would be sure to leave some area exposed to attack.

Just after receiving his commission as lieutenant general and before taking up his headquarters at Culpepper, Grant had gone West for about ten days conferring with Sherman at Nashville, after which the two generals rode together from Nashville to Cincinnati. They laid plans for the major features of what Grant called "sanguinary war." [1] They pored over maps and planned simultaneous attacks with Richmond and Atlanta—the armies of Lee and Johnston—as targets. Thus they proposed to nullify the enemy's advantage of interior lines; incidentally they hoped to prevent Confederate soldier furloughs for the planting of crops. The new strategy was reducible to two points: unity of command and "attrition to powder of the Confederate armies by a continuous series of battles." [2] In addition to the two most prominent commanders—Grant and Sherman—other campaigns were intrusted to such commanders as Butler in Virginia and Banks in the far Southwest.

---

[8] *Ibid.*, 83. [9] *Ibid.*, 156.
[1] Grant, *Memoirs*, II, 119. [2] *Harper's Pictorial History of the Civil War*, II, 600.

While at Culpepper in late March and April, Grant planned the spring and summer offensive of the eastern army, keeping in touch with Lincoln by occasional personal visits to nearby Washington. Lincoln gave Grant a free hand, but it would be a mistake to suppose that the President had nothing to do with strategy or that he was passively inattentive to military matters. Too much should not be made of Lincoln's statement to Grant, as to other generals, disclaiming military expertness while leaving the field commander to act as the effective military leader. It is true that on the eve of the Virginia campaign the President wrote: "The particulars of your plans I neither know nor seek to know." [3] In his *Memoirs* Grant records that Lincoln "told me he did not want to know what I proposed to do." [4] (This was probably a misinterpretation of the Chief's statement that he did not seek to know the "particulars" of the general's plans.) In those same *Memoirs,* written long after the war, the general related that the President "submitted a plan of campaign of his own," illustrating it with a map. The general "listened respectfully," but knew that the President's plan was unworkable.[5] The full truth as to the respective attitudes of Lincoln and Grant is not easy to state. In a careful study T. Harry Williams discounts the validity of some of the general's comments in his *Memoirs.* The general, he said, wrote "under the influence of the postwar Grant and Lincoln myths." "Grant had forgotten much in the years after the war, and his account [of Lincoln's unworkable plan] was wide of the truth." [6]

On May 4, 1864, Grant moved out from his Culpepper headquarters, crossed the Rapidan, and began a slugging campaign of forty days, in which the most frightful and bloody slaughter of the war brought little apparent success while it produced agony and heartache by its terrific Union casualties. The chief phases of these forty days were: (1) the battle of the Wilderness, May 5 and 6; (2) the shifting of the armies to Spottsylvania and the engagement there; (3) operations on the North Anna River; (4) the unsuccessful and shockingly costly assaults at Cold Harbor, June 1–3; and (5) the Union change of front as Grant's army crossed the James River and attempted the quick taking of Petersburg. Each of these operations could be set down as a Union failure, beginning with the confused struggle in the Wil-

---

[3] *Works,* X, 90 (Apr. 30, 1864). [4] Grant, *Memoirs,* II, 123.
[5] *Ibid.* [6] T. Harry Williams, *Lincoln and His Generals,* 304–305.

derness, where Grant had not intended to fight, and ending with the shifting of the "line" which he had said he would not do. At the end of the forty days the assault on Petersburg failed, so that the Union effort against that Confederate stronghold resolved itself, much to Lincoln's disappointment, in a long siege.

Yet such was war: it looked like failure, but because of ceaseless pounding while Union soldier morale kept at high pitch, the enemy was not only prevented from conducting an offensive operation (had that been Lee's purpose), but was progressively weakened for the (as yet unforeseen) final chapter. Grant was sustained both by his basic character and by his star. He seems to have had a reserve of endurance as well as a surplus of prestige. Otherwise his lack of success in the spring and summer of '64 might have relegated him to the fate of McDowell, Pope, Burnside, and Hooker.

As for the Wilderness, the obvious disadvantages of that impossible area will serve to confirm the reasons why McClellan, two years before, had preferred the Peninsular approach. The two-day battle (May 5 and 6) has been described as "a battle which no man saw or could see." [7] It was a series of attacks and repulses without co-ordinated control, fought in brush and thickets which made artillery ineffective and made it almost impossible to find the wounded who remained lying in the field, with a renewed engagement about to begin.[8] Neither side claimed victory; on the Union side the only justification for the encounter was that the Confederates brought on the operation before Grant's dispositions could be developed, and that by hammering continuously, "by mere attrition, if in no other way," the enemy would be forced into "submission." [9]

III

Despite Grant's over-all leadership and the much emphasized principal of co-ordinated strategy there were two fairly ambitious operations in 1864 which resulted in sorry fiascos: the Red River expedition of General N. P. Banks in the Southwest and the frustrated advance of B. F. Butler on the James River in Virginia. Only a brief mention of these episodes can be allowed.

The Union expedition up the Red River in western Louisiana,

---

[7] *Offic. Rec.*, 1 ser., XXXVI, pt. 1, 218.   [8] *Ibid.*, 218, 231.   [9] *Ibid.*, 13.

Ten Reasons why Abraham Lincoln should not be elected President of the United States a second term.

1. Because after having taken an oath to support the Constitution, he falsified his oath, and trampled the Constitution under foot, by adopting the slaveholders' *construction* of it, instead of the plain language of the instrument itself.

2. Because he did not "let the oppressed go free" when, according to his own theory he had the power, as in the Border States, but *pretended* to emancipate in those States and parts of States where he had not the power, the rebels having military possession.

3. Because his Emancipation and Amnesty proclamations, taken together and translated into plain Saxon-English, mean just this: "If you will come back into the Union and help elect me President for another term I will agree that your slavery shall be guaranteed to you and your posterity forever, but if you will not, I will then emancipate your slaves."

4. Because during the time this billing and cooing was going on with the slaveholding rebels, our President was spending two millions of dollars a day and allowing our brave soldiers to be sacrificed at the rate of a hundred thousand lives per annum, in the criminal attempt to drive a sharp bargain with the rebels, that would put him in the Presidential chair for a second term, against which he was virtually pledged.

5. Because he returned to slavery 50,000 slaves, embraced in Gen. Fremont's proclamation of emancipation, and superceded him and every other General in favor of emancipation.

6. Because, after the rebels—mean and cruel as they are—had spurned the bribe, Pres. Lincoln would neither emancipate their slaves himself nor allow any of his Generals, so disposed, to do so, but permitted others of them, without let or hindrance, to return fugitive slaves to their former masters, and *compel* our soldiers to stand guard over rebel property, and act as slave catchers generally, for the miserable scamps in rebellion.

7. Because he hypocritically *says* he is "naturally anti-slavery," while *really* he *chooses to establish* slavery where he has the power to *abolish* it, (as in the Border States), thus *acting* in *favor* of slavery while *professing* to be *against* it.

8. Because he has used the major part of his *first* presidential term, more to conserve slavery, and get himself elected a *second* term than to *conquer* the rebellion.

9. Because after Congress passed a law excluding the States in rebellion from the Electoral College, and making a republican form of government (of course, without slavery) a condition of readmission to the Union, the President coolly pocketed the bill without signing or vetoing it, until Congress had adjourned, so that it could not be passed by a Constitutional majority of two thirds over his veto, but left the door open for him to reconstruct, before election, the States in rebellion, on his old plan of one tenth of the people, and by that means obtain a majority of Electoral votes.

10. Because his plan of re-constructing the Slave States on a slaveholding basis, is now so transparent that the wayfaring man though a fool need not err in the matter.

Robert Todd Lincoln Coll., Lib. of Cong.

THE CASE OF THE RADICALS

A pro-Fremont, anti-Lincoln campaign circular issued by Radical Republicans in the summer of 1864.

FOR McCLELLAN

A lithographic broadside issued by Currier & Ives for sale to Democrats during the campaign of 1864. McClellan is trying to prevent Lincoln, on the left, and Jefferson Davis, on the right, from tearing the United States apart.

THE POLITICAL "SIAMESE" TWINS
THE OFFSPRING OF CHICAGO MISCEGENATION.

AGAINST McCLELLAN

Currier & Ives sold their lithographs to Republicans as well as Democrats. In this one the two Union soldiers on the left say good-bye to "little Mac" because of his "party tie" with Pendleton. On the right Vallandigham and Seymour tell Pendleton that they support the ticket because a victory for him will also be a victory for the Peace Democrats and for Jefferson Davis.

FREEMAN AND FREEDMAN

Left: John H. Rock, a Boston lawyer, the first Negro to be admitted to practice before the U. S. Supreme Court (on Feb. 2, 1865). Never a slave, Rock exemplified the successful freeman. From *Harper's Weekly*, Feb. 25, 1865. *Right:* Frederick Douglass, abolitionist and friend of Lincoln. Born in slavery on the Eastern Shore of Maryland, Douglass was an outstanding freedman.

March to May 1864, was designed as a combined army-navy operation in which Banks had (presumably) the military command while Admiral D. D. Porter was called upon to assist with a formidable fleet of gunboats. Sherman reluctantly "loaned" 10,000 of his men under General A. J. Smith for the purpose, while General Frederick Steele, moving from Arkansas, added a fourth unit to the clumsy enterprise. The purposes of this far-off trans-Mississippi adventure were political, military, and economic: if successful, it was expected that the operation would promote Lincoln's free-state organization in Louisiana (very dear to the President's heart), extend the line of Union occupation, discourage the French in their imperial Mexican designs, encourage Unionists in eastern Texas, capture Shreveport, and result in Union seizure of immense quantities of cotton. By getting started in March, it was expected that the operation would require only a month, after which Sherman's troops could be returned for use in the Atlanta campaign. The plan was largely Halleck's, though Lincoln approved it. It was vigorously opposed by Grant, yet this was supposed to be the period of unified Grant strategy on all fronts.

From first to last the execution of the operation went wrong. The army and navy were distrustful of each other; Porter disliked Banks; no one commander had recognized authority in the field; Sherman himself did not participate; commanders criticized each other; professionals of the army had little confidence in the politically minded Banks who was not of West Point; and the whole scheme brought into play the bitter antagonism between the pro-Lincoln plan of reconstruction personified in Banks and the radicals who detested him and were determined to undo his efforts.

Faulty marching arrangements, a miserable surplus of wagons on narrow roads, unwise tactics, and failure of the diverse units to concentrate—such factors as these contributed to what has been called "one of the most humiliating and disastrous [expeditions] . . . to be recorded during the war." [1] At Sabine Cross Roads (April 8, 1864), some miles south of Shreveport, the Confederates struck when Union forces were at a serious disadvantage. Artillery was useless and the Union line falling back was hampered by wagons clogging the road; Federal retreat was covered and the army mainly

---

[1] *Battles and Leaders of the Civil War,* IV, 366.

"saved" but all hope of taking Shreveport was destroyed. On April 9 the Union army did better at the battle of Pleasant Hill, but Banks was now in retreat. Moreover, a new complication had arisen; the drying river had fallen to such an extent that Porter's gunboats were in serious danger of being grounded and lost; this misfortune was narrowly averted by brisk and expert engineers who built dams to raise the water level and allow the fleet to get through in the nick of time. Losses were heavy—about 2200 army casualties in the one day of Sabine Cross Roads; the navy lost a few gunboats and over 300 men.[2] Banks was demoted—i. e., superseded in military command by E. R. S. Canby—and the force under A. J. Smith was sent, not to Sherman, but to the Army of the Potomac in the war's main theater. As to the cotton, many of the speculators came back "without their sheaves";[3] their disappointment as to profits had much to do in spreading false reports concerning Banks. Much of the cotton had been burned by the Confederates, and the emphasis on speculators getting cotton behind enemy lines was not so much a policy of Banks as of Lincoln and the government at Washington. The whole enterprise was one of the sorry episodes which tended to discredit the Lincoln administration in an election year.

IV

Simultaneously with Grant's Wilderness drive, B. F. Butler made his contribution, if such it could be called, to the Union effort. Having been for some months established at Fort Monroe in command of the Army of the James (about 36,000 men), he now moved up that river, pointing toward Richmond, and hoping to achieve a spectacular result by entering the Confederate capital, though at times it appeared that Petersburg was his objective. The scheme was conceived in terms of Grant's broad strategy of concerted Union attacks from different directions. Yet the effort was poorly co-ordinated with the work of the Army of the Potomac. Moreover, Butler being the man he was, the adventure cannot be judged apart from the general's prominence as a frequently mentioned rival of Lincoln for

---

[2] Fred H. Harrington, *Fighting Politician; Major General N. P. Banks*, 156; *Battles and Leaders*, IV, 366.

[3] *Battles and Leaders*, IV, 361.

the presidential nomination. All this, of course, was in terms of radical support. Had Butler been able to "take" or enter Richmond in May of 1864, it is hard to believe that such an event would not have been exploited for political advantage.

As it turned out, this subsidiary operation of Butler was a fiasco. On May 5 he "occupied" City Point and Bermuda Hundred on the James River less than twenty miles southeast of Richmond; this was easily done without opposition. Moving slowly up the river, and giving his antagonist, Beauregard, time to improve his defensive arrangements, Butler reached Drewry's Bluff, but soon withdrew and "intrenched" in "a position" which he could "hold," assuming he received supplies.[1] Little more need be said of Butler's part in the campaign. Beauregard, unharmed by Butler, was able with an inferior force to keep him penned in at Bermuda Hundred, in a corner between the Appomattox and James Rivers, where the much-advertised general was useless to Grant, who wrote: "His [Butler's] army . . . , though in a position of great security, was as completely shut off from . . . Richmond as if it had been in a bottle strongly corked. It required but a . . . small force of the enemy to hold it there." [2]

For this phase of the war one finds elaborate and important sounding military dispatches in Butler's published correspondence, but when they are boiled down they relate to such things as failure of an "attempt on the railroad," orders "for the purpose of" cutting communications between Richmond and Petersburg, criticisms of his corps commanders (Quincy A. Gillmore and William Farrar Smith), requests to Washington for reinforcements, references to his orders not being executed, comments on the safety of his force, and repeated mention that he had not taken Petersburg.[3]

---

[1] *Battles and Leaders of the Civil War*, IV, 147.

[2] This was Grant's statement in his official report (*Offic. Rec.*, 1 ser., XXXVI, p. 1, 20; *Battles and Leaders*, IV, 147). Years later, in writing his Memoirs, he softened his words. Without substantially modifying the impression as to Butler's ineffective position, he showed that the simile of the bottle and the cork, which caused annoyance to Butler, was not his own, but was only a repetition without quotation marks, of the words of his "chief engineer, General Barnard." *Memoirs*, II, 150–152. There is no reason to believe that in this effort to "correct history" and rectify an "injustice," the famous general had undergone any change of opinion as to the facts.

[3] *Private and Official Correspondence of B. F. Butler*, IV, *passim*, especially 168, 169, 171, 411, 417, 426.

V

In the shift to the North Anna the superiority of Lee's maneuvering was demonstrated. In the operations on that river the Confederates, contrary to usual procedure in this campaign, took the offensive and made unsuccessful assaults. Aside from the slaughter little was accomplished in this battle.

Meanwhile, in addition to Grant's shifting and pounding with the main army, there were ambitious cavalry operations in which Sheridan, Hunter, and Custer were active on the Union side, against Confederate commanders Stuart, Early, and Mosby. One of the most striking of the cavalry episodes, though minor in results, was Sheridan's raid toward Richmond in the period of Grant's severe fighting against Lee's army. With the idea of cutting Lee's communications and diverting Confederate cavalry, Sheridan pushed rapidly toward the Southern capital, destroying railroad equipment, seizing food supplies, and releasing Union prisoners. At Yellow Tavern on May 11, six miles north of Richmond, a sharp engagement between Sheridan's force and that of the redoubtable J. E. B. Stuart resulted in Union repulse, yet sadly for the Confederates it resulted also in the fatal wounding of Stuart. The Union cavalry leader then swept back toward the Army of the Potomac without attempting to enter Richmond. Had he made that entry, it would have been only for a quick raid and prompt withdrawal.

After the continued slaughter in the Wilderness, at Spottsylvania, and on the North Anna, there was more of the same, though intensified, at Cold Harbor, where in a series of assaults Union troops were hurled against solid enemy defense positions. The enemy were taking no risks and the human sacifice was tremendous. In this battle, which was a failure, Grant lost 12,000 men in killed and wounded.[1] Charging bravely but hopelessly, the troops were simply mowed down at close range. If this was Grant's type of warfare, he nevertheless admitted that Cold Harbor was a mistake. In his *Memoirs* he wrote: I have always regretted that the last assault at Cold Harbor was ever made." [2] He was conducting a seemingly reckless "war of attrition,"

---

[1] Thomas L. Livermore, *Numbers and Losses in the Civil War in America, 1861–1865,* 114.

[2] Grant, *Memoirs,* II, 276.

yet even in terms of that kind of "strategy" he realized that such losses could not be continued. Beginning with the Wilderness (May 5) and running on through Cold Harbor and the cavalry raids, the total of Grant's casualties have been figured at 54,000 men, of whom 7621 were killed.[3] Casualties were running far above a thousand a day, much more for days of actual fighting, and Grant could not point to sufficient advantage to justify the excessive human cost. He wrote: "Without a greater sacrifice of life than I was willing to make, all could not be accomplished that I had designed north of Richmond." [4]

It was part of Grant's fitness for the grim business of war that he did not permit his emotions to be revealed. At the time of Cold Harbor an observer wrote: "His is a face that tells no tale—a face impassive in victory or defeat; face of stone; a sphinx face! Not of him can it be said, as Lady Macbeth to her lord: 'This face, my thane, is as a book, wherein one may read strange things.' Rather it is a *palimpsest,* whose obscured characters escape the scrutiny of the keenest-eyed searcher."

The writer then thought of Meade and added: "Nothing, indeed, could be more striking than the contrast presented by the two commanders, as they stooped in consultation on that bare hill, with their faces turned Richmond-ward. The small form with the slight stoop in the shoulders, sunken gray eyes; still, reserved demeanor, impassive face, and chin as of a bull-dog or close-set steel-trap—that is Grant; the tall figure, with the nervous, emphatic articulation and action, and face as of antique parchment—that is Meade—and the antipodes could not bring together a greater contrast." [5]

With a fundamental shift of plan Grant decided to cross the James River, place the Army of the Potomac south of Richmond, and pursue his further operations against Lee's army from Petersburg in the hope that that place could be quickly reduced. At the outset of his 1864 campaign he had written (May 11) Halleck: "I . . . propose to fight it out on this line if it takes all summer." [6] Yet after weeks of incessant hammering and ghastly losses he changed his "line." The shift was successfully made in mid-June. The crossing by bridge and ferry occupied several days beginning on June 14. In this movement

---

[3] *Offic. Rec.,* 1 ser., XXXVI, pt. 1, 188. [4] *Ibid.,* 22.
[5] Moore, *Rebell. Rec.* (Doc.), XI, 560–561. [6] *Offic. Rec.,* 1 ser., XXXVI, pt. 1, 4.

Lee was surprised, but on the other hand Grant's expectations were not fulfilled. His first effort south of the James was to conduct assaults upon Petersburg which failed, after which his great army settled down to a long-drawn-out siege, which was the type of war that he had hoped to avoid.

Lincoln was always generous toward Grant, and when the Army of the Potomac was in the thick of its death grapple with Lee, the President wrote: "My previous high estimate of General Grant has been maintained and heightened by what has occurred in the remarkable campaign he is now conducting . . . . He and his brave soldiers are now in the midst of their great trial . . . ." [7]

The President, with his beloved son Tad, visited Grant's army for several days at City Point in late June, leaving Washington on June 20 and returning to Washington on the 23rd. At this stage in the war the President was "deeply disappointed" that the costly campaign had resolved itself into a siege of Petersburg; he may then have felt "perhaps some doubts of Grant's generalship." [8] The shocking extent of the slaughter was weighing upon the President's mind. Shortly before his visit to the army, he had wired to Grant: "I do hope you may find a way that . . . shall not be desperate in the sense of great loss of life." [9] The war had now reached an unprofitable stage; it would be months before the burdened Chief could see prospects of ending the conflict.

VI

Military failure and national anger produced, or gave occasion for, grave and sometimes sensational manifestations behind the lines. Because of the overwrought feelings of the time a newspaper hoax in New York which should have stirred up a mere ripple, was magnified into a kind of tidal wave. In two of that city's newspapers there appeared on May 18, 1864, a purported proclamation of President Lincoln, allegedly dated May 17, in which, because of "the general state of the country," the President set a day for "fasting, humiliation, and prayer"; called forth an additional 400,000 men, and ordered that the troops "be raised by an immediate and peremptory

---

[7] *Works*, X, 112 (June 3, 1864).   [8] Williams, *Lincoln and His Generals*, 320.
[9] *Works*, X, 160 (June 17, 1864).

draft." The author of this daring forgery was one Joseph Howard, Jr., a prolific writer who had been private secretary to Henry Ward Beecher and had floated about on various journalistic assignments. His motive apparently was to make money by a disturbance in the stock market. He has been identified by Nicolay and Hay as having perpetrated the disgustingly false report that Lincoln, on his way through Baltimore to Washington in February 1861, had worn a Scotch cap and long military coat as a disguise, an invented yarn which led to caricatures belittling the President Elect and holding him up to ridicule.[1]

Though the effort was made to play the trick upon all the leading New York papers, only two of them—the *World* and the *Journal of Commerce*—permitted the issuance of editions containing the bogus proclamation. The *Herald* discovered the forgery after its edition had been put through the press; the edition was then destroyed and a new one printed.[2] As for the papers that were tricked, it was but a coincidence that they were both strongly hostile to the Lincoln administration. What happened to them was a matter of deception; there was no intention of fraud on the part of editors and proprietors. The false document came in by messenger at night, written on the kind of thin manifold paper used for Associated Press dispatches. In handwriting and physical appearance it looked like a regular news report. A boy opened the envelopes with the A. P. dispatches and the bogus telegram between three and four o'clock and handed them to the night editor who thought they were all from the same legitimate source. When the fraud was discovered it was too late to stop the edition in the case of the *World* and the *Journal of Commerce*.

At this point the stern and impulsive secretary of war, Stanton, entered the picture. Without waiting for an investigation, Stanton caused the immediate issuance of a sharp order, for which he obtained Lincoln's signature, which soon became revealed as a serious executive blunder. The order declared that the proclamation had been "wickedly and traitorously . . . published" with the "design to give aid and comfort to the enemies of the United States." Gen-

[1] Nicolay and Hay, *Lincoln*, III, 315 n.
[2] Typed memorandum by Frank A. Flower to accompany an original of Joseph Howard's bogus proclamation sent to C. F. Gunther, MS., Chicago Hist. Soc.

eral Dix was accordingly "commanded forthwith to arrest and imprison" the editors and proprietors, to hold them "in close custody until they can be brought to trial before a military commission," to take forcible military possession of the printing establishments of the papers, and to "prohibit any further publication thereof." [3]

This was indeed an amazing order. It was issued on snap judgment without knowledge of the facts, though on that very day General Dix was instituting an investigation which would promptly reveal that the papers and their publishers were not guilty. It was done in the arrogant fashion and with the peremptory language of a military despotism most uncongenial to the mind and nature of Lincoln. It was an attack on freedom of the press, and was inconsistent with the prevailing policy of the Lincoln government, which was to leave opposition newspapers unmolested—a policy of which the *World* and the *Journal of Commerce* were standing examples. It opened up a wretched conflict of state against Federal power and of civil against military procedures. In its mention of trial before a "military commission" it seemed to presage a proceeding which could have subjected the Lincoln administration to serious embarrassment and censure. Finally it gave a handle to Lincoln's unfair partisan critics who used the episode for much more than it was worth; it seemed to give validity to their attacks upon the President as a tyrant and a destroyer of civil rights.

What made it more amazing was that the action taken was quite unnecessary. Neither of the papers concerned was so blind to its own self interest as to publish a fake proclamation of the President intentionally for a treasonable purpose. The accusation was preposterous, however hostile the papers had been to the Republican administration. The *World* managers promptly discovered the fraud; they announced the fact in their bulletin; they withheld copies of the May 18 edition from the steamer which took dispatches to Europe and offered a reward of $500 for information leading to detection of the perpetrator. The angry and elaborate sequel to the affair was due not so much to the forgery, which had its brief hour, but to the post-mortems and voluminous legal proceedings against Dix and his officers, but with Lincoln, Stanton, and the Republicans, as the ultimate targets.

[3] Randall, *Constitutional Problems Under Lincoln,* 496–497.

The suppression, or suspension, was very brief. General Dix, whose attitude differed notably from that of Burnside in the cases of Vallandigham and of the Chicago *Times,* reluctantly executed the Stanton order (for so it should be called) so far as arresting some of the editors and proprietors. This was a military arrest and if a trial had been sought it would presumably have been a military trial, but on discovering that the men were innocent, Dix released them on May 20 and on May 23 the papers were allowed to resume publication.

It might now have been supposed that there had been enough ado about the freakish occurrence, and the matter would have been dropped so far as the Washington authorities were concerned, but Governor Seymour of New York would not allow the episode to be so terminated. By instruction of the governor accusations were brought against Dix and other officers before a New York grand jury. That body refused to vote an indictment and recommended that it would be inexpedient to pursue the case further. Even then the governor would not let the matter drop, and indeed if appropriate legal procedure could be found here was a flagrant misuse of military authority and a shocking violation of the freedom of the press, which the governor, with his anti-Lincoln attitude, would quite naturally wish to expose and exploit, as he could do with civil rights on his side. Seymour now instructed A. Oakey Hall, district attorney of the County of New York, to have the case further prosecuted.[4] Accordingly elaborate proceedings were begun before a local magistrate, Judge A. D. Russell, city judge in New York City.

The case was titled: *The People of New York* versus *John A. Dix and Others,* in which the defendants were charged with kidnaping and inciting to riot; it was thus a somewhat eccentric hearing in that the charges were whittled down to fit a merely local court and to be comprehended within state law, though in reality large Federal issues were at stake. Dix and his men were not in fact imprisoned; they were free on verbal recognizance while arguments long enough to fill a book were presented to the judge. On the side of the prosecution were A. Oakey Hall and John Cochrane, the latter being attorney general of New York; the defense was conducted by Edwards Pierrepont and William M. Evarts. Weighty questions were brought

---

4 Stewart Mitchell, *Horatio Seymour of New York,* 358.

into the long discussion: the war power, martial law in relation to civil government, the habeas corpus act, application of military rule outside the area of war, the duty of an officer to execute the order of a superior, and the problem whether an officer of the general government acting under an order from Washington could be rightfully arrested by local authority and subjected to trial before a state judge.

When at last Judge Russell issued his decision the result was an anticlimax. It is true that portentous words were used on broad points of law. The Federal authorities were strongly criticized and the habeas corpus act was denounced, but after the decision the defendants were free, with the possibility of any follow-up in an actual trial remaining a matter of doubt.

In the strict sense this was not a "trial" of Dix and the others; the judge was giving out a statement in a preliminary hearing. The question was whether the case could and should come to trial in a New York court in spite of the habeas corpus act of March 3, 1863 (especially the indemnity feature of that law) by which those who made military seizures or arrests under the President's order were protected from prosecution in any court for such acts, with the further provision that such cases belonged within Federal, not state, jurisdiction.[5] As showing the preliminary nature of the proceeding Judge Russell explained that he did not "deem it proper" to state his views on the legal principles involved; then he added: "Such an exposition of the law would be more appropriate should this case come before the court for trial." In the whole proceeding the judge's words were stronger than his judicial deeds. He could not approve the "very novel and startling doctrine" of the Federal indemnity (habeas corpus) law, since in his opinion it made the President "an absolute monarch . . . incapable of doing any wrong." The existing war, he argued, did not justify a system by which "the President can direct anything to be done in this state he pleases." The government, he declared "must not only enforce but obey the laws." Having so expressed himself, the judge ended somewhat harmlessly by announcing that "The complaints will . . . pass to the grand jury in the usual way for its action." A verbal recognizance was accepted; no written one being required. Though the decision has a certain dignity in its treatment of fundamental matters of government, it was

---

[5] Randall, *Constitutional Problems Under Lincoln,* chap. ix.

probably intended less for a showdown with the Federal government than for a public declaration in the heat of a presidential campaign.[6]

Thus the case in the courts was closed, but the criticism of Lincoln, which may be regarded as one of the motives of the New York proceedings, continued. For this criticism the *World* was the main spokesman; on August 8, 1864 that newspaper declared "The liberties of the people have been invaded. The war . . . has been made the instrument of usurpation and oppression . . . ."

In judging official Washington it must be concluded that the real blunderer was Stanton, who had seen to it that an order was issued in Lincoln's name. It was a hasty order based upon mere suspicion of wrongful intent; its wording was excessive and inappropriate; it made accusations that were soon found to be baseless; and the Lincoln administration felt that the arrests and seizures were unnecessary and ill advised. Welles commented that the seizure of the papers was "hasty, rash, inconsiderate, and wrong." As for Howard, author of the miserable forgery, Welles remarked: "He is of a pestiferous class of reckless sensation-writers for an unscrupulous set of journalists who misinform the public mind." [7] On May 20 Howard had been arrested; he was thrown into Fort Lafayette and kept for three months; he was then released by special intervention of the President. Howard had gone wrong, but he had influential friends, chief of whom was Henry Ward Beecher. On August 2, 1864, Beecher wrote earnestly to another man of influence, John D. Defrees, superintendent of public printing in Washington. The preacher felt that the sting and prostration of his punishment would be a lesson to the young man. He continued: "He was the tool of the man who turned states evidence and escaped; & Joe, had only the hope of making some *money,* by a stock broker, he had not foresight or consideration enough to perceive the relation of his act to the Public Welfare." Admitting his personal interest, Beecher wrote: "You must excuse my earnestness. He has been brought up in my parish & under my eye and is the *only* spotted child of a large family." Defrees wrote promptly to Lincoln [8] and on August 22 the President wrote to Stanton: "I very much wish to oblige [Henry Ward] Beecher by relieving Howard

<hr>

[6] Russell's opinion is given in the New York *World,* August 8, 1864, p. 1, c. 6.

[7] Welles, *Diary,* II, 38 (May 23, 1864).

[8] Henry Ward Beecher to John D. Defrees, New York, Aug. 2, 1864, R. T. L. Coll., 35002-3; John D. Defrees to John Hay, Washington, Aug. 3, 1864, *ibid.,* 35025.

. . . ." Several communications were exchanged between the President and the secretary of war; then on August 23 came Lincoln's order: "Let Howard, imprisoned in regard to the bogus proclamation, be discharged." [9] In compliance with this order the actual release came on August 24 and Howard continued to float about in the journalistic world for many years. The President himself had had but little to do directly with the affair, though it was "said to have angered Lincoln more than almost any other occurrence of the war period." [10]

VII

In the despair that hung over the nation in July 1864, with the certainty that the country's heavy woes would be capitalized for partisan or factional advantage, there occurred a remarkable episode of peace agitation. That irrepressible editor, Horace Greeley of the New York *Tribune* was now cast in the prominent role of attempted "negotiator" between Confederate emissaries and the President of the United States. As Greeley himself wrote, "the very darkest hours of our contest . . . were those of July and August, 1864." [1] Grant's campaign seemed a failure; the North was horrified by casualties such as those at Cold Harbor; attacks upon Petersburg were unavailing; the mine explosion there was a flash in the pan; and the whole war, though greatly intensified, seemed to have degenerated into an unprofitable stalemate. Increasing war weariness of the Northern people could be exploited by opponents of the Lincoln administration; this might give a considerable advantage to Northern Democrats in this year of a presidential election, to be held in the midst of a shattering war. Added to all this were two factors not to be overlooked: Greeley's ardent if eccentric personality, and his deep distrust of Lincoln.

To give an appraisal of this peacemaking episode one should seek to understand the whole Greeley and that is not easy. The problems of the age were a challenge and a disturbance to his active mind and sympathetic heart. He felt social ills so keenly that one could think

9 Stanton MSS., 54446, Lib. of Cong.
10 F. A. Flower to C. F. Gunther, Washington, Feb. 14, 1904, MS., Chicago Hist. Soc.
1 Greeley, *Amer. Conflict*, II, 664.

of the Greeley quest for solutions as the quest, or dilemma, of the age. He had the restless instinct of the reformer. In the depths of his nature there was Christianity, deep Puritan respect for moral virtue, and a consuming interest in humanitarian advance and achievement. Others were complacent, or inattentive, toward the needs of the time, but not Greeley. He could not help thinking earnestly and writing prolifically. If the demands of quick journalism led to superficiality in some of his declarations, it was nevertheless true that few editors could match him in informed study of the stresses of a changing industrial America. Though he had known the cruel hard knocks of life, he was notable for the uplift of his thought and the optimism of his fundamental outlook. In his friendliness toward socialism and his concern for the working man he did not slip off the track into Marxian radicalism or economic excess. His interest in Fourierism and in Brook Farm was genuine, yet he kept an element of conservatism in his idealistic nature. He decisively rejected communism. Though he should not be set down as a mere utopian dreamer, he burned with righteous discontent as he saw the working of the greedy capitalism of mid-century America. If the times were out of joint, his sense of mission prompted him to set them right.

His intense opposition to human slavery was an authentic part of his humanitarian concept; it was in harmony with his transcendentalism, his strong religious (yet not dogmatic) sense, his universalist viewpoint, his thought of the Over-Soul, and his deep devotion to the democratic faith.[2] Despite his "On to Richmond" drive and his earlier belief that war was necessary to rid the country of slavery, the bent of Greeley's mind was toward hatred of war and friendliness to peace crusades. He had once favored letting the cotton states "go in peace," and though his attitude on this question was complex and a bit hard to define, the result was that the editor was associated with the concept of peaceable separation.[3]

In addition to all his other qualities and outshining them all, Greeley was a great power in journalism. As a newspaper to give the people what they wanted, the *Tribune* had become a notable success. No one had done more to give importance to the editorial page

[2] The mind of Greeley, in a wide range of social and intellectual attitudes, is presented in Theodore Fisch's scholarly and readable treatment entitled "Horace Greeley: A Yankee in Transition," ms. doctoral dissertation, Univ. of Ill., 1947.

[3] David M. Potter, *Lincoln and His Party in the Secession Crisis*, 52–55.

as a force for shaping, not merely reflecting, opinion. In his editorial capacity Greeley had outstanding eminence as a pundit; his words were accepted by thousands of readers, including many in the West, as political gospel.

The Baltimore convention had not been to Greeley's liking. No political solution had materialized in terms of his radical preferences. He doubted whether Lincoln could lead the country either to military triumph or to terms of peace. He did not, nor did others in the country, foresee that a more favorable situation would be reached later in the year; these were the defeatist days of dark July. As a man keenly devoted to politics without being a politician, he desired the success of the Republican party; he did not relish the prospect that the Democrats might have, in their own peace drive, a popular and perchance a winning issue. It was not that his ultimate motives were so different from Lincoln's—they had in fact much in common—but if the President needed prodding in order to turn motives into accomplishment, Greeley stood ready to apply the editorial spur.

VIII

Such were the factors at work when, in early July, Greeley received word that "two Ambassadors of Davis & Co." were in Canada "with full & complete powers for a peace." [1] His informant was William Cornell ("Colorado") Jewett, a man notorious for wild schemes, an agitator in America and abroad who had been bombarding Lincoln with unpleasant letters giving vociferous advice and demanding that the war be terminated. There were indeed commissioners or emissaries of the Confederate President operating in Canada—Clement C. Clay of Alabama, Jacob Thompson of Mississippi, and J. P. Holcombe who had been a professor at the University of Virginia—but their instructions, which were not fully known, were vastly different from what was implied in recommending them to Greeley as promising peace negotiators. They had no authority whatever to confer on terms of peace in the name of the Confederate

---

[1] William Cornell Jewett to Greeley, Niagara Falls, July 5, 1864, R. T. L. Coll., 34281. Next day (no. 34298) Jewett wired Greeley: "Will you come here? Parties have full power." Jewett's numerous letters to Lincoln, reposing in the R. T. L. Collection, might have been a considerable annoyance, except that, according to Hay, the President did not read them.

government. They were part of the Confederate secret service and their purposes were to cause mischief by a variety of means to the Union cause, as for instance by rigging the gold market, creating Northern disaffection, subsidizing newspapers, making contact with "Copperheads," plotting the release of Confederate prisoners in the North, and building up for a major revolt in the Northwest. (Not that a revolt in terms of a "Northwest Confederacy" to withdraw from the United States and join the Southern Confederacy was feasible, but it was among the anti-Union schemes that were agitated and on which hopes were built.) Later in the year 1864 there would be fantastic Canadian-based efforts of Confederate agents to stir up violence and insurrection behind the lines in the United States, promoted with small concern for Canadian neutrality. Though these schemes involved more of melodramatic intrigue than real menace, they were part of the hidden history of the time and it was for such purposes that the Confederate secret service in Canada was set up.

Among these agents in Canada was George N. Sanders of Kentucky who was concerned with business matters on behalf of the Confederate government, such as arranging for the building of ships abroad, to be paid for in cotton deliverable at any port of the Confederacy.[2] Sanders had a considerable Canadian acquaintance and had made it his business to invite citizens of the United States to take part in various conferences at Niagara Falls, such invitations being given only to those understood to be hostile to the Lincoln administration. Thus Sanders offered a kind of liaison between Americans and Confederate agents, while Jewett in his self-made capacity assisted Sanders in obtaining contact with Greeley.

On hearing of these Confederate "ambassadors" (Jewett's word) ready to talk peace, Greeley was sufficiently impressed to undertake an appeal to Lincoln. On July 7 he wrote the President urging him to invite these gentlemen to Washington, "there to open their budgets." Referring to the Confederate desire for peace, he reminded the nation's Chief "that our bleeding, bankrupt, almost dying country also longs for peace—shudders at the prospect of fresh conscriptions, of further wholesale devastations, and of new rivers of human

---

[2] *Offic. Rec.* (Nav.), 2 ser., III, 529, 1235. For the general subject of these schemes and maneuvers from across the Northern border, see John W. Headley, *Confederate Operations in Canada and New York.*

blood." [3] From that point there followed an elaborate series of communications, letters, telegrams, and interviews, in which on Lincoln's part a safe conduct was offered to "any person, anywhere," bringing from Jefferson Davis a proposition for peace with Union and abolition of slavery. [4] On the other side, however, it was soon revealed that the "commissioners" were utterly lacking in credentials as Confederate agents authorized to negotiate peace.

Lincoln not only agreed to confer with accredited Confederate representatives, promising them safe conduct; he went farther in an adroit maneuver by assigning to Greeley himself the task of bringing the emissaries to see the President. For this purpose the editor was expected to meet the Confederates at Niagara Falls and accompany them to Washington. To have done so would have been understood as signifying that Greeley was vouching for these men as authorized negotiators. The editor, now greatly embarrassed, dallied and seemed disposed to pass the ball to the President. In a letter of July 13 he informed him of the names of the agents and expressed the hope that the President would take appropriate action. [5] At that rate the matter would have dragged on indefinitely, since the Confederate gentlemen were reluctant to show their hand, but Lincoln decided not to have it so. A famous editor was sponsoring a peace movement; the matter was being widely discussed; the national government was being distrusted or misrepresented; and the President could not afford to allow the question to remain dangling in uncertainty. Accordingly he sent John Hay to see Greeley, bearing a communication expressing disappointment that nothing had been done to produce the commissioners and concluding "I not only intend a sincere effort for peace but I intend that you shall be a personal witness that it is made." [6]

Greeley was now annoyed, feeling that the President had put him at a disadvantage. Proceeding to Niagara Falls and acting through Jewett, he sent a note addressed to Clay, Holcombe, and Thompson.

---

[3] *Ann. Cyc.*, 1864, 780; Horace Greeley to Lincoln, New York, July 7, 1864, R. T. L. Coll., 34316–18.

[4] *Works*, X, 154 (July 9, 1864); R. T. L. Coll., 34278.

[5] Nicolay and Hay, *Lincoln*, IX, 189; Horace Greeley to Lincoln, New York, July 13, 1864, R. T. L. Coll., 34458–9.

[6] *Works*, X, 159; Lincoln's draft of this letter, all in his own hand, is in R. T. L. Coll., 34492 (July 15, 1864).

Being "informed," he wrote, that these gentlemen were "duly accredited from Richmond as bearers of propositions . . . [for] peace," he extended safe conduct to them on authority of the President and offered to accompany them to Washington.[7] In this proceeding there was a strange omission: Greeley said nothing to the Southern agents about Lincoln's essential conditions of peace. The President had stated these conditions clearly enough in his letter to Greeley of July 9: "the restoration of the Union and abandonment of slavery." [8] Lincoln knew that no "negotiation" was worth trying if it did not presuppose these simple but indispensable terms. Lincoln's understanding with Greeley was not that the Commissioners should be asked merely to talk peace, but that they should come to Washington with Greeley "on the terms stated" in his letter of July 9.

At this point there came a hitch in the proceedings. The motive of the Confederate gentlemen was not to take constructive measures toward peace by negotiations at Washington, but to cause all possible trouble to the Lincoln administration and the Union cause. Clay and Holcombe now informed Greeley truly enough that Lincoln's safe conduct had been tendered them under a "misapprehension," inasmuch as they had "not been accredited to him (Lincoln) from Richmond as the bearers of propositions looking to . . . peace." [9] Greeley then telegraphed Washington for "fresh instructions," though Lincoln's previous statement of terms had been clear enough.

The President was now determined to see the thing through, to crystallize the trying situation for what it might signify, and to close the episode with national dignity if no favorable results were possible. He now entrusted Hay, for delivery to the appropriate persons, a paper which is of such significance that it may be quoted in full:

Executive Mansion, July 18, 1864

Whom it may concern

Any proposition which embraces the restoration of peace, the integrity of the whole Union, and the abandonment of slavery, and which comes by and with an authority that can control the armies now at war against the United States, will be received and considered by the Executive government of the United States, and will be met by liberal terms on other

---

[7] *Ann. Cyc.*, 1864, 780 (July 17, 1864).   [8] *Works*, X, 154.
[9] *Ann. Cyc.*, 1864, 781 (July 18, 1864).

substantial and collateral points; and the bearer or bearers thereof shall have safe-conduct both ways.

Abraham Lincoln [10]

There followed a fruitless interview at the Cataract House, Niagara Falls, between Hay and Greeley on one side and Holcombe on the other. Nothing came of the interview except that the Confederates now had the President's statement of minimum terms. As for a Confederate reply, that was delayed until Holcombe and Clay could prepare a rather ambitious paper which turned out to be an elaborate manifesto in the manner of Confederate propaganda. (This reply was prepared by the agents without consulting the Confederate government at Richmond, but such consultation was impracticable and if it had occurred the result would hardly have been different.) The commissioners had been assured of safe conduct, they declared, and they had expected a "most gratifying change in the policy of the President." It had seemed "that the President had opened a door . . . previously closed" against the Confederate States. Then came Lincoln's "To whom it may concern." They could not claim safe conduct "in a character . . . [they] had no right to assume." They could only express "profound regret" that the peace spirit "had not continued to animate the counsels of the President." Instead of the requested safe conduct, they received (so they declared) a document which provoked "as much indignation as surprise." It precluded negotiation; it constituted a "sudden and entire change in the views of the President." This "rude withdrawal of a courteous overture for negotiation" meant only "fresh blasts of war to the bitter end."

The President, as they represented it, was fully to blame. They therefore concluded that they could publish the correspondence and if any Confederate citizen still hoped that peace was "possible with this administration," the documents in the case would "strip from his eyes the last film of such delusion." [11]

Greeley had departed for New York with some haste, Hay left at about the same time, the Niagara "conference" was terminated, Jewett was left to receive any further Confederate communication, the *Tribune* carried a report, and the incident was closed. Lincoln, of

---

10 *Works*, X, 161; Lincoln's autograph draft, with his notation: "Copy of Doc sent by John Hay," is in R. T. L. Coll., 34536.

11 *Ann. Cyc.*, 1864, 782.

course, had never been inconclusive as to conditions of peace. He had not changed as the Confederate agents asserted, but the President's side of the controversy had not been adequately impressed upon the alleged negotiators and it was they, with Greeley, who captured the journalistic headlines. In the words of E. C. Kirkland, excellent historian of these peace moves: "The public was furnished with no evidence to dispute the charge of the Confederates that the President had, in bad faith, changed his policy in the course of negotiations." [12]

As for these Confederate gentlemen in Canada, it is to be noted in the first place that they never were authorized negotiators for peace,[13] and in the second place that their purpose—namely, to forestall peace drives in the South while sowing defeatism and anti-Lincoln sentiment in the North—was the opposite of Lincoln's. There was ample reason for Lincoln's attitude, which combined full willingness for genuine peace with a clear statement of the indispensable national aims of Union and abolition of slavery. The non-vindictiveness of the President's position was well expressed in his July 18 statement that Union and emancipation would "be met by liberal terms on other substantial points." Once the essential conditions were met, there would be no reprisals, no undue punitive measures, and no postwar policy of revenge so far as the President was concerned.

When Greeley was well started he was hard to stop, and thus it happened that the Niagara conference discussion did not end when the conference ended. Greeley's demand now was for publication of the correspondence between himself and Lincoln and his letters on this subject made a vexatious sequel to the July episode.

Misunderstood by his friends and under fire from his enemies, the troubled editor felt that such publication would help his case. The subject of peace, which he deemed imperative, still burned in his soul, and besides, the permission to publish would afford reading matter for the *Tribune*. He wrote to Hay broaching the idea of publication, and the next day his *Tribune* suggested that the whole of the correspondence be made public.[14] Lincoln saw a danger here; he therefore proposed that, in the event of publication, some of

[12] Edward Chase Kirkland, *The Peacemakers of 1864*, 85.

[13] *Offic. Rec.* (Nav.), 2 ser., III, 1194, 1236.

[14] Greeley to Hay, Aug. 4, 1864, R. T. L. Coll., 35055.

Greeley's phrases, of the sort that would disturb public thought, be omitted. Since the matter had become tense and personally difficult between them, Lincoln further proposed that Greeley come to Washington and talk the matter over, but to this Greeley demurred. Perhaps he felt that the meeting would put him at a further disadvantage; what he wrote was that it might "only result in farther mischief, as at Niagara." [15] The editor then launched into a reproach of Lincoln, bringing up old scores and telling him that he had made a great mistake in not letting Alexander H. Stephens come to Washington for consultation on peace in 1863. [16] Next day the editor continued in the same vein in another letter to the President. He feared that his usefulness had passed, but he knew that "nine-tenths of the whole American People, North and South, . . . [were] anxious for Peace—Peace on almost *any* terms." He knew that "to the general eye" the "rebels" were "anxious to negotiate, and that we repulse their advances." So the people understood it, and if that impression were not removed he feared "we shall be beaten out of sight next November." He therefore begged and implored the President "to inaugurate or invite proposals for peace forthwith." He thought that a national convention should be held, and if peace could not be at once made, he favored an armistice for a year. If this were done he thought that "at all events" (which meant regardless of terms or conditions of settlement) "there will surely be no more war." [17]

There came one more Greeley letter. On August 11 he wrote the President again suggesting that the entire correspondence be published. [18] This, however, was at variance with the President's wish who wanted certain "discouraging and injurious parts" deleted. [19] As a result, the correspondence that preceded the Niagara conference "was not published until after the President's death." [20] Having to choose between two undesirable things, Lincoln thought it was better to allow a false impression as to his own position to continue than to incur consequences (in terms of Greeley's phrases) which would

---

[15] Horace Greeley to Lincoln, New York, Aug. 8, 1864, R. T. L. Coll., 35139.

[16] *Lincoln the President: Midstream*, 242–245.   [17] R. T. L. Coll., 35171.

[18] *Ibid.*, 35228.

[19] Lincoln to H. J. Raymond, Aug. 15, 1864, *Works*, X, 191–192. In the Lincoln Papers (R. T. L. Coll., 34277–80) there is a printed pamphlet giving the correspondence of Jewett, Greeley, Lincoln, etc. and ending with the statement "To Whom it May concern." Parts have been crossed out in red pencil. Did Lincoln make these deletions?

[20] Nicolay and Hay, *Lincoln*, IX, 199.

have been unfortunate for the nation. Thus the North was largely misjudging Lincoln at the same time that Southern foes were assailing him in almost the same terms, as shown by the following statement in the Richmond *Sentinel:* "We want to treat, to bargain, to negotiate for peace, and Mr. Lincoln will not deign to show his face to us . . . but slams the door rudely in our faces." [21]

IX

Simultaneously with the Greeley fiasco there occurred a minor peace effort which at least resulted in an interview between Jefferson Davis and two unofficial Northerners. One of these was Colonel James Jaquess of Illinois, a preacher of great piety, a commander of a regiment under Rosecrans, and a soldier of gallant record. In his combination of military fervor with religious enthusiasm he has been compared to Cromwell's Ironsides. He had been president of a small Methodist college and it burned deeply into his conscience that Christians, especially Methodists, North and South should be killing each other. The other amateur diplomat was J. R. Gilmore, a man of business and of literature who had visited the South and had become known as the colorful author of *Among the Pines,* under the pseudonym of Edmund Kirke. He had written much else and was regarded as an authority on Southern conditions. Yet he was anti-slavery and by no means shared pro-Confederate views in the existing war. In 1863 Colonel Jaquess was given a furlough, was passed through the military lines with Lincoln's permission, and reached Richmond; at that point his mission broke down in that he failed to obtain an interview with President Davis.

The effort was renewed in 1864, and in July of that year Gilmore and Jaquess, with Gilmore in responsible charge, reached the Confederate capital by passes through the lines. From President Lincoln's standpoint there was little to be expected from such a mission, but on the experimental principle that no harm would be done and that no well meant effort for peace should be rebuffed, possibly also with the intent of exposing false representations of peace prospects at the North, the President gave his consent, though not his official accrediting, to the mission. On reaching Richmond the peacemakers con-

---

[21] Quoted in New York *Daily News,* Aug. 9, 1864; clipping in R. T. L. Coll., 35173.

ferred with the Confederate secretary of state, Judah P. Benjamin, and through him obtained an interview with President Davis which occurred on July 17 in Benjamin's office in the old customs house. Lincoln's terms were presented—reunion, abolition of slavery, amnesty, restoration of the rights of the states, and generous compensation for emancipated slaves.[1] (These terms had been drawn up by the President before the peacemakers had left Washington.)

The result of the pious effort was a decisive refusal on the part of Davis whose actual words at the interview are a matter of some doubt (there having been no verbatim report on the spot), but the essential point was that Lincoln's demand for a reunited country was indignantly spurned by the Southern leader as the equivalent of defeat and surrender.[2] Gilmore published his report of the episode in the Boston *Transcript* of July 22, 1864, but this was denounced by Confederate authorities as grossly inaccurate; it was a matter of coincidence that the Gilmore report appeared on the same day as Greeley's account (in the *Tribune*) of the unsuccessful Niagara Falls conference.

No better result followed when in midsummer of 1864 the names of three former members of Buchanan's cabinet—Jeremiah S. Black, Edwin M. Stanton, and Jacob Thompson—were involved in a footless conference in Canada between Black and Thompson. Black had been attorney general and later secretary of state under Buchanan; Thompson had been secretary of the interior (until he withdrew in the sharp secession crisis); and Stanton had been appointed in the last phase of Buchanan's administration as attorney general. Stanton's part in the 1864 affair consisted in the fact that he had a talk with Black in Washington, but the stern secretary of war, denying that Black was his envoy, avoided all responsibility for the episode.

In an elaborate letter to Stanton, August 24, 1864, Black reported the conversation to the secretary of war. Thompson, according to this

---

1 Kirkland, *Peacemakers of 1864*, 92; *Offic. Rec.* (Nav.), 2 ser., III, 1193.

2 "The President [Davis] answered that . . . the offer was in effect a proposal that the Confederate States should surrender at discretion, admit that they had been in the wrong from the beginning of the contest, submit to the mercy of their enemies, and avow themselves to be in need of pardon for crimes; that extermination was preferable to such dishonor." Report of Judah P. Benjamin, Confederate secretary of state, to James M. Mason, "Commissioner to the Continent" (circular), *Offic. Rec.* (Nav.), 2 ser., III, 1193. Coming from a high Confederate source, this may be considered a more authentic report of Davis's statement than that which Gilmore caused to be published in the Boston *Transcript* of July 22, 1864.

account, expressed fear of subjugation, insult, degradation, control by enemies of the South, confiscation, spoliation, military execution of the best men, and total suppression of free speech and personal liberty. (In so expressing himself he was certainly not speaking with understanding of Lincoln's views.) He spoke bitterly of the abolitionists, and opposed forcible emancipation of Negroes. On one important point there was doubt as to what was really said and intended. Black reported that the terms indicated by Thompson did "not mean the separate nationality of the South" but rather Southern control of their own domestic affairs. Yet in a postscript Black stated that "nothing positive" was said as to the restoration of the Union. Then he added: "My desire to see a restoration may have helped me to the conclusion. If you wish you may cross-examine me . . . ."

The main point of Black's letter was a suggestion to Stanton to "advise the President to suspend hostilities for three or six months and commence negotiations in good earnest . . . ." Stanton's reply was entirely negative as to the prospect of any favorable result to come from dealings with Thompson. The secretary was all the more convinced that the "rebels" would accept no peace except with dissolution of the Union. He had no wish to cross-examine Black, he would not give the President the suggested advice, and he made it clear that Black's conversation with the Confederate gentleman was not in accord with his (Stanton's) wishes. As to an armistice, he considered it "fatal to the Government and the national existence." [3] The Thompson-Black conversation was informal and unofficial. It seemed that the two men were not so far apart as, for instance, Lincoln and Davis, but neither man had authority in the premises, and it would be a mistake to consider the episode as a "negotiation." Whatever Thompson may have said, he was not authorized to speak for the Confederate government and Lincoln knew that so long as that government remained intact and its armies unbeaten, any agreement for reunion was impossible.

---

[3] The Black-Thompson episode is treated in E. C. Kirkland, *Peacemakers of 1864*, 118–124. The letter of Black to Stanton and Stanton's reply are in the Stanton MSS., Lib. of Cong. nos. 57801–57822.

CHAPTER IX

CONGRESS: MEANS AND ENDS

THE first session of Lincoln's second Congress adjourned on July 4, 1864, after having done less, and more, than the President had hoped. Necessarily he had looked to the law-making branch for money and men, for the means of carrying on the war to a successful conclusion. With him, victory and reunion were the main considerations in such matters as conscription and public finance. With many congressmen, however, there were other considerations, including the protection and promotion of the profits of Northern business. Going beyond means and looking toward ends, some in Congress attempted to dictate the President's choice of cabinet advisers and to thwart his reconstruction program. In the Wade-Davis Bill they presented their alternative to his "ten per cent" plan, and though he disposed of the bill with a pocket veto, he did not silence all his congressional critics. Already a climax was approaching in the conflict between Congress and President—a conflict that was to eventuate in deadlock between congressional Radicals and Lincoln's successor during the "tragic era" of postwar reconstruction.

I

As summer approached in 1864, with Grant fighting his stubborn and costly campaign in northern Virginia, the Union government faced a crisis in regard to military manpower. In replenishing the armies the procedure was for the President first to issue a call for volunteers, designating a period of time within which each locality was to fill a specified quota. Then, in those areas which failed to meet their quotas by volunteering, he set going a draft. As a means of recruiting, the draft was a last resort; its main purpose was to threaten men into volunteering. The conscription threat was supplemented by rewards in the form of bounties (local, state, and national) held out to volunteers. Despite both the threat and the rewards, Lincoln's call for troops in the summer of 1863 yielded disappointing results, and so did his three additional calls during the winter of 1863–64.

The conscription law itself (even as amended on February 24, 1864) was defective. Its most serious faults were its provisions for commutation and substitution, by which a drafted man had the privilege, if he had the money, of buying exemption or procuring a substitute. Such discrimination in favor of the rich and against the poor was not only undemocratic: it was also inefficient, for it caused the poor to resent the calls to military service, and it enabled the rich to escape such service entirely. So the number of men willing and eligible to serve was decreasing at the very time when the needs of the army—its ranks depleted by the expiration of short-term enlistments and by desertion, disability, and death—were reaching new heights.[1]

In June, 1864, Lincoln received an appeal for new legislation which Provost-Marshal-General James B. Fry had submitted to the secretary of war. Fry cogently demonstrated the faults in the existing law (of February 24, 1864) with figures on the returns from the latest draft. Too many men were buying their way out. The congressional session now drawing to a close, Lincoln hastily added his endorsement to Fry's recommendations and submitted them, without change, to the Senate and the House. A bill "to prohibit the discharge of persons from liability to military duty by reason of the payment of money" happened to be in Congress already, having been introduced by Senator Edwin D. Morgan, of New York. Within two days the Morgan bill, embodying the essence of the administration's own proposal, was under debate.[2]

The Democrats in Congress generally opposed this plan, as they did any plan, for strengthening the conscription act, and the Republicans divided in regard to it, most of them unwilling to compel the businessman to fight. Such Radicals as James G. Blaine and Thaddeus Stevens voted consistently with the opposition and against a repeal of the commutation or the substitution clause. Blaine believed that

[1] Fred A. Shannon, *The Organization and Administration of the Union Army, 1861–1865*, II, 34–36.
[2] *Ibid.*, 35.

commutation was indispensable to "the great 'middle interest' of society—the class on which the business and the prosperity of the country depend." He warned: "Just let it be understood that whoever the lot falls on *must go,* regardless of all business considerations, all private interests, all personal engagements, all family obligations; that the draft is to be sharp, decisive, final, and inexorable, without commutation and without substitution, and my word for it you will create consternation in all the loyal States." Stevens urged a generous bounty policy, rather than an inexorable draft, as the proper means for raising adequate troops. He insisted that volunteers should be allowed to enlist not only in their home district but in whatever district paid the highest bounty. "If one [district] is willing to pay $500, and another refuses to pay anything," he said, "why should not these poor men be permitted to go and take the $500 for the benefit of their families? In that way you will fill the army with volunteers instead of drafted men." As Fred A. Shannon has remarked, Stevens' argument "centered on the discrimination against the poor, as if the whole mercenary system were intended as a device for the dispensation of national charity." [3] Of course, if Stevens had been sincerely opposed to discrimination, he might have sought to eliminate the rich man's privilege of buying personal safety rather than to insure the poor man's opportunity of selling his military service to the highest bidder.

Nevertheless, the view prevailed in Congress that the business class must not be compelled, and that the working class must be enticed, to enlist. The Morgan bill, after being emasculated, was set aside entirely and replaced by another measure (June 28, 1864) which was passed just before the end of the session. In this bill the President was authorized to call for volunteers for terms of one, two, or three years, and the volunteer was granted (in addition to local bounties) a war department bounty of one hundred dollars for each year of his enlistment period. Commutation was abolished, except for conscientious objectors, but the right to furnish substitutes, without restriction, was expressly guaranteed. Though it fell far short of the recommendations he had submitted to Congress, Lincoln signed this bill and made it a law on the last day of the session, July 4.[4]

---

[3] *Ibid.,* 32, 38–40, 89. On the question of the repeal of the commutation clause, see also *Lincoln the President,* III, 127–130.

[4] Shannon, *Union Army,* II, 37, 38, 87.

On July 18, under the new law, the last conscription act to go into effect during the war, he issued the third of his draft calls. His proclamation asked for a half million men and allowed fifty days for them to volunteer, setting September 5 as the date for the beginning of the draft.[5]

His call could not have been expected to be popular, nor was it. Some critics thought the proclamation should have been couched in language more eloquent and less matter of fact, though, as *Harper's Weekly* commented, the country needed soldiers, not rhetoric. Other critics thought that a military leader, General Sherman or General Grant, should have appealed directly to the people for troops.[6] The *New York Herald* argued that the people, at least in New York, would have responded more eagerly if Lincoln first had restored McClellan to a command. One small-town newspaper editor in New Jersey was arrested for publishing articles tending to discourage enlistments.[7]

State governors of both political extremes, such as John A. Andrew of Massachusetts and Horatio Seymour of New York, objected to the terms of the President's new call. On the day of the proclamation Andrew telegraphed Lincoln urging him to make a succession of calls for two hundred thousand men at a time, rather than one call for five hundred thousand.[8] After the proclamation Seymour resumed his complaints of the unfairness of the quotas for New York, even though Lincoln had gone to great lengths to appease Seymour after the governor's contest with the federal government the previous summer. In response to Seymour's original grievances Lincoln had authorized a special commission to look into the New York quotas, and the commission had drawn up a new table for the state, increasing the quotas in some districts and decreasing them in others. "For the now ensuing draft," Lincoln had instructed the secretary of war, February 27, 1864, "let the quotas stand as made by the enrolling officers, in the Districts wherein this table requires them to be increased; and let them be reduced according to the table, in the others." But Seymour was not to be appeased. In a letter dated August 3, 1864, addressed to

---

[5] Nicolay and Hay, *Works*, X, 164–166.

[6] *Harper's Weekly*, VIII, 514 (Aug. 13, 1864); Shannon, *Union Army*, II, 130–131.

[7] New York *Herald*, July 19, 1864, p. 4, c. 2; Washington *Constitutional Union*, Aug. 13, 1864.

[8] Andrew's telegram was not received at the War Department until 8:45 p. m., July 18. R. T. L. Coll., 34537.

the secretary of war, and printed as a campaign circular, the governor repeated his familiar objections against the "draft lately ordered by the President" that the quotas for New York State, and especially for New York City and Brooklyn, were "unequal and oppressive," a "heavy drain," and a "great injustice." [9]

Lincoln's call of July 18, 1864, produced less volunteering than his calls under the two previous drafts. According to Provost-Marshal-General Fry, volunteering was discouraged by a growing fear of Confederate brutality to prisoners. "Men who would cheerfully enlist in the cause of the Union and would take all the chances of civilized warfare," said Fry afterwards, "were not so willing to expose themselves to the protracted torture that awaited them if, by the fortunes of war, they fell into the hands of the enemy." By this time, stories of Andersonville prison were circulating throughout the North.

If, for whatever reason, the new call raised fewer troops through voluntary enlistment than either of the previous calls, it raised more by direct conscription than both of them combined. More than half of the conscripts, however, were substitutes. The price of substitutes, now that commutation had been abolished, rose so high that only the very well-to-do could afford them. "Men of wealth served in the army," as Professor Shannon has said, "but never by compulsion." [10]

II

The army's need for men was but one of Lincoln's worries in connection with the draft. He also faced the problem, less serious for the Union cause but equally trying to him personally, of what to do with the unwilling conscript, the conscientious objector. The law allowed no exemption on grounds of conscience. The objector could keep from shouldering arms if he could afford to pay the commutation fee of three hundred dollars and if his conscience would permit him to pay it; otherwise he had no choice but to join the army when he was drafted. Once in uniform, he ran into hardships of more or less severity, depending upon the attitude of his superior officers, and his only recourse was an appeal to the secretary of war or to the President.

Seldom, if ever, did Lincoln fail to provide relief in some way for conscientious objectors whose cases were brought to his personal at-

[9] R. T. L. Coll., 5407–8–9, 35096.   [10] Shannon, *Union Army*, II, 42, 131.

tention.[1] One of the earliest cases was that of Henry D. Swift, a Quaker of South Dedham, Massachusetts, who was drafted in 1863. Refusing to take part in military drills, Swift was court-martialed and sentenced to be shot. When prominent members of the Society of Friends appealed to Lincoln and Stanton, the President directed the issuance of an honorable parole, which was delivered to Swift shortly before his execution was to have taken place.[2]

A more fully reported case was that of Cyrus Pringle, another Quaker, from Vermont. When conscripted, Pringle would neither pay commutation money nor allow anyone else to pay it for him. He was hustled into a railroad car along with other conscripts and taken to a camp near Boston, where he was put into the guardhouse for refusing to perform fatigue duty. Later he was transported to Alexandria, Virginia, to be equipped, but he would not handle a gun, even to clean it. "Two sergeants soon called for me," he recorded in his diary, "and taking me a little aside, bid me lie down on my back, and stretching my limbs apart tied cords to my wrists and ankles and these to four stakes driven in the ground somewhat in the form of an X." Still he would not give in, would not "purchase life at the cost of peace of soul." He was not merely being stubborn but was holding to his principles, resisting the military way of life, in which, as he said, "the man is unmade a man" and "is made a soldier, which is a man-destroying machine." As he lay in the hot sun, staked down on the rainsoaked ground, the cords cutting his wrists, he wept not from his own suffering but "from sorrow that such things should be in our own country, where Justice and Freedom and Liberty of Conscience have been the annual boast of Fourth-of-July orators so many years."

Already a group of Friends had interceded with Lincoln, who had agreed to detail Pringle and some Quaker companions to hospital duty or to the care of colored refugees, but Pringle and his fellows had declined to accept either of these alternatives, since acceptance would have released other men for active service. Then, on the same morning as he was staked down (October 6, 1863), Pringle received orders to report to the war department in Washington. There he learned from one of the Friends who again had interceded for him:

"That the Secretary of War and President sympathized with

---

[1] *Ibid.*, 252.
[2] Edward N. Wright, *Conscientious Objectors in the Civil War*, 124–125.

Friends in their present suffering, and would grant them full release, but that they felt themselves bound by their oaths that they would execute the laws, to carry out to its full extent the Conscription Act. That there appeared but one door of relief open,—that was to parole us and allow us to go home, but subject to their call again ostensibly, though this they neither wished nor proposed to do. That the fact of Friends in the Army and refusing service had attracted public attention so that it was not expedient to parole us at present. That, therefore, we were to be sent to one of the hospitals for a short time, where it was hoped and expressly requested that we would consent to remain quiet and acquiesce, if possible, in whatever might be required of us. That our work there would be quite free from objection, being for the direct relief of the sick; and that there we would release none for active service in the field, as the nurses were hired civilians."

A month later, after further repeated visits at the White House, Pringle's sponsor reported that Lincoln had exclaimed to him: "I want you to go and tell Stanton that it is my wish that all those young men be sent home at once." And they were.[3]

Lincoln's action in the Pringle case became a precedent for the regular policy thereafter in dealing with conscientious objectors. A war department instruction, issued on December 15, 1863, directed that such objectors, if they declined to pay commutation or provide substitutes, should be put on parole, "to report when called for." [4] They continued to be drafted under the amended enrollment act of February 24, 1864, which did not exempt them, though it made service or commutation easier for them to accept. It provided that, if they served, they should be considered as noncombatants and assigned to hospital work or the care of freedmen; or, if they chose commutation, their money should be used for medical purposes and not for hiring substitutes. Since many conscientious objectors continued, as Pringle had done, to reject these alternatives, Lincoln found it necessary to go on granting individual paroles.

His heart, as the Hicksite Friends of Philadelphia gratefully resolved after his death, was "imbued with a regard for conscientious scruples in relation to war." [5] He felt, as his own, the dilemma of a

[3] Rufus M. Jones, ed., *The Record of a Quaker Conscience: Cyrus Pringle's Diary*, *passim*.

[4] *Offic. Rec.*, 3 ser., III, 1173.   [5] Wright, *Conscientious Objectors*, 125.

religious people who shrank from a bloody conflict while they embraced its presumably righteous aims. "Your people—the Friends—have had, and are having, a very great trial," he said in his well-known letter to Eliza P. Gurney, a letter written (September 4, 1864) on the eve of a new draft. "On principle and faith, opposed to both war *and* oppression, they can only practically oppose oppression by war. In this hard dilem[m]a some have chosen one horn and some the other." Lincoln himself managed to keep from grasping either horn, though with him the dilemma was complicated by his oath of office. As he had protested, when he first received an appeal in Pringle's behalf, he had sworn to execute the laws, including the conscription act. "For those appealing to me on conscientious grounds," he now repeated to Mrs. Gurney, "I have done, and shall do, the best I could and can, in my own conscience, under my oath to the law." [6] It was, of course, an evasion of the law for him to release conscripted men and let them go home, there to remain subject ostensibly though not actually to recall at some future time. He never tried to resolve his dilemma by requesting Congress to change the law so as to grant outright exemption to conscientious objectors.

III

As summer came in 1864 Congress had to cope with serious emergencies in public finance as well as military manpower, with problems of finding ways and means to uphold the national credit, restore confidence in the currency, and carry on the war. Wartime finance, as evolved during the three years since the firing on Fort Sumter, was a hodgepodge of expedients. There were loans on a great variety of terms, paper money issues and national banknotes, and taxes on almost every taxable object, though much the greater part of the government's income was derived from borrowing. Now the government's currency was depreciating badly, the national banking system (as established in 1863) was proving defective, and the public credit was in jeopardy. In dealing with these problems, as with that of raising troops, congressmen and their constituents were inclined to confuse their special interests with the national interest.

The most drastic, and the least successful, of the financial reme-

---

[6] R. T. L. Coll., 35907–8.

dies proposed by Congress was a measure to prevent speculation in gold. This evil had arisen as a perhaps inevitable consequence of the issuance of irredeemable paper money, to which Congress first had resorted as an emergency expedient at the end of 1861, when a bank crisis led to the suspension of specie payments and left the country flooded with state banknotes not exchangeable for cash. Congress then (February 2, 1862) authorized an issue of "United States notes," and in succeeding years authorized two further issues, a total of $432,000,000 actually being put into circulation. These notes, popularly dubbed "greenbacks," were declared legal tender for all debts public and private but not for the payment of customs duties or interest on government bonds. Though the greenbacks were, in a vague sense, promises to pay hard money, no provision was made for their redemption in gold.

The way was open for fluctuations in the price of gold as expressed in greenbacks, and on the Gold Exchange in New York dealers bought and sold "gold futures" as they did those of other commodities on other exchanges. The daily gold quotations became an index of Union morale: the worse the prospects for the armies in the field, the higher the price of gold in New York. During June, 1864, as the casualty lists lengthened, the price rose to a point where nearly two dollars in greenbacks were needed to buy an ordinary dollar's worth of the precious metal.[1]

Congress reflected a popular demand to do something about this gambling in gold, which looked like gambling on the lives of Union soldiers. On June 17, 1864, a "gold bill" was enacted forbidding speculative trading in gold futures and making it illegal for anyone to contract for the delivery of gold not actually in his possession.[2]

This did not go far enough in the opinion of some congressmen, such as Thaddeus Stevens, who was later to demand legislation simply prohibiting the acceptance of legal-tender notes for less than their face value.[3] Doubtless such a law would have been unenforceable, but certainly the one actually passed was inadequate. After the enactment the price of gold rose even faster than before, so that by June 29 two and a half dollars in greenbacks were necessary to buy an ordinary

---

[1] Randall, *Civil War and Reconstruction*, 450–453; Horace White, *Money and Banking*, 5th ed., 126–127.

[2] *U. S. Stat. at Large*, XIII, 132–133.   [3] Current, *Old Thad Stevens*, 205.

dollar's worth of gold. Though the bankers, brokers, merchants, and money-changers of Wall Street disagreed among themselves as to whom the law was hurting or helping the most, they united in sending a committee to Washington to lobby for its repeal.[4] On July 2, after only a day more than two weeks of the experiment, Congress decided to abandon it. The price of gold fell suddenly, then rose again, and thereafter fluctuated wildly for several weeks.

Despite this experience the congressional advocates of paper money, including Stevens, desired to authorize another issue of greenbacks, but the majority chose instead to rely on a new loan. The wartime loans, through a personal arrangement made by Secretary of the Treasury Chase, were handled exclusively by the country's foremost investment banking firm, Jay Cooke and Company. By means of high-pressure selling methods, including newspaper advertisements and appeals to workingmen to invest their savings in government bonds, Cooke succeeded in disposing of the loans readily enough—for a handsome profit to himself as the "financier of the Civil War." The largest purchasers were not day laborers, of course, but bankers and men of wealth who acquired government securities on terms which made them an unusually attractive investment.[5] The bonds, though purchasable in greenbacks, paid interest in gold, and some of them the principal as well. The government paid its other creditors, among them its officers and soldiers of the armies, in mere "legal currency," that is, in greenbacks. According to Stevens, who repeatedly insisted that all the government's creditors should be treated alike, the government's own demand for gold, to pay its bondholders, accounted for the exorbitant prices on the Gold Exchange.[6]

To provide a large market for bonds, and at the same time to create a uniform and stable national currency, Chase had planned and Congress had authorized (in an act of February 25, 1863) the establishment of a national banking system. Further legislation was needed, however, and Congress supplied it in the law of June 3, 1864, on which the system, as it was to operate from the Civil War to the first World War, was actually based. Under the system, federally chartered banks purchased United States bonds and, with these as

[4] New York *Herald*, June 23, 1864, p. 4, c. 5.

[5] Randall, *Civil War and Reconstruction*, 444–448, 454–455; E. P. Oberholtzer, *Jay Cooke: Financier of the Civil War* (2 vols., 1907).

[6] Current, *Old Thad Stevens*, 195.

security, issued national banknotes guaranteed by the Federal government. The banknotes circulated as money, and unlike the greenbacks they were accepted at par, since they were exchangeable for gold.

The national banking system, at least as it operated in the beginning, should not be viewed as a purely fiscal instrument, free from politics or favoritism. As George La Verne Anderson has said, it "soon developed into something that was neither national nor a banking system." Instead, it was a "loose organization of currency factories" designed to serve "commercial communities" and confined "almost entirely to the New England and Middle Atlantic States." [7] Even within these states, as for example in the vicinity of Stevens' home in Pennsylvania, the system discriminated against certain areas, and here businessmen were hard put for money, especially after a prohibitory tax on state banknotes went into effect in 1866. In this light Stevens's partiality for greenbacks becomes understandable. "In my judgment this whole national banking system was a mistake," he was finally moved to say. "I think every dollar of paper circulation ought to be issued by the Government of the United States." [8]

While legislating on gold, loans, and banks, Congress did not neglect the perennial problem of taxes but made a successful effort to increase considerably the proportion of Federal income derived from tax revenues. Early in the war (act of August 5, 1861) Congress had provided for an income tax, imposing a flat rate of 3% on all incomes over $800. Now (act of June 30, 1864) the base was broadened and the rate increased and made progressive. The new law put a tax of 5% on incomes from $600 to $5,000, one of 7½% on those from $5,000 to $10,000, and one of 10% on those over $10,000.[9] Though this was a graduated tax, it was not by modern standards very steeply graduated, and it placed a relatively heavy burden on citizens with low and moderate incomes.

During the second year of the war (act of July 1, 1862) Congress also had levied a wide range of excise taxes. These fell on manufactures of all sorts: liquor, tobacco, stamps, cotton, wool, flax, hemp, iron, steel, wood, stone, earth, carriages, billiard tables, yachts, gold and silver plate, and so forth. The taxes also had to be paid as a price of doing business by every butcher, baker, pawnbroker, lawyer, horse

---

[7] Randall, *Civil War and Reconstruction*, 455–458.
[8] Current, *Old Thad Stevens*, 246.   [9] *U. S. Stat. at Large*, XII, 309; XIII, 223, 281.

dealer, physician—indeed, by practitioners of almost every calling except that of minister of the gospel. Having cast this very broad net, Congress in subsequent years had only to raise the rates in order to increase the yield, and with the new rates of 1864 the excise along with the income tax produced the unprecedented sum of $209,000,000 for the ensuing fiscal year. If the excise was a hardship to many producers and to most consumers, it was nevertheless a boon to commodity speculators who managed to get advance notice of forthcoming tax boosts and consequent price increases.[10]

The excises, payable as they were by domestic but not by foreign manufacturers, put the former at a competitive disadvantage and gave them a pretext for demanding increased protection in the form of "countervailing" duties. Such compensatory protection was the chief feature of the tariff of June 30, 1864. American manufacturers now "found their opportunity in the necessity of the government"; they "had only to declare what rate of duty they deemed essential, and that rate was accorded to them." [11] Most of the new duties were outrageously high, some as high as 100%, the average being 47%, or approximately double the average rate of the last prewar tariff act, that of 1857. After the war this high level was maintained even after the wartime excise taxes, which ostensibly justified it, had been eliminated. A habit of protectionist thinking had been established.

The wartime tariffs, including that of 1864, received the signature of Lincoln as President, but that fact does not necessarily indicate that he favored extreme protectionism as a permanent principle. During the war years the government was indeed confronted with what a later President, with connotations of his own, was to call a "condition" and not a "theory." The government desperately needed revenue, and whatever else they may have been, the tariff bills were also revenue measures. No one can say what stand Lincoln might have taken on the protectionist issue in later years if he had lived. "For decades following his death, however," writes Reinhard H. Luthin, "protectionists, in summoning testimony from 'the Fathers,' made full use of Lincoln's high-tariff record to bolster their claims that huge duties on imports were economically sound and socially desirable; at

10 Blaine, *Twenty Years of Congress*, I, 433; Report, Sec. of the Treas., *House Ex. Doc. No. 3*, 39 Cong., 1 sess., p. 18; Current, *Old Thad Stevens*, 192.
11 Stanwood, *American Tariff Controversies in the Nineteenth Century*, II, 129–130.

times the more zealous, in combating free trade, misquoted Lincoln and even concocted orations which they attributed to him." [12]

In Lincoln's own party there were a number of critics of extreme protectionism during and right after the war. The scholarly Francis Lieber, for example, writing to Senator Sumner soon after the final Emancipation Proclamation, insisted that New England in fairness to the rest of the country should give up her demands for unreasonable protection, and he argued that there could be "no better accompaniment for *the Proclamation* than *Free Trade*." [13] Many practical businessmen themselves opposed high tariffs, at least on certain products.

The promoters of railroads in the West objected to protection for iron rails, though otherwise they could hardly complain that they were being neglected by the Federal government. Congress (in an act of July 2, 1864) further extended the largess already granted in the form of public lands and loans (act of July 1, 1862) to the Central Pacific and Union Pacific railroads for constructing a line from the Missouri River to California,[14] and Congress was yielding readily enough to the demands of other enterprisers for similar favors. As a congressional agent of both the railroad and the iron interests, Stevens found himself in a rather difficult position, but he managed to satisfy both groups fairly well. Himself an ironmaster, he included in a bill for land grants to the projected People's Pacific railroad a stipulation against the use of imported rails. "I go for nothing but American iron, of course," he frankly explained. On the other hand, when the tariff bill of 1864 was impending, he assured the worried president of the St. Croix and Lake Superior Railroad Company that the company's recently imported rails, on which the duties had not yet been paid, would be exempt from the new rates.[15]

While using his position as Ways and Means chairman to further the railroad schemes of Eastern capitalists, Stevens also exerted his power to thwart the internal improvements projected by certain Western interests. On behalf of his Illinois constituents Congressman Elihu B. Washburne repeatedly introduced a bill for a Federal appropriation to improve the Illinois-Michigan canal, and each time Stevens brought to bear his sarcastic eloquence and his mastery of

---

[12] Luthin, "Abraham Lincoln and the Tariff," 49 *A. H. R.* 629 (1944).
[13] Lieber to Sumner, Jan. 10, Jan. 16, 1863, Lieber MSS., Huntington Lib.
[14] *U. S. Stat. at Large*, XII, 492; XIII, 358.   [15] Current, *Old Thad Stevens*, 195–196.

parliamentary rules to defeat it.[16] Many Westerners, more interested in access to markets than in tariff protection, accumulated a sense of outrage which seemed likely to provoke a sectional controversy between East and West as soon as the one between North and South had been disposed of. "The South cannot be kept out of Congress forever," Horace White, an editor of the *Chicago Tribune,* was to threaten early in 1866. "When the south does come back the south & west will join hands & rule this country." [17]

So the question of economic measures—of tariff protection, money, the banking system, and the public debt—was linked to the question of the future of the seceded South, the question of reconstruction. However seriously the interests of various groups in the Northeast might conflict, these groups had a common concern in preventing an early restoration of political power to the South. This consideration, underlying many of the maneuvers of Congress against President on the reconstruction issue, gives meaning to legislative stratagems not easily explained otherwise.

IV

At the end of June, 1864, the final resignation of Treasury Secretary Chase raised new questions about government finance and complicated the relations between Congress and President. His resignation climaxed the long-raging feud in Congress between his adherents and those of Seward, Welles, and the Blairs.

After Frank Blair's repeated philippics in the House against the treasury secretary, the friends of Chase twice demanded that Lincoln dismiss Montgomery Blair as postmaster general in order to repudiate his brother. But Lincoln not only declined to get rid of Montgomery; he also showed favor to Frank by telegraphing Grant, late in April, to restore him to his position as major general. Infuriated, Chase thought of resigning, going home to Ohio, and rallying the people to support him against Lincoln and the Blairs. The Governor of Ohio, John Brough, talked him into withholding his resignation —for the good of the country.[1]

Though Chase was quieted for the moment, his adherents in both

---

[16] *Ibid.,* 165–166, 175, 185–186, 195–196.
[17] White to Justin S. Morrill, Feb. 15, 1866, MS. in Cornell Univ. Lib.
[1] Smith, *Blair Family in Politics,* II, 258–260.

houses of Congress were not. Some of the representatives muttered about impeaching the President, and the Senate approved a resolution, introduced by Garrett Davis of Kentucky, which rebuked Lincoln along with Stanton for violating the Constitution by permitting Blair to serve as a military officer while a member of Congress. Unable to get at the cabinet representative of the hated Blair family, the Radicals became the more determined to make an example of his more vulnerable brother. Stevens introduced and the House passed a resolution calling on the Executive to provide information about Frank Blair's dual character, military and congressional. Responding fully and yet somewhat defiantly, Lincoln gave Congress a complete report, including a copy of a letter he had written the previous December advising that Blair give up his military commission temporarily, aid in organizing the House of Representatives, and then remain in Congress if elected Speaker. Their fury redoubled by this revelation, the Radicals took occasion at the Baltimore convention to strike at the Blairs by seating the anti-Blair delegation from Missouri and by inserting in the platform the sixth resolution, which called for a reorganization of the cabinet in the interests of harmony. In Congress they succeeded in unseating Blair before the end of the session.[2]

Blair's ouster did not entirely appease Chase and his friends, for Chase was already encountering the Blair charges of corruption and mismanagement from another quarter, and these charges became involved in and gave added bitterness to a deadly patronage fight. Thurlow Weed, replying in his Albany *Evening Journal* to attacks on Seward in the pro-Chase New York *Evening Post,* elaborated on the alleged corruption of Chase's treasury appointees in New York. In the midst of this journalistic bickering the Assistant Treasurer in New York, John J. Cisco, decided to leave his job. Chase was ready to name as Cisco's successor the Assistant Secretary of the Treasury, Maunsell B. Field. But Weed objected to Field's appointment.

Lincoln faced a dilemma. If he appointed Field he would antagonize not only Weed and Seward but also the New York senators, one of whom was Edwin D. Morgan, chairman of the Republican National Committee. The rule of senatorial courtesy as well as relations with the New York machine was at stake. Lincoln regularly consulted with

---

[2] *Ibid.,* 250–251, 259, 265, 267, 268. On the Blairs and Lincoln, see also *Lincoln the President,* III, 280–284.

Republicans in the Senate before making major appointments in their respective states.[3] After consulting with Senator Morgan, who protested against Field and suggested three others as possibilities for a compromise appointment, Lincoln submitted the three names to Chase and requested him to approve one of them or suggest someone else not obnoxious to the senators.[4] Chase refused to consider anyone except Field for Cisco's job but, rather than force the issue, he persuaded Cisco to withdraw his resignation for the time being. Lincoln meanwhile was putting pressure on Chase by hinting that, if Field was to be appointed, another Chase man, Hiram Barney, might have to be removed from the lucrative and powerful position of collector of the port of New York.[5]

Chase replied in a two-page letter with a couple of enclosures which Lincoln received on the evening of June 29. Hastily scanning the first page, Lincoln noticed the words: "The withdrawal of Mr. Cisco's resignation, which I enclose, relieves the present difficulty . . . ."[6] This was most welcome news, and happy that the troublesome matter was thus disposed of, Lincoln put the papers in his pocket without finishing the letter. Hours later, sitting down to pen a congratulatory note to the secretary, he looked at the letter and the enclosures again. He now discovered that, while Cisco was taking back his resignation, Chase was putting forth his own![7]

That same evening Lincoln happened to see Governor Brough, visiting in Washington, and invited him into the White House to discuss Chase's resignation. Brough thought he could get the Ohio congressmen together and, with them, prevail upon Chase to retract it. "But," protested Lincoln, as Brough quoted him in a memorandum he dictated two weeks afterward, "this is the third time he has thrown this at me, and I do not think I am called on to continue to beg him to take it back, especially when the country would not go to destruction in consequence."[8] The next day Lincoln penned a note to Chase

---

[3] Carman and Luthin, *Lincoln and the Patronage*, 264–265.

[4] Dennett, . . . *Diaries* . . . *of John Hay*, 198–199 (entry for June 30, 1864); Nicolay and Hay, *Works*, X, 137–138.

[5] Carman and Luthin, *Lincoln and the Patronage*, 265–266; Nicolay and Hay, *Works*, X, 138–139.

[6] R. T. L. Coll., 34119–20–21.

[7] Dennett, . . . *Diaries* . . . *of John Hay*, 199 (entry for June 30, 1864).

[8] MS. transcription of shorthand record, dictated by John Brough and dated July 12, 1864, Vol. 20, Letters and Papers of William Henry Smith, Ohio State Arch. and Hist. Soc.

—"you and I have reached a point of mutual embarrassment in our official relations which it seems can not be overcome"—accepting the resignation.[9]

In naming Chase's successor Lincoln at first seemed to be most concerned about appeasing the Ohio Republican organization rather than Congress or Wall Street. He promptly thought of David Tod, Brough's predecessor as Ohio governor. "Dave Tod. He is my friend, with a big head full of brains," the President told John Hay. True, he lacked experience in government finance, but, said Lincoln, "He made a good Governor, and he has made a fortune for himself. I am willing to trust him." The Senate finance committee, however, was not willing. Headed by William Pitt Fessenden, the committeemen called on the President to tell him Tod had too little experience and was too little known. Lincoln assured them of his own confidence in Tod, acknowledged their duty and responsibility of passing on Tod's fitness, and declared that he could not "in justice to himself or Tod" withdraw the nomination.[10]

In another talk with Governor Brough the President emphatically repeated his refusal to withdraw it. "The Governor," according to Brough's own account, "advised him to request the Senate Committee to delay their report until the next morning, as he was satisfied Tod w^d decline the appointment, and in that way the President, the Senate, Tod and the country would be relieved from embarrassment." Lincoln wanted to know Brough's reasons for thinking Tod would decline. Brough gave his reasons: "the state of his [Tod's] health, and the fact that in the nomination he got all the honor without the hard work; and that Tod was a man of good common sense and would not willingly place himself in a position which he was not capable of filling" Lincoln "accepted this advice, and apparently with great pleasure." [11]

Tod did decline, but Lincoln continued to talk of appointing an Ohioan, either former Governor Dennison or Governor Brough himself. Brough, again according to his own story, argued against any such appointment and recommended Senator Fessenden instead.[12]

The next morning, July 1, Lincoln sent Hay to the Senate with

[9] Lincoln to Chase, June 30, 1864, R. T. L. Coll., 34148.
[10] Dennett, . . . *Diaries* . . . *of John Hay*, 198–199 (entry for June 30, 1864).
[11] Brough MS.   [12] *Ibid.*

Fessenden's nomination. It was "instantly confirmed, the executive session not lasting more than a minute," as Hay recorded. At this very moment, unaware of his appointment, Fessenden was in the White House in conversation with the President. "I could not help being amused," Lincoln told Hay afterwards, "by seeing him sitting there so unconscious and you on your way to the Capitol." When Fessenden began to speak of the qualifications of Hugh McCulloch for the treasury office, Lincoln answered: "Mr. Fessenden, I have nominated you for that place. Mr. Hay has just taken the nomination to the Senate." Fessenden sputtered in protest, but Lincoln closed the interview by saying firmly: "If you decline, you must do it in open day, for I shall not recall the nomination." [13]

If, in this business of finding a new secretary of the treasury, Lincoln's behavior seems rather airy and impulsive, one should not forget his characteristic and habitual shrewdness in such matters. It is possible, indeed probable, that he all along expected Tod to refuse the job. By insisting at first on naming an Ohio man, he could expect to disarm much of the opposition that might otherwise have arisen in behalf of Chase. He was doubtless pleased at Brough's impressions because they confirmed his own, and he doubtless had Fessenden in mind even before Brough recommended him, if indeed Brough did so. (Hay quoted Lincoln as remarking: "It is very singular, considering that this appointment of F's is so popular when made, that no one ever mentioned his name to me for that place." [14]) Fessenden was as nearly an ideal choice as could have been made in the circumstances, and Lincoln knew it, summarizing Fessenden's qualifications in Hay's presence as follows: 1. "he knows the ropes"; as chairman of the Senate finance committee, he was as well informed as Chase on financial questions; 2. he had a national reputation and the confidence of the country; 3. he was "a radical—without the petulent [sic] and vicious fretfulness of many radicals." [15]

The inner meaning of the cabinet change was interpreted in various ways, even by Chase himself, who provided a whole series of explanations for his departure from the administration. Surprised and hurt when his resignation actually was accepted, he complained of Lincoln's ill will toward him. "Had his feelings been kind," he told a

---

[13] Dennett, . . . *Diaries* . . . *of John Hay,* 201–203 (entry for July 1, 1864).
[14] *Ibid.,* 202.   [15] *Ibid.*

friend, ". . . he would have invited an interview and all might have been harmonized." [16] He attributed this ill will to the Pomeroy Circular. "Then the course of some of my friends in making my name prominent in connection with the Presidential canvass tended to cool his regard for me; and the shameless assaults of the Blairs upon whom a Jacksonian 'down!' from him would have silenced the hounds cooled my regard for him." [17] He also blamed the President for the "embarrassment" in their official relations, saying: "I had found a good deal of embarrassment from him but what he could have found from me I could not imagine unless it has been created by my unwillingness to have offices distributed by spoils or benefits with more regard to the claims of divisions, factions, cliques and individuals than to fitness of selection." [18] Besides: "He had never given me the active and earnest support I was entitled to & even now Congress was about to adjourn without passing sufficient tax bills, though making appropriations with lavish profusion, and he was notwithstanding my appeals taking no pains to assure different results." [19] The administration, Chase further complained, had failed to support him earnestly in his efforts to "give the people a uniform currency, made in the end equivalent to gold everywhere." [20] Whatever the explanation for his departure—whether it was personal jealousy, the Blairs, the patronage, or differences about fiscal policy—Chase was sure that the fault was the President's.

His admiring and sympathizing correspondents confirmed Chase in his conviction that he had been grossly wronged.[21] Some other observers, however, thought they saw a different meaning in his separation from the cabinet. The task of a treasury secretary—"the great practical problem regularly recurring," as Congressman Samuel Hooper put it, "to raise one hundred millions a month"—was most difficult. Chase had been widely criticized as personally responsible for the financial ills of the nation, and, according to Hooper, he had been "attempting to throw unfair responsibilities on Congress." Then came

---

[16] Chase to Col. R. C. Parsons, July 8, 1864, Chase MSS., Box 15, Pa. Hist. Soc.
[17] *Ibid.*   [18] Chase MS. diary, June 30, 1864, Lib. of Cong.   [19] *Ibid.*
[20] Chase to Joseph Cable, July 11, 1864, Buffalo *Morning Express*, Aug. 15, 1864, p. 2, c. 3.
[21] See letters to Chase from M. C. Meigs, June 30; R. D. Mussey, July 1; H. G. Stebbins, July 1; E. T. Carson, July 4; M. Goodrich, July 7; E. G. Cooke, July 11, 1864, Chase MSS., Lib. of Cong.

the acceptance of his resignation, "to relieve him of all responsibility." [22] So Hooper said, and an English journalist expressed a similar opinion. This writer, observing that "Mr. Chase's strategic movement" had occurred "just when gold had risen to 270 per cent," called it a "timely retreat from overwhelming difficulties," a retreat which might save Chase's reputation and his presidential availability.[23]

For a while some of Lincoln's friends as well as Chase's partisans feared that the loss of Chase might prove disastrous to the administration and to the Union cause. At a time of "military unsuccess, financial weakness," and "Congressional hesitation on question of conscription," Representative Washburne said, Lincoln's acceptance of the resignation would be "ruinous." [24] The financiers in Wall Street, however, did not consider Chase an indispensable man. Though distressed by Tod's nomination, they were reassured by Fessenden's appointment and by the coincident repeal of the gold bill.[25] Nor was Lincoln himself inclined to fear for the public finances. All along he had disagreed with some of Chase's policies and had agreed with the Blairs that the trade in Southern cotton should not be monopolized by favored agents holding treasury department permits. On the day he accepted the resignation he told Hay "he had a plan for relieving us to a certain extent financially: for the Government to take into its own hands the whole cotton trade and buy all that [was] offered; take it to New York, sell for gold, & buy up its own greenbacks." [26]

The political consequences of the cabinet change were more dangerous for the administration than the financial consequences. So far as Lincoln's re-election prospects were concerned, Abram Wakeman, the New York postmaster, believed that Chase's departure would be a help rather than a hindrance, for "henceforward the fifty thousand Treasury agents would be friends of the President instead of enemies." [27] But a newspaper correspondent warned that, if the people

[22] Dennett, . . . Diaries . . . of John Hay, 199–200. For criticism of Chase's conduct of finances, see for example New York Herald, June 20, 1864, p. 2, c. 1.

[23] London Saturday Review, July 23, 1864, quoted in Boston Daily Advertiser, Aug. 12, 1864, p. 2, c. 4.

[24] Dennett, . . . Diaries . . . of John Hay, 198 (entry for June 30, 1864).

[25] New York Herald, July 1, 1864, p. 2, c. 1; July 2, 1864, p. 2, c. 1; July 4, 1864, p. 2, c. 1; July 6, 1864, p. 2, c. 1; New York Post, quoted in Cincinnati Daily Gazette, July 2, 1864, p. 3, c. 4.

[26] Dennett, . . . Diaries . . . of John Hay, 203 (entry for July 1, 1864).

[27] Ibid., 201.

generally should get the impression that Chase had been "wrongly treated," then Lincoln, though re-elected, might "find himself *in a minority of Congress*" during his second term.[28]

Certainly the affair did bode ill for Lincoln's relations with Congress, immediately as well as remotely. Though Fessenden was a Radical of sorts and "the Senate's man," the Radicals in Congress did not consider him a sufficient offset to such cabinet Conservatives as Montgomery Blair. With Chase out, the Radicals were to increase their clamor for Blair's removal. Already one of the most extreme among them in the House, Blair's Maryland rival Henry Winter Davis, was preparing in collaboration with Benjamin F. Wade in the Senate an explosive challenge to the President's authority over the reconstruction of the Southern states.

V

While the President was beginning the re-establishment of Southern state governments with his "ten per cent plan," many of his fellow partisans in Congress were denouncing it, frustrating its purposes, and preparing an alternative of their own. "We may conquer rebels and hold them in subjection," Stevens told the House in reply to Lincoln's message of December, 1863, but it was a "mere mockery" of democratic principles to say that a "tithe" of the inhabitants of a conquered state could carry on government because they were "more holy or more loyal than the others." Stevens refused to hear of giving seats in Congress to representatives seeking admission from states reorganized under the presidential plan. The record of Republicans, he said, should not so "entangle" them that later they might be "estopped from denying the particular condition of those states." [1] When, before the end of the session, senators elected by the reconstructed legislature of Arkansas appeared in Washington, they were turned away.

Meanwhile Henry Winter Davis had induced the House to refer the reconstruction passages of the President's message to a special committee, of which he became chairman. From the committee he reported a bill (February 15, 1864) to guarantee a "republican form of government" to certain states whose governments had been "usurped or overthrown." A preamble to the bill implied that these

---

[28] Cincinnati *Daily Gazette*, July 8, 1864, p. 1, c. 2.
[1] Current, *Old Thad Stevens*, 189–190.

states were no longer in the Union: they were entitled neither to be represented in Congress nor to take any part in the national government. Some of the bill's provisions coincided with features of the President's plan, but others ran counter to it. As in his program, slavery was to be prohibited, the post-secession public debts disavowed, and representation in Congress permitted only with congressional assent. A majority of the white male citizens, however, and not a mere ten per cent of the 1860 voters, was to start the remaking of a state government—a majority taking an oath to support the Constitution of the United States. Not all members of this majority were to be allowed actually to participate in the creation of a new state constitution: only those who could swear that they had never voluntarily borne arms against the United States, nor given aid to persons in armed hostility thereto, nor supported any hostile "pretended government." Nor was any former officeholder under a "usurping power" to vote or hold office in the recreated state.[2]

In support of his bill Davis made a characteristically fiery speech in the House. He asserted that only Congress, not the President, had the constitutional authority to provide for the reorganization of state governments. He argued—as if the President's plan did not already include abolition—that slavery was "really, radically inconsistent with the permanence of republican governments" and must be eliminated. By denouncing those who, he said, clamored for "speedy recognition of governments tolerating slavery," he left the implication that he opposed speedy recognition of any governments, since those being restored under the Lincolnian process did not, in fact, tolerate slavery, and it was the recognition of such governments as these to which he was objecting.[3]

On May 4, by a strict party vote of 73 to 59, the House passed the Davis bill. Extreme though it was, it still did not go far enough to suit all the Radicals who voted for it. Stevens, for one, desired a measure providing for the reversion to the Federal government of all lands, in the "so-called states" or "territories" of the South, belonging to rebels who owned a hundred acres or more. When a colleague voted for the Davis bill under protest, Stevens spoke up: "I ought to say that I refused to vote, under protest."[4] Other Radicals agreed with him that

---

[2] *Cong. Globe*, 38 Cong., 1 sess., 3448–3449.   [3] *Ibid.*, App., 82–85.
[4] *Ibid.*, 38 Cong., 1 sess., 2108; *Old Thad Stevens*, 198, 201.

the bill should embody more explicitly the principle that the Southern states, once recovered from the Confederacy, were no more than conquered provinces, which Congress might dispose of as it pleased, even with a general confiscation of rebel property.[5]

In the Senate Ben Wade took charge of the bill. Wade tried, without success, to strike the word "white" from the clause directing provisional governors to enroll "all white male citizens" for taking the loyalty oath. Sumner tried, without success, to add an amendment by which the Emancipation Proclamation would have been "adopted and enacted as a statute of the United States." Other Senators succeeded in attaching amendments, none of them drastic, and the minor differences between the House and Senate versions had to be reconciled by a conference committee. The Senate finally passed the bill on July 4, 1864, within an hour of the *sine die* adjournment of the session.[6]

The last hours of any session were confused and chaotic, and the last hours of this one were unusually so. Though both houses had agreed to adjourn at noon, they found it necessary to make three ten-minute postponements, in order to take care of the final rush of business. Toward the very end important bills were still being "pitchforked into shape"—not only the reconstruction measure but also a bill amending the Pacific Railroad Act so as to increase the compensation of the railroad builders, and another bill providing for a whiskey tax. "Cabinet ministers were numerous on the floor of the House," as Noah Brooks recalled, "and lobbyists in the general disorder slipped in through the doors and buttonholed members, while the mill of legislation slowly ground out its last grist."[7] A clerk of the House droned out the Declaration of Independence, which was being read in observance of the Fourth of July, despite the objection of the congressional jester, the Democrat "Sunset" Cox, who said the Declaration was an insurrectionary document and would give aid and comfort to the rebels.[8] As the hands of the clock neared the closing time, some of the congressmen began to wonder whether the President was going to sign the Wade-Davis bill. Word came that he had no further communication for the House, and Speaker Colfax adjourned the

[5] Williams, *Lincoln and the Radicals*, 319.

[6] S. S. Cox, *Three Decades of Federal Legislation*, 341.

[7] Brooks, *Washington in Lincoln's Time*, 166–167.

[8] Dennett, . . . *Diaries* . . . *of John Hay*, 204.

session and dismissed the members to their homes. "In the disorder which followed, Davis standing at his desk, pale with wrath, his bushy hair tousled, and wildly brandishing his arms, denounced the President in good set terms." [9]

The President all the while was in the room set apart for his use in the Senate wing of the Capitol, where he had been conferring with members of the cabinet and the Congress as he considered newly passed bills for his signature. During the morning Zachariah Chandler had warned him not to veto the Wade-Davis measure, for, he said, a veto would have a disastrous political effect in the states of the Northwest. Lincoln, who had made no move to discourage Congress from passing the bill, now patiently explained to Chandler his constitutional doubts about it. As Lincoln left the Capitol that day he told John Hay that Chandler and the Radicals could "do harm" politically on the reconstruction issue. "At all events," he went on, "I must keep some consciousness of being somewhere near right: I must keep some standard of principle fixed within myself." [10]

Unless the President signed the bill within ten days, it would fail to become law, no positive veto being necessary after the adjournment of Congress. Lincoln could have let the ten days pass in silence on his part. Instead, he chose the unusual course of issuing a proclamation on the subject, and a most remarkable proclamation it proved to be. He announced (July 8, 1864) that he was "unprepared, by a formal approval of this bill, to be inflexibly committed to any single plan of restoration," and that he was "also unprepared to declare that the free-State constitutions and governments already adopted and installed in Arkansas and Louisiana" should be "set aside and held for nought." Nevertheless he was "fully satisfied with the system for restoration contained in the bill as one very proper plan for the loyal people of any State choosing to adopt it," and he was "prepared to give the executive aid and assistance to any such people." [11] That is to say, he was willing to give effect to a mere proposal—a bill that had not become law—and he left the Southern people to take their choice between his plan and that of Davis and Wade.

"What an infamous proclamation!" exclaimed Old Thad Stevens

[9] Brooks, *Washington in Lincoln's Time*, 168.
[10] Dennett, . . . *Diaries . . . of John Hay*, 204–206.
[11] Nicolay and Hay, *Works*, X, 152–154.

in a letter to an intimate. "The idea of pocketing a bill and then issuing a proclamation as to how far he will conform to it . . . ." Though Lincoln had intended to mollify the Radicals, he had succeeded only in exasperating them with his conditional approval of their plan. "But what are we to do?" Stevens asked his friend, then answered his own question: "Condemn privately and applaud publicly!" [12] His colleagues Wade and Davis, however, were in no mood for applause, and in a month the President and the nation were to hear from them.

VI

Lincoln based his ten per cent plan on his assumption of a strong potential unionism in the South. He counted upon the good will of his countrymen, even in their hour of defeat, and he intended to nourish that sentiment rather than take for granted, and thereby foster, the perpetuation of wartime hatreds. But the Radicals did not share his faith in this regard. Stevens, for one, expected guerrilla warfare to go on indefinitely even after the Confederate armies should all have surrendered.[1] And Winter Davis declared: "There is no fact that we have learned from any one who has been in the South and has come up from the darkness of that bottomless pit which indicates . . . repentance." There was no fact "at all reliable," he went on, which indicated that "any respectable proportion of the people of the southern states" were willing to accept even such terms as the Northern Democrats might grant them.[2] Davis and his associates in Congress looked for continuing disunionism and strife; the President hoped for peace.

The differing approaches of President and Congress, in planning for the defeated South, followed naturally from their differing assumptions. Lincoln aimed to conciliate the recent rebels and to adapt his program, if necessary, to meet conditions that might vary from state to state. He was unprepared, as he said in his proclamation on the Wade-Davis bill, "to be inflexibly committed to any single plan of restoration," and he was also unprepared to see the free-state constitutions of Arkansas and Louisiana set aside, "thereby repelling and

---

12 Stevens to Edward McPherson, July 10, 1864, Stevens MSS.
1 Current, *Old Thad Stevens*, 207.   2 *Cong. Globe*, 38 Cong., 1 sess., App., 84.

discouraging the loyal citizens" in those states.[3] The bill, by contrast, would have provided a fixed and invariable program for all areas of the South, regardless of differences in the time and circumstances of the rebuilding of state governments.

The difference in spirit between the presidential and the congressional plans is clearly seen in the different oaths the two required. The Wade-Davis bill prescribed the "ironclad oath" that a man had not willingly supported the rebellion, before he could participate in politics or government. Thus, in the bill, loyalty was made a matter of past conduct, not of present attitude or future promise, and no allowance was made for a possible change of heart. In Lincoln's plan the concept of loyalty was forward and not backward looking. "On principle I dislike an oath which requires a man to swear he *has* not done wrong," Lincoln explained. "It rejects the Christian principle of forgiveness on terms of repentance. I think it is enough if the man does no wrong *hereafter*." [4]

Whether or not Lincoln's was the more Christian way, the Radicals argued that it was the less democratic. As Stevens said, to allow a "tithe" of the people to govern the rest was a "mere mockery" of democratic principles. Of course the Wade-Davis bill did require a majority and not merely a tenth of the loyal voters to start the constitution-making process. But Lincoln intended his tenth as a nucleus around which a loyal majority might, with his simple oath, soon develop. His was a minority that had possibilities of rapid growth. The majority principle of Wade and Davis, on the other hand, was deceptive. Under their program no one could participate in politics who could not take the ironclad oath, which would eliminate hundreds of thousands and very likely leave political power in the hands of a minority. And this minority could grow only with the aging and death of former Confederates and the rise of a new generation too young to have participated in the war. (A majority could have been created, of course, by the enfranchisement of former slaves, but the Senate had defeated Wade's proposal to strike the word "white" from the bill's provision for enrolling all "adult white males.")

The President and the Congress disagreed on issues of constitutionality as well as loyalty. Could a state secede from the Union? Had some of the states actually done so? The Wade-Davis bill implied that they

---

[3] Nicolay and Hay, *Works*, X, 152–153.   [4] *Collected Works*, VII, 169.

had, and Radicals like Stevens made the point explicit. "This bill and this position of these gentlemen seems to me," Lincoln commented in Hay's presence, "to make the fatal admission (in asserting that the insurrectionary States are no longer in the Union) that States whenever they please may of their own motion dissolve their connection with the Union." Lincoln thought the Federal government could not survive such an admission. "If that be true," he said, "I am not President, these gentlemen are not Congress." He preferred not to argue about the question whether certain states were in or out of the Union. To him this was a "merely metaphysical question." The real problem was a practical one—how to "restore the Union"—and he believed the Union could best be restored without a quarrel over abstractions.[5] In discussing the future of the Southern states he habitually used the term "restoration" in preference to "reconstruction," with its connotations of change drastic, forcible, and delayed.

Both Lincoln and the Radicals, including Davis himself, favored an amendment to the Federal Constitution as an ultimate measure for disposing of slavery in the states of the South. Pending the adoption of such an amendment, there were sharp differences of opinion about presidential and congressional powers in the sphere of abolition. In urging Lincoln to sign the Wade-Davis bill, Senator Chandler said: "The important point is that one prohibiting slavery in the reconstructed States." Lincoln: "That is the point on which I doubt the authority of Congress to act." Chandler: "It is no more than you have done yourself." Lincoln: "I conceive that I may in an emergency do things on military grounds which cannot be done constitutionally by Congress." After Chandler had left and Fessenden had come in, Lincoln continued: "I do not see how any of us now can deny and contradict all we have always said, that Congress has no constitutional power over slavery in the States." Fessenden agreed, but added that he had doubts about the "constitutional efficacy" of the President's own emancipation decree.[6]

Lincoln inclined to the belief that, in time of war, the Constitution restrains the President less than it does Congress. Yet the Supreme Court was later to rule that Congress may exercise belligerent powers in disregard of the ordinary restraints of the Constitution.[7] This opin-

---

[5] Dennett, . . . *Diaries* . . . *of John Hay*, 204–205.   [6] *Ibid.*, 205.
[7] Randall, *Constitutional Problems under Lincoln*, 514–515.

ion (though the Court was not deciding the specific question of the war power of Congress to abolish slavery) suggests that the abolition clause of the Wade-Davis bill was based on constitutional grounds no more dubious than those on which stood the Emancipation Proclamation or the presidential order prohibiting slavery under the ten per cent plan.

As for the practical consequences of the presidential and congressional programs, there would have been no immediate difference in respect to slavery, at least within the states of Louisiana, Arkansas, and Tennessee, where Lincoln's plan was being put into operation. There might (theoretically) have been a difference later on. That is, if Radical fears were justified, pro-slavery governments might eventually have come into power and re-established slavery in the restored states. Or, in other states yet to be restored under the presidential plan, flexible and variable as it was, Lincoln conceivably might have made concessions to slavery—might, for example, have directed gradual rather than immediate emancipation. Such fears were idle. The President was, in fact, already committed to an antislavery constitutional amendment (and was, within a year, to press it upon Congress). Wade and Davis were only confusing the issues when they tried to give the impression that their bill was an antislavery alternative to proslavery policies on the part of the President.

Their bill, if enacted would have had other consequences very different from those of the President's plan, if he had been free to carry it out. His kind of "restoration" would have meant the early return of the Southern states to a normal and natural place in the Union. The Radicals' brand of "reconstruction," however, might have delayed the return indefinitely. Even to begin the process would have been difficult, if not impossible, so long as a majority of adult white males, willing to take an oath of loyalty to the Constitution of the United States, was required. And after the process was begun, the disfranchisement of the former political leaders would doubtless have led to complications, conflicts, and delays.

On the part of some of the Radicals the postponement of restoration was deliberately intended. As Stevens was to say, the Southern people must "eat the fruit of foul rebellion" before receiving all the rights of citizenship again. He was to calculate that, as soon as Southern representatives should be readmitted to Congress, they along with the

Northern Democrats would have a clear majority there. His own aim, he was frankly to state, was to "secure perpetual ascendancy to the party of the Union," that is, to the Republican party. If Republicans should lose the ascendancy, then their entire economic program—the protective tariff, the national banking system, the subsidization of railroads—would be jeopardized.[8]

But the Wade-Davis bill was not nearly so effective an instrument for perpetuating disunion and Republican supremacy as the Radicals later were to devise. Radical reconstruction, in the fullness of its development, was to include military rule, Negro suffrage, and hopelessly complicated procedures for reorganizing and recognizing new state governments in the South. Indeed, as the Radical Congressman George W. Julian was to say, the "somewhat incongruous bill" of Wade and Davis, if the President had accepted it, would have become "a stumbling-block in the way of the more radical measures which afterwards prevailed." [9]

Even without achieving the enactment of the bill, the Radicals accomplished at least part of their purpose in passing it. "It was commonly regarded," Blaine later recalled, "as a rebuke to the course of the President in proceeding with the grave and momentous task of reconstruction without waiting the action or invoking the council of Congress." [10] The bill was also a rebuke to Lincoln for his presidential aspirations, or so it was intended by some of the Radicals, who intimated that his real purpose in hastening the restoration of Southern state governments was to use them in building a personal political machine which would assure his renomination and re-election in 1864.[11] The rebuke was the perhaps inevitable outcome of his habit of playing scant regard to the prerogatives and sensitivities of Congress. If he had sedulously cultivated congressional support, he might possibly have avoided the rebuke and the impasse to which it led. But that is doubtful, in view of the fundamental divergences in spirit and purpose between him and the majority of his fellow partisans in Congress.

This much is certain, that in consequence of the bill's passage and pocket veto, Congress and the President had reached a stalemate in

8 Current, *Old Thad Stevens*, 207, 226–229.

9 Julian, *Political Recollections*, 247–248.

10 Blaine, *Twenty Years of Congress*, II, 42.   11 Current, *Old Thad Stevens*, 190.

the conflict over policy with regard to the Southern states. And this conflict boded ill for the success of the party in general and the President in particular in the coming political campaign. Some of the bills recently passed and signed—tax laws, the conscription act—were dubious party assets in an election year, but the bill passed and not signed was likely to make far more trouble for the party. Congress adjourned with worse relations between legislative and executive than at any time since the foundation of the Republic under the Constitution, or at least since the days of Andrew Jackson. The prospects for fruitful co-operation between Congress and President, even if Lincoln should be re-elected with a Republican majority in both houses, seemed rather poor.

CHAPTER X

DARK SUMMER

DURING all the four years of the Civil War there were, for President Lincoln, no darker months than those from the summer solstice to the autumnal equinox in 1864. In September the skies were to brighten for him, but in July and still more in August the days brought little but increasing gloom. These were the days of abortive peace missions, of lagging recruitments, of cynical speculation in gold, of widespread defeatism throughout the North. The war dragged on, and Grant made no noticeable dent in the great ring of earthworks that kept him from Richmond and Petersburg. While the enemy Capital remained beyond the reach of Union troops, Washington itself was threatened by the Confederates.

I

Besieged as he was in Richmond and Petersburg, General Lee looked for relief, as he informed Jefferson Davis on June 20, 1864, from a stratagem for drawing the attention of the Federals to their own territory. Thereby he might induce Grant to weaken his besieging force by sending part of it northward or, better yet, to bleed his army further by assaulting the strong Confederate defenses. So Lee sent Jubal A. Early with nearly twenty thousand men up the Shenandoah Valley, that convenient approach to the unguarded rear of Washington, a route already well worn by Confederate raiders, who had used it every summer of the war. The Union forces under David Hunter having previously retreated out of the way, over the mountains into West Virginia, Early advanced unopposed through the Valley. During the first days of July his troops crossed the upper Potomac. On July 11, just a week after the adjournment of Congress, his army was on the northern outskirts of Washington, in sight of the Capitol dome.[1]

For a couple of days Washington had a small taste of what was becoming familiar and routine in Richmond—a state of siege—but Washington knew far less than Richmond about the nature and intentions of the besieging force. Communications with the North by rail and telegraph were cut off. No one in the city, not even the President and his cabinet, could do more than guess how large the enemy force was, precisely where it was concentrated or whether it was concentrated at all, and when or whether it was going to attack. In his diary Secretary Welles railed against the "dunderheads" at the War Office, the stupid Stanton and the confused Halleck, and expressed no satisfaction when told that intelligence was poor because fresh cavalry was lacking.[2] Grant himself suffered from defective information, though from his own intelligence and from Washington reports he had a broadly accurate picture of Early's movement. Unaware that Hunter had removed himself from the possibility of effective action, Grant counted upon him to pursue and entrap Early's army.[3]

Fortifications dotted the circumference of Washington, but most of the garrisoning troops had been sent to Grant as replacements for his heavy losses, and the forts were manned by a motley collection of invalids and raw militiamen. At the enemy's approach, civilian employees of the navy and war departments were called into service.[4] When Grant offered to come to the relief of the city, Lincoln suggested but did not order that he do so. On second thought Grant decided to send two corps but not to go himself, and Lincoln calmly accepted this arrangement.[5]

Much alarmed about the President's personal safety, Stanton on July 9 sent Lincoln a note telling him his carriage had been followed by a mysterious horseman and warning him to be "on the *alert.*" Nevertheless Lincoln with his family went out as usual on the next evening to spend the night at the Soldiers' Home, in the northern part of the city, where the enemy was expected to appear. At ten that evening Stanton drafted another warning note, in which he started to tell Lincoln to "come into town at once," then corrected the last two

---

[1] Nicolay and Hay, *Abraham Lincoln: A History*, IX, 158, 160, 169–173; Williams, *Lincoln and His Generals*, 324.

[2] Welles, *Diary*, II, 69–70, 72–74.   [3] Williams, *Lincoln and His Generals*, 325–326.

[4] Nicolay and Hay, *Abraham Lincoln: A History*, IX, 163–164; Welles, *Diary*, II, 72.

[5] Williams, *Lincoln and His Generals*, 325–326.

words to read, a little less peremptorily, "tonight." [6] The President, though reluctant, did return with his family that night, in a carriage which Stanton had sent for him, but he was considerably annoyed. He was further annoyed to learn that a gunboat was being readied so that he might flee the city.[7]

The next day he determined to "desert his tormentors" and make a tour of the city's defences. He went out to Fort Stevens, beyond the Soldiers' Home, near the northern corner of the District of Columbia, on the 7th Street Road. He was on the parapet when the Confederates, advancing through heat and dust from Silver Spring, first opened fire on the fort. A soldier standing beside him—long afterward identified as Oliver Wendell Holmes, Jr.,—"roughly ordered him to get down or he would have his head knocked off." [8] The expected assault did not develop, as Early spent the afternoon in feeling out the strength of the works.

On the following day the President again was under fire at Fort Stevens. Though Early still ordered no attack, he kept up his reconnaissance, and a "continual popping" of gunfire came from pickets and skirmishers on both sides. An officer a few feet from Lincoln on the parapet fell with a mortal wound. A few minutes later Secretary Welles and Senator Wade entered the fort together and found the President sitting in the shade, his back against the parapet towards the enemy. Shells fired from the fort were setting fire to houses in which rebel sharpshooters were hiding.[9] Learning that "the military officers in command thought the shelling of the houses proper and necessary," Lincoln, as he afterwards stated, "certainly gave" his "approbation to its being done." [10]

Smoke arising in the distance indicated that the Confederates also were burning houses, and one of these was the mansion of Montgomery Blair at Silver Spring. "The Rebels have done him this injury," Welles was to reflect later, on viewing the blackened walls of Blair's house, "and yet some whom they have never personally harmed denounce him as not earnest in the cause, as favoring the Rebels and their views." One of Blair's foremost detractors, personally unharmed by the rebels, was of course Welles' uncongenial companion on the

6 R. T. L. Coll., 34399, 34405.   7 Brooks, *Washington in Lincoln's Time*, 175.
8 Dennett, . . . *Diaries . . . of John Hay*, 208   9 Welles, *Diary*, II, 72, 74–75.
10 Lincoln Memorandum, Oct. 10, 1864, Box 162, House of Rep. Coll., Lib. of Cong.

Fort Stevens visit, Senator Wade.

From the fort, after the shelling had let up, Lincoln had a chance to see at first hand a little of the drama of soldiers in action. There, only a few hundred yards away, in the broad valley below, were men in blue (newly arrived veterans) advancing across open fields, and ahead of them were men in grey running for the wooded cover on the brow of the opposite hills. And here, nearer at hand, were Union stretcher bearers bringing in their wounded comrades. By nightfall the action had ceased, and campfires lighted up the woods around the fort, while the road was clogged with Union stragglers, some weary and worn out, others drunk.[11] In the darkness to the north Early was withdrawing his troops.

All the while Lincoln had worried little if at all about his own safety or that of the city. "With him," as Hay noted on July 11, "the only concern seems to be whether we can bag or destroy this force in our front." And when the force had begun to leave, he became doubly anxious lest it get away. On July 13 Hay recorded again: "The President thinks we should push our column right up the River Road & cut off as many as possible of the retreating raiders." But there was no one to give the necessary orders in time. Grant was too far away. Halleck, never a man to assume responsibility, declined to act without instructions from Grant. And Lincoln, unwilling to interfere with the general-in-chief, restrained whatever impulses he may have had to take personal command in the emergency. Finally a telegram from Grant started General Wright in pursuit with all available forces. "Wright telegraphs that he thinks the enemy are all across the Potomac but that he has halted & sent out an infantry reconnoissance [sic], for fear he might come across the rebels & catch some of them." So, on July 14, Lincoln said to Hay. And Hay observed to himself, "The Chief is evidently disgusted." [12]

Wright, of course, was not really to blame for his delayed and seemingly timid pursuit. As T. Harry Williams has written, "Early got away because the tangled command system in the Washington military area did not make anybody responsible for catching him." Both Lincoln and Grant soon recognized this fact and saw the necessity

---

11 Welles, *Diary*, II, 74–75, 80.
12 Dennett, . . . *Diaries . . . of John Hay*, 209–210; Brooks, *Washington in Lincoln's Time*, 177.

for reorganizing the command system so as to put the troops in the Capital and the adjacent departments under the control of a single general. Otherwise Early could threaten Washington again and again, Grant would have to keep on detaching troops from the Richmond and Petersburg area, and Lee would never be finally hemmed in and compelled to surrender.[13] This military lesson for the President and his general-in-chief was one of the important consequences of the Early raid.

Another consequence, less favorable to the Union cause, was an aggravation of the defeatism prevailing throughout the North. The people of the country did not realize how little panic, how little sense of real danger, the raid had aroused in Washington itself. After communications had been reopened, however, the people got from the Washington papers, such as the *Chronicle* and the *National Intelligencer*, the impression that there had been a miraculous deliverance from imminent peril and that the narrow escape was cause for national humiliation.[14] Prophets of disaster drew what seemed to them an obvious moral from the idea that, even at this late date in the war, the Capital, the government records and treasures, and the person of the President were not safe.[15]

II

The Lincoln government had to deal not only with overt military threats, such as the Early raid, but also with threats, rather obscure and ill defined, of what in a later day would have been called "fifth column" activity. Confederate plotters were full of schemes for exploiting defeatism and disloyalty in the North during the gloomy summer of 1864. Though the exact dimensions of the conspiracy were not known to Lincoln and his advisers at the time, there were signs and rumors aplenty which both exaggerated and underestimated its extent.

In Peoria and Springfield, Illinois, in Syracuse, New York, and in other cities of the North the Peace Democrats during August sponsored mass demonstrations which to Republicans seemed sinister and ominous. At the Peoria "Copperhead Convention" on August 3 there

---

[13] Williams, *Lincoln and His Generals*, 326–327.   [14] Welles, *Diary*, II, 77.
[15] Brooks, *Washington in Lincoln's Time*, 179–180.

was a crowd of between ten and twenty thousand, according to the estimate of the sympathetic Chicago *Times*. Conspicuous at the meeting were such prominent Democrats as Clement L. Vallandigham, George H. Pendleton, and Fernando Wood. The resolutions of the convention condemned Lincoln for his reply to the Niagara peace proposal and demanded an immediate armistice to end the war.[1]

Governor Richard Yates of Illinois saw in the peace movement signs of serious trouble for his state. Already, as in Coles County during the spring, mob violence had flared up between critics and defenders of the Lincoln administration, and passions still were simmering. After the Peoria demonstration Yates feared a general uprising might begin in Illinois. He said, privately, that if he had only himself to consider, he would be for "shooting the home traitors" as he would "so many dogs." He refrained from giving guns to loyal citizens, however, because his doing so might give rise to the accusation that he was "arming the abolitionists," and this might be made a "pretext for arming the copperheads." Then "hostilities might be provoked & civil war precipitated."[2]

From time to time President Lincoln received warnings of a "great conspiracy" which extended far beyond the borders of Illinois. He sent Hay to Missouri to find out what General Rosecrans knew. The general gave Hay some papers to take back, and dispatched others by another courier—documents giving "the details of evidence covering a thousand pages of foolscap." This detailed report, the general said (in a letter of June 22), would show the following:

"1. That there exists an oathbound secret society, under various names but forming one brotherhood both in the rebel and loyal states, the objects of which are the overthrow of the existing national government, and the dismemberment of this nation.

"2. That the secret oaths bind these conspirators to revolution and all its consequences of murder arson pillage and an untold train of crimes, including assassination and perjury under the penalty of death to the disobedient or recusant.

"3. That they intend to operate in conjunction with rebel movements this summer to revolutionize the loyal states, if they can.

---

[1] *Weekly Illinois State Journal* (Springfield), Aug. 10, 1864, p. 2, c. 7; New York *Herald*, Aug. 19, 1864, p. 5, c. 4.

[2] Yates to J. Berden and others, Aug. 12, 1864, Reavis MSS., Chicago Hist. Soc.

"4. That Vallandingham [*sic*] is the Supreme Commander of the Northern wing of this society . . . .

"5. That the association is now and has been the principal agency by which spying and supplying rebels with the means of war are carried on between the loyal and rebel states, and that even some of our officers are engaged in it.

"6. That they claim to have 25000 members in Missouri, 140000 in Illinois, 100000 in Indiana, 80000 in Ohio, 70000 in Kentucky and that they are extending through New York New Jersey Penn^a Delaware & Maryland." [3]

A Canadian wrote to Lincoln on July 7 to give additional information about the plot. His country and many of his countrymen, this man said, were involved in it. Vallandigham while in exile in Canada had organized Union deserters and draft dodgers, together with thousands of Canadians and Irishmen living in Canada, into a force which, together with civilians in the Northern states and officers and men in the Union army, totalled at least three hundred thousand, "all anxiously waiting for the time to arrive to strike a deadly blow." Arms were being cached against the day of revolution. "It is not intended to make any demonstration before the presidential election comes on if the South can hold out successfully until that time and then they will concentrate their forces and commence their work of destruction on the lakes and the frontiers." [4]

From other sources also the war department was warned that Confederate agents in Canada were "setting on foot expeditions of the most dangerous character," and Republican newspapers published rumors of Confederate and Copperhead intrigue.[5] In these stories there was a considerable element of truth.

The Confederate government was in fact carrying on a campaign to exploit the war weariness of the Northern people, the organized peace movement, the partisan opposition to Lincoln, and the financial difficulties of the Union government. The peace offensive (as a later generation would have termed it), which Jacob Thompson and his colleagues launched from Canada during the summer, was only a part of a large and ambitious enterprise. From Jefferson Davis, in

[3] R. T. L. Coll., 33944–45.   [4] M. C. Moe to Lincoln, R. T. L. Coll., 34323–24.
[5] Maj. Gen. S. A. Hitchcock (Sandusky, Ohio) to Stanton, Sept. 23, 1864, *Offic. Rec.*, 1 ser., XXXIX, 448; New York *Tribune*, Oct. 29, Nov. 5, 1864.

Richmond, Thompson had received oral instructions to proceed at his discretion to do what would "seem most likely to conduce to the furtherance of the interests of the Confederate States of America." [6] From Thompson other agents got unwritten instructions.[7] Most colorful and resourceful of these agents was a young Kentuckian, Thomas Henry Hines, who is said to have shaken hands with Lincoln once, while the bonds that were to finance his efforts stuck boldly out of his pockets.[8] Despite the poor condition of Confederate finances, Thompson was fairly well supplied with funds.

The Confederate conspirators counted on the co-operation of the Sons of Liberty in Illinois, Indiana, Ohio, and other states of the North. The Sons of Liberty—a name adopted early in 1864 for its patriotic connotations from Revolutionary days—were successors of the Knights of the Golden Circle. Thompson enjoyed the confidence of some of the leading Liberty men, and through them he helped to finance the Peoria peace demonstration. He also managed to gain interviews with Vallandigham, Pendleton, and other prominent Peace Democrats. Thompson and his fellow plotters hoped, through their connection with the Sons of Liberty, to do more than merely stimulate pacifist demands. At the most, the Sons were expected to rise up in rebellion, "throw off the galling dynasty at Washington," and create an independent Confederacy of the Northwestern states. At the least, the Liberty men were expected to collaborate in various undertakings for the harassment of the Union.[9]

If the conspiracy had succeeded, a United States gunboat on Lake Erie would have been captured and the rebel prisoners on Johnson's Island freed. Prisoners at other camps from Illinois to New York also would have been turned loose. River boats on the Mississippi would have been sabotaged or destroyed. Fires would have been started in New York, Boston, Philadelphia, Chicago, Pittsburgh, Washington, and other cities, all of which would have been reduced to ashes. Chicago would have been captured. Settlements along the

6 *Offic. Rec.*, 4 ser., III, 278, 322.

7 J. W. Headley, *Confederate Operations in Canada and New York*, 221, 227.

8 For a recent and exaggerated account of the conspiracy in general and of Hines's career in particular, see James D. Horan, *Confederate Agent: A Discovery in History* (New York, 1954).

9 *Offic. Rec.*, 1 ser., XLIII, pt. 2, 930–931; 2 ser., VIII, 523–525; *Offic. Rec.* (Nav.), 2 ser., III, 1235.

Canadian border would have been plundered. And the Union government would have been forced to make peace on the basis of the
independence of the Confederate States of America.[10]

The actual accomplishments of the conspirators fell somewhat short
of this grand design. In September an attempt on Johnson's Island
failed. In October a band of raiders from Canada fell upon St. Albans,
Vermont, a border town of about five or six thousand, and attempted
to burn the place after robbing the three local banks. In November
arsonists set fires in several New York hotels and on vessels on the
North River, but all the fires were put out before significant damage
was done. The hoped-for revolt of the Sons of Liberty did not even
start.[11]

The idea of revolutionizing the Northwest and establishing a new
Confederacy was never more than a fantastic dream. Only a few of
the Sons of Liberty themselves were implicated in the plot, and still
fewer outsiders would have been willing to have anything to do with
it. From the outset even the conspiring leaders of the Liberty organization recognized the futility of an armed uprising. "We are willing to
do anything which bids fair to result in good," one of them wrote
to Thompson and his associates on August 8, "but shrink from the
responsibility of a movement in the way now proposed." The writer
added: "You underrate the condition of things in the Northwest." [12]
Thompson's partner C. C. Clay informed Judah P. Benjamin, the
Confederate secretary of war, in September, that the Northern people
showed little sympathy for the Liberty men.[13]

Nothing was done except when the Confederates themselves did
it, and all their efforts failed except for the St. Albans raid, which was
only a partial success. The other undertakings were frustrated by the
vigilance and the prompt counteraction of Union authorities.

Meanwhile, though the President had not been able to ignore the
rumblings of the Confederate underground, he had refused to give
them any more attention than they deserved. At the time of Rose-

10 Headley, *Confederate Operations*, 230; *Offic. Rec.*, 1 ser., XLIII, pt. 2, 229–230, 932,
934.
11 Headley, *Confederate Operations*, 259–261, 274–277; *Offic. Rec.*, 1 ser., XLIII, pt.
2, 932–933; XLV, pt. 1, 1077–1079; Welles, *Diary*, II, 152; New York *Herald*, Oct. 21,
1864, p. 5, c. 4; Oct. 23, 1864, p. 5, c. 1; New York *Tribune*, Dec. 16, 1864; *Ann. Cyc.*,
1864, 588.
12 Quoted in Headley, *Confederate Operations*, 225.   13 *Offic. Rec.*, 4 ser., III, 639.

crans' warning, he had stated "in reply to Rosecrans' suggestion of the importance of the greatest secrecy, that a secret which had already been confided to Yates, Morton, Brough, Bramlette, & their respective circles of officers could scarcely be worth the keeping now," as Hay noted. Hay observed further: "He treats the Northern section of the conspiracy as not especially worth regarding, holding it as a mere political organization, with about as much of malice and as much of puerility as the Knights of the Golden Circle." [14] His calmness and sanity in that time of wild rumor and equally wild plot make a refreshing contrast to the hysteria of men like General Rosecrans, with his make-believe of mystery, and Governor Yates, with his mutterings about shooting down home traitors like dogs.

III

A month and a day after the adjournment of Congress the authors of the Wade-Davis bill replied to Lincoln's pocket veto and his proclamation with a joint statement published in the New York *Tribune*. Their "manifesto" was a most remarkable document for two so prominent Republicans to hurl at the candidate of their own party in the midst of a presidential campaign.

Mincing no words, Senator Wade and Representative Davis savagely denounced Lincoln for proceeding with his own reconstruction plan in disregard of the aims of Congress. They charged him with "grave Executive usurpation" and with the perpetration of a "studied outrage on the legislative authority." They condemned his "shadows of governments" in Arkansas and Louisiana as "mere oligarchies" and "mere creatures of his will." Referring to his "personal ambitions" and his "sinister" motives, they insinuated that his real purpose in hastening the readmission of Southern states was to assure himself of additional electoral votes. They questioned whether the Supreme Court sooner or later would not disapprove his plan. Then they turned to strong hints of immediate retaliation against him. They declared that his pocket veto—"this rash and fatal act"—had been "a blow at the friends of his Administration" as well as a blow at the "rights of humanity" and the "principles of Republican Government." He "must understand that our support is of a cause and

---

[14] Dennett, . . . *Diaries . . . of John Hay*, 192.

not of a man," and "if he wishes our support" he must "confine himself to his Executive duties" and "leave political reorganization to
Congress."[1]

Throughout the North the Wade-Davis Manifesto made sensational
news. The immediate reaction among many of the Radical Republicans was highly favorable, though Greeley himself, on publishing it,
said only that it was "a very able and caustic protest." "Better late
than never," crazy old Adam Gurowski told his diary. "Two *men* call
the people and Mr. Lincoln to their respective senses."[2] The *National
Anti-Slavery Standard* opined that the Wade-Davis bill had been well
devised (and left the implication to be drawn that Lincoln's plan had
not been) to accomplish the triple aim of eliminating slavery, forestalling traitors, and disavowing rebel debts in the reorganized states.
"We certainly shared in the general regret that the bill was not permitted to become law," the *National Anti-Slavery Standard* now observed.[3] To Wade and Davis the old abolitionist Gerrit Smith sent a
letter of congratulation, saying Lincoln had "good intentions" but
lacked "nerve" and "stern justice," and this letter was published in
John W. Forney's Philadelphia *Press*.[4]

Generally Republicans who approved the manifesto discussed the
subject of congressional and presidential relations in bitterly personal terms. In a few cases, however, they based their approval of it
on fairly sober constitutional grounds. "Our government is strictly
a government of law," one Republican paper reminded its readers.
Procedures and policies not prescribed by legislation but laid down
by arbitrary executive action were "alien and repugnant" to the
Constitution, the *Evening Post* went on. Congressmen were entitled
to protest when the President, at his own whim, "put aside action of
Congress" and "left the restoration of the rebel states to their proper
place in the Union wholly unprovided for, except by methods which
the Executive might think proper to dictate."[5]

Some conservative Republicans came wholeheartedly to the Presi-

---

1 New York *Tribune,* Aug. 5, 1864; *Ann. Cyc.,* 1864, 307–310.

2 Gurowski, *Diary, 1863–1864,* 309–310.

3 Quoted in the New York *Times,* Aug. 13, 1864, p. 3, c. 4.

4 Smith to Wade and Davis, Aug. 8, 1864, Philadelphia *Press,* Aug. 17, 1864, p. 2,
c. 4.

5 New York *Evening Post,* Aug. 6, 1864. Welles listed the *Evening Post* as one of the
"Administration journals" in New York. Welles, *Diary,* II, 104 (Aug. 13, 1864).

dent's defense. The New York *Times*, edited as it was by Lincoln's campaign manager, Henry J. Raymond, deplored the "ultra radicalism and barbarism" of "these gentlemen," Wade and Davis. They were dangerous revolutionaries, the *Times* alleged. "They have sustained the war not as a means of restoring the Union, but to free the slaves, seize the lands, crush the spirit, destroy the rights and blot out forever the political freedom of the people inhabiting the Southern States." [6] A Buffalo newspaper saw the issue as one of patronage, not revolution. "It is suggested that if Mr. Lincoln had granted Winter Davis what he modestly asked a year ago—the control of all the military and civil appointments for Maryland—Winter wouldn't have issued his protest." [7]

"As President of the United States he must have sense enough to see and acknowledge he has been an egregious failure," was the moral that James Gordon Bennett's New York *Herald* drew on the day after the publication of the protest in the rival *Tribune*. "One thing must be self-evident to him, and that is that under no circumstances can he hope to be the next President of the United States." [8] The Democratic New York *World* observed: "Wade's charge amounts to an impeachment, and may be followed by one." [9]

Among members of Lincoln's cabinet the protest aroused as much alarm as it did rejoicing in extreme Radical circles. Welles assumed that Wade had been motivated by presidential aspirations of his own.[10] J. P. Usher, the secretary of the interior, noted that, except for Chase, everyone in the cabinet had approved the President's amnesty proclamation. Usher thought that Wade and Davis were seeking to "gratify their malignity" at the expense of Republican success in the election. Lincoln, he wrote, had tried to "oblige this class of men," had given them little "cause & reason to assail him," but they were unappeasable and would never be satisfied.[11] Montgomery Blair saw them as enemies of the Union and the administration, which had to face Jefferson Davis, R. E. Lee, and the rebels on one side and

---

6 New York *Times*, Aug. 18, 1864, p. 4, c. 3; Williams, *Lincoln and the Radicals*, 325.

7 Buffalo *Morning Express*, Aug. 24, 1864.

8 New York *Herald*, Aug. 6, 1864, p. 4, c. 3.

9 Quoted in Washington *Constitutional Union*, Aug. 13, 1864, p. 2, c. 1.

10 Welles, *Diary*, II, 95–96.

11 Usher to R. W. Thompson, Aug. 14, 1864, MS., Lincoln Nat'l Life Foundation, Fort Wayne, Ind.

"Henry Winter Davis & Ben Wade and all such hell cats on the other." [12]

Seward read the manifesto to Lincoln on the night of August 5, and the President (as a state department visitor heard the next day, apparently from Seward himself) commented: "I would like to know whether these men intend openly to oppose my election—the document looks that way." [13] Not long afterward he said to Noah Brooks: "To be wounded in the house of one's friends is perhaps the most grievous affliction that can befall a man." He felt that he had done his best to meet the wishes of Wade and Davis while also keeping in mind his "whole duty to the country." Their bill, however, seemed to him like the bed of Procrustes: "if a man was too short to fill the bed he was stretched; if too long, he was chopped off"; and if any state "did not fit the Wade-Davis bedstead, so much the worse for the State." Grieved though he had been by the passage of the bill, the President was even more distressed by the manifesto, "so needless" and "so well calculated to disturb the harmony of the Union party," as Brooks reported, doubtless expressing Lincoln's attitude as well as his own. [14]

IV

Lincoln had guessed right about the intentions of Davis and Wade when he suspected that these men meant openly to oppose his re-election. Their "protest" was, in fact, the first public sign of a move to replace him as the Republican candidate in mid-campaign. Davis soon was circulating among prominent party men, for their signatures, a paper calling for a new national "Union" or "Peoples" convention to meet in September and nominate another candidate. This document, said to be a "powerful arraignment" of the administration's "shortcomings in the conduct of the war," demanded the nomination and election of a President who could and would "save the country from anarchy and rebellion." [1] If the "call" gained the support of enough politicians, it was to be brought out into the open at a suitable time.

---

[12] J. K. Herbert to B. F. Butler, Aug. 6, 1864, *Private and Official Correspondence of Gen. Benjamin F. Butler during the Period of the Civil War*, V, 8–9.

[13] *Ibid.*   [14] Brooks, *Washington in Lincoln's Time*, 170–171.

[1] Albany *Journal*, Aug. 12, 1864, p. 1, c. 4; Washington *Constitutional Union*, Aug. 16, 1864, p. 1, c. 5.

Once launched, the movement was directed (in so far as it had any central direction) by a secret council of party leaders who met on August 14 and from time to time thereafter in New York. The chief conspirators included not only such chronic dissidents as Davis and Greeley, but also the Mayor of New York, George Opdyke; the prosperous merchant, David Dudley Field; and the president of the New York Bank of Commerce and treasurer of the Union (i. e., Republican) National Committee, John Austin Stevens.[2] Among other schemers were three outstanding Massachusetts politicians: Senator Sumner, Governor Andrew, and General Butler. Chase was expected to co-operate, and so were Seward's friend Weed and Lincoln's campaign manager Raymond. As the project attracted both numbers and respectability, it developed into something far more serious than a mere gesture of Lincoln haters and party irresponsibles.

What gave it sense, during those dark days of August, was the seeming hopelessness of Lincoln's chances for re-election in the fall. Republican politicians gloomily assured one another that the people would have no more of him. "Among the masses of the people a strong reaction is setting in, in favor of the Democrats & against the war," said one. "I have been among the mechanics, and the high prices . . . are driving them to wish a change."[3] Said another, in upstate New York: "It is certainly true that in this region the President has lost amazingly within a few weeks, and if the public sentiment here affords a fair indication of the public sentiment throughout the country, the popular suffrage today would be 'for a change.' "[4] And still another wrote: "Things in a political way do not look so favorable as they did some time ago. Pennsylvania, New York, and all the New England States are getting down on *Old Abe* as they call him."[5] Many others found, or thought they found, that Republican voters were "utterly spiritless,"[6] were "sick and dispirited,"[7] were

---

[2] The New York *Sun,* June 30, 1889, p. 3, published a collection of documents illustrating the "secret movement to supersede Abraham Lincoln in '64." Actually, the movement was not entirely secret, since news of it was given in contemporary newspapers, such as those cited in the footnote above.

[3] A. Brisbane (Buffalo, N.Y.) to H. Greeley, Aug. 2, 1864, Greeley MSS., N. Y. Pub. Lib.

[4] G. Martindale (Rochester, N.Y.) to Butler, Aug. 16, 1864, *Private and Official Correspondence of Gen. Benjamin F. Butler during the Period of the Civil War,* V, 54–55.

[5] G. C. Rice to E. B. Washburne, Aug. 14, 1864, Washburne MSS., Lib. of Cong.

[6] Schurz, *Reminiscences,* III, 102.

[7] J. W. Grimes to C. H. Ray, Aug. 3, 1864, Ray MSS., Huntington Lib.

completely apathetic,[8] and would either stay away from the polls or mark their ballots for Frémont or for the Democratic candidate. To some Republican leaders it seemed hardly worth while to bother with campaigning for Lincoln. Senator Grimes, of Iowa, wondered whether Senator Trumbull, of Illinois, would take the stump. "There was not a very great inclination among Senators to do so when I left Washington," Grimes believed.[9]

Who, if not Lincoln, could inspirit Republicans, unite the party, and salvage victory on election day? On this question the malcontents disagreed. Davis himself was said to favor some man like Charles Francis Adams,[10] but most of the others preferred a military man like General Grant or, if he was unavailable, then some lesser general like Sherman, Hancock, or Butler.[11] Grant, endorsing the re-election of Lincoln, refused to allow himself to be made a rallying point for political opposition to his commander-in-chief. Butler however, was willing enough, as always. To Andrew's friends he was unacceptable, but to Wade he appeared available enough. To his wife, to his admirer J. K. Herbert, and to some men on his staff Butler seemed an ideal candidate—indeed, to one of them, he was "the greatest Intelligence on this continent." The Butler men visited and corresponded with dissaffected politicians to boom the general's cause, while their hero himself remained discreetly at Fort Monroe, until late in August, when he visited his home in Lowell and conferred with politicians in New York on the way back.[12]

The leaders of the anti-Lincoln movement disagreed on questions of tactics as well as personnel. Some of them wished to go ahead with a new nomination regardless of Lincoln's attitude. Others, like Sumner, were willing to proceed only if Lincoln first could be induced voluntarily to resign as the party's candidate.[13] Most of them came to agree that both Lincoln and Frémont should withdraw, so that the followers of both could reunite behind a single nominee, who might be expected also to attract many of the War Democrats if the Demo-

---

[8] D. Dickinson to S. Cameron, July 26, 1864, Cameron MSS., Lib. of Cong.

[9] Grimes to Ray, Aug. 3, 1864, Ray MSS., Huntington Lib.

[10] W. J. Gordon to S. J. Tilden, Aug. 25, 1864, Tilden MSS., N. Y. Pub. Lib.

[11] Albany Statesman, quoted in Baltimore Daily Gazette, Aug. 23, 1864, p. 2, c. 1.

[12] Louis Taylor Merrill, "General Benjamin F. Butler in the Presidential Campaign of 1864," Miss. Valley Hist. Rev., XXXIII, 558–562.

[13] Sumner to Andrew, Aug. 24, 1864, Andrew MSS., Mass. Hist. Soc.

cratic party, at its forthcoming convention, should choose a peace man or a peace platform.

Frémont indicated his willingness to consider the plan when he replied to an appeal from six Bostonians. "You must be aware of the wide and growing dissatisfaction, in the republican ranks, with the Presidential nomination at Baltimore; and you may have seen notices of a movement, just commenced, to unite the thorough and earnest friends of a vigorous prosecution of the war in a new convention which shall represent the patriotism of all parties," the six had written. "Permit us, sir, to ask whether, in case Mr. Lincoln will with-draw, you will do so, and join your fellow citizens in this attempt to place the Administration on a basis broad as the patriotism of the country and as its needs." In reply, Frémont said he could not resign his nomination without consulting the party that had nominated him at Cleveland, but he suggested that his correspondents confer with leaders of both his own and Lincoln's party, then organize a "really popular convention," one broader than factions or cliques. This exchange of letters was published on August 27.[14]

Meanwhile the proponents of a new convention found reason to believe that Lincoln also would co-operate. Lincoln's political expert Weed, his former law partner Swett, and his campaign manager Raymond all seemed to think so. After a two-hour conversation with Weed, Butler's man Herbert wrote to the hopeful general on August 11: "He says Lincoln can be prevailed upon to draw off. Swett, who I sent to Maine for, is of the same opinion." Herbert added: "Raymond says Lincoln has gone up, all we can expect of him is to get him to help choke [others] off the track." [15]

On or about that same August 11 Weed told Lincoln frankly "that his re-election was an impossibility," and he repeated this conviction in a letter of August 22 to Seward. "Mr. Swett," he added, in confirmation of his own view, "is well informed in relation to the public sentiment. He has seen and heard much." [16] While Weed was writing to Seward, Raymond wrote to Lincoln a letter detailing the hopelessness of the outlook. Said Raymond:

14 Boston *Daily Advertiser*, Aug. 27, 1864, p. 1, c. 6. The letter to Frémont was signed, by George L. Stearns, S. R. Urbino, James M. Stone, Elizur Wright, Edward Habich, and Samuel G. Howe.

15 *Correspondence of Gen. Benjamin F. Butler*, V, 67–68.

16 Weed to Seward, Aug. 22, 1864, R. T. L. Coll., 35490–91.

I feel compelled to drop you a line concerning the political condition of the country as it strikes me. I am in active correspondence with your staunchest friends in every State and from them all I hear but one report. The tide is setting strongly against us. Hon. E. B. Washburne writes that "were an election to be held now in Illinois we should be beaten." Mr. Cameron writes that Pennsylvania is against us. Gov. Morton writes that nothing but the most strenuous efforts can carry Indiana. This State [New York], according to the best information I can get, would go 50,000 against us to-morrow. And so of the rest.[17]

But neither Weed nor Raymond proposed to Lincoln, at this time, that he should step out of the presidential race. Instead, Raymond urged upon him a stratagem by which, as Raymond thought and Weed concurred, the President might yet save the day for the party and for himself. "Two special causes are assigned for this great reaction in public sentiment," Raymond explained, "—the want of military successes, and the impression in some minds, the fear and suspicion in others, that we are not to have peace *in any event* under this administration until Slavery is abandoned. In some way or other the suspicion is widely diffused that we *can* have peace with Union if we would." Now, said Raymond, the thing for Lincoln to do was to disperse these fears and suspicions with a shrewd propaganda stroke. The President should appoint a special commission *"to make* [a] *distinct proffer of peace to* [Jefferson] *Davis, as the head of the rebel armies, on the sole condition of acknowledging the supremacy of the Constitution,"* all other questions to be settled later in a convention representing the people of the states North and South. This offer, which would require no armistice, would put Davis and the Confederate government into a dilemma. If they accepted, the war would be ended and the Union saved. If, as was much more likely, they rejected the proposal, they would thereby "plant seeds of disaffection in the South" and "dispel the delusions about peace that prevail in the North." They would "unite the North as nothing since the firing on Fort Sumter" had done. "Even your radical friends could not fail to applaud it when they should see the practical strength it would bring to the common cause." [18]

In fact, however, the Radicals were most unlikely to applaud an offer of peace on the basis of Union alone, with such matters as slavery to be postponed for discussion at some later time. The Radi-

---

[17] Raymond to Lincoln, Aug. 22, 1864, R. T. L. Coll., 35478–79–80–81.　　[18] *Ibid.*

cals were pressing Lincoln in exactly the opposite direction, that is,
in the direction (to use the hackneyed phrase of the time) of a "vigorous prosecution" of the war. Some of them urged upon him a quite
different strategem by which, if he did not delay too long, he might
presumably save himself and also the Republican cause. They were
merely repeating the familiar demand that he purge his cabinet of
lukewarm advisers and replace them with "sound, energetic, reliable"
men.[19] Thaddeus Stevens, for one, called at the White House in mid-
August and tried to argue him into forming a new cabinet with
Montgomery Blair left out. Otherwise, said Stevens, party workers in
his state could not put their hearts into the campaign. Lincoln answered that he desired re-election but not on terms which would make
him a mere puppet. Returning unsatisfied to his home in Lancaster,
Stevens let it be known that he could no longer canvass for the President. "If the Republican party desires to succeed," he was heard
to say, "they must get Lincoln off the track and nominate a new
man." [20]

Lincoln was caught between extremes. The Radicals complained
because, they said, he was too friendly with Conservatives. And Conservatives "who have been acting with us," as Blair heard from a
Missouri correspondent, intended to go for the Democratic candidate
"because the President countenances the Radicals." [21]

He knew of the movement against him within his own party, as
he also knew of the consensus among political experts that his chances
of re-election were slim, at best. Yet, rather than make concessions to
the politicians who beset him on either side, he was willing to accept
defeat, if defeat must come. On August 23, the day after Raymond had
penned his pessimistic letter on "the political condition of the country," Lincoln wrote the remarkable memorandum which he folded,
pasted, and gave to his Cabinet members to endorse, sight unseen.
In it he put himself on record thus:

This morning, as for some days past, it seems exceedingly probable
that this Administration will not be re-elected. Then it will be my duty to
so co-operate with the President elect, as to save the Union between the

[19] N. G. Upshur to Butler, Aug. 12, 1864, *Correspondence of Gen. Benjamin F. Butler,*
V, 43–44.
[20] Current, *Old Thad Stevens,* 202.
[21] M. Blair to B. Able, Aug. 22, 1864, Blair MSS., Lib. of Cong.

election and the inauguration; as he will have secured his election on such ground that he can not possibly save it afterwards.[22]

This, as Lincoln was to recall after the election, was at a time "when as yet we had no adversary, and seemed to have no friends." [23] The Democratic convention was six days away. Even when defeat seemed most probable, however, Lincoln had not quite abandoned hope. Earlier he had been reported as saying that the people blamed him for Grant's failure to take Richmond, and that he knew as well as anyone that he was going to be *"badly beaten"*—unless "some great change" occurred in the military situation.[24] Pessimistic though he became, he still counted on that great change. "Lincoln said," according to a letter of August 26, citing a recent White House visitor, "the public did not properly estimate our military prospects, results of which would change the present current," but he himself "relied on this confidently." [25]

V

The gloomier the Republicans became, the more hopeful the Democrats had reason to be as they looked ahead to the meeting of their own nominating convention, scheduled for the unprecedentedly late date of August 29, in Chicago. They ran the risk, however, of exposing fissures in their own party as wide and deep as any in administration ranks. To win, they must unite, War Democrats with Peace Democrats. "The greatest danger of Mr. Lincoln's succeeding in another term of office, whether by fair or foul means, and thus dragging our poor country still deeper down his road to Ruin seems to consist in the . . . possible division of the Democratic Party," one worried Democrat believed. Unless the Democrats could agree upon a popular candidate and a "people's" platform, they must expect a second and possibly a third term for the man in the White House—"another four years, *or more,* of Lincolnism." [1]

The pre-convention favorite was the erstwhile hero of the Army of the Potomac, General George Brinton McClellan. Would Mc-

---

[22] *Collected Works*, VII, 514.   [23] *Ibid.*

[24] Herbert to Butler, Aug. 11, 1864, *Correspondence of Gen. Benjamin F. Butler,* V, 35–37.

[25] H. A. Tilden to S. J. Tilden, Aug. 26, 1864, Tilden MSS., N. Y. Pub. Lib.

[1] W. R. Skidmore to W. Kelly, Aug. 18, 1864, Tilden MSS., N. Y. Pub. Lib.

Clellan run? "It is very doubtful whether anything would now induce me to consent to have my name used," he wrote as late as June 25.[2] But he must run, the War Democrats told one another. Only he could "control any large portion of the army vote in the field and at home"; only he could "prevent the use of the army by Mr. Lincoln" to deprive the opposition of free expression at the polls.[3] McClellan was not the choice, however, of such party leaders as Vallandigham, Pendleton, and Wood. These men stood to gain by the long delay in the opening of the convention. "The democrisy have postponed their convenshun till it is ascertained how Lee *agt* Grant comes out," explained Petroleum V. Nasby, one of Lincoln's favorite humorists. "Ef Lee whales Grant—Peace Platform." [4] And the Ohio Congressman S. S. Cox grew "really mortified, vexed, and discouraged" at the postponement, which he feared would give the extreme peace men a chance to "dirk" McClellan. Cox thought there was "no denying that since Grant's failure or seeming failure," there had been "an increase of the peace sentiment—irrespective of consequences." [5]

Some Republican as well as Democratic politicians believed that McClellan, if nominated, could beat Lincoln in the campaign. During the darkest days of July and August the Blairs, Cameron, and others toyed with a stratagem for nullifying the general's supposed popularity or converting it into an administration asset. Here was another of those last-minute schemes for salvaging Lincoln's chances. In pursuance of it the elder Frank Blair called upon McClellan in New York, about July 20, and told him he would be restored to command if he would disavow any presidential aspirations he might have. McClellan was noncommittal.[6] When Blair returned to Washington the President listened to him without comment, though, according to Frank Blair, Jr., the President himself "had concluded with Genl Grant to bring again into the field as his adjunct Gen McClellan if he turned his back on the proposals of the peace junto at Chicago." [7]

---

2 McClellan to Manton Marble, June 25, 1864, Marble MSS., Lib. of Cong.

3 S. L. Barlow to Manton Marble, Aug. 21, 1864, Marble MSS.

4 Buffalo *Morning Express*, Aug. 26, 1864, p. 2, c. 4.

5 Cox to Manton Marble, June 20, 1864, Marble MSS.

6 Smith, *Blair Family*, II, 280–281.

7 F. P. Blair, Jr., to the editor of the *National Intelligencer*, Oct. 15, 1864, Blair MSS., Lib. of Cong.

Despite the failure of Blair's mission, some Republicans continued to hope that Lincoln might appease McClellan and the War Democrats.[8] On August 26 Cameron was reported as having recently said that Lincoln could not win against McClellan and so was "disposed to be friendly" toward him. "He [Cameron] also says, which is even more important, that Lincoln told him last week that if McClellan was not nominated he should at once appoint him to his 'old place.' Whether he means in command of the army of the Potomac, or in Hallecks place I do not know." [9]

Nothing came of all this, except for some campaign propaganda later on,[10] and McClellan still led all contenders when the Democratic convention finally met. The delegates disposed of their business within a remarkably few days. Vallandigham, dominating the resolutions committee, saw to it that the platform denounced the war and declared for an early peace, though he insisted that a "dishonorable peace" was not to be considered. "Whoever charges that I want to stop this war in order that there may be Southern independence and a separation," he declared, "charges that which is false, and lies in his teeth, and lies in his throat!" [11] The key plank, as reported and adopted, read in part: ". . . after four years of failure to restore the Union by experiment of war . . . justice, humanity, liberty, and the public welfare demand that immediate efforts be made for a cessation of hostilities, with a view to an ultimate convention of the states, or other peaceable means, to the end that at the earliest practicable moment peace may be restored on the basis of the Federal Union of the States." After the adoption of the platform, McClellan was nominated on the first ballot. Then, unexpectedly, and as another sop to the peace faction, Pendleton was selected as his running mate.

These Chicago proceedings had the close attention of the politician in the White House. His secretary Nicolay gave instructions: "Save all the Chicago papers so that we may have a full report of the convention." [12] His journalist friend Brooks attended the convention

---

[8] J. D. Kellogg to S. Cameron, Aug. 6, 1864, Cameron MSS., Lib. of Cong.

[9] S. L. Barlow to Manton Marble, Aug. 26, 1864, Marble MSS.

[10] See Washington *Daily National Intelligencer*, Oct. 3, 1864, p. 3, c. 1; Oct. 20, 1864, p. 2, c. 4; Oct. 21, 1864, p. 3, c. 1.

[11] Cincinnati *Daily Commercial*, Aug. 27, 1864.

[12] Nicolay to Mr. Neill, MS., Lib. of Cong.

and, "agreeably to the expressed wish of the President," sent back letters in which he gave facts and insights which the newspapers overlooked. In one of his letters Brooks reported that, at every stop west of Pittsburgh, crowds "attracted by the music and the cannon on our train" were "blindly and ignorantly bawling for 'Peace.' " In Chicago most of the delegates were similarly peace-minded, even though the majority of them clearly favored the war man, McClellan. The Democrats seemed confident as they began their work. "These men are making the most of our own dissensions and have published as a campaign document the Wade-Davis manifesto . . . ," Brooks wrote. "These things create a great deal of despondency among our own people, of course, and many of the weak-kneed already predict defeat and disaster . . . ." In a second letter, written from Dixon, Illinois, after the adjournment of the convention, Brooks was able to report a more optimistic spirit among Republicans. First, he detailed the complicated deals to which the Democrats had had to resort in completing their work, and he made clear the bitter intra-party feeling which nevertheless persisted. He had gathered from Democrats themselves that "McClellan's nomination was made for the soldiers' vote, which, they think, will be the decisive power in the next election," and that only this consideration had enabled Vallandigham to "swallow the bitter pill, which he did with a very ill grace." Finally Brooks noted: "Our people hereabouts are confident and hopeful. The nomination has already served to unite them, and I feel more encouraged than when I left Washington." [13]

Another observer, in not-so-distant Naperville, got a very different impression of the reaction among Illinois Republicans. "Since I came home," this man wrote to Senator Trumbull, "I learn of a number who have been, *and are*, Republicans, who have been supposed to be all right for Lincoln, who declare, since the Chicago Nomination, that as between Lincoln and McClellan, *they are for McClellan*." [14] But Lincoln heard directly from Governor Dennison, in Columbus, Ohio: "The Chicago nominations are welcomed with no enthusiasm here, nor, so far as I can learn, anywhere in the State." [15] And he heard from Henry Wilson, in Natick, Massachusetts, that the nomination

---

[13] These letters were dated Aug. 29 and Sept. 2, 1864. R. T. L. Coll., 35638–39 and 35828–29.
[14] G. Marton to Lyman Trumbull, Sept. 2, 1864, Trumbull MSS., Lib. of Cong.
[15] Dennison to Lincoln, Sept. 2, 1864, R. T. L. Coll., 35833–34.

had aroused "our friends" to action and that they were now "fighting up in New England." [16]

Whether or not it served to unite and inspirit Republicans, the Chicago convention had the effect of exacerbating the factional quarrel among the Democrats. They had nominated McClellan because of his war record but had provided a peace platform for him to run upon. Now they would be handicapped by a fundamental contradiction in their position—unless McClellan somehow could resolve their dilemma for them.

In composing his letter of acceptance he faced that impossible task. The issue between the factions of his party was not one of peace *or* union, since even Vallandigham insisted that no cessation of hostilities should be considered on the basis of a separation of the states. The question was, which should come first—union, or peace? Vallandigham and his followers desired an armistice without prior stipulations in regard to reunion; they took it for granted that reunion would follow. The other faction demanded that reunion be made a precondition of any cease-fire agreement. For days, prominent men of both groups pelted McClellan with contradictory advice. On the one hand, August Belmont, the Prussian-born New York banker who was chairman of the Democratic National Committee, told him he must stand squarely and unequivocally upon Union ground.[17] On the other hand, Vallandigham urged him not to listen to his Eastern friends, not to "*insinuate* even a little war" into his letter of acceptance, lest he lose at least a hundred thousand votes in the West.[18] Thus beset, McClellan wavered as he drafted and redrafted his letter. For a time he seemed willing to accept an armistice even at the risk of disunion. At last, in the fourth and final version, dated September 8, he came out for union as the prerequisite of peace.[19]

The publication of his letter provoked new disagreements within his party, setting the separate factions to quarreling among themselves. Some of the peace men desired to repudiate him and reas-

---

[16] Wilson to Lincoln, Sept. 5, 1864, R. T. L. Coll., 35963–64.

[17] Belmont to McClellan, Sept. 3, 1864, cited by Charles R. Wilson, "McClellan's Changing Views on the Peace Plank of 1864," *Amer. Hist. Rev.*, XXXVIII, 503.

[18] Vallandigham to McClellan, Sept. 4, 1864, McClellan MSS., Lib. of Cong.

[19] Wilson, *Amer. Hist. Rev.*, XXXVIII, 498–505. McClellan's biographer William Starr Myers is "not able to agree entirely" with Wilson that McClellan "really wavered." Rather, "he merely was trying shrewdly to meet the *political* necessities of the campaign, but without any compromise of principle." Myers, *McClellan*, 455 n.

semble the convention for nominating a new candidate.[20] Others preferred to make the most of a bad situation by endorsing him, acceptance letter and all. The Ohio Sons of Liberty, in a meeting at Columbus on September 12, decided by a majority of only two to adhere to the ticket as it was.[21] George N. Sanders, the Confederate agent in Canada, assured Benjamin Wood, a New York Peace Democrat, that the peace plank would be binding on McClellan, no matter what he had said in his acceptance letter. "Genl McClellan has accepted the nomination," Sanders said, "and he cannot as an honorable man, and will not, reject a suspension of hostilities and a convention of the states; so clearly marked out, and required by the platform." [22]

At least a few of the War Democrats declined to support McClellan for the same reason that Sanders urged Peace Democrats to stay with him, namely, that he would be bound to carry out the party resolutions, even the peace plank. While McClellan's own statement was a "manly declaration," there was serious doubt "whether he would be permitted to pursue the line of policy indicated in his self-constructed platform." Lincoln often had been forced to give way to extremists within the Republican party. McClellan, if elected, would "have as violent and unreasonable men to deal with" in the Democratic party. So declared one group of War Democrats who announced their decision to vote for Lincoln.[23] Other War Democrats gave thought to the possibility of reassembling the convention and getting "Genl McClellan's letter adopted as their manifesto." [24] Still others considered calling a convention to present to the voters a new candidate as well as a new platform.[25] The party seemed about to split again, as it had done in 1860.

As September came in 1864, Democrats were bickering among themselves at least as bitterly as Republicans lately had been doing. The Democrats, too, were troubled by factious enterprises for setting aside their duly nominated candidate. Yet, though increasingly defeatist, they were not defeated. They had declared the war a failure, as conducted by the Lincoln administration, and if the news of battle

20 New York *Herald*, Sept. 11, 1864, p. 4, c. 2; Cincinnati *Daily Gazette*, Sept. 12, 1864, p. 1, c. 5.

21 Washington *Evening Star*, Sept. 15, 1864, p. 2, c. 5.

22 Sanders to Wood, Sept. 11, 1864, Tilden MSS.

23 Buffalo *Commercial Advertiser*, Oct. 5, 1864, p. 2, c. 2.   25 Bates, *Diary*, 421.

24 D. E. Sickles to Dem. Union Club, N. Y., Sept. 19, 1864, Sickles MSS., N. Y. Pub. Lib.

should continue to bear them out, they could expect success on election day. In this sense bad news would be good news for them. But not for Lincoln.

VI

Focusing most of their attention on the fortunes of the Army of the Potomac, the Northern people during the summer of 1864 kept looking for news that Grant had taken Richmond. They were inclined to measure Federal success or failure in terms of this objective, and hence their growing pessimism as the August days went by. They might and did read reports of victories by the Union Navy, but these alone were not enough to change the Northern temper, so long as Grant still faced an undefeated Lee. Finally, before the summer's end, news came of land engagements which, in outcome, seemed so spectacularly favorable to the Union cause that Northerners at last began to revise their hopes, even without any significant change in the opposing lines of Lee and Grant.

Early in the summer the most dramatic naval duel of the war—except, perhaps, for the duel of the *Monitor* and the *Merrimac*—was fought and won by a Union ship, the *Kearsarge,* against the most notorious and most successful of the Confederate commerce raiders, the *Alabama.* This vessel was one of those built for the Confederate Navy in a British shipyard. Its captain was the doughty sea fighter and confirmed Yankee-hater, Raphael Semmes, but its officers and men were mostly English. Roving the oceans for two years, the *Alabama* destroyed the U. S. S. *Hatteras* (one hundred tons larger than herself) and captured sixty-two merchant ships, burning or sinking most of them after taking off the persons on board. The actual destruction by this and other such raiders was only a small part of the damage done by them, for they created a hazard which raised insurance rates to prohibitive heights, caused the transfer of hundreds of ships from the American to the British flag, and helped to set the American merchant marine upon a decline lasting until the first World War. The Union cruiser *Kearsarge,* Captain John A. Winslow, finally trapped the *Alabama* in the port of Cherbourg, France, and (June 19, 1864) ended her career in a blazing fight which sent her to the bottom, leaving 26 of her complement of about 146 dead and

70 others as prisoners (the rest being taken off on a British steam yacht and a French pilot boat).[1] Gratifying though this news was to Northern hearts, it was soon overshadowed by reports of action much closer to home, by reports of Early's raid and the supposedly narrow escape of the national Capital itself.

Less than a month after Early's raid, the Navy gained another notable victory in the battle of Mobile Bay (August 5, 1864). Here Admiral David G. Farragut forced his large wooden ships, monitors, and gunboats through the difficult channel and into the bay defended by shore forts and a fleet including the famous ram *Tennessee*. The old admiral, lashed to the rigging of his flagship, the *Hartford,* damned the torpedoes and ordered full speed ahead into a fatal storm of shot and shell. He maneuvered so skillfully that the *Tennessee* failed to ram any of his vessels, and the torpedoes did little damage, though "the fire of the Confederate fleet and of Fort Morgan fell with butchering precision upon the Union decks, piling them with mangled fragments of humanity." Mobile fell, the Confederacy lost one of its few remaining ports, and the Union blockade was drawn tighter by another notch.[2] Significant though the victory was, it did not suffice to dispel the August gloom in the North nor even to lessen the effect of the Wade-Davis manifesto, published on the very same day.

The capture of Atlanta, a few weeks later, made far more glorious news than did the capture of Mobile. Atlanta was the reward for a long, strenuous, and expertly conducted campaign by General Sherman. At first he had been held in check by the defensive skill of his opponent, General Joseph E. Johnston, who had the disadvantage of an army only a little more than half as large as Sherman's but had the partly conmpensating advantage of a rough and mountainous terrain. "His resistance to Sherman was comparable to Lee's performance in delaying Grant." In mid-July, however, the Confederate war department, disliking his Fabian tactics, replaced him with the less cautious J. B. Hood, who promptly exposed his army to unequal battle. Hood had to withdraw to Atlanta and then (September 1, 1864) had to evacuate the city. The next day Sherman occupied it. The effect of this news, immediately and throughout the North, would be hard to exaggerate.[3] "The good news from Atlanta has set the

---

[1] Randall, *Civil War and Reconstruction,* 587–590.   [2] *Ibid.,* 592–593.
[3] *Ibid.,* 551–554.

people wild," General Butler, stopping in New York on September 5, wrote to his wife in Massachusetts.[4]

After a few weeks more, news almost as cheering came from the Shenandoah Valley in Virginia. There, after Early's retreat from Washington, Grant had sent his ablest cavalry commander, Sheridan, to dispose of Early and devastate the farmland which comprised the chief Confederate granary. In a campaign of quick movement and sharp fighting, with frequent costly engagements, Sheridan outpointed Early in the battles of Winchester (September 19, 1864) and Fisher's Hill (September 22), then drove him southward up the Valley. A little later, returning from Washington after consulting with Halleck and Stanton, Sheridan was to make the ride that became famous in song and story.[5] Already his exploits, coming as they did on top of Sherman's occupation of Atlanta, were enough to convince many of the Northern people that the tide of the war was turning fast. To some of them, the battle of Winchester alone seemed like an "overwhelming defeat for the rebs." [6]

VII

While McClellan was being nominated and Atlanta was about to fall, the anti-Lincoln movement within the Republican party reached a climax. On August 30 a council of the malcontents in New York concluded that it was "useless and inexpedient" to run Lincoln "against the blind infatuation of the masses in favor of McClellan." They agreed to call a new convention, which was to meet in Cincinnati on September 28 "and, if need be, to nominate some candidate who can unite the entire loyal vote." [1] Before publishing the call, however, they decided to reassure themselves that Lincoln's prospects were indeed hopeless. To all the Republican governors they dispatched copies of a circular letter—signed by Horace Greeley, Parke Godwin, and Theodore Tilton—inquiring whether the governors could carry their respective states for Lincoln and whether he could be elected or whether another candidate should be nominated.

"The fall of Atlanta puts an entirely new aspect upon the face of

4 *Correspondence of Gen. Benjamin F. Butler*, V, 125.
5 Randall, *Civil War and Reconstruction*, 569–570.
6 J. Galt to E. B. Washburne, Sept. 23, 1864, Washburne MSS., Lib. of Cong.
1 George Wilkes to E. B. Washburne, Aug. 31, 1864, Washburne MSS., Lib. of Cong.

affairs," a New Yorker who professed to be a student of public opinion said on September 3, just three days after he had insisted that Lincoln had no chance and should withdraw.[2] "If you want to know who is going to vote for McClellan," the Albany *Journal* suggested, also on September 3, "mention Atlanta to them. The long face and the low muttered growl is sufficient. On the other hand, every Lincoln man bears a face every lineament of which is radiant with joy." [3] The war now seemed to be a success, yet the Chicago platform of the Democrats called it a failure. Disaffected Republicans were beginning to admit to one another that the Chicago platform had made Lincoln's re-election possible and McClellan's defeat necessary.[4] As Sumner put it, "Lincoln's election would be disaster, but McClellan's damnation." [5]

The governors had a chance to read the war news before they replied to the letter of Greeley, Godwin, and Tilton. Governor Yates, in his reply, declared that the re-election of Lincoln was a "strong probability," that Illinois could be carried for him and "not for any other man," and that any substitution would be "disastrous": "It is too late to change now." [6] Yates sent copies of his own letter to the other governors.[7] Governor Andrew was less positive and enthusiastic. He feared that, with a candidate like Lincoln, "essentially lacking in the quality of leadership," the party could not be so certain of success as it could be "under the more energetic influence of a positive man, of clear purpose and more prophetic nature." Nevertheless, said Andrew, "Massachusetts will vote for the Union cause at all events and will support Mr. Lincoln so long as he remains its candidate." [8]

The war news, together with the opinions of the governors, caused the arch-plotters in New York to abandon their project for a new convention within a week after deciding to go ahead with it. On September 5 they held their last council meeting, most of them agreeing that

---

[2] H. H. Elliott to G. Welles, Sept. 3, 1864, Welles MSS., Lib. of Cong.

[3] Albany *Journal*, Sept. 3, 1864, p. 2, c. 2.

[4] W. Dennison to Lincoln, Sept. 2, 1864, R. T. L. Coll., 35833–34; Anna E. Dickinson to "My dear friend," Sept. 3, 1864, Dickinson MSS., Lib. of Cong.; C. Sumner to F. Lieber, Sept. 3, 1864, Pierce, *Memoirs and Letters of Charles Sumner*, IV, 198; G. W. Julian to Sumner, Sept. 4, 1864, Sumner MSS., Widener Lib.; B. F. Butler to Mrs. Butler, Sept. 5, 1864, *Correspondence of Gen. Benjamin F. Butler*, V, 125; Henry Wilson to Lincoln, Sept. 5, 1864, R. T. L. Coll., 35963–64.

[5] Lillie B. Chace to Anna E. Dickinson, Sept. 19, 1864, Dickinson MSS.

[6] Yates to Greeley *et al.*, Sept. 6, 1864, Mass. Hist. Soc. *Proceedings*, LXIII, 86–87.

[7] James Conkling to Lincoln, Sept. 6, 1864, R. T. L. Coll., 35983–84.

[8] Andrew to Greeley *et al.*, Sept. 3, 1864, Andrew MSS., Mass. Hist. Soc.

recent developments had made it "the duty of all Unionists to present a united front." [9] On the same day Tilton wrote to Andrew: *"The Tribune* and *The Independent* [Tilton's own paper], and I suppose *The Post* also, will take the ground that all the Republican forces ought to rally round the Baltimore platform & candidates (not because these candidates are the best) but because we cannot afford to run the risk, by division, of giving a victory to the outrageous principles put forth at Chicago." [10] A few days later Seward heard from Weed: "The conspiracy against Mr. Lincoln collapsed on Monday last." [11]

The state elections in Vermont and Maine, held during the second week in September, seemed to confirm the belief that Lincoln would have a good chance to win in November. The New York *Herald* had conceded that, if the Republicans should carry those states, McClellan would have little if any chance. And the Republicans did carry both states, by majorities considerably larger than in the previous elections.[12]

Even after these returns were in, a few diehards among the malcontents still wanted and thought they could get a new candidate. Sumner, for one, "had not quite given up the hope that someone else might be substituted for Lincoln." [13] George Wilkes, fanatic editor of the *Spirit of the Times,* remained reluctant to abandon the proposed convention and, unlike Sumner, continued to think that Lincoln should be forced to retire. Winter Davis, he informed Butler on September 15, would send a delegation to Cincinnati, and so would others. But, Wilkes went on, even if the convention plan should fail, mass meetings could be held in every state, and these, "as a *dernier resort,"* could denounce Lincoln and endorse another man, presumably Butler. "I confess, however, the prospect now looks very slim." Greeley, said Wilkes, was deserting the cause, and so was John Austin Stevens, one

---

[9] Tilton to Anna E. Dickinson, Sept. 5, 1864, Dickinson MSS.

[10] Tilton to Andrew, Sept. 5, 1864, Andrew MSS.

[11] Weed to Seward, Sept. 10, 1864, R. T. L. Coll., 36155–56. Weed now attempted to dissociate himself entirely from the conspiracy, writing: "It was equally formidable and vicious, embodying a larger number of leading men than I supposed possible. Knowing that I was not satisfied with the President, they came to me for co-operation, but my objection to Mr. L. is that he has done too much for those who now seek to drive him out of the Field."

[12] New York *Herald*, Sept. 2, 1864, p. 4, c. 2; Sept. 15, 1864, p. 4, c. 2.

[13] Lillie B. Chace to Anna E. Dickinson, Sept. 19, 1864. Dickinson MSS.

of the original arch-plotters.[14] Indeed, Stevens soon gave up the movement as dead and pronounced an autopsy on it. The replacement of
Lincoln, he said on September 19, had become an impossibility because of "the outrage to the nation offered at Chicago, the glorious
result of the Georgia campaign, the steady attitude of Vermont and
the vote of Maine." [15]

All along, loyal Republican politicians had kept the President well
informed of the plot against him. He had watched it rise and grow
and die down, without his having to lift a hand to appease anybody.
No longer did he need to fear that dissident Republicans might put
up a new rival candidate. One rival, however, was already in the
field, and that of course was Frémont. Some of the Radical leaders,
Wade and Davis among them, though not intending to campaign for
Frémont, remained unwilling to come out for Lincoln. "You must lose
no time in the work of putting all our friends in the fight," Henry
Wilson advised the President. Wade and Davis in particular "should
be brought in if possible," Wilson said, so as to "take the force" out of
their late manifesto.[16] But Wade and Davis and others like them would
probably go on sulking unless Lincoln should make a gesture toward
conforming with the plank in the Baltimore platform that called for
a reorganization of the cabinet. Chase had gone: Blair must go.

VIII

Finally, on September 22, Frémont announced his withdrawal from
the presidential race. The next day Lincoln requested and received
Blair's resignation from the cabinet. This conjuncture has given rise
to a story that the President, to insure his re-election, had made a
"bargain" with Frémont. "To prevent almost certain defeat," the
biographer of the Blairs has written, "he entered into a bargain with
the Frémont Radicals, they to support the Union National ticket in
exchange for the decapitation of Postmaster-General Blair." [1] Some
historians, including Frémont's biographer, have questioned the
bargain story, and one of Lincoln's biographers has dismissed it as a

---

[14] Wilkes to Butler, Sept. 15, 1864, *Correspondence of Gen. Benjamin F. Butler*, V,
134–135.

[15] Stevens to Andrew, Sept. 19, 1864, Andrew MSS.

[16] Henry Wilson to Lincoln, Sept. 5, 1864, R. T. L. Coll., 35963–64.

[1] Smith, *Blair Family*, II, 284.

myth.[2] To find what truth there is in it, the rather fragmentary bits of evidence must be re-examined.

The chief source for most of the accounts of the supposed Lincoln-Frémont deal is the official biography of Senator Zachariah Chandler, of Michigan, who undertook to serve as the go-between. Himself one of the most extreme Radicals, Chandler was an intimate of Wade and a friend of both Davis and Frémont, but he was also on fairly good terms with Lincoln, who allowed him to dispose of an ample share of the federal jobs in Michigan.[3]

At the end of August, according to his official biography, Chandler left home to mediate among the party factions. Stopping in Ohio, he found Wade apparently willing to take the stump for the Union cause if Lincoln would "make some sacrifices" in concession to the Radicals and if Davis was satisfied. Going on to Washington, "he obtained from the President what were practical assurances that Mr. Blair would not be retained in the Cabinet in the face of such strong opposition if harmony would follow his removal." In Baltimore he consulted Davis, who "promptly recognized the logic of the situation, and expressed his willingness to accept Blair's displacement as an olive branch and give his earnest support to the Baltimore ticket." Proceeding to New York, he "opened negotiations there with the managers of the Frémont movement," and after much delay they finally "agreed that, if Mr. Blair (whom General Frémont regarded as a bitter enemy) left the Cabinet and all other sources of Republican opposition to the Baltimore nominees were removed, the Cleveland ticket should be formally withdrawn from the field." Hastening back to Washington to see Lincoln and "ask the fulfillment of the assurances," he was "admitted to an immediate private interview with the President in preference to a great throng of visitors, and reported in detail the successful result of his labors." That was on September 22, the day the newspapers published Frémont's letter of withdrawal.[4]

This account, at certain of its significant points, is borne out by contemporary correspondence. Thus Butler's man Herbert wrote in Washington on September 3 that he had had a long conversation with

[2] Nevins, *Frémont*, II, 665; Stephenson, *Lincoln*, 507–508 n.

[3] See Winfred A. Harbison, "Zachariah Chandler's Part in the Reelection of Abraham Lincoln," *Miss. Valley Hist. Rev.*, XXII, 267–270.

[4] *Zachariah Chandler: An Outline Sketch of His Life and Public Services* (Detroit, The Post and Tribune Company, 1880), 273–276.

Chandler. "But, briefly, he is sent here by Wade and others from the west to say to Mr. L., & he & Washburn & Harlan did say to him to-day, throw overboard your Cabinet or we can't save you." Herbert added: "He is to see Mr. L. tomorrow again to get his ultimatum." [5] Presumably Lincoln's "ultimatum" sent Chandler to New York to confer with Frémont. From New York he wrote to his wife, on September 8, that Wade had disappointed him by not joining him there. "If he were here I could accomplish all I started to do but without him I fear I shall fail," Chandler complained. "The President was most reluctant to come to terms *but came* & now to be euchered is hard. I saw Frémont yesterday & shall see him again today when the matter will be decided one way or another." [6] The "terms" to which Lincoln and Chandler had come, implicit in this last sentence, were more definitely implied in the subsequent correspondence of Chandler and Wade. A week after Frémont had withdrawn, that is, on September 29, Chandler wrote to Wade and rebuked him for his non-appearance in New York. Wade replied: ". . . I did not understand that in your opinion it was essential that Frémont should withdraw from the canvass." He explained: "I mentioned that thing to you while here and that I ought to have some influence with Frémont and thought I could persuade him to withdraw, but concluded from your manner that you attached but little importance to the idea . . . ." [7] From all these interchanges, it seems safe to infer that Lincoln did agree to remove Blair on the condition that Frémont be persuaded to quit. Lincoln made a bargain, all right, at least with Chandler, or so Chandler certainly understood.

That Frémont himself entered into the bargain is not so clear, in the light of other contemporary evidence. Rather, it appears, from McClellan's correspondence, that he was more willing to make a deal with McClellan than with Lincoln. McClellan was informed, on September 20, that Frémont had authorized an agent to make whatever arrangement the Democrats considered best for themselves in regard to his withdrawing or continuing to run. [8] McClellan was told further,

[5] Herbert to Butler, Sept. 3, 1864, *Correspondence of Gen. Benjamin F. Butler,* V, 120–121.

[6] *Miss. Valley Hist. Rev.,* XXII, 273.

[7] Wade to Chandler, Oct. 2, 1864, Chandler MSS., Lib. of Cong.

[8] Charles R. Wilson, "New Light on the Lincoln-Blair-Frémont 'Bargain' of 1864," *Am. Hist. Rev.,* XLII, 71–78.

in a cipher telegram a few days later, that Chase and Wilson had promised Frémont a place in Lincoln's cabinet and the dismissal of both of the Blairs, Frank from the army as well as Montgomery from the cabinet, "if he would withdraw and advocate Lion [Lincoln]. He replied that it was an insult." [9] After his withdrawal, Frémont denied that he had been motivated either by a guarantee of Blair's removal or by promises of political favors for himself. He also insisted that his "only consideration was the welfare of the Republican party." [10] This does not seem to have been his only consideration, for, as Charles R. Wilson concludes from his study of the McClellan manuscripts, "Frémont came very close to withdrawing in favor of McClellan and the Democrats rather than in favor of [Lincoln and] the Republicans." [11]

In the public letter announcing his retirement, Frémont did not mention such a possible alternative. On the contrary, he now denounced McClellan's candidacy, though he did not quite endorse Lincoln's. He was stepping aside, he declared, "not to aid in the triumph of Mr. Lincoln" but to do his part toward "preventing the election of the Democratic candidate," which because of the Chicago platform would signify "either separation or re-establishment with slavery." He did hint, however, that he and his followers would not give Lincoln their wholehearted support unless he reformed his cabinet. "I consider," he said, "that his administration has been politically, militarily and financially a failure, and that its necessary continuance is a cause of regret to the country." [12]

Lincoln took the hint. Commenting in cabinet, the day Frémont's statement was published, he said the remark that his administration was a failure—"politically, militarily, and financially"—included at least the secretaries of state, treasury, and war, and the postmaster-general.[13] In asking, the next day, for the postmaster-general's resignation, he reminded Blair of Blair's repeated assurance that it was at his disposal whenever it would be a "relief" to him. "The time has come," Lincoln wrote. "You very well know that this proceeds from no dissatisfaction of mine with you personally or officially." [14] The inference to be drawn was that he was dissatisfied politically, and

---

[9] Fragmentary telegram from General Rosecrans, Sept. 23, 1864, McClellan MSS., Lib. of Cong.

[10] Nevins, *Frémont*, II, 665.   [11] Wilson, *loc. cit.*

[12] Quoted in Smith, *Blair Family*, II, 286.   [13] Welles, *Diary*, II, 156.

[14] Lincoln to Blair, Sept. 23, 1864, R. T. L. Coll., 36580.

Blair and his friend Welles both drew that inference. Welles believed, and Blair agreed, that Lincoln would not have yielded to the pressure for "pacifying the partisans of Frémont" if Seward and Weed had not advised him to do so. Lincoln assured Blair, however, that Washburne had recommended it, and Welles thought it strange that Lincoln should listen to such a man. "But Washburne thinks it will help the President among the Germans." [15]

If Frémont had not withdrawn, Lincoln possibly might have dismissed Blair anyhow, to conciliate such Radicals as Davis and Wade.[16] But probably not. For, if Chandler understood aright, Lincoln had come to "terms" most reluctantly and had presented the "ultimatum" that Frémont must give up if Blair was to go. To the last, he remained extremely loath to sack Blair. As he told Blair's father, not long before the dismissal, Blair was a good and true friend who should not be sacrificed for false friends.[17] The day came, however, when Lincoln apparently felt that he had to choose between imposing on the one and antagonizing the other. His decision can be criticized, as Rhodes has criticized it, as beneath the dignity of a President of the United States, though worthy of a shrewd politician.[18] Or it can be defended as Nicolay and Hay have defended it. "He felt," they wrote of Lincoln, "that it was his duty no longer to retain in his Cabinet a member who, whatever his personal merits, had lost the confidence of the great body of Republicans." [19]

IX

The sacrifice of Blair was not in vain. True, it outraged some of Blair's political friends, one of whom wrote to him to exclaim: "Great God has it come to this. That a man who is . . . Honest cannot . . . hold an office under this administration. . . . I had concluded to vote for Mr. Lyncoln but I cannot support him any longer . . . ." [1] But Blair himself loyally took the stump and doubtless won back most of those among his admirers who at first might have been tempted to stray from the Lincoln party.

15 Welles, *Diary*, II, 156–157.   16 So believes Wilson, *loc. cit.*

17 F. P. Blair, Sr., to Montgomery Blair [Sept., 1864], Blair MSS., Lib. of Cong.

18 Quoted in Smith, *Blair Family*, II, 284.

19 Nicolay and Hay, *Lincoln*, IX, 340. These authors evince a strongly anti-Blair bias in their account of the dismissal.

1 R. W. Y. to Blair, Sept. 30, 1864, Blair MSS.

As September turned to October the sulking Radicals one by one indicated a renewed optimism and a determination to carry the election for the regular candidate as well as the Radical cause. "Everybody who voted for him four years ago will vote for him now, while others, like Edward Everett, who voted against him before, will gladly range among his supporters," Charles Sumner assured a cheering crowd in Faneuil Hall on September 28.[2] Winter Davis wrote to Sumner the next day: "The Chicago platform compelled people to swallow their disgust and elect Lincoln: but," he added ominously, "will the Senate hold him to a proper responsibility & compel respect for the will of the nation . . . ?"[3] Theodore Tilton wrote to Anna E. Dickinson at the end of September: "As to politics, the field grows clearer—the prospect brightens." He confessed: "I was opposed to Mr. Lincoln's nomination; but now it becomes the duty of all Unionists to present a united front."[4] Early in October, Ben Wade assured "Brother" Chandler that Lincoln could be elected "by an overwhelming majority" and that he was "doing all for *him*" that he could have done "for a better man."[5] Ben Butler, in a public letter to Simon Cameron, averred that it was "the plain duty of every loyal man to support the election of Lincoln and Johnson."[6] Thad Stevens began to tell the Pennsylvania voters that Lincoln had risen above "the influence of Border State seductions and Republican cowardice" and would make no peace with slavery. "Let us forget that he ever erred, and support him with redoubled energy."[7]

Now, with the election hardly more than a month away, it was time for every good man to come to the aid of the party, and every good man came. At last the campaign got seriously under way.

[2] Sumner, *Works*, VIII, 68.

[3] Davis to Sumner, Sept. 29, 1864, Sumner MSS., Widener Lib.

[4] Tilton to Anna E. Dickinson, Sept. 30, 1864, Dickinson MSS., Lib. of Cong.

[5] Wade to Chandler, Oct. 2, 1864, Chandler MSS., Lib. of Cong.

[6] Cincinnati *Daily Gazette*, Oct. 5, 1864, p. 3, c. 7.

[7] Current, *Old Thad Stevens*, 203.

CHAPTER XI

RE-ELECTION

I<sup>F WE come triumphantly out of this war, with a presidential election in the midst of it," Francis Lieber wrote to Charles Sumner at the end of August, 1864, ". . . I shall call it the great-est miracle in all the historic course of events." [1] There was, indeed, something marvelous if not miraculous in the very fact that a presiden-tial election was being held, and still more in the fact that its being held was taken pretty much for granted. In all the historic course of world events, there had been few if any examples of a great people doing what the American people were now about to do. In the midst of a desperate civil war they were about to assess their leadership and, if they so decided, to change their rulers by the same orderly processes as in times of peace. If these processes, as usual, involved a certain amount of "dirty" politics, the dirt must not be allowed to obscure the shining truth that American democracy now met and surmounted one of its supreme tests of all time.

I

When, in September, the Republicans reunited themselves and began their campaign in earnest, the outcome of the election in No-vember was still far from a foregone conclusion. The polling was to be by no means a mere formality or a manipulated plebiscite, even though the administration with the powers of government at its dis-posal could powerfully influence the behavior of the people at the polls. If Lincoln, weeks ahead of time, could have foreseen the final returns, he could have spared himself much troubling of spirit.

Political forecasting, even in this present day of public opinion

---

[1] Freidel, *Francis Lieber,* 351.

polls and "scientific" sampling, is a somewhat hazardous business. In 1864 no such techniques were known. One could attempt prediction by appraising the reports of politicians with their ears to the ground, but, in the fall of 1864, the wiseacres were hearing uncertain and contradictory noises. The New York financier and Democratic leader August Belmont bet $4,000 that his state would go for McClellan; at the same time James Gordon Bennett was positive that the state would go for Lincoln, though "by a very close vote." [1] In Indiana, Republicans breathed confidence while Democrats quoted a "very shrewd politician" who regarded Lincoln's chances as *"very doubtful."* [2] As for Pennsylvania, John W. Forney gave Lincoln alternately optimistic and pessimistic estimates, Simon Cameron was consistently sanguine and Alexander K. McClure cautious most of the time, yet as late as November 1 a Democratic worker found the prospect "exceedingly encouraging"—for McClellan. [3]

If such politicians' guesses were undependable, there was in those days an indicator of election trends in several of the states which was much more reliable, even more reliable than modern samplings of public opinion seem to be. In Maine and Vermont the voters chose various state officers in September, and, by the time the national campaigning got seriously under way, these states already had gone Republican by increased majorities. In Indiana, Ohio, and Pennsylvania the state elections were to be held in October, and the results would give an even more significant indication of the voting trend— at least in those three important "October states."

On the night of October 11 Lincoln watched anxiously for the returns from Indiana and Pennsylvania, both of which balloted that day. At eight o'clock he went to the telegraph office in the war department. The place was locked, and Stanton had taken the keys upstairs, but "a shivering messenger was pacing to and fro in the moonlight over the withered leaves," and he let the President and his party in at a side door. When there was a lull in the dispatches coming in over the wires, Lincoln—as he so often did in worried moments—took a volume of Petroleum V. Nasby from his pocket and read aloud several chapters. Later the good news from Indiana became better, but the

---

1 W. O. Bartlett to Lincoln, Oct. 20, 1864, R. T. L. Coll., 37390–91.

2 G. W. Adams to Manton Marble, Sept. 21, 1864, Marble MSS., Lib. of Cong.

3 Dennett, . . . *Diaries* . . . *of John Hay*, 230; McClure, *Lincoln and Men of War-Times*, 183; G. W. Adams to Manton Marble, Sept. 20, 1864, Marble MSS.

fat reports from Pennsylvania began to be "streaked with lean." When, a few days afterward, the final returns were in, Indiana like Ohio had gone Republican by a gratifying margin but Pennsylvania by a less satisfactory one. The "wild estimates of Forney & Cameron" were not fulfilled, "but we did not expect them to be," Hay reflected.[4]

After the October elections Lincoln was by no means overconfident about his own chances in November. On October 13, again at the war department's telegraph office and writing on its stationery, he jotted down his estimate of the forthcoming electoral vote. In the Democratic column he listed the states of New York, Pennsylvania, New Jersey, Delaware, Maryland, Missouri, Kentucky, and Illinois, and tallied 114 electoral votes. In the Republican column he listed the rest of the states and got a total of 117.[5] The conclusion thus was that he probably would win—but by the very narrow majority of three in the electoral college.

Yet, even if this probable majority had been an absolutely certain one, he would not have been satisfied with it. He longed for a decisive vindication of his party and his administration, for a victory made glorious by the numbers of Republican congressmen and governors elected as well as by the size of the popular and electoral votes for himself. McClure, having talked with him just after the October returns, went away impressed with the idea that it was "of the utmost importance" to gain such a "majority on the home front" as would "give moral force and effect to the triumph." [6] At about the same time Hay told Lincoln that the defection of two such states as Indiana and Illinois would be "disastrous and paralyzing," and that, as for himself, he would be willing to sacrifice some votes in Pennsylvania if those states could be held. Lincoln, however, could approve no such sacrifice. "He said he was anxious about Pennsylvania because of her enormous weight and influence which, cast definitely into the scale, w^d close the campaign & leave the people free to look again with their whole hearts to the cause of the country." [7]

There was a device by which the President could have tried to swell his electoral vote—the device of hastening the admission of new states or the readmission of old ones before election day. In the West the

4 Dennett, . . . *Diaries* . . . *of John Hay*, 227–229.

5 Lincoln, *Collected Works*, VIII, 46.

6 McClure, *Lincoln and Men of War-Times*, 184.

7 Dennett, . . . *Diaries* . . . *of John Hay*, 229–230.

territories of Nebraska, Colorado, and Nevada had enthusiastic aspirants and sponsors for statehood. In the South the conquered states of Louisiana and Tennessee were in different stages of Lincolnian reconstruction. If a couple of states—say, Tennessee and Nevada—could be hurried into the Union, Lincoln would be assured of several additional votes in the electoral college, since Republican majorities could be counted on in both. But Lincoln himself expressed little interest in such schemes, apparently feeling that, at best, they would give him only a contrived and not a real vindication.

In Tennessee, on September 30, the military governor and vice-presidential candidate Andrew Johnson issued a proclamation setting forth plans, authorized by the constitutional convention, for the election of presidential electors in that state. A group of Tennesseans protested to Lincoln against the announced proceedings. In reply to them Lincoln, on October 20, refused to disavow what Johnson and the convention had done, and he also refused to interfere in any way.[8] The votes of Tennesseans were not to be counted in the presidential election of 1864.

Nevada was a different case. The territorial governor, James W. Nye, was eager for the territory to be made a state in time for its electoral vote to be counted, and so was his intimate friend Seward. To Lincoln's own list of probable electoral votes, someone (possibly it was Seward) added the prospective three votes of Nevada, making a total of 120 instead of 117 and a victory margin of six instead of three. If the final result should have proved as close as Lincoln had calculated, the three Nevada votes, few though they were, would have been of considerable comfort to him. So that there would be ample time to make it possible for Nevadans to vote, Congress, in response to Governor Nye's appeal, had moved the date for the territory's constitutional referendum ahead from October 11 to September 7. After the constitution had been thus early ratified, Seward was eager for Lincoln to proclaim Nevada as a state,[9] but, as Earl S. Pomeroy has written, Lincoln "was curiously slow to take advantage of the change." He refused to act until he had seen a copy of the constitution as ratified, even though he had already seen a copy as sent to him before ratification. Finally the governor telegraphed him the full text of the ratified constitution, at an expense of $4,303.27. This long telegram

---

[8] Cincinnati *Daily Gazette*, Oct. 24, 1864, p. 3, c. 7.   [9] Welles, *Diary*, II, 163–164.

was received in Washington on October 28. "Lincoln did not issue the proclamation until October 31—eight days before the election!" The oft-repeated story that the admission of Nevada was instigated by the President and was a pet project of his is, as Professor Pomeroy has shown, a fabrication put forth by the journalist Charles A. Dana.[10]

Lincoln was little concerned about the three votes of Nevada, but he was intensely interested in the twenty-six votes of Pennsylvania and the thirty-three votes of New York.

II

Lincoln once protested that he could not see personally to all the details of his campaign. "Well, I cannot run the political machine; I have enough on my hands without *that*," he wrote. "It is the *people's* business—the election is in their hands." [1]

The people and the politicians pursued the business with elaborate organization. As chairman of the Union (that is, Republican) National Committee, Henry J. Raymond provided general direction in the management of the campaign. Members of his committee, such as Simon Cameron in Pennsylvania, ran the party organization within their respective states and provided a link between the national chairman and the local workers. "We have had our County Committee appointed for some time," one of these workers informed Cameron in September, "and we are trying to have an organization in every township—so that we may hold meetings in every school district." [2] Nowhere was any prospective voter likely to escape the over-arching influence of the party hierarchy.

Supplementing the regular machinery were other campaigning groups. The Republicans in Congress set up their own Union Executive Congressional Committee consisting of three senators, headed by James Harlan of Iowa, and three representatives, headed by Elihu B. Washburne of Illinois. Lest this committee duplicate some of the work of the national committee, Raymond early sounded out Washburne on ways to "arrange matters so as not to have the two organizations go over the same ground." [3]

---

10 Earl S. Pomeroy, "Lincoln, the Thirteenth Amendment, and the Admission of Nevada," *Pac. Hist. Rev.*, XII, 366–368.

1 Hertz, *Abraham Lincoln: A New Portrait*, II, 941.

2 G. E. Minor to Cameron, Sept. 7, 1864, Cameron MSS., Lib. of Cong.

3 Raymond to Washburne, June 20, 1864, Washburne MSS., Lib. of Cong.

The Union Leagues, those secret societies which had appeared in time to serve the Republican party in 1862, were strengthened and expanded for 1864. "It is all important to the success of the Union cause," an organizer declared, ". . . that Union Leagues be established in every County, and if practicable in every Township in the District." [4] Though not so universal as the Union Leagues, there were in many localities organizations of War Democrats supporting Lincoln and Johnson, such as the War Democratic General Committee of the City and County of New York. Also active throughout the North were the Lincoln and Johnson Clubs and such miscellaneous groups as, in New York, the Young Men's Republican Union. And the Loyal Publication Society now devoted itself to electioneering.

All the various Republican organizations, in their efforts to outdo the Democrats, had enough work to keep their members fairly busy for a couple of months. They staged the usual torchlight processions, the ward rallies, the great meetings with fireworks, cannon, bells, brass bands—and speeches.[5] In the small town of Polo, Illinois, the local Republicans built a Wigwam of their own, a building over a hundred feet long, "to accommodate a crowd as well as any place west of Chicago," in which to hold their meetings during the campaign.[6]

Speakers were routed through this or that state or district in response to the appeals of local leaders. Joshua Giddings, of Ohio, went into Illinois and Wisconsin. Frederick Douglass, the famous Negro abolitionist, was steered into some areas and away from others as prejudice and prudence seemed to dictate. "I think he would do pretty well in some parts of Wisconsin," a Chicago worker informed Washburne, but "for fear that our people would be driven off by the cry of 'Nigger' and a prejudice be raised in the Southern portion of the State," he should postpone his appearance in Illinois.[7] Thaddeus Stevens not only stumped his own district in Pennsylvania but also addressed a monster rally in Philadelphia. Naturally the Democrats noted with some concern the peregrinations of Republican orators, which amounted at times to something like a mass movement. "Indi-

[4] E. H. Berry (Indianapolis) to R. W. Thompson, April 20, 1864, Lincoln National Life Foundation, Fort Wayne, Ind.

[5] See, for example, Baltimore *Sun,* Sept. 2, 1864, p. 1, c. 5; Washington *Daily Morning Chronicle,* Oct. 6, 1864, p. 1, c. 4.

[6] H. Norton to E. B. Washburne, Sept. 19, 1864, Washburne MSS.

[7] Z. Eastman to Washburne, Sept. 19, 1864, Washburne MSS.

ana has sent up a Republican cry for help!" a Hoosier Democrat exclaimed early in the campaign. "The Republicans have sent out *twenty* new speakers. *Gov. And. Johnson,* candidate for V. P. is among them." [8]

Campaign literature was distributed in such tremendous quantities and such numerous varieties that, if it was all read, the voters must have had little time for several weeks to do anything but read it—and listen to speeches. "We are now sending out from fifty to a hundred thousand documents a day," Washburne reported on September 15, when his congressional electioneering committee had scarcely begun its work. [9] Between early September and early November the Loyal Publication Society alone broadcast more than a half-million pieces of literature, mostly among the German voters of New York City. [10] The publisher of the campaign biographies of Lincoln (which Raymond had authored) and of Johnson offered the books for circulation as campaign documents at twenty dollars the hundred, a price low enough to encourage wide distribution. [11] Another publisher, Mason & Company, of Philadelphia, was ready with a Lincoln campaign songbook, "containing a number of good songs, set to the most popular tunes," the whole collection being "excellent to circulate throughout the country," and the price only "$25 per 1000 copies." [12] Oliver Ditson, of Boston, published "Liberty's Call, or Hurrah for Abe and Andy," a piece of sheet-music widely sold during the campaign. A celebrated composer, publisher, and songster of the time, James D. Gay, of Philadelphia, entertained hundreds of crowds with his "Abe Lincoln's Union Wagon" and his "Abe Lincoln's Battle Cry." [13]

The election was indeed, as Lincoln said, in the hands of the people, but despite his protestations he was not content to leave it entirely in their hands. While burdened with his duties as the country's President, he did not evade his obligations as the party's leader. He was himself the master strategist of his own campaign. He did not al-

---

[8] G. W. Adams to Manton Marble, Sept. 25, 1864, Marble MSS.

[9] Washburne to E. D. Warner, Sept. 15, 1864, Warner MSS., Illinois Historical Survey, Urbana, Ill.

[10] Freidel, *Francis Lieber,* 351–353.

[11] Derby & Miller to E. B. Washburne, Sept. 13, 1864, Washburne MSS.

[12] Mason & Co. to Simon Cameron, Oct. 15, 1864, Cameron MSS.

[13] Philip D. Jordan, "Some Lincoln Civil War Songs," *Abr. Linc. Quar.,* II, 133–134.

ways leave even the details to Raymond or Washburne or the workers in the field, many of whom reported directly to him about ordinary tactical questions. Little that went on escaped his eye, and certainly nothing of significance.

He sometimes took a hand in the management of the Republican speakers' bureau, as when he requested General John A. Logan to leave his command in Sherman's army and miss the march to the sea, in order that he might apply his talents as a colorful and persuasive stump speaker in Indiana and Illinois.[14] Apparently Lincoln also suggested to Gustav Koerner that he, as a leading German-American of Illinois, might do much good among the German voters of the Midwest. "My German friends seem to agree with me that I can do a great deal more good by not taking a prominent stand on the stump," Koerner wrote, at Belleville, Illinois, to Lincoln. "The opposition papers have already charged that I had been called home by you to the great detriment of public bussiness [sic], to regulate the Dutch, and set them right." [15]

Lincoln did not hesitate to interfere in the operations of the regular party organization when he thought they were being poorly carried on. After the somewhat disappointing results of the October election in Pennsylvania he had reason to believe, from the complaints of Pennsylvanians returning to Washington after having gone home to vote, that Cameron had "botched the canvass badly" in that state.[16] He promptly called Cameron's factional foe Alexander K. McClure from Harrisburg to Washington, discussed the Pennsylvania situation carefully with him, and requested him to devote himself to aiding the state committee. McClure objected that his own participation would antagonize Cameron, but Lincoln promised to take care of that difficulty. Two days later McClure got a letter from Cameron inviting him to join in the committee's work. From that time on, Lincoln kept in close touch with McClure and, through him, with the progress of the Pennsylvania campaign. He even sent Postmaster General Dennison to Philadelphia to talk confidentially with McClure.[17]

---

14 McClure, *Lincoln and Men of War-Times*, 83.

15 Koerner to Lincoln, Sept. 22, 1864, R. T. L. Coll., 36559–60.

16 Dennett, . . . *Diaries . . . of John Hay*, 232.

17 McClure, *Lincoln and Men of War-Times*, 184–185. In the *Collected Works*, VIII, 81, there is a telegram from Lincoln to McClure, Oct. 30, 1864: "I would like to hear from you."

WOULD-BE PEACEMAKERS

Upper left: Alexander H. Stephens, Vice President of the Confederacy.
Upper right: William H. Seward, Lincoln's Secretary of State.
Lower left: John A. Campbell, Ass't. War Secretary of the Confederacy.
Lower right: Robert M. T. Hunter, Confederate Senator from Virginia.

The three Confederates, as peace commissioners, met with Lincoln and Seward in the abortive Hampton Roads Conference of February, 1865.

This is like a Dream I once had in Illinois—

UNCLE ABE'S VALENTINE SENT BY COLUMBIA.

AN ENVELOPE FULL OF BROKEN CHAINS.

"*Now, Jeffy, when you think you have had enough of this, say so, and I'll leave off.*"—(*Vide* President's Message.)

CARTOON COMMENT FROM *LESLIE'S*

Left: A comment on Lincoln's message to Congress of Dec. 6, 1864. Lincoln, pummeling Davis, says: "Now, Jeffy, when you think you have had enough of this, say so, and I'll leave off." *Frank Leslie's Illustrated Newspaper,* Dec. 24, 1864.

Right: A comment on the House of Representatives' passage of the resolution for a thirteenth amendment, Jan. 31, 1865. *Leslie's,* Feb. 25, 1865.

"All seems well with us."—A. LINCOLN.

"CITY POINT, VA., *April —,* 8.30 A.M.

THE PEACE COMMISSION.

Flying to ABRAHAM's Bosom.

CARTOON COMMENT FROM *HARPER'S*

Left: The Confederate peace commissioners—Stephens, Hunter, and Campbell—fly to Abraham's bosom. *Harper's Weekly,* Feb. 18, 1865.

Right: Lincoln at City Point writes: "All seems well with us." This was published in the issue of *Harper's* for April 15, 1865, the day Lincoln died.

THE SECOND INAUGURATION

Chief Justice Chase administering the oath to Lincoln, March 4, 1865.
This drawing, published in *Harper's Weekly* for March 18, 1865, was made
from an Alexander Gardner photograph which has since disappeared.

In the disposal of the federal patronage Lincoln participated in the campaign more intimately and more continuously than in any other way. He did not always consult or even inform his party leaders about his use of job offers. When Senator Harlan suggested to Hay that the pro-McClellan editor James Gordon Bennett be offered a foreign mission, Hay reflected that Bennett was "too pitchy to touch" and that Lincoln probably thought so, too.[18] Yet Lincoln apparently did touch him.

Lincoln did not go out and campaign for himself: he could not have done so, of course, because of the taboo which, as late as 1864, still showed no signs of breaking down. He would not even "write a general letter to a political meeting" when requested to do so.[19] And yet, when delegations of soldiers or civilians appeared from time to time in the White House yard, he addressed them with remarks which were intended to influence the voters who heard them and the many more who read them in the newspapers. Indeed, he could scarcely have done or said anything without its having, consciously or unconsciously, some electioneering effect. He, after all, was the President and a candidate for re-election. More than that, he was himself the foremost issue of the campaign.

III

In addition to the personalities of the candidates, the issues most frequently and most thoroughly discussed during the campaign were those of Union and disunion, freedom and slavery, war and peace. These were not really discrete questions but, rather, closely intertwined themes. Nor were the differences between the two parties made entirely clear by the stump speakers, pamphleteers, and journalists on either side.

In the contest of semantics the Republicans held a distinct advantage as a result of their appropriation of the term "Union." Their official name, for the duration of the campaign, was the "National Union Party," and the word "Union" appeared prominently on their tickets and throughout their literature. Often the politicians forgot themselves, however, and reverted to the term "Republican," espe-

---

18 Dennett, . . . *Diaries* . . . *of John Hay*, 215.
19 Lincoln to I. M. Schermerhorn, Sept. 12, 1864, *Collected Works*, VIII, 2.

cially in their private correspondence, but sometimes in their public pronouncements. A Massachusetts circular calling for the formation of a "Union Club" in every town bore the heading "Headquarters, Republican State Committee." [1] Of course, the existence of a coalition ticket of Lincoln and Johnson, the latter a man of Democratic antecedents, lent some color to the Republican claim to the "Union" designation, as did the support which many War Democrats gave to the ticket. But even Lincoln, in a passing reference to it after the election, spoke of it as "the Union ticket, so called." [2]

To reinforce the implication that the Democrats, in presuming to oppose the administration, were advocates of disunion and treason, the Republicans during the campaign, as before and after it, commonly referred to them as "Copperheads," without discriminating between War and Peace factions or between innocent Sons of Liberty and actual plotters of sedition. In Indiana, Governor Morton drove home the "treason" issue by bringing about military trials of leaders of the Sons at election time. "The most ludicrous aspect of this 'secret' society," writes Kenneth M. Stampp, "was the fact that it was never able to conceal its secrets, and that, so far from aiding the Democracy, its very existence was a source of infinite satisfaction to the Republicans." [3]

The Democrats also tried to benefit from the magic in the "Union" name. At the time of the regular Democratic convention in Chicago, a group of prominent party members staged a "Union Conservative National Convention" in the same city, to denounce the Lincoln government. Later the Democrats organized a series of "Young Men's Democratic Union Clubs," whose members adopted McClellan's letter of acceptance as their manifesto.[4] Democratic speakers appealed again and again to "the friends of the Union and the Constitution." [5] A Tammany Hall broadside—printed in patriotic colors: red and blue ink on white paper—declared for the "preservation of the Union," the "perpetual Union." [6] But the Democrats were never able to identify themselves with the Union cause so convincingly as the Republicans did.

---

1 John A. Andrew MSS., Mass. Hist. Soc.   2 Nicolay and Hay, *Works*, II, 613.
3 Stampp, *Indiana Politics During the Civil War*, 241.
4 H. Liebenau and others to S. J. Tilden, Sept. 15, 1864, Tilden MSS., N. Y. Pub. Lib.
5 F. H. Churchill and others to S. J. Tilden, Sept. 1, 1864, Tilden MSS.
6 Tilden, MSS.

The Chicago Platform, which McClellan's letter could not entirely cancel, put the Democrats on the defensive. That platform, the Republicans kept insisting, "gives a silent approval of the Rebellion itself, and an open condemnation of the war waged for its suppression." [7] And many Democrats themselves feared, as one of them expressed it: "That platform will cost the Democratic party the defeat of McClellan. Tens of thousands of Republicans & War Democrats votes would have been polled for McClellan, who will now vote for Lincoln unpleasant as it may be." [8] That platform gave Republican orators golden opportunities, and they took advantage of them. "There is but one question before the country in the approaching canvass," General John A. Dix told a Philadelphia mass meeting. "Shall we prosecute the war with unabated vigor until the rebel forces lay down their arms; or shall we, to use the language of the Chicago Convention, make 'immediate efforts' for 'a cessation of hostilities,' with a view to an ultimate convention of all the States, etc." [9] General James A. Garfield, addressing a Cincinnati crowd, found apt alliteration in the names of the Democratic candidates for governor and vice president as he declaimed against those Ohioans who were "for Pugh and Pendleton, and Peace at any price." [10]

A number of Republican papers harped incessantly upon the charge that every rebel and every sympathizer with rebellion was working and praying for Lincoln's defeat. But the opposition press could quote Southern opinion to show that the Confederacy could hope for no advantage from a victory by the Democrats. "They would like peace on condition of our return to the Union, and they are fools enough to believe that a majority of the people in the Confederacy are in favor of reunion," the Richmond *Dispatch* had said, long before the campaign of 1864 began. "But they are as bitterly opposed to separation as Lincoln himself, or any of the thieves and murderers who lead his armies." [11] Robert C. Winthrop, an eloquent Boston Democrat, once a Whig friend of Daniel Webster, turned the Republican charge back upon the Republicans by insinuating that Southerners preferred Lincoln for President of the United States. "We all know that the seces-

[7] "Appeal of the National Union Committee to the People of the United States," circular dated N. Y., Sept. 9, 1864.

[8] J. W. Rathbone to Manton Marble, Nov. 4, 1864, Marble MSS.

[9] Cincinnati *Daily Gazette*, Oct. 12, 1864, p. 1, c. 3.

[10] *Ibid.*, p. 1, c. 4.   [11] Quoted in *ibid.*, Jan. 27, 1863.

sion leaders of the South . . . exulted in the election of Abraham Lincoln," Winthrop declared at a great New York "ratification" meeting, harking back to 1860, ". . . because it supplied the very fuel which was needed for kindling this awful conflagration." [12]

Democrats repeated their familiar cry that the war, as carried on by the Republican administration, was not a war for the preservation of the Union. "If Lincoln is re-elected, the war will last at least four years longer," one of their journals said. "He is waging it, sacrificing the white population of the North, to free the degraded negro slaves of the South." [13] Such Radical Republican spokesmen as Salmon P. Chase frankly avowed abolition as a leading war aim. "People are resolved on Union & Freedom & recognize in Lincoln & Johnson the representatives of these great ideas," Chase averred.[14] In Missouri, where he had gone as Lincoln's personal mediator, John G. Nicolay appealed to the quarreling factions, as he reported back to Lincoln, to patch up their differences so as to elect Republican congressmen and help "get a two-thirds vote in the House and thus be able to pass the Constitutional Amendment about Slavery." [15]

In an effort to get the labor vote, some Republicans sought to define the issue of freedom in broader terms than the mere abolition of Negro slavery. The wealthy Boston merchant J. M. Forbes urged "bringing into prominence the great Issue—*Democratic Institutions against Aristocratic ones.* Mr. Lincoln must not depend upon the rich or aristocratic classes." The party must concentrate upon "appealing to the *plain people.*" [16] One of Cameron's correspondents suggested a different approach to the laboring man. "But Pa. has a peculiar class of interests, mining, manufacturing & rail road, deeply interested in the reelection of Mr. L.," Cameron was reminded, "& a combination of which, by securing funds, & also by influencing the operatives in their employ, would secure a very decided success in the Octr election." [17] The tariff issue was the means thus to get the operatives' vote, and at least in Pennsylvania the perennial protection-

[12] Pamphlet in McClellan MSS., Lib. of Cong.
[13] Pittsburgh *Daily Post,* Sept. 9, 1864.
[14] Chase to Z. Eastman, Oct. 24, 1864, Chicago Hist. Soc.
[15] Hay to Lincoln, Oct. 18, 1864, R. T. L. Coll., 37371–76.
[16] J. M. Forbes to F. P. Blair, Sept. 18, 1864, R. T. L. Coll., 36422–23.
[17] M. Ryerson to Cameron, Sept. 10, 1864, Cameron MSS.

ist arguments were not entirely neglected during the campaign. But the Democrats outdid the Republicans in workingclass appeal. They made the most of such labor grievances as the high cost of living, which they blamed upon the Lincoln administration.[18]

Lincoln stated his own view of the interconnection between the issues of Union, freedom, and war when he was interviewed, in August, by Governor Alexander Randall and Circuit Judge John T. Mills of Wisconsin. This interview, first reported in the Grant County, Wisconsin, *Herald,* was afterward reprinted by Republican newspapers and was also circulated as a campaign broadside throughout the North. "There is no programme offered by any wing of the Democratic party but that must result in the permanent destruction of the Union," the President told his Wisconsin visitors at the Soldiers' Home. "But, Mr. President," one of them protested, "General McClellan is in favor of crushing out the rebellion by force. He will be the Chicago candidate." Then Lincoln patiently explained how "arithmetic" would prove his point. There were, he said, nearly two hundred thousand able-bodied colored men in the service of the United States, most of them under arms. "Abandon all the posts now garrisoned by black men; take 200,000 men from our side and put them into the battlefield or cornfield against us, and we would be compelled to abandon the war in three weeks." His enemies pretended, Lincoln went on, that he was carrying on the war for the sole purpose of abolition, but this was not true. "So long as I am President it shall be carried on for the sole purpose of restoring the Union. But no human power can subdue the rebellion without the use of the emancipation policy, and every policy calculated to weaken the moral and physical forces of the rebellion." [19]

When, on the evening of October 19, a group of Marylanders serenaded Lincoln at the White House, his impromptu response reinforced the standard Republican argument that a Democratic victory would mean unconditional peace with disunion and slavery. He said he believed the people were "still resolved to preserve their country and their liberty," but how they voted was their own business. "If they should deliberately resolve to have immediate peace even at the

---

18 New York *Herald,* July 26, 1864, p. 5, c. 4.

19 Clipping from Grant County *Herald* as reprinted in unidentified newspaper, R. T. L. Coll., 36047; Republican broadside, n. p., n. d.

loss of their country, and their liberty, I know not the power or the right to resist them." [20]

IV

Even those who saw little difference in issues between the two parties, asserted that there was a vast difference in the personal fitness of the two candidates for the high office of President. Partisans of both sides considered as woefully unfit the candidate they opposed. So a good deal of the campaigning consisted of sheer defamation.

Among Republicans the favorite epithets for McClellan were "traitor" and "coward," and they ransacked his military record for evidences of his craven ways and his downright villainy. In search of new scandal the zealous editor John W. Forney looked to Lincoln. "Can you tell me whether the arrest of the members of the Maryland Legislature [in 1861] was opposed by General McClellan, or whether it was recommended by him?" Forney inquired. "A single word in reply to this will enable me to complete what I think will be a most damaging article for him for to-morrow's paper." [1] But Lincoln was not the man to abet such a campaign of vilification. "I never heard him speak of McClellan in any other than terms of the highest personal respect and kindness," testified another editor, Alexander K. McClure, who spent a fair amount of time with the President during the electioneering season. "He never doubted McClellan's loyalty to the government or to the cause that called him to high military command." [2]

Lincoln was a target for even more mud than McClellan was. Lincoln was a power-mad dictator, a "scoundrel" and a "tyrant," according to indignant stump speakers, who seemed to think that his opponent would be far less dangerous in the presidency, though that opponent was a military man who once had shown some signs of a Napoleonic complex. The former Whig President, Millard Fillmore, now a McClellan supporter, admitted that he did not favor the election of "military chieftains" as a general rule, but he believed that a "military man of disinterested devotion to his country" (meaning

---

20 *Collected Works*, VIII, 52–53.

1 Forney to Lincoln, Sept. 1, 1864, R. T. L. Coll., 35800.

2 McClure, *Lincoln and Men of War-Times*, 207.

McClellan) could "do more to save it from ruin than any other" (meaning Lincoln).[3] Certainly, in the view of Democrats, Lincoln was not an indispensable man.

The Republicans did not exactly say he was, but they did advise the voters: "It is no time to change leaders when you are confronting a powerful and wily foe—'No time to swap horses in the middle of the stream.' "[4] Lincoln himself had put this "swap horses" expression into currency, when the Baltimore convention was meeting in June. And he did seem to think that, in the circumstances, his continued services were indispensable to the nation. In running for re-election he was motivated not by "personal vanity or ambition," as he told his Wisconsin visitors in the well-publicized August interview, but by "solicitude for his great country."[5]

When not denouncing him for his alleged dictatorial proclivities, the Democrats condemned him for what they considered his loutish ways. The New York *World* characterized the Lincoln-Johnson ticket as made up of "a rail-splitting buffoon and a boorish tailor, both from the backwoods, both growing up in uncouth ignorance."[6] And the New York *Herald,* while editor Bennett was still in an anti-Lincoln phase, had this to say: "Mr. Lincoln is a country lawyer of more than average shrewdness, and of far more than the average indelicacy which marks the Western wit."[7] McClellan, on the other hand, was a gentleman with the dignity becoming to the White House, at least according to the Democrats. When installed in the presidential mansion, he would see that callers would "put on their best clothes & make themselves clean," as one of his admirers wrote to Mrs. McClellan. "It is the cultivation of the feeling that the President is no better than any other citizen, that has brought us to the election of such ordinary men as Abraham Lincoln."[8]

Such phrases as "rail-splitting buffoon," the "indelicacy" of his "Western wit," and "Abe, the vulgar joker" were intended to turn against Lincoln one of the traits that most endeared him to the people

---

[3] Fillmore to Mrs. McClellan, Mar. 24, 1864, McClellan MSS.

[4] Union League circular, dated Washington, Oct. 18, 1864, R. T. L. Coll., 37382.

[5] Clipping from Grant County, Wisconsin, *Herald,* as reprinted in unidentified newspaper, R. T. L. Coll., 36047.

[6] Quoted in Washington *Daily Morning Chronicle,* June 20, 1864, p. 2, c. 3.

[7] New York *Herald,* Sept. 9, 1864, p. 4, c. 2.

[8] J. S. Fay to Mrs. McClellan, Sept. 22, 1864, McClellan MSS.

—his sense of humor. A more elaborate piece of propaganda, adorning the theme of his crudeness and insensitivity, was an old story about the "Antietam song-singing," which the Democrats revived, elaborated, and then repeated, with variations, throughout the campaign.

One version of the canard, published in the New York *World*, was this: "While the President [after the battle of Antietam in September, 1862] was driving over the field in an ambulance, accompanied by Marshal Lamon, General McClellan, and another officer, heavy details of men were engaged in the task of burying the dead. The ambulance had just reached the neighborhood of the old stone bridge, where the dead were piled highest, when Mr. Lincoln, suddenly slapping Marshal Lamon on the knee, exclaimed: 'Come, Lamon, give us that song about Picayune Butler; McClellan has never heard it.' 'Not now, if you please,' said General McClellan, with a shudder; 'I would prefer to hear it some other place and time.'" But Lamon went ahead and sang the funny song, and Lincoln relished it.[9]

Another version, printed in the *Essex Statesman* and (like the *World's* version) reprinted by other Democratic papers, told how, "soon after one of the most desperate and sanguinary battles," Lincoln was being shown over the field by an unnamed commanding general, who was of course McClellan. Finally, Lincoln said, "This makes a fellow feel gloomy." Turning to a companion, he asked, "Jack, can't you give us something to cheer us up. Give us a song, and give us a lively one." Obligingly, Jack "struck up, as loud as he could bawl, a comic negro song," and he kept it up until the general, in deference to the feelings of his soldiers, requested the President to quiet his friend. "We know that the story is incredible," commented the *Essex Statesman* as it proceeded to point the moral of the tale. "The story can't be true of any man fit for any office of trust, or even for decent society; but the story is every whit true of Abraham Lincoln."[10]

Referring to the anecdote as given in the New York *World,* a Democrat wrote to McClellan and asked if it was true.[11] What reply McClellan gave to this inquiry, if any, is not on record, but he issued no public denial to scotch the story.

---

9 Quoted in Lamon, *Recollections of Abraham Lincoln*, 141–142.

10 Clipping from *Essex* [Massachusetts] *Statesman*, as reprinted in unidentified newspaper, R. T. L. Coll., 35007.

11 J. S. Philip to McClellan, Oct. 1, 1864, McClellan MSS.

A Republican appealed to Lamon for a repudiation. Already Lamon had begged Lincoln to refute the slander, but Lincoln had said: "Let the thing alone." Now Lamon took it upon himself to write out a refutation and a protest, which he showed to Lincoln. Lincoln criticized Lamon's remarks as too belligerent and thought it would be better simply to state the facts. The facts were that the incident had occurred sixteen days after the battle and several miles from the battlefield (and, as Lamon recalled in his reminiscences, Lincoln had requested "a little sad song," not a comic one). "Let me try my hand at it," said Lincoln, and he himself wrote out a statement, then told Lamon to keep it until the proper time to make it public. But Lincoln never found the proper time.[12]

At the close of the campaign he remarked to John Hay: "It is a little singular that I, who am not a vindictive man, should have always been before the people for election in canvasses marked for their bitterness: always but once; when I came to Congress it was a quiet time." [13]

V

"The Democrats will enter the coming canvass," the New York *World* complained on August 25, 1864, "under the great disadvantage of having to contend against the greatest patronage and the greatest money-power ever wielded in a presidential election." [1] And an Indiana Democrat predicted confidentially that Lincoln would "in all probability be re-elected," because the group that controlled "legitimately nine hundred millions of Dollars a year," and would control "corruptly" much more than that, could hardly be dislodged.[2] There was considerable justice in these Democratic complaints. As the campaign got under way, Lincoln and his campaign directors proceeded with a determination that Federal jobholders and other beneficiaries of the government must do their part for the administration party and all its candidates.

After removing the Chase man Horace Binney from the New York

---

12 Lamon, *Recollections of Abraham Lincoln*, 142–146.

13 Dennett, . . . *Diaries* . . . *of John Hay*, 233.

1 Quoted in Carman and Luthin, *Lincoln and the Patronage*, 293.

2 W. S. Holman to Allen Hamilton, Mar. 17, 1864, MS., Lincoln Nat'l Life Foundation, Fort Wayne, Ind.

Custom House, Lincoln rapidly brought into line the employees of this politically most important of all such establishments. The new collector, Simeon Draper, had to dismiss only a few of the deputy collectors, weighers, inspectors, and debenture officers in order to discipline the rest. In September Lincoln himself removed the surveyor of the port, Rufus F. Andrews, and appointed the New York postmaster, Abram Wakefield, in his place. Then he named James Kelly as postmaster. "The appointment of Draper as collector, Wakeman as surveyor, and Kelly as postmaster of New York City," say the two most thorough students of Lincoln's patronage policies, "indicated that Lincoln fully realized that the Seward-Weed faction of Republicans must be awarded more recognition if the Empire State was to be made secure for Lincoln in November." [3]

He used his patronage power not only in his own behalf but also on behalf of those members of Congress who were loyal to his administration. He rebuked the Philadelphia postmaster for restraining a couple of hundred postal employees from aiding in the renomination of William D. Kelley. He checked the Chicago postmaster, who was working against Isaac N. Arnold. When George W. Julian, of Indiana, complained to him that Commissioner of Patents David P. Holloway, also a Hoosier, refused to recognize Julian as the regular party nominee, he replied to Julian: "Your nomination is as binding on Republicans as mine, and you can rest assured that Mr. Holloway shall support you, openly and unconditionally, or lose his head." [4]

Lincoln expected officeholders to act as loyal party workers, and the great majority of them did. They performed the lowly chores necessary for holding rallies, distributing campaign documents, and otherwise garnering votes. At a big meeting at the Cooper Institute in New York, the Federal officials in that city turned out "almost *en masse,*" according to the New York *World,* which listed the names of many of them. And, according to the Indianapolis *Daily State Sentinel,* a hundred government clerks were kept busy in congressional committee rooms with mailing out Lincoln propaganda. They "continue to draw their salaries while engaged in re-electing Abraham Lincoln. They neglect the business of the country, for which only they ought to be paid." [5]

---

[3] Carman and Luthin, *Lincoln and the Patronage,* 280–281.
[4] *Ibid.,* 282–285. See also R. T. L. Coll., 34600.   [5] Carman and Luthin, 287, 296–297.

Some of the government employees balked, presenting touchy problems to Lincoln and his deputy dispensers of the patronage. The most serious problem of this sort arose at the Brooklyn Navy Yard, and it was an especially urgent one because of Lincoln's desperate need for votes in the crucial state of New York. The chairman of the Union State Committee, Charles Jones, reported in August to campaign-manager Raymond: "It cannot be questioned that nearly one half of the employees of the Govt. in the Brooklyn Navy-Yard are hostile to the present Administration, and will oppose the reelection of Mr. Lincoln. Of this number there are Mechanics in the different departments who must be retained, but I have no doubt that of the 6,000 to 7,000 employed it will not be necessary for the efficient working of the departments to retain as many as 1,000 who are opposed to us." [6]

Wholesale dismissals were needed to rid the Navy Yard of men who were "actually loud mouthed and insulting in their expressions of hostility to what they call the Black Republican Administration." But the existing rules of employment stood in the way, and the President or the secretary of the navy would have to intervene. Raymond went to Washington and "explained these matters" to Lincoln and Gideon Welles and, according to his own account, "received from the Secretary assurances of a disposition to remedy all these evils." [7] But Welles, a month later, left a different impression in his diary: "I am not sufficiently ductile for Mr. Raymond, Chairman of the National Executive Committee, who desires to make the navy yard a party machine." Welles indicated a disinclination to aid Raymond "by the arbitrary and despotic exercise of power" from his own office. [8]

At last, a few weeks before election day, a number of workmen were discharged—not thousands of them but enough (fifty-one out of a total of fifty-three employed in one particular shop) to serve, perhaps, as a healthy example to the rest. When the Democratic papers protested that the only grounds for the dismissal of the fifty-one was their avowed intention to vote for McClellan, the Republican Brooklyn *Daily Eagle* explained that only loyal men should be allowed to work on Union ships, and added: "The only questions asked were,

---

[6] Jones to Raymond, Aug. 2, 1864, MS., N. Y. Pub. Lib.
[7] Raymond to Seward, Aug. 5, 1864, MS., N. Y. Pub. Lib.   [8] Welles, *Diary*, II, 136.

whether they were loyal men or not, and whether they were Union men or Democrats, which amounted to just the same thing." [9]

Federal employees, from the highest to the lowest, were expected not only to work and vote for Lincoln but also to contribute to the Republican campaign chest. The various committees—national, state, and congressional—all gave considerable attention to money-raising activities. "Does your State Committee expect to make *exclusive* assessments upon Federal officeholders within the State for the purpose of the canvass," Raymond inquired of Cameron, "or is our Committee to go over the same ground?" [10] Raymond collected five hundred dollars apiece from cabinet members, directed the assessing of employees in all the departments, and levied "an average of three per cent of their yearly pay" on the workers in the New York Custom House. Senator Harlan, on behalf of the congressional campaign committee, franked letters to postmasters throughout the North, demanding from them sums ranging from two to one hundred and fifty dollars, depending on the size of the post office. When a jobholder declined to pay, the campaign directors used their influence to have him discharged. "Pressure was brought to bear upon Lincoln, who," say Professors Carman and Luthin, "seems to have had full knowledge of this expedient and at least did nothing that served to discourage it." [11]

The fund-raisers did not confine themselves to Federal employees but also turned to individuals and firms doing business with the government. Raymond sent out a circular appealing to war contractors, and from one of them alone—Phelps, Dodge and Company, New York dealers in metals—he received at least $3,000. Cameron got large sums from a Philadelphia businessman who expected him to secure government contracts in return.[12] "Simonds, a fortunate contractor and builder of wagons for Govt. has given $50,000," an envious Democratic worker reported to one of his own party's strategists. "An officer has been detailed both at Phila. and New York, to ascertain from Quarter Masters in charge of those places, the names of those who have been favored with Govt. patronage, for the purpose of levying assessments upon them." [13] Jay Cooke and Company, the bankers and

[9] Carman and Luthin, *Lincoln and the Patronage*, 298.
[10] Raymond to Cameron, July 17, 1864, Cameron MSS.
[11] Carman and Luthin, *Lincoln and the Patronage*, 288–289, 292–293.
[12] *Ibid.*, 290–292.   [13] Samuel North to Manton Marble, Sept. 28, 1864, Marble MSS.

sellers of government bonds, gave Cameron a checking account of $1,000, to be drawn upon as needed for his committee's expenses.[14]

How much money the Republicans raised and spent, all together, would be impossible to guess. One Democratic worker thought they had a fund of a million dollars exclusively for the October election in Pennsylvania, but another Democratic worker estimated the true figure as being nearer a half million.[15] The Democrats themselves, by their own accounting, spent only $32,475 in that same October election.[16] There can be no doubt that, whatever the exact sums, the Republicans received and disbursed a tremendous and unprecedented total and one far larger than the Democrats could aspire to. Lincoln certainly had the advantages of patronage and the purse.

VI

If the President's appointive powers comprised an asset in a political campaign, so too, in war time, did his powers as Commander-in-Chief of the Army and Navy. The Democrats were "impressed with the opinion that Lincoln's best prospects of re-election" were "based on his power to control the votes of the army."[1] To politicians on both sides it seemed that the votes of soldier citizens might prove decisive, and to Lincoln himself the utilization of those votes was a matter of deep personal interest.

Politicians both Republican and Democratic hoped to get a party endorsement from leading army officers, for this presumably would influence both civilian and soldier voters. The officers whose commitments were most eagerly sought were, of course, Sherman and Grant. Sherman inclined toward McClellan, or so at least some of the Democrats thought, and one of them, a Boston cotton broker, wrote McClellan to ask whether they could outflank the Republicans "by getting a letter from Gen Sherman (who it is very generally believed here advocates your election) endorsing the Chicago nominations?"[2] But Sherman remained noncommittal. Grant favored Lincoln,

[14] J. K. Moorhead to Cameron, July 22, 1864. Cameron MSS.
[15] S. North to Marble, Sept. 28, 1864, and H. M. Phillips to Marble, Sept. 30, 1864, Marble MSS.
[16] H. M. Phillips to R. E. Randall, Nov. 5, 1864, Marble MSS.
[1] Washington *Daily Constitutional Union*, Aug. 10, 1864, p. 1, c. 6.
[2] E. H. Kettell to McClellan, Sept. 24, 1864, McClellan MSS.

or so Republicans said, but Lincoln himself seems to have doubted whether he really had Grant's wholehearted support.[3] At any rate, the Republicans were able to make extensive use of a letter which Grant and written in August opposing the election of any "Peace candidate." [4] Among the officers in the Army of the Potomac, the Democrats started a subscription to buy a testimonial gift for McClellan, but abandoned the project because their opponents "misconstrued" it and because they themselves feared it might offend McClellan's successor as commanding officer, Meade, whom they aspired to win over.[5] "Genl. Meade is on the fence as far as I can learn," a Democrat in the Army of the Potomac reported to McClellan, "but the prevailing sentiment at his Hd. Qrs. is in your favor." [6] Rosecrans also wavered, sometimes talking like a McClellan man, but Nicolay, after seeing Rosecrans in Missouri, advised Lincoln on ways to bring him definitely to the administration side.[7]

Whatever the consensus among Army officers may have been, Republicans became more and more confident, as the campaign progressed, that the overwhelming majority of the men in the ranks were for Lincoln. "There were in the Western Army many McClellan men at the time of his nomination," an Illinois soldier in Sherman's army reported from Atlanta at the end of September, "but since the platform has been read and then to know that the nomination of McClellan was made unanimous on the motion of that Traitor Valindlingham [sic] is more than the admirers of little 'Mac' could stand and I can assure that 'Mac' has lost thousands of votes within three weeks." [8] A straw vote in this soldier's regiment, the 45th, produced 329 votes for Lincoln and only 16 for McClellan. A few weeks later a test ballot in one corps of the Army of the Potomac gave "3,500 votes Union and 500 for McClellan," and soldier ballotings elsewhere yielded similar results.[9]

---

[3] "Well, McClure," Lincoln is quoted as saying late in October, "I have no reason to believe that Grant prefers my election to that of McClellan." McClure, *Lincoln and Men of War-Times*, 185–187.

[4] Washington *Evening Star*, Sept. 9, 1864, p. 2, c. 1.

[5] Arthur McClellan to George B. McClellan, Sept. 26, 1864, McClellan MSS. See also Washington *Daily Morning Chronicle*, Sept. 25, 1864, p. 2, c. 2.

[6] M. F. McMahon to McClellan, Oct. 10, 1864, McClellan MSS.

[7] Nicolay to Lincoln, Oct. 12, 1864, R. T. L. Coll., 37168–69.

[8] Evans Blake to Washburne, Sept. 30, 1864, Washburne MSS.

[9] Cincinnati *Daily Gazette*, Oct. 18, 1864.

But Republican party workers did not take the soldier vote for granted. Their congressional campaign committee sent an agent to scatter "Union" literature among the soldiers, and he reported shortly before election day that he had "distributed nearly a million of documents, nearly all to the Army from Maine to La." [10] McClellan's brother, at the Harrisonburg headquarters of the 6th Army Corps, complained to McClellan: "Nothing is seen by the troops but Republican papers and the Democrats seem to be afraid to open their mouths or do anything." [11] A Democratic worker in the Army of the Potomac, pleading for "papers, tracts and so forth," said that the Republicans were "sending them down by the wagon loads" while there was "not one yet for our side." [12] But some Democratic officers found ways of dealing with the excess of Republican propaganda. "Maj. Hancock (brother of the General) tells us that the McClellan colonels destroy whole boxes of Republican documents sent to them," a Democrat proudly informed his own national committee. "They don't allow the soldiers to see them." [13]

Lincoln himself was careful not to offend soldier opinion. Whenever he addressed groups of uniformed men in Washington, as he did on several occasions during campaigning season, he praised them for their labors and sacrifices in upholding the Union.[14] And he gave heed to soldier feelings when, late in September, he faced the difficult question of going ahead with the scheduled new draft. Some of the frightened politicians, especially Governor Morton of Indiana, begged him to postpone the draft until after election day. Otherwise, the Indiana Republicans insisted, they would lose their state.[15] But Lincoln had a dispatch from Sherman, dated September 17, 1864, which he recopied in his own hand and which he no doubt pondered carefully. "The Secretary of War tells me the draft will be made on Monday next. If the President modifies it to the extent of one man, or wavers in its execution," Sherman had warned, "he is gone over. The Army would vote against him." [16] Lincoln went ahead with the draft.

10 G. T. Brown to Lyman Trumbull, Nov. 5, 1864, Trumbull MSS.

11 Arthur McClellan to G. B. McClellan, Oct. 2, 1864, McClellan MSS.

12 Unsigned letter to Manton Marble, Sept. 22, 1864, Marble MSS.

13 G. W. Adams to Marble, Sept. 27, 1864, Marble MSS.

14 Cincinnati *Daily Gazette,* June 13, 1864, p. 3, c. 6; Baltimore *Sun,* Aug. 23, 1864, p. 2, c. 1, and Sept. 2, 1864, p. 1, c. 7.

15 Stampp, *Indiana Politics during the Civil War,* 250–251.   16 R. T. L. Coll., 36417.

Well before the election every Northern state (except Oregon) considered the matter of amending its constitution or passing legislation so as to make possible the counting of soldier votes cast in the army. Most of the states—those with Republican-controlled legislatures—made provision either for voting in the field or for voting by proxy at home, but none of the states with Democratic-controlled legislatures did so.[17] In these states, only those soldiers home on furlough at election time could legally vote. Lincoln watched with keen interest the action of the various states on soldier voting, and when, in California, the voting arrangement was declared unconstitutional, he "was sorry to see the Courts there had thrown *out* the soldier's right to vote," and he thought "it a bad augury for the success of the loyal cause on Nov. 8th." [18]

He was prepared to co-operate fully with his party's managers when they undertook, in accordance with state laws, to gather in the votes of men in the armed forces far from home. These votes were especially needed in New York. When the chairman of the New York state committee appealed to Lincoln "to obtain facilities for taking the votes of Seamen & Sailors," Lincoln obliged him with a note to Secretary of the Navy Welles: "Please do all for him in this respect which you consistently can." [19] The next day Lincoln, with Seward, called personally at Welles' office. "Wanted one of our boats to be placed at the disposal of the New York commission to gather votes in the Mississippi Squadron," Welles noted. Welles did not like the idea, "and yet," he thought, "it seems ungracious to oppose it." He gave his permission.[20]

Some of the Democrats were even more eager than Lincoln and Seward to get the New York soldier vote, so eager indeed that they were willing to steal it. According to the New York proxy system, a soldier in the field sealed up his ballot and sent it to his home county to be opened for him on election day. A couple of zealous Democratic workers in Washington intercepted large numbers of these ballots, unsealed the envelopes, put in ballots marked for the Democratic ticket, and sent them on. These "ballot-box stuffers" were said to have had more than twenty men at work for them and to have been "sending off the ballots, as fabricated by them, in dry-goods boxes full."

17 Benton, *Voting in the Field*, chap. xxx.
18 H. Bellows to his son, Nov. 2, 1864, Bellows MSS., Mass. Hist. Soc.
19 Lincoln to Welles, Oct. 10, 1864, Lincoln Coll., N. Y. Pub. Lib.
20 Welles, *Diary*, II, 175.

Before election day the two ringleaders were apprehended, tried, and sentenced to long prison terms, with the approval of Stanton and Lincoln.[21]

Although Pennsylvania had authorized its soldiers to vote in the field, "as fully as if they were present at their usual place of election," [22] Lincoln after the rather unsatisfactory returns in October was unwilling to depend on their absentee ballots for victory in November. "He knew that his election was in no sense doubtful," according to McClure, "but he knew that if he lost New York and with it Pennsylvania on the home vote, the moral effect of his triumph would be broken and his power to prosecute the war and make peace would be greatly impaired." McClure told him there was no reasonable prospect of carrying Pennsylvania on the "home vote." Lincoln asked: "Well, what is to be done?" McClure advised him to see that Meade and Sheridan each furloughed five thousand Pennsylvania troops in time to vote at home. Lincoln did so.[23]

In Indiana, where the unamended state constitution forbade voting in the field, Governor Morton and Representative Colfax desperately sought soldier votes for the October election. Colfax repeatedly begged Sherman to send his Indiana soldiers home, but Sherman wrote him that this was "impossible." Colfax was not satisfied, and he wrote to Lincoln. "About ⅓ of each Regiment are minors," he pointed out to the President. "Why not leave them, & let the voters come . . . ?" Lincoln endorsed Colfax's letter and turned it over to Stanton.[24] Still Sherman did nothing. Finally Morton went to Washington to see Lincoln, and Lincoln sent a note direct to Sherman, suggesting that he let some Indiana men go home. Even then, Sherman's response was far from satisfactory to the Hoosier politicians.[25]

In Illinois, where (as in Indiana) there was a stalemate between governor and legislature and no arrangement had been made for absentee balloting, Governor Yates became frantic about furloughs as the November election approached. In response to his appeals Secre-

---

[21] Cincinnati *Daily Gazette*, Oct. 27, 1864, p. 3, c. 5; Oct. 31, 1864, p. 3, c. 3; Nov. 3, 1864, p. 1, c. 8; Nov. 5, 1864, p. 3, c. 4 and 8.

[22] Washington *Daily Morning Chronicle*, Mar. 12, 1864, p. 2, c. 1.

[23] McClure, *Lincoln and Men of War-Times*, 185–187.

[24] Colfax to [Lincoln], Aug. 29, 1864, Stanton MSS., Lib. of Cong. On the back of the letter is the endorsement: "Submitted to the Sec. of War Sept. 3/1864 A Lincoln."

[25] Stampp, *Indiana Politics during the Civil War*, 251–252.

tary Stanton on October 28 ordered General Rosecrans to furlough several regiments of Illinois troops to enable them to vote. But on October 30 the war department, faced with a military emergency on top of a political one, ordered these troops sent to Nashville to reinforce General Thomas, who expected an attack from the approaching Confederate army of Beauregard. Immediately, on November 1, Yates sent a long and frenzied telegram directly to Lincoln. "Defeat in Illinois is worse than defeat in the field," Yates argued, "and I do hope that you will immediately order that these Regiments may be allowed to remain and vote, on the route to Tennessee." Lincoln did not flatly turn down this candid appeal from Yates. He directed that a reply be wired to him saying merely that, until the Illinois regiments had reached St. Louis on their way from Missouri to Tennessee, his telegram could not be "fully answered." [26]

VII

In some parts of the country the Republicans, expecting violence, awaited election day with apprehension. In Illinois, Stanton was informed, more than five thousand armed Confederates were roaming at large. "They intend to vote at the coming election and by terrorism to keep from the polls more than 5,000 *citizens*." [1] In the city of New York, Stanton heard, the rebels intended not only to jam the polls with "enemies" but also to start a general conflagration.[2] From New York and a number of other cities the War Department received appeals for troops to protect the polls, and a regiment was sent to New York, but General Halleck exclaimed that if the army were to respond to only half of the requests, "we would not have a single soldier to meet the rebels in the field!" [3]

When November 8 came, however, no serious disturbances interfered with the polling anywhere. In Illinois the qualified voters—white men over twenty-one with a year's residence in the state—patiently waited their turns to vote, standing single file in long lines

---

[26] Yates to Lincoln, Nov. 1, 1864, and T. M. Vincent to Yates, Nov. 2, 1864, *Offic. Rec.*, 3 ser., IV, 871–872.

[1] H. E. Payne to Stanton, Sept. 8, 1864, Stanton MSS.

[2] Stanton to Dix, October 23, 1864, and Grant to Dix, October 24, 1864, *Offic. Rec.*, 1 ser., XLIII, pt. 2, pp. 463–464.

[3] Halleck to Lieber, Oct. 26, 1864, Lieber MSS., Huntington Lib.

at many polling places. Saloons were closed, and in Springfield, where it rained steadily most of the day, the *Illinois State Journal* noted that "fewer drunken people were seen upon the streets than usual." [4] From New York, General Butler, in command of the Federal troops, telegraphed laconically to the war department at noon: "The quietest city ever seen." [5]

But Butler had not seen Washington that day. It was even quieter. The day was dark and rainy, and the city was considerably depopulated by the homeward exodus of more than eighteen thousand voters, mostly government employees. "The rush to the cars of those going home to vote was too much for the railroads," a news dispatch reported two days before the election. "Some four hundred were left behind, but by the aid of extra trains, all have been able to get off to-day." [6] The White House was almost deserted, and the President, beginning to look "care-worn and dilapidated," [7] was by himself when Noah Brooks called at noon. Lincoln did not attempt to hide his anxiety about the election. "I am just enough of a politician to know that there was not much doubt about the results of the Baltimore convention," he told Brooks; "but about this thing I am very far from being certain. I wish I was certain." [8]

In the evening, the weather still rainy and "steamy," Lincoln went with a party including Brooks and Hay to the telegraph office, to get the returns as they came in. "We splashed through the grounds to the side door of the War Department where a soaked and smoking sentinel was standing in his own vapor with his huddled-up frame covered with a rubber cloak." Upstairs, the President was handed the reports of the early returns, which were extremely favorable. He sent out the "first fruits" to Mrs. Lincoln. "She is more anxious than I," he explained. [9] Later in the evening the reports began to come in slowly because of the rainstorm, which interfered with the telegraph, and during the lulls he entertained the group around him with anecdotes.

By midnight, though to his great disappointment he had not heard

[4] Paul G. Hubbard, The Lincoln-McClellan Presidential Election in Illinois (MS. doctoral dissertation, Univ. of Ill., 1949), 191–192, 196–197.

[5] Dennett, . . . *Diaries* . . . *of John Hay*, 233.

[6] Cincinnati *Daily Gazette*, Nov. 7, 1864, p. 3, c. 3.

[7] L. D. Campbell to Andrew Johnson, Nov. 12, 1864, Johnson MSS., Lib. of Cong.

[8] Brooks, *Washington in Lincoln's Time*, 216–217.

[9] Dennett, . . . *Diaries* . . . *of John Hay*, 233–234.

from Illinois (or Iowa), Lincoln could be "tolerably certain" that Maryland, Pennsylvania, most of the Middle West, and all of New England would go for him.[10] A midnight supper was brought in, and Hay observed how "The President went awkwardly and hospitably to work shovelling out the fried oysters." [11] As he received congratulations on what looked like a sure and decisive victory, Lincoln appeared utterly calm, with no trace of elation or excitement. He did say "he would admit that he was glad to be relieved of all suspense, and that he was grateful that the verdict of the people was likely to be so full, clear, and unmistakable that there could be no dispute."

About two o'clock in the morning a messenger brought the information that a crowd of Pennsylvanians were serenading the White House. Lincoln went home and, in response to cries for a speech, he talked for a few minutes, concluding: "If I know my heart, my gratitude is free from any taint of personal triumph. I do not impugn the motives of any one opposed to me. It is no pleasure to me to triumph over any one, but I give thanks to the Almighty for this evidence of the people's resolution to stand by free government and the rights of humanity." [12]

VIII

Slightly more than four million votes were cast, and counted, for presidential electors in 1864. Of these, Lincoln's electors received approximately 55 per cent, or about four hundred thousand more than McClellan did (but McClellan got practically as many popular votes as Lincoln had got in 1860). Lincoln's majority of the electoral vote was even more impressive—234 to 21—as he carried every state in the Union except Delaware, New Jersey, and Kentucky. Yet, as an analysis of the voting will show, the election was actually closer than it seemed, and the worries that beset Lincoln even as late as election day were by no means far-fetched.

His strength varied considerably from place to place. The state he carried by the largest proportion of the votes cast was Massachusetts, where he got more than 125,000 of a total vote of 175,000. The state he carried by the smallest proportion was New York, the most popu-

---

10 Brooks, *Washington in Lincoln's Time,* 217–218.
11 Dennett, . . . *Diaries . . . of John Hay,* 235–236.
12 Brooks, *Washington in Lincoln's Time,* 218–219.

lous of all, where he had a margin of fewer than 7,000. He made his poorest showing in the big cities. The heaviest majority against him in any city was that in New York, where McClellan got nearly two-thirds of the approximately 100,000 votes. In Chicago and Cincinnati, Lincoln did best in the wards with a predominantly German population and worst in those where the Irish were most numerous.[1] In Detroit, McClellan captured nearly three-fourths of the votes in the heavily Irish eighth ward and carried both the city and Wayne County, although the county had gone for Lincoln in 1860.[2]

Lincoln "received an almost unanimous vote," as Frank Blair believed, from the army.[3] Indeed, it has been calculated that Lincoln was given roughly three-fourths of the ballots cast by soldiers in the field or through proxies at home. The total of this vote—not more than 235,000—was relatively very small, both in proportion to the size of the army (it contained at least ten times as many men as voted in the field or by proxy) and in proportion to the size of the popular vote as a whole.[4] But this does not mean that soldier voting had little or no effect upon the outcome of the election. It should be remembered that, in addition to the soldiers who voted in the field or by proxy, many others on furlough voted at home (their numbers cannot be determined, since their ballots were not counted separately from those of civilians). It should be noted also that most of the votes of soldiers on furlough were concentrated in certain large and pivotal states. William B. Hesseltine has estimated that in New York, Pennsylvania, Illinois, Indiana, Maryland, and Connecticut the Republican majorities—which ranged from 2,000 (Connecticut) to 30,000 (Illinois)—resulted from the presence of soldiers as guards or as voters at the polls. "Without the soldiers' vote in six crucial states," concludes Professor Hesseltine, "Lincoln would have lost the election."[5]

Just what factors (other than habitual party allegiance) were most important in making up the minds of the more than four million voters, soldier and civilian, it would be difficult to say. Frank Blair believed that "no effort upon the part of any officer of rank" had been

1 Cincinnati *Daily Gazette*, Nov. 22, 1864, p. 1, c. 4.

2 W. A. Harbison, "Detroit's Role in the Re-Election of Abraham Lincoln," *Bulletin of the Detroit Hist. Soc.*, V, No. 6, pp. 8–9.

3 Frank Blair to F. P. Blair, Sr., Nov. 10, 1864, Blair MSS., Lib. of Cong.

4 Benton, *Voting in the Field*, chap. xxx.

5 Hesseltine, *Lincoln and the War Governors*, 384 n.

made to "influence the votes of the troops," and that they had "voted their own unbiased sentiments." [6] (Democrats charged, however, "the War Department and our commanding generals" had "adopted a rule to refuse furloughs to Democratic soldiers and to grant them *ad libitum* to those of Republican proclivities." [7]) As for civilian voters, many who marked their ballots for McClellan doubtless were influenced more by anti-Negro prejudice and by dislike of high prices, high taxes, draft calls, and arbitrary arrests than by the arguments of Democratic politicians. On the other hand, large numbers of habitual Democrats, at least in the Northwest, voted for Lincoln because they did not like the "peace plank" in the Democratic platform. They were for "war to the knife and the knife to the hilt," as a Detroit Democrat told McClellan after the election. "The Chicago Platform . . . defeated us in this state." [8] Very likely the Chicago platform, together with the news of victories on the battlefield, refuting the resolution that declared the war a failure, also confirmed many Republicans in their inclination to support Lincoln and the "Union" party. Yet considerations of patronage and personal gain seem to have had as much influence on many Republicans as did political issues.

The real issues, as between Lincoln and McClellan, were much less sharp than they had been made to appear to the voters. There was no question of Union or disunion. As Lincoln himself put it (in his message to Congress, December 6, 1864): "There has been much impugning of motives, and much heated controversy as to the proper means and best mode of advancing the Union cause; but on the distinctive issue of Union or no Union the politicians have shown their instinctive knowledge that there is no diversity among the people." [9] Certainly McClellan did not think that the Union had been at stake. As he looked back upon the election, it seemed to him "a struggle of honor, patriotism & truth against deceit, selfishness & fanaticism." [10] The truth is that he, like Lincoln, had been a Union candidate. In his attitude toward the war he had much more in common with Lincoln than with the Peace Democrats. And Lincoln, in his attitude toward

[6] Blair to F. P. Blair, Sr., Nov. 10, 1864, Blair MSS.

[7] Washington *Daily Morning Chronicle*, Nov. 3, 1864, p. 2, c. 2.

[8] R. McClelland to W. Wright, Nov. 10, 1864, McClellan MSS.

[9] Nicolay and Hay, *Works*, X, 305.

[10] McClellan to Manton Marble, Nov. 28, 1864, Marble MSS.

the South, had much more in common with McClellan than with the Radical Republicans.

What difference would it have made, for the Union cause, if McClellan had won? It is inconceivable that he would have considered peace on the basis of disunion. Even the so-called "peace plank" of his party's platform did not sanction such a thing. That plank called for peace discussions with a view to restoration of the Union, and the man who wrote it, Vallandigham, in supposing that the rebel leaders would make peace without the independence of the Confederacy, was not traitorous but misinformed. Anyhow, there is little reason to suppose that McClellan, if elected, would have been guided by Vallandigham. It is possible, of course, that McClellan's anti-emancipation views, if he had put them into effect, would have weakened the Union Army by depriving it of Negro troops and auxiliaries (as Lincoln had argued in his August interview). It is also possible that a change in Presidents, with a kind of four-month interregnum between election and inauguration, might have unsettled policies and jeopardized the Union cause. But Lincoln stood ready, if he lost, to cooperate fully with McClellan in minimizing the break between administrations. After the election Lincoln showed the cabinet his memorandum of August 23, which the secretaries had signed without reading, and in which he recorded his intention of inviting McClellan's co-operation if McClellan should be elected. Seward commented that McClellan would have said yes, yes, and would have done nothing about it.[11] But Seward, for all his perspicuity, was something less than a fair and impartial judge in this case.

Yet the election did hold a profound meaning for the future of both the Union and democracy, a meaning that occurred simultaneously to Grant, to Lincoln, and to dozens of newspaper editors throughout the North. The election showed, according to the Detroit *Free Press*, that "in the very midst of the most gigantic revolution" the American people could "execute a freeman's will with the same dignity and respect, with the same quiet and regard for the forms of law witnessed in the most ordinary peaceful times." [12] Grant, in a telegram congratulating Lincoln, said: "The election having passed off quietly,

---

[11] Dennet, . . . *Diaries* . . . *of John Hay*, 237–238.
[12] Quoted by Harbison, *Bull. of the Detroit Hist. Soc.*, V, No. 6, p. 9.

no bloodshed or riot throughout the land, is worth more to the country than a battle won." [13] Addressing a crowd that surged about the
White House two nights after the election, Lincoln said: "It has long
been a grave question whether any government, not *too* strong for
the liberties of its people, can be strong *enough* to maintain its own
existence, in great emergencies." The election, "a political war," had
"partially paralyzed" the loyal people and so had weakened them,
temporarily, for the war against the rebellion. And yet the election had
been a necessity. "We can not have free government without elections;
and if the rebellion could force us to forego, or postpone a national
election, it might fairly claim to have already conquered and ruined
us." [14]

---

[13] Grant to Stanton, Nov. 10, 1864, *Correspondence of Gen. Benjamin F. Butler*, V, 336.
[14] *Collected Works*, VIII, 100–101.

CHAPTER XII

POLICY, POLITICS, AND PERSONNEL

RE-ELECTED, Lincoln would have liked to end his first term and begin his second with as little change as possible in the personnel, both high and low, of his government. He was weary of the interminable demands of friendship and faction, which he had to try to reconcile with his needs for competence and for loyalty to the administration. After more than three years of shuffling men and places, he had achieved a fair balance between his needs and the politicians' demands. But he had not set up a stable equilibrium, nor could he. Vacancies continued to occur through resignation, dismissal, or death, and hungry politicians continued to clamor for patronage. So the President, while wrestling with problems military and financial and diplomatic, still had to concern himself with the problem of readjusting personnel in such a way as to serve the ends of both politics and policy.

I

Of all the places that Lincoln now had to fill, the most important was the Chief Justiceship of the Supreme Court, which had become vacant only a few weeks before election day, when John Marshall's successor Roger Brooke Taney finally died. His death broke the tension which, ever since Lincoln's inauguration, had existed between the Republican President and the Republicans in Congress, on the one hand, and the Democratic Chief Justice on the other.

Taney's infamy among Republicans dated back to the Dred Scott case (1857). He and a majority of the Court then held that a Missouri Negro could not be an American citizen and therefore could not sue in the Federal courts, but they had gone on to say in an *obiter dicta* that Congress could not constitutionally exclude slavery from the territories. This opinion struck at the key plank of the Republican platform, the Free Soil plank. Republicans denounced Taney and the concurring judges as tools of slavery, and Lincoln in the debates with Douglas intimated that he and his party, once in power, would somehow set aside the decision of the Supreme Court.

At Lincoln's inauguration it was of course this same Taney who, by virtue of his office, administered the oath to the new President, in the presence of the other justices. And Lincoln, in his inaugural address, gave a word of warning to Taney and the court when he said: ". . . if the policy of the government, upon vital questions affecting the whole people, is to be irrevocably fixed by decisions of the Supreme Court, the instant they are made, in ordinary litigation between parties in personal actions, the people will have ceased to be their own rulers . . ." [1] Soon Taney defied Lincoln when, sitting as a circuit judge in *ex parte Merryman,* he denied the constitutionality of the President's suspension of the writ of *habeas corpus.*[2] And Lincoln, in his message to the special session of Congress (July 4, 1861), again answered Taney. He noted that the Federal laws were being violated wholesale in almost a fourth of the states, then asked whether "all the laws but one" (the one concerning the *habeas corpus* writ) were "to go unexecuted, and the government itself to go to pieces lest that one be violated." [3]

Neither then nor later did Lincoln call upon Congress to curb the Supreme Court, but when the first regular session of Congress met, he did suggest that the circuit courts be reorganized so as to provide a circuit of approximately equal population for each of the Supreme Court justices. The congressional Radicals, led by Senator John P. Hale of New Hampshire, took it upon themselves to eliminate the judiciary as an obstacle to their program. After debating at length Hale's proposal to abolish the Court and set up a new one, they had to be satisfied with nothing more than the President's re-organization plan, most of which became law. The Conservative Republicans were willing to wait for the President to capture the Court by appointing new judges.[4]

---

[1] Nicolay and Hay, *Works,* II, 5.   [2] See *Lincoln the President,* III, 161 ff.

[3] Nicolay and Hay, *Works,* II, 59–69.

[4] David M. Silver, "The Supreme Court during the Civil War" (doctoral dissertation, Univ. of Ill., 1940), 40–50.

When the Court convened for the first time under Lincoln, there were already three vacancies on it, and some of the remaining justices appeared to be too old to last much longer. The three oldest came from slaveholding states and two of them from seceding states—Taney from Maryland, James M. Wayne from Georgia, and John Catron from Tennessee. The rest had been appointed by Democratic (and two of them by Southern) Presidents—Samuel Nelson, of New York, appointed by Tyler; Robert C. Grier, of Pennsylvania, by Polk; and Nathan Clifford, of Maine, by Buchanan. One vacancy existed already when Lincoln was inaugurated, Buchanan having been unable to get Senate approval for his last appointee. Another vacancy occurred when, exactly a month after Lincoln's inauguration, the seventy-six-year-old John McLean died. And the third vacancy arose when John A. Campbell, of Alabama, resigned to go with his state into the Confederacy.[5]

Lincoln was in no hurry to appoint new justices but preferred to wait until Congress had rearranged the circuits. When the Court met in December, 1861, however, there was no quorum, Taney and Catron being ill. So, in January, 1862, Lincoln nominated Noah H. Swayne, a Virginia-born Ohio lawyer who had once been a Jacksonian Democrat and who possesed no judicial experience of any kind. He was so little known in the East that the newspapers there usually misspelled his name as "Swain." But he was the choice of the Ohio Republican leaders, including Senators Sherman and Wade and Governor Dennison, and that was enough.[6]

Lincoln made his second appointment in July, 1862, on the day after the circuit reorganization had become law. Samuel F. Miller, the new justice, born in Kentucky, had taught himself law while practicing medicine there, then had moved to Iowa and gone into law and politics. Before his Supreme Court appointment, when the Iowa congressman, John A. Kasson, visited Lincoln in his behalf, Lincoln had confused him with a Daniel F. Miller he had known, and after his appointment some of the eastern newspapers kept referring to him as Daniel F. rather than Samuel F. Miller. He was the nominee of the Iowa Republicans, of Senators Harlan and Grimes and Governor Kirkwood.[7]

Not till October, 1862, did Lincoln get around to naming a third

[5] Ibid., 13 ff., 108 ff.   [6] Ibid., 37–39, 68 ff.   [7] Ibid., 76–82.

Supreme Court justice, though the friends of David Davis had been urging his appointment ever since the death of McLean. David Davis, a Maryland-born cousin of the Marylander Henry Winter Davis, had been a judge of the eighth Illinois circuit where Lincoln used to practice and had been Lincoln's manager at the Chicago convention of 1860. His friends, among them Leonard Swett, expected him to be rewarded for his part in making Lincoln President, and they became increasingly impatient at Lincoln's long delay. Davis himself said that so many friends were mentioning him for a Supreme Court position that he was beginning to feel a desire for one. Finally they and he got their wish.[8]

Except for Davis, none of Lincoln's three appointees had had judicial experience or was known outside his own state. All of them, including Davis, had been born in slave states. All were chosen primarily for political reasons. Yet all were men of ability, all were strongly pro-Union and antislavery, and all could be depended upon to uphold the administration. But they comprised only a minority of the Supreme Court, and when the first test of the President's war powers came up, in the *Prize Cases* (decided in March, 1863), the legality of Lincoln's blockade proclamation during the first three month's of his administration could have been sustained only with the aid of at least two of the older justices. Two of them—Justices Grier and Wayne—did join with the three Lincoln appointees in the five-to-four decision.[9]

Meanwhile Congress was enlarging the Supreme Court by adding a tenth justiceship and a tenth circuit. Lincoln signed the bill and it became law on March 3, 1863. He named a judge to fill the new place, Stephen J. Field, on March 6. The Court's decision in the *Prize Cases* was announced on March 10 (Field did not, of course, participate in this). It has been said that the creation of the additional judgeship and the appointment of the extra judge were closely related to the *Prize Cases*, though the timing of the events indicates that the actual vote in this decision could not have been the cause of the action by Congress and the President. Nevertheless, the President and Congress, anticipating a close vote or possibly an adverse one, may have been "packing" the Court so as to lessen the danger of judicial "sabo-

---

[8] *Ibid.*, 86–94.
[9] See Randall, *Constitutional Problems under Lincoln*, 51–59, and *Lincoln the President*, III, 153–156.

tage." [10] Or Congress may have been merely following through on the President's earlier recommendation that it provide a circuit for each justice and a justice for each circuit. The new circuit, bringing California and Oregon into the regular court system, needed a judge familiar with the tangled land laws and land claims of California. Stephen J. Field—one of the famous family of brothers, including David Dudley, Cyrus W., and Henry M.—was such a man. He had gone to California as a forty-niner and had served for several years on the Supreme Court of that state. Incidentally, while on the California court, he had written an opinion which impugned Federal authority to the extent of arguing that the legal-tender act did not apply to state debts.[11] If Lincoln had been deliberately packing the Court, he might have picked a man with fewer qualms about the greenbacks than Field.

Some members of Congress had a continuing interest in increasing the number of Republicans on the Court, as was indicated by the bill which Senator Harlan introduced in December, 1863. This would have made it possible for a justice to retire on a pension which, depending on the length of his service, would range from $4,000 to $6,000 (as compared with the salaries of $6,000 for the associate justices and $6,500 for the Chief Justice). If Harlan's bill had passed, a few of the older judges—including Unionists like Wayne and Grier—might have been lured from their positions by the promise of generous retirement pay. "The 4 seniors, Taney, Wayne, Catron, and Grier, are evidently failing . . ." Attorney-General Bates noted on April 11, 1864. "I think all four of them would gladly retire, if Congress would pass the proposed bill—to enable the justices to resign, upon an adequate pensi[o]n." [12] But Congress never passed the bill. Even without it, the preponderance of age on the Court was considerably reduced by Lincoln's appointments, the average age of the judges being 71 years in 1861 and 62 in 1864.

The Taney Court had been converted into a Lincoln Court, with a majority generally loyal to the administration. "If it could not sustain the administration in war cases," as David M. Silver has written, "it denied that it had jurisdiction." [13] The greatest danger of judicial sabotage had already passed by the time of Taney's death, but Repub-

---

10 Swisher, *Taney*, 652–663, and *Stephen J. Field*, 115–116.

11 Silver, "Supreme Court during the Civil War," 99–105.

12 Bates, *Diary*, 358.   13 Silver, "Supreme Court during the Civil War," 138.

licans had not forgotten the case of Dred Scott, and there were questions regarding slavery which they expected the Court yet to pass upon.

II

From week to week during 1864 Chief Justice Taney, going on eighty-seven, feeble, incapacitated much of the time, was expected to die. The Radicals could hardly wait. Senator Wade quipped: "No man ever prayed as hard as I did that Taney might outlive James Buchanan's term, and now I'm afraid I have overdone it." [1] So efficacious had been Wade's prayers that it looked as if Taney might outlive Abraham Lincoln's term also!

During one of Taney's illnesses Lincoln made up his mind that the next Chief Justice should be Salmon P. Chase, then secretary of the treasury.[2] He did not change his mind when he accepted Chase's resignation from the treasury department. Chase learned of the President's intention from Representative Samuel Hooper, of Massachusetts, who reported to him on June 30 (the day after Chase resigned) a recent White House conversation. As Chase recorded the gist of it in his diary: ". . . the President expressed regret that our relations were not more free from embarrassment . . . . At the same time he expressed his esteem for me & said that he had intended in case of vacancy in the Chief Justiceship to tender it to me & would now did a vacancy exist." [3] The next day Lincoln remarked privately that Chase ought to "go home without making any fight and wait for a good thing hereafter, such as a vacancy on the Supreme Bench." [4]

Taney held out for more than three months longer, until October 12. Few mourned him, even among the Conservative Republicans. Attorney-General Bates, who had been with him on the night of his death, was the only cabinet member who attended the funeral. Secretary of the Navy Welles "felt little inclined to participate" in any ceremony, for he believed that by the Dred Scott decision Taney had "forfeited respect" both as a man and as a judge.[5] President Lincoln himself, along with Secretary of State Seward and Postmaster-General Dennison, "attended the body from the dwelling to the cars" after

---

[1] Nicolay and Hay, *Lincoln*, IX, 386.　　　　[2] Browning, *Diary*, I, 687.
[3] Chase MS. diary, entry for June 30, 1864, Lib. of Cong.
[4] Dennett, . . . *Diaries* . . . *of John Hay*, 203.　　　[5] Welles, *Diary*, II, 176–177.

services in Washington, but did not go on to the burial in Frederick, Maryland.[6]

Meanwhile some of the rejoicing Radicals got busy on behalf of Chase. Secretary of War Stanton sent him a terse telegram: "Chief Justice Taney died last night," [7] and Chase promptly replied that for three or four months he had been "afraid" it was the President's intention to appoint him; he thought he would accept, but he wondered whether he should.[8] Professor Lieber, the moment he heard the glad news in his Columbia College classroom, sat down in front of his students and dashed off a note to his friend Senator Sumner, suggesting that the Senator go at once from Boston to Washington. "The subject is so vitally important," Lieber wrote, "and we ought to show our gratitude, practically, for God's having removed at last this fearful incubus." [9] But Sumner needed no prodding. Already, on the very night of Taney's death, he had written to Lincoln a whole-hearted endorsement of Chase. "Thus far the Constitution has been interpreted for Slavery," he said. "Thank God! it may now be interpreted solely for Liberty." [10]

After a week Lincoln let Chase know, through Secretary of the Treasury Fessenden, that he had not forgotten what he had said about appointing him, "but as things were going on well he thought it best not to make any appointment or say anything about it, until after the election was over." [11] Meanwhile Chase kept on campaigning for Lincoln, amid rumors of a "bargain" by which Lincoln had persuaded Chase to support him in return for a promise of the Chief Justiceship.[12] Election day came and went, and still Lincoln sent no nomination to the Senate. Chase's friends became impatient. "The President, in my opinion, errs by his delay," Sumner said. "The appointment ought to have been made on the evening of Taney's funeral; but sooner or later Mr. Chase will be nominated." [13] Chase himself also became restless. He needed to go to Washington on business but,

[6] Bates, *Diary*, 418–419.

[7] Stanton to Chase, Oct. 13, 1864, Chase MSS., Hist. Soc. of Pa.

[8] Chase to Stanton, Oct. 13, 1864, Stanton MSS., Lib. of Cong.

[9] Lieber to Sumner, Oct. 13, 1864, Sumner MSS., Harvard Coll. Lib.

[10] Sumner to Lincoln, Oct. 12, 1864, R. T. L. Coll., 37179–80.

[11] Fessenden to Chase, Oct. 20, 1864, Chase MSS., Hist. Soc. of Pa.

[12] J. K. Herbert to Butler, Sept. 26, 1864, *Correspondence of Gen. Benjamin F. Butler,* V, 167–168.

[13] Pierce, *Sumner,* IV, 208.

rather than give the impression that he would "solicit or even ask such an appointment as a favor or as a reward for political service," he stayed at home in Cincinnati, hoping from day to day that the President would act.[14]

Meanwhile strong opposition to Chase was arising in several quarters, even in Lincoln's own household, on the part of his wife. Several other candidates were being urged, or were pressing their own claims, among them Associate Justice Swayne, Secretaries Stanton and Bates, the New York legal light William M. Evarts, and the former Postmaster-General, Montgomery Blair.[15] Stanton himself did not seek the job, but Mrs. Stanton sought it for him, and at her request O. H. Browning interceded with Lincoln. The President "said nothing . . . except to admit Mr. Stantons ability, and fine qualifications," and also to confide that Bates "had personally solicited the Chief Justiceship" for himself.[16]

Having been sacrificed to appease the Radicals, Blair deserved the Chief Justiceship as his consolation, or so his father thought. Old man Blair wrote to everyone he could think of who might possibly appeal to Lincoln in the son's behalf.[17] He had no trouble in enlisting Mrs. Lincoln's support. "Mr. Blair," she told him, as he reported their conversation, "Chase and his friends are beseiging my Husband for the Chief-Justiceship. I wish you could prevent them." The elder Blair finally went to Lincoln himself and, though the President was noncommittal, came away with great expectations. "From the tenor and manner of his remarks I infer that he is well disposed to appoint Montgomery." [18]

The Supreme Court was to meet on December 5, and when that day arrived, the Court still lacked a Chief Justice. No one knew— unless Lincoln himself did—when it would have one or who he would be. Welles remained confident that, while the President sometimes did "strange things," he would not make such a "singular mistake" as to appoint Chase.[19] Welles thought Blair was the man, and the New York *Times* predicted that Blair probably would be ap-

14 Chase to John Sherman, Nov. 12, 1864, Sherman MSS., Lib. of Cong.
15 Silver, "Supreme Court during the Civil War," 208–214.
16 Browning, *Diary*, I, 687–688.
17 Silver, "Supreme Court during the Civil War," 211–214.
18 Blair to John A. Andrew, Nov. 19, 1864, Mass. Hist. Soc. *Proc.*, LXIII, 88–89.
19 Welles, *Diary*, II, 187.

pointed. The New York *Herald* predicted that Swayne would be.[20]

On December 6, without an advance word to the cabinet or to anyone else, Lincoln sent the name of Chase to the Senate. The Senate, as it usually did with appointees who were or had been senators, promptly and unanimously confirmed the appointment.[21] Republican newspapers hailed it as marking a revolution in the history of the Court and the Constitution. "Five years ago, had any one suggested Salmon P. Chase as the probable successor of Roger B. Taney," observed the New York *Tribune*, ". . . he would have been regarded as in need of a straight jacket." [22]

Chase wrote to Lincoln on the day of the nomination: "Before I sleep I must thank you for this mark of your confidence, and especially for the manner in which the nomination was made." [23] The next day the new Chief Justice paid a brief social call at the Executive Mansion.[24] Whatever Lincoln may have told him at that time, Lincoln told another visitor at about the same time, as Welles had it, "that he would rather have swallowed his buckhorn chair than to have nominated Chase." [25]

Why, then, did he nominate him? He explained to Representative George S. Boutwell, of Massachusetts, that there were three reasons. First, Chase was a prominent figure with a considerable following. Second, as Chief Justice he would uphold the administration on the issues of emancipation and the legal tenders, if and when these issues came before the Court. Third: "We cannot ask a man what he will do, and if we should, and he should answer us, we should despise him for it. Therefore we must take a man whose opinions are known."

But Lincoln added that there was a strong reason against the appointment of Chase. "He is a candidate for the Presidency, and if he does not give up that idea, it will be very bad for him and very bad for me." [26] Chase's overweening ambition doubtless accounted for Lincoln's long hesitation. Blair did not suffer from the same defect; he was certainly as deserving on account of political services as was Chase; and he could have been counted on as well or better to sustain the administration. One consideration alone, however, was enough

20 Silver, "Supreme Court during the Civil War," 219–220.
21 Washington *Daily Chronicle*, Dec. 7, 1864.
22 Silver, "Supreme Court during the Civil War," 222.
23 Schuckers, *Chase*, 513.   24 New York *Herald*, Dec. 8, 1864, p. 4, c. 5.
25 Welles, *Diary*, II, 196 (Dec. 10, 1864).   26 Boutwell, *Reminiscences*, II, 29.

to disqualify Blair. He was anathema to the Radicals, and his nomination would never have been confirmed by the Senate. Whatever other motives Lincoln may have had, his naming of Chase was a concession to the Radicals.

For them, the first of February, 1865, was an epoch-making date. On that day Sumner moved in the Supreme Court that John S. Rock be admitted to practice before it. Chase, consulted in advance by Sumner, had made sure of favorable action on the motion. It carried, and Rock was admitted. The Dred Scott decision was indeed a thing of the past, for Rock was a Negro, the first of his race to appear as a lawyer before the Supreme Court.[27] Here was an auspicious beginning, from the Radical point of view, and the Radicals expected other great things in the new era under Chase.

However reliable Chase might be on questions involving the Negro and emancipation, Lincoln soon was told that he could not be depended upon when such questions as the constitutionality of the greenbacks came up. Chase, it was said, would "fail the Administration," but Lincoln, recalling the "committals of Chase," refused to believe it.[28] Chase was indeed to fail the administration, after Lincoln was dead, when he ruled the legal-tender act unconstitutional, even though, as secretary of treasury, he had been largely responsible for its passage in the first place. And Chase was to justify Lincoln's fear that he would never give up his intriguing for the Presidency.

He was also to disappoint the hopes of the Radicals—as when, presiding at the impeachment trial of President Johnson, he behaved with judicial impartiality instead of abetting the impeachers. Once he was on the Court he seemed to grow more conservative—or perhaps only more independent—than he formerly had been. He did not agree with the Radicals in Congress who refused even to let money be spent to provide the Supreme Court chamber with a bust of Taney, that "wicked" man.[29] At least in private conversation, he was willing to be generous and just to his predecessor. He once remarked to Browning "that he, Taney, had been cruelly misrepresented in regard to his opinion in the Dred Scott case—that what he said about the rights of negroes was but the statement of a historical fact, and that there was nothing in it derogatory to the Judges integrity or hu-

---

[27] Pierce, *Sumner*, IV, 209.   [28] Welles, *Diary*, II, 245–246 (Feb. 22, 1865).
[29] Silver, "Supreme Court during the Civil War," 230–231.

manity—that he was a man of great talents and attainments—a very able jurist—unusually kind and gentle in his nature, and of very pure and exalted character." [30]

III

Though the Radicals hailed the Chase appointment as a victory for themselves, they were not content with that alone. In the sixth plank of the Baltimore platform they had called for a reorganization of the Cabinet in the interests of "harmony," which meant of course the interests of Radicalism. The removal of Blair, as they saw it, was only a beginning. After the election of 1864 they renewed their old criticisms of the Lincoln ministry, and—though not for the same reasons —reformers with Conservative leanings joined them in the demand for changes in the cabinet.

All kinds of rumblings and rumors about the cabinet were to be heard on the streets and in the offices and salons of Washington during the fall and winter of 1864–65. One visitor in the Capital reported with heavy irony his "joy" at finding that, among some of Lincoln's friends, his re-election was taken to mean "the people were overwhelmingly in favor of trusting the Government in the hands of the Administration! and this, notwithstanding the unpopularity of many members of the Cabinet, Stanton & Welles particularly. Seward is by no means wholly satisfactory to the people. Lincoln himself lacks the power to content the fastidious & the highly conservative, or the strongly radical." [1] Another observer in Washington predicted that the cabinet would "all bust up" soon after Lincoln's re-inauguration in March. Stanton was "worse than ever," or so Blair was swearing "on corners of the streets"; Welles was "listless"; Seward was "devilish"; and the observer himself was "disheartened—disgusted." [2] The President did have defenders, such as the eloquent Edward Everett, who in a Boston speech replied to the charge that Lincoln's administration "wanted unity of counsel" by pointing out that George Washington's had included "the heads of two radically opposite parties," Hamilton and Jefferson. "It rarely happens," protested Everett, "that

[30] Browning, *Diary*, II, 54 (Dec. 22, 1865).
[1] H. W. Bellows to his son, Nov. 13, 1864, Bellows MSS., Mass. Hist. Soc.
[2] L. G. Hews to J. A. Andrew, Dec. 17, 1864, Andrews MSS., Mass. Hist. Soc.

any other course is practicable in difficult times."[3] Yet the gossips persisted in saying that Lincoln's cabinet was a "solemn failure" and that the President himself had come to realize it. "Having violated what is known to have been his original intention to make no changes till the close of his Administration, by accepting Mr. Chase's resignation and requesting Mr. Blair's, he may be reasonably presumed to be contemplating others."[4]

He was indeed. When Congress met, early in December, he was ready with two names to send to the Senate. Neither of these names attracted much attention, since they were overshadowed in the news by the nomination of Chase to the Chief Justiceship at the same time.[5] One was that of William Dennison, an interim appointee already designated (September 24) to replace Blair as Postmaster General.[6] The choice of Dennison, a former Ohio governor, implied that the President had both geographical and factional considerations in mind. Dennison, a loyal Lincoln campaigner, was "preaching the gospel to the heathen" of southern Ohio at the moment he received word of his nomination.[7] He was also a Radical and a friend of Chase, and his accession to the cabinet would presumably compensate to some degree for Chase's departure, so far as Ohio Republicans were concerned.

The other place which Lincoln was ready to fill when Congress met was that of the Attorney General. Edward Bates, viewing himself as the last of the old Whigs, had begun to feel that he was "among strangers." During the campaign of 1864 Bates told Lincoln he wanted to retire after the election, and at the end of November Lincoln accepted his resignation.[8] Since Bates was a Missourian, Lincoln looked for a successor from a border state, first offering the job to Joseph Holt, the Judge Advocate General, a Kentuckian. When Holt declined, Lincoln sent a telegram (December 1) to another Kentuckian, James Speed.[9] For this selection, Lincoln had personal as well as geographical reasons, James being the brother of Joshua F. Speed, Lincoln's intimate of the early Springfield days. "The appointment of James

[3] Washington *Daily Chronicle*, Nov. 18, 1864, p. 1, c. 5.
[4] Cincinnati *Daily Gazette*, Nov. 23, 1864, p. 1, c. 4.
[5] Washington *Daily Chronicle*, Dec. 7, 1864.
[6] Dennett, . . . *Diaries* . . . *of John Hay*, 216.
[7] Carman and Luthin, *Lincoln and the Patronage*, 277–278.
[8] Bates, *Diary*, 428.   [9] *Collected Works*, VIII, 126.

Speed, of Louisville, to the vacant Attorney-Generalship," said a Washington commentator, "is owing rather to the President's old friendship and high appreciation of his abilities, than to any specific political interest." [10] In fact, a "political interest" also was involved, at least incidentally, since Speed could be expected to help balance the cabinet on the Conservative side.

A third and more important vacancy appeared in the offing when, in February, 1865, William Pitt Fessenden indicated his intention of resigning as secretary of the treasury. After entering the cabinet reluctantly, Fessenden soon had become anxious to leave it, so as to return to the Senate, for which his talents better fitted him. In anticipation of his departure, several Radicals were mentioned for his place, among them George S. Boutwell, John W. Forney, and Thaddeus Stevens.[11] As chairman of the House committee on appropriations—corresponding to the Senate finance committee, of which Fessenden had been chairman—Stevens seemed, to the Pennsylvania Republicans in Congress, to be logically next in line for the treasury post. If, by his inflationary views, he had pleased many of the manufacturers of his own state, he had antagonized the "sound money" men of Wall Street. His latest gaucherie in their eyes was a bill to prohibit any greenback from being "received for a smaller sum" than was specified on its face, a proposal which led the New York *World* to sneer at him as one who expected to "legislate fair weather in finance." Even had Lincoln been inclined to appoint him in appeasement of the Radicals, Stevens would have been disqualified because of his monetary aberrations.[12]

But Lincoln was not inclined to appoint him, anyhow. Apparently he did consider naming Hannibal Hamlin, the retiring Vice President, whose ambition for a Senate seat from Maine was frustrated by Fessenden's desire for the same seat. According to Hamlin's son, Fessenden objected to his rival's succeeding him in the cabinet, and so Lincoln promised him the Boston collectorship as a consolation prize (and President Johnson later gave him the Boston job).[13] Lincoln then called in Thurlow Weed for a consultation, and Weed recommended Senator Edwin D. Morgan, of New York, for the treas-

---

10 Cincinnati *Daily Gazette*, Dec. 5, 1864, p. 3, c. 3.
11 *Ibid.*, Feb. 25, 1865, p. 1, c. 1.   12 Current, *Old Thad Stevens*, 205–206.
13 C. E. Hamlin, *Hannibal Hamlin*, 495.

ury.[14] Morgan had no special qualifications as a financial expert, but he was thought to deserve a cabinet place on account of his political services—"for," as Washington gossips asked, "was he not Chairman of the National Executive Committee that insured Mr. Lincoln's nomination by refusing to postpone the call for the National Convention?" [15] But Morgan could not be persuaded to accept.

His reiterated refusals left Hugh McCulloch as Lincoln's favorite candidate. McCulloch was a banker, not a politician. Chase as treasury secretary had brought him to Washington from Indianapolis to serve as comptroller of the currency. Both Chase and Fessenden recommended McCulloch to head the treasury department, though McCulloch did not entirely approve the policies of either of them. He thought Chase had erred in consenting that the government paper money should be made a legal tender, and he thought Fessenden had erred in attempting to dispense with the services of the middleman Jay Cooke in the sale of government bonds. Indeed, he feared that the treasury had become "considerably embarrassed" and the government credit considerably "impaired" as a result of Fessenden's timidity and administrative incompetence. McCulloch was "taken aback" when, a day or two after the second inauguration, Lincoln called him by messenger to the Executive Mansion, grasped his hand, and told him he was needed as secretary of the treasury. McCulloch protested that he doubted his own capacity to do what the "existing financial condition of the Government" would make necessary. "I will be responsible for that," said Lincoln, as McCulloch afterward recalled, "and so I suppose we will consider the matter settled." [16]

Lincoln had one final cabinet change to make. He had been growing more and more dissatisfied with John P. Usher's administration of the interior department. Early in 1865 he conferred with Governor Yates and Senator Trumbull, of Illinois, about a successor to Usher. They recommended Senator Harlan, of Iowa.[17] Others, however, urged the appointment of Representative Isaac N. Arnold, of Illinois. "Representative Arnold insists that he is a candidate for no place and wants nothing; but his position as peculiarly the President's man in Congress entitles him to something; and the arrangers of the

[14] Carman and Luthin, *Lincoln and the Patronage*, 310.
[15] Cincinnati *Daily Gazette*, Feb. 25, 1865, p. 1, c. 1.
[16] McCulloch, *Men and Measures*, 190–191.
[17] Carman and Luthin, *Lincoln and the Patronage*, 311–312.

Cabinet hold that he would make as good a Secretary of the Interior as anybody." [18] Arnold was fighting the President's fight for the Thirteenth Amendment in the House at this time, and the President thought highly of him. But Lincoln thought highly also of Harlan, who was a loyal political lieutenant, having headed the congressional campaign committee in 1864, and a family friend as well. Harlan escorted Mrs. Lincoln to the second inauguration, and his daughter was often escorted by her son, Robert Todd Lincoln (who later married Miss Harlan). When Usher submitted his resignation, to take effect May 15, Lincoln named his friend Harlan as secretary of the interior (March 9), but Lincoln was dead a month before Harlan took office.

By the personnel changes he made after his re-election, Lincoln probably improved and certainly did not impair the administrative efficiency of the departments. But he did not succeed in adding political strength to his administration, nor did he achieve greater unity, though he managed to maintain a fairly even Radical-Conservative balance. McCulloch was a Conservative in politics as much as a conservative in finances. Speed, however, who as a Kentuckian was originally thought to be a Conservative, aligned himself with the Radicals Stanton and Dennison before Lincoln's death.[19]

The policy-making significance of the appointments, apart from their bearing on the broad issue of Radicalism and Conservatism, was not very clear. By his choice of a new treasury secretary the President might have been expected to indicate his own financial preferences. The fact is, however, that Lincoln disagreed profoundly with McCulloch about the relation of government finances to the national economy.

McCulloch was bearish. He had the dour outlook proverbially associated with a man of his Scotch ancestry. As comptroller of the currency he had issued to the National Banks in December, 1863, a circular embodying his pessimistic views. The states of the North, he then warned, appeared to be prosperous but actually were not, for the war was "constantly draining the country of its laboring and producing population, and diverting its mechanical industry from works of permanent value to the construction of implements of warfare."

18 Cincinnati *Daily Gazette,* Feb. 25, 1865, p. 1, c. 1.
19 Carman and Luthin, *Lincoln and the Patronage,* 312.

The "seeming prosperity," he explained, was due primarily to "the large expenditures of the Government and the redundant currency." He advised the bankers to prepare for a depression: "manage the affairs of your respective banks with a perfect consciousness that the apparent prosperity of the country will be proved to be unreal when the war is closed, if not before . . . ." When he received the offer of the treasury position, McCulloch assumed that Lincoln had been motivated by "the impression which was made upon him" by this gloomy circular.[20]

But Lincoln in his message to Congress of December, 1864, expressed an entirely different spirit. Part of the message was a paean to wartime progress and prosperity. "It is of noteworthy interest," the President declared, "that the steady expansion of population, improvement and governmental institutions over the new and unoccupied portions of our country have scarcely been checked, much less impeded or destroyed, by our great civil war, which at first glance would seem to have absorbed almost the entire energies of the nation." Sales of public land soared high, the Pacific railroad was being pushed to completion, new sources of gold and silver and mercury were being opened in the West. The popular vote in the recent election—larger in the free states, despite the non-voting of most of the soldiers, than it had been in 1860—demonstrated an important fact: "that we have *more* men *now* than we had when the war *began* . . . ." Besides: "Material resources are now more complete and abundant than ever." [21]

IV

William H. Seward (who, with Welles, was to remain in the cabinet from the beginning of Lincoln's administration to the end of Johnson's) was doing a thoroughly satisfactory job as secretary of state, and Lincoln's working relations with him were excellent, the secretary's foreign-war panacea of 1861 long since forgotten. The President still took an occasional hand in diplomatic affairs, as in such ceremonials as the presentation of the credentials of the Baron de Vetterstedt, the first fully accredited Envoy Extraordinary and Minister

20 McCulloch, *Men and Measures*, 195–198.   21 *Collected Works*, VIII, 145–146.

Plenipotentiary ever sent from Stockholm to Washington. In a rather quaint interchange of pleasantries the President told the Baron: "My memory does not recall an instance of disagreement between Sweden and the United States." [1]

With respect to few other countries could Lincoln honestly have said such a thing, but he could and did announce, in his annual message of December 6, 1864, that the United States was on fairly good terms with most of the world. He went so far as to suggest that, "if it were a new and open question," the maritime powers "would not concede the privileges of a naval belligerent to the insurgents," as Great Britain and others had done at the start of the war.[2] But he and Seward did face two serious problems of diplomacy in the winter of 1864–65. One, the problem of the French intervention in Mexico, he passed over lightly in his message to Congress. The other, the problem of the use of Canadian soil for Confederate raids across the border, he discussed more fully.

He announced that, because of the border threat (he did not refer specifically to such recent events as the St. Alban's raid), it had been "though proper to give notice that after the expiration of six months, the period conditionally stipulated in the existing arrangement with Great Britain, the United States must hold themselves at liberty to increase their naval armament upon the lakes." While thus denouncing the Rush-Bagot agreement of 1817, he also indicated that he was ready to modify the reciprocity treaty of 1854, so as to raise tariffs on Canadian goods and discontinue certain privileges of transit from Canada through the United States.

He made these announcements in no bellicose tone. He wished to be understood that the Canadian authorities were "not deemed to be intentionally unjust or unfriendly" and that they, "with the approval of the imperial government," would "take the necessary measures to prevent new incursions across the border." [3] In British government circles his remarks were received in the spirit in which he had intended them. "The resolution of the Federal government to place an additional force on the great lakes is not to be complained of," said the authoritative *Times* of London. "So long as the war lasts

---

[1] Washington *Daily Chronicle,* Jan. 21, 1865, p. 2, c. 1.
[2] *Collected Works,* VIII, 136, 140.   [3] *Ibid.,* 141.

it will be the object of the Confederates to make the British provinces the basis of some kind of operations against their enemy." [4]

Lincoln was careful to see that zealous Americans did not go beyond the intent of his Canada policy. When General Dix, in command in New York, instructed all military commanders on the frontier to shoot down raiding groups on sight, whatever their nationality, and to cross the boundary in pursuit of them if necessary, Lincoln disapproved the order and it was revoked.[5] He also declined an offer of the Fenian Brotherhood, a revolutionary organization of armed Irish-Americans, to prevent invasions from the North.[6] (A few years later the Fenians were to reverse the border problem by themselves undertaking incursions into Canada.) Lincoln did order that crossings into the United States be denied to all who lacked appropriate passports. The Canadian authorities co-operated by providing a few thousand militia to patrol the border, at an estimated expense of $100,000 per month.[7]

No patronage matter arose to complicate relations with Canada and Great Britain, but such a matter did momentarily jeopardize relations with France. In December, 1864, the American minister in Paris, the rather ineffectual William L. Dayton, died. Fortunately there was an ideal successor to Dayton already on the ground, namely, John Bigelow, the American consul general, who already was performing many of the functions of an ambassador, who in fact was more nearly than Dayton the equivalent in France of Minister Charles F. Adams in England.[8] But, unfortunately, Lincoln during the presidential campaign had promised the French mission to the newspaperman whose help he then had needed—James Gordon Bennett.

And Bennett was not likely to be *persona grata* in Paris. Though Bigelow sometimes was impatient with Seward's policy of speaking softly on French intervention in Mexico, Bennett was becoming fanatical on the subject. His New York *Herald* criticized Lincoln's annual message for its neglect of the Monroe Doctrine.[9] Reviving the essence of the forgotten Seward formula—reunion at home through a war abroad—the *Herald* kept hammering at the theme of combining the Blue and the Gray into an army that would drive the puppet em-

---

[4] Quoted in Cincinnati *Daily Gazette,* Jan. 10, 1865, p. 1, c. 3.

[5] *Ann. Cyc.,* 1864, IV, 360–361.   [6] New York *Herald,* Dec. 19, 1864, p. 5, c. 6.

[7] *Ann. Cyc.,* 1864, IV, 178.   [8] See Margaret Clapp, *John Bigelow.*

[9] Dec. 7, 1864, p. 4, c. 2.

peror Maximilian out of Mexico and at the same time reconcile the North and the South in a common cause. "In the struggles and triumphs of a foreign war," as the *Herald* bluntly put it, "we shall recement the sundered sympathies of loyal and rebellious states." [10]

Even though Bennett as minister to France could thus be expected to work against Seward's temporizing policy, Lincoln was not a man to forget his political promises. Of course, he may have counted upon Bennett's declining the appointment. If so, he was taking a risk, for he had no way of knowing for sure that Bennett would decline it. On the contrary, Bennett seemed eager for the offer, if not also for the position itself. In any case, when Lincoln offered it he turned it down.[11] Later Lincoln nominated Bigelow, another experienced newspaperman, a former part owner of the New York *Evening Post*. The French mission thus happened to fall into able hands.

V

With U. S. Grant as general-in-chief, the army was led by a man whom the President could depend upon. From time to time Lincoln still "interfered" in military affairs, though the myth persists that he allowed Grant to have his own way completely. As late as August, 1864, for example, he insisted that the general come to Washington for consultation about the pursuit of Early's army after the raid on Washington. "In the remaining months of 1864," T. Harry Williams writes, "Lincoln watched intently and sometimes anxiously over the conduct of the vast Union war effort, but he intervened in the management of it only at rare intervals because in general he was satisfied with Grant's direction." [1]

During these months the most spectacular military activity was conceived and initiated by General W. T. Sherman, with the somewhat doubtful approval of Grant and Lincoln. With the capture of Atlanta, Sherman had not won his main objective, which was the capture or destruction of the opposing army under General J. B. Hood.[2] Moreover, Sherman had lost the initiative. To recover it, he proposed to divide his forces and, with about 60,000 men, strike out

---

10 Nov. 8, 1864, p. 4, c. 3; Nov. 9, 1864, p. 4, c. 4.   11 See above, pp. 42–45.

1 Williams, *Lincoln and His Generals*, 336.

2 Randall, *Civil War and Reconstruction*, 554.

boldly from Atlanta to some point on the coast, effecting a "devastation more or less relentless" [3] on the way, while he sent General George H. Thomas back with about 30,000 men to hold Tennessee. Grant thought Sherman should dispose of Hood's army before he started off. Lincoln let Grant know that he himself had doubts about the plan. Yet he accepted it when Grant told him that nothing better seemed available. [4]

Early in November Sherman's men moved out of Atlanta and headed southeast, with orders to advance fifteen miles a day by four parallel roads, foraging on the country and laying waste mills, houses, cotton gins, public buildings, and especially railroad tracks and bridges. [5] Sherman did not attempt to maintain lines of communication or supply, and the North had little news of his three-hundred-mile march while it was in progress. The President referred to it cautiously in his annual message on December 6. "It tends to show a great increase in our relative strength that our General-in-Chief should feel able to confront and hold in check every active force of the enemy, and yet to detach a well-appointed large army to move on such an expedition," he said. "The result not yet being known, conjecture in regard to it is not here indulged." He left out of the address one sentence which would have revealed to the people his own very real fear of possible disaster. In this sentence he had written that the general-in-chief must have concluded that "our cause could, if need be, survive the loss of the whole detached force." [6]

Before Sherman left Atlanta, Hood had moved northward into Tennessee, in the hope of maneuvering Sherman out of Georgia, but Sherman relied on Thomas to deal with Hood. Though defeated at Franklin, Hood pushed stubbornly on to Nashville and besieged Thomas there. Lincoln, as he anxiously watched events from Washington, kept expecting Thomas to come out and fight. Finally he directed Stanton to consult with Grant about Thomas's failure to attack, and he got more of a reaction from Grant than he had bargained for. Grant advised that Thomas be removed from command and, despite Lincoln's unwillingness to approve such a drastic step, sent General John A. Logan to supersede him. [7] Finally Grant went to

3 Sherman, *Memoirs*, II, 175.   4 Williams, *Lincoln and His Generals*, 339–340.
5 Sherman, *Memoirs*, II, 171–172, 175.   6 *Collected Works*, VIII, 148.
7 Williams, *Lincoln and His Generals*, 341, 345; Randall, *Civil War and Reconstruction*, 675–676.

consult Lincoln, intending to go on from Washington to Nashville to see personally that Thomas was relieved.

On December 15, Lincoln presided at a conference of Grant, Stanton, and Halleck. The President was now in the position, unusual for him, of arguing for the retention of a general who seemed to be afflicted with what, in the case of McClellan three years earlier, he had called the "slows." Lincoln pointed out that Thomas, on the ground, was better able to judge the tactical situation than was Grant, hundreds of miles away. Angrily and stubbornly Grant persisted in demanding Thomas's removal, and at last Lincoln gave in.

That night, before Grant had left Washington, a telegram came to the war department with news of a great victory at Nashville. Stanton immediately drove to the White House, where Lincoln in a nightshirt and with a candle in his hand appeared at the head of the main stairway to hear the news. He smiled and went back to bed.[8]

Next day he telegraphed his congratulations to Thomas on the "good work." Remembering other "victories" which had proved abortive, he also admonished: "You made a magnificent beginning. A grand consummation is within your easy reach. Do not let it slip." [9]

Thomas did not let it slip. He followed up the shock of his first assault with a vigorous pursuit of Hood, who escaped across the Tennessee River with only a sorry remnant of the fine army he had taken out of Atlanta several weeks before. "The victory at Nashville was the only one in the war so complete that the defeated army practically lost its existence," says T. Harry Williams. "It was also a complete vindication of Lincoln's faith in Thomas. Again the President had been more right than Grant." [10]

Grant as well as Lincoln had complete faith in Sherman, who was approaching the end of his march to the sea at the time of the battle of Nashville. He took Savannah in time to give it to Lincoln as a Christmas present. On December 26 the President sent his thanks to Sherman and his whole army. "When you were about leaving Atlanta for the Atlantic coast," Lincoln confessed to him, "I was *anxious*, if not fearful; but feeling that you were the better judge, and remembering that 'nothing risked, nothing gained' I did not interfere. Now, the undertaking being a success, the honor is all yours; for I believe

8 Williams, *Lincoln and His Generals*, 343–344.   9 *Collected Works*, VIII, 169.
10 Williams, *Lincoln and His Generals*, 344–345.

none of us went farther than to acquiesce. And, taking the work of Gen. Thomas into the account, as it should be taken, it is indeed a great success." [11]

As the year 1864 ended and the fateful new year began, the President had reason to be satisfied with Thomas, Sherman, and Grant. The army now was commanded by professional soldiers—with one very notable exception—and the professionals were doing excellent work.

VI

The last of the politician-generals to hold important army commands were Nathaniel P. Banks and Benjamin F. Butler, whose careers provide interesting comparisons and contrasts. Both men were former Democrats with backgrounds as labor champions in Massachusetts, Banks as the "Bobbin Boy" of Waltham and Butler as an agitator for the ten-hour day in Lowell. Both had become Radical Republicans and, like many another politico when the war was young, had received commissions in the army by virtue of their political influence rather than their military skill. In the spring of 1864 each had demonstrated his unfitness for a field command, Banks in the fiasco of his Red River expedition into Texas, Butler in allowing his Army of the James to be "as completely shut off from further operations directly against Richmond as if it had been in a bottle strongly corked" (to quote Grant's report of Butler's withdrawal into Bermuda Hundred, at the forks of the James and the Appomattox). Both Banks and Butler had had experience in administering occupied territory, Banks having succeeded Butler as military commander in occupied New Orleans. But Banks had proved a much better administrator, at least from Lincoln's point of view, and he was willing to co-operate loyally in carrying out the presidential plan for restoring loyal state governments. Butler, equipped with a kind of audacity and a talent for publicity which Banks lacked, devoted his truly remarkable talents to sabotaging the presidential plan while continuing his military blunders. Of all Lincoln's many personal problems, this man Butler must be singled out as the most persistently troublesome.

By comparison, Banks was a minor nuisance. During the fall of

---

[11] *Collected Works*, VIII, 181–182.

1864, in Washington on leave from his command of the Gulf Department, where he no longer exercised more than civil functions, he tried for weeks to persuade Lincoln to restore the military powers of which Lincoln had deprived him in May. "I cannot . . . ," said the President. Referring presumably to Grant, he explained: "He whom I must hold responsible for results, is not agreed." Banks then offered to resign, but Lincoln dissuaded him, needing him to continue working in behalf of the new state government of Louisiana, the launching of which Banks had already overseen. "I know you are dissatisfied, which pains me very much," said Lincoln, "but I wish not to be argued with further." [1] In November he extended Banks' leave indefinitely,[2] and Banks stayed on in Washington throughout the winter to lobby, ex-congressman that he was, in behalf of the reconstructed Louisiana government. He became a source of comfort rather than pain to the President.

Butler, however, continued as the storm center of one personality clash after another. While in New York, where with his troops he was supposed to prevent violence at the November polls, he got into a controversy with General John A. Dix, the commander of the Department of New York, by insisting on precedence over Dix even though he did not outrank him.[3] As commander of the Department of Virginia and North Carolina, a position he had held since late in 1863, he was continually at odds with Francis H. Pierpont, the governor of the "Restored Government" of Virginia, with presumed authority over what was left of that state after West Virginia and the Confederate-controlled area were subtracted from it. General Butler, in Norfolk, repeatedly challenged the authority of Governor Pierpont, in Alexandria, and Lincoln finally had to step in to decide the issue of military as against civilian rule.

In the spring of 1864 Pierpont published in pamphlet form a long letter, addressed to the President and Congress, in which he described the "abuses of military power" in Virginia and North Carolina. According to Pierpont's indictment, Butler was guilty of an imposing list of arbitrary actions, most of them intended to line his own pockets or those of his friends. He levied taxes on oyster boats in Chesapeake Bay and on other vessels using the port of Norfolk. He set up a pro-

---

[1] Harrington, *Fighting Politician*, 159–160, 163–164.   [2] *Collected Works*, VIII, 106.
[3] F. E. Howe to John A. Andrew, Nov. 6, 1864, Andrew MSS.

vost marshal's court in competition with the courts of the Pierpont government, and his provost marshal turned out of jail prisoners awaiting trial in the state courts. Setting up a monopoly of the liquor traffic, he placed it in the hands of his associates from Boston, as he also did the management of the Norfolk gas plant. He issued an order that every fourth dog should be killed; any dog-lover desiring to rescue a pet had to pay two dollars which, along with other Butler exactions, went into a "provost marshal's fund." [4]

In reply, Butler dismissed Pierpont as "the *soi disant* Governor of Virginia." During the summer of 1864 he further showed his contempt for Pierpont by holding a referendum in Norfolk on the question of abolishing the civil government there. The vote favored Butler and military rule. He then put forth an order forbidding any exercise of authority by "persons pretending to be elected to civil office" in Norfolk. Pierpont protested to Lincoln and assured him that most of the loyal voters had boycotted the election, that Butler's majority had come chiefly from "Uncompromising seceshinists" and "Non residents Mostly liquor sellers." [5] Attorney-General Bates took up Pierpont's cause and wrote a long letter to Lincoln.[6] Butler, also writing to Lincoln, attacked Bates and Pierpont as men of doubtful loyalty and defended his own assumption of civilian powers as necessary for the preservation of order and the protection of his troops.

"This subject has caused considerable trouble, forcing me to give a good deal of time and reflection to it," Lincoln wrote at last, on August 9, in a letter he intended to send to Butler. Pierpont and Bates were as loyal as Butler himself, the President patiently reassured the general. True, Pierpont did not actually govern much of Virginia, and the "insignificance of the parts" which were "outside of the rebel lines" gave a "somewhat farcical air to his dominion." But Pierpont, as well as Lincoln himself, had "considered that it could be useful for little else than a nucleus to add to" a nucleus, in other words, for the reconstruction of Virginia. "Coming to the question

<hr>

[4] *Letter of Governor Peirpoint, to His Excellency the President and the Honorable Congress of the United States, on the Subject of Abuse of Military Power in the Command of General Butler in Virginia and North Carolina* (Washington, D. C.: McGill & Witherow, Printers and Stereotypers, 1864), *passim*. The Governor then spelled his name *Peirpoint* but in 1881 changed it to *Pierpont* to conform to an earlier spelling which had been corrupted. See Ambler, *Pierpont*, 3–4.

[5] Peirpoint to Lincoln, July 8, 1864, R. T. L. Coll., 34359.

[6] Ambler, *Pierpont*, 232 ff.

itself," Lincoln went on, "the Military occupancy of Norfolk is a necessity with us." If Butler, as commander of the department, found it necessary to take complete control of the city and provide such services as street cleaning and lighting, fire protection, wharfage, and poor relief, he could of course do so. "But you should do so on your own avowed judgment of military necessity, and not seem to admit that there is no such necessity, by taking a vote of the people on the question." And then Lincoln added a sentence which was more than an afterthought: "I also think you should so keep accounts as to show every item of money received and how expended." [7] The President finished the letter, then laid it aside. The time was not auspicious for sending it, this being dark August, the Wade-Davis Manifesto still fresh, and Butler himself the Radical favorite for replacing Lincoln on the presidential ticket. Grant wanted Butler removed as unfit for command, but Lincoln for the time being would not assume personal responsibility for removing him, though willing to let Grant do it on his own. For Lincoln to remove Butler, or even to rebuke him, would be most impolitic until after the election. And, as Lincoln thought, the Pierpont-Butler controversy was dying down anyhow.

Before the end of the year it flared up again. On December 21, 1864, Lincoln finally sent Butler a copy of his letter of August 9 and with it a note: "I now learn, correctly I suppose, that you have ordered an election, similar to the one mentioned, to take place on the Eastern Shore of Virginia. Let this be suspended, at least until conference with me, and obtaining my approval." On December 27 Butler wired back that the inhabitants of the Eastern Shore (the peninsula above Norfolk and east of Chesapeake Bay) had petitioned for such an election but he had not ordered it. [8]

Just as this old issue was coming to a head again, Butler was busy with his final enterprise as a military commander. This was a joint army-navy expedition against Fort Fisher on the Cape Fear River, near Wilmington, the only port of any size still accessible to Confederate blockade-runners. For some time the navy department had contemplated such an undertaking but had delayed it because of difficulties in enlisting army co-operation. Then Butler came forth eagerly with an original plan of his own. He had read in the newspapers about the terrible damage recently done by the accidental explosion of a gunpowder dump in England. This gave him the idea

---

[7] R. T. L. Coll., 35159–62.   [8] *Collected Works*, VIII, 174.

that, "by bringing within four or five hundred yards of Fort Fisher a large mass of explosives, and firing the whole," he could do such damage that "the garrison would at least be so far paralyzed as to enable, by a prompt landing of men, a seizure of the fort." Welles agreed to provide naval assistance in carrying out Butler's scheme, and Grant consented to Butler's participation as commander of the troops to be landed. The navy prepared a "powder boat," packed with 235 tons of explosives, through which ran a complicated fuse designed to set off the whole mass at once. After repeated delays the expedition finally got under way.[9]

At a cabinet meeting on December 27 Lincoln was "very pleasant over a bit of news in the Richmond papers, stating that the fleet appeared off Fort Fisher, one gun boat got aground and was blown up," as Welles noted. "He thinks it is the powder boat which has made a sensation." Welles himself expected little from Butler's stratagem but trusted that the expedition itself would succeed, in spite of Butler's presence. Welles's doubts were confirmed and Lincoln's hopes were dashed two days later, when dispatches arrived from Rear Admiral David D. Porter, the naval commander in the Fort Fisher assault. "The powder-ship was a mere puff of smoke, doing no damage so far as is known," said Welles, summarizing the admiral's report. The navy nevertheless had succeeded in silencing the fort's batteries, but Butler had not gone ahead with the landing of his troops. Welles and his assistant secretary, Gustavus Vasa Fox, took Porter's dispatches to the President, and the President read them carefully. What now? Welles asked. Lincoln referred him to General Grant.[10]

For Lincoln, the Butler problem had now become a complication in the larger problem of co-ordinating the army and the navy. Butler himself blamed the navy—which, he said, had put too much powder into the boat and had exploded it too soon and in water too deep— and was convinced that *"Porter did not intend that the attack of the army should succeed."* [11] The secretary of war did not try to justify Butler to the President but did say that Porter was no better. The naval officers denounced Butler while Lincoln "listened calmly," and Welles sided with them, while regretting to himself that he had ever sanctioned the powder boat. "That was not regular military," he re-

9 Butler, *Autobiography* . . . *Butler's Book*, 775 ff.　　10 Welles, *Diary*, II, 210.
11 Butler, *Autobiography* . . . *Butler's Book*, 808.

flected, "and had it been a success, the civilian General would have had a triumph." [12] Grant telegraphed that he would immediately organize another expedition, and Lincoln told Welles to see that the navy co-operated better this time.[13] The second attack by combined land and naval forces brought the capitulation of Fort Fisher, on January 15, 1865.

The Butler question remained. A possible way to dispose of it was to shift the trouble-making general from Virginia to Kentucky. The commander in the Kentucky area, General S. G. Burbridge, was unpopular with many Republicans, one of whom complained to the President: ". . . he lost us the vote of Kentucky by his offensive manner of carrying into effect your orders as to Coloured troops." [14] On January 2, 1865, a delegation of Kentuckians asked Lincoln to assign Butler to the command including their state. "Somebody has been howling ever since his assignment to military command," Lincoln replied. "How long will it be before you, who are howling for his assignment to rule Kentucky, will be howling for me to remove him?" [15]

A couple of days after that, Grant wrote to Stanton and requested that Butler, for "the good of the service," be removed as commander of the Department of Virginia and North Carolina. "In my absence General Butler necessarily commands, and there is a lack of confidence felt in his military ability, making him an unsafe commander for a large army," Grant explained. "His administration of the affairs of his department is also objectionable." Learning that Stanton was out of town, Grant on January 6 telegraphed directly to Lincoln and asked for "prompt action." Next day an order came from the war department relieving Butler "by direction of the President of the United States" and instructing him to "repair to Lowell, Mass." When Butler asked Lincoln for permission to publish his own report of the Fort Fisher assault, Lincoln replied that he could not grant permission until he had seen the report, "and not then, if it should be deemed to be detrimental to the public." So, as Butler later complained, "while the newspapers of the country were filled with extract's from Porter's reports and abusive criticisms of my conduct, I

---

[12] Welles, *Diary*, II, 212–217.   [13] Williams, *Lincoln and His Generals*, 348.
[14] T. Ewing to Lincoln, Dec. 1, 1864, Ewing MSS.
[15] New York *Tribune*, Jan. 4, 1865, quoted in *Collected Works*, VIII, 195.

could not say one word as to what that conduct had been." [16]

Butler soon had an opportunity to air his whole collection of grievances and to defend his record from beginning to end. The committee on the conduct of the war moved quickly to investigate the Fort Fisher failure and invited Butler to be heard. Lincoln, after having ordered him home to Lowell, had little choice but to grant him leave to come to Washington, though as Welles observed: "Allied with Wade and Chandler and H. Winter Davis, he will not only aid but breed mischief. This is intended." [17] When Butler arrived in Washington (on the day after the fall of Fort Fisher) the Radicals gave him a hero's reception and asserted that they would restore both his reputation and his command.[18] On the floor of the House Thaddeus Stevens was heard to mutter that Congress would rather have Butler than Lincoln for President.[19]

The Butler question now embraced not only the issue of Radical as against Conservative politics but also the issue of the civilian general—the latter-day Cincinnatus—as against the professionals, both military and naval. Given wide latitude on the witness stand, Butler assured the sympathetic committeemen that Admiral Porter and the navy were entirely responsible for the repulse from Fort Fisher and that he himself and also Grant, whom he exculpated, were victims of a clique of West Pointers who had conspired to disgrace him because he was the last of the civilian generals in an important command.[20] In the committee's unanimous report, Chairman Wade declared that, under the circumstances, "the determination of General Butler not to assault the fort" seemed to have been "fully justified." [21]

Though the Radicals thus cleared Butler's name, at least to their own satisfaction, they did not succeed in getting his command restored to him. He retired to Lowell, whence he kept Wade supplied with documents incriminating Porter, while the committee continued its investigation by calling Grant to testify and then going to Fort Fisher to look for evidence on the spot.[22] At least, Lincoln's Norfolk

16 Butler, *Autobiography . . . Butler's Book*, 827–830; *Collected Works*, VIII, 207; Williams, *Lincoln and His Generals*, 347–348.

17 Welles, *Diary*, II, 223–224 (Jan. 14, 1865).

18 Williams, *Lincoln and the Radicals*, 366.   19 Current, *Old Thad Stevens*, 206.

20 Williams, *Lincoln and the Radicals*, 367–368.

21 Butler, *Autobiography . . . Butler's Book*, 820–821.

22 Williams, *Lincoln and the Radicals*, 368–372.

headache was gone. Civil government was restored in the city, and Pierpont had no difficulty in collaborating with Butler's successor, General E. O. C. Ord.[23]

VII

The removal of the bold political general, the partial reorganization of the cabinet, the appointment of a Chief Justice—these personnel changes at the policy-making level Lincoln could not well have avoided after his re-election. With respect to presidential patronage at a lower level he would have liked to maintain the *status quo* almost intact. "Can't you and others start a public sentiment in favor of making no changes in office except for good and sufficient causes?" he appealed to Senator John B. Clark of New Hampshire not long after election day. "It seems as though the bare thought of going through again what I did the first year here, would *crush* me." [1] So as to win a decisive victory in the late campaign, he had been willing to use his appointing power vigorously, even ruthlessly. Once the victory had been won, however, he was unwilling to use that power punitively. When Henry J. Raymond, "breathing fire and vengeance," demanded the dismissal of certain employees of the New York custom house, who he thought had been disloyal to him and to the party, Lincoln refused to comply, saying: "I am in favor of a short statute of limitations in politics." [2]

Yet the President could not ignore entirely the well-established patronage rule of punishing enemies and rewarding friends. The pressure on him was too great. From November throughout the winter and spring jobseekers crowded into Washington in numbers inferior only to those of 1860–61. Some friends of Lincoln worried lest he, like Presidents Harrison and Taylor before him, suffer a physical breakdown as a result of his hounding by the spoilsmen. Despite his determination against a large-scale shift of officeholders, he had a number of political debts arising from the campaign, and he paid off many of them.[3] Up to the day of his death in April, 1865, he was busy with appointments of collectors of internal revenue and other

---

23 Ambler, *Pierpont,* 243.   1 Carpenter, *Six Months in the White House,* 276.
2 Dennett, . . . *Diaries* . . . *of John Hay,* 239.
3 Carman and Luthin, *Lincoln and the Patronage,* 301–302.

such officers, sometimes making the appointments in batches.[4] On the eve of his assassination he penned a note to the secretary of the treasury in which he said he "would like to oblige Gen. Schenck by the appointment of his nephew" to a collector's job in California.[5]

If Schenck had a nephew to place, Lincoln had a son: Robert Todd, twenty-two, fresh out of Harvard. "Could he, without embarrassment to you, or detriment to the service, go into your Military family with some nominal rank, I, and not the public, furnishing his necessary means?" Lincoln wrote diffidently to Grant, after beginning his letter with a request that it be read as though he were not the President "but only a friend." Whether as a favor to a friend or as a response to the suggestion of his superior, Grant consented gracefully to accepting Robert Todd as a captain on his staff.[6] This was a family affair. Mrs. Lincoln could not stand the thought of her son's being exposed to death in battle, and Lincoln had tried to calm her fears and save her sanity by having him put into a relatively safe army berth, though she persisted in seeing him as any other soldier, exposed to all the risks of war.[7]

The case of John G. Nicolay and John Hay, the President's private secretaries, was also a family matter. Mrs. Lincoln did not like them, and they did not like the "hellcat," as they called her. She was fond of Noah Brooks, a dapper young newspaperman and literateur, much like John Hay except that his sense of humor was less cruel than Hay's. Hay, technically, was never Lincoln's secretary, but first as a pension office clerk and then as an army officer, was assigned to special service at the White House as Nicolay's assistant.[8] He and Nicolay slept at the White House and were practically members of the presidential family, too much so to please the President's wife. Early in 1865 she undertook a campaign to get Nicolay out and Brooks in.[9] Nicolay and Hay, tiring of their secretarial routine, were glad to accept Lincoln's offer to send them off to Paris, Nicolay as consul general and Hay as secretary of the legation under Minister Bigelow.[10] Brooks, the Wash-

[4] Cincinnati *Daily Gazette*, Apr. 8, 1865, p. 3, c. 6.   [5] *Collected Works*, VIII, 408.

[6] Lincoln to Grant, Jan. 19, 1865, *ibid.*, 223. Robert Todd Lincoln was appointed on February 11, 1865.

[7] Ruth Painter Randall, *Mary Lincoln*, 333–334, 367–368.

[8] Dennett, *John Hay,* 35 ff.

[9] A. G. Henry to Mrs. Henry, Mar. 13, 1865, Henry MSS., Ill. St. Hist. Lib.

[10] Dennett, *John Hay,* 57.

ington correspondent of the Sacramento *Union*, had already accepted from Lincoln "the promise of a lucrative place in San Francisco," and Lincoln hesitated to ask him to sacrifice this in order to become the President's private secretary. He told Brooks he could continue his work as a correspondent to supplement the secretary's income, and Brooks accepted the less remunerative position, though he never served in it, since Lincoln died before the change was actually made.[11]

Among the applicants for government jobs who filled the streets and hotel lobbies of Washington were numerous one-armed or one-legged men, disabled veterans of the war which still was adding daily to the total of the seriously scarred or maimed. A United States Sanitary Commission committee, headed by the former general-in-chief, Winfield Scott, set itself to the task of finding employment for such men as these. If the Federal government would hire as many as possible, a part of the growing total would thus be taken care of, and the rest might then get work from state governments and from private employers who, presumably, would follow the fine example which the Federal government should set.[12] Scott's committee looked to the President, not to Congress. In a public letter Scott asked Lincoln to recommend to the heads of departments that they give preference to badly crippled soldiers for whatever jobs these men could fill. Lincoln replied on March 1, 1865, with "hearty concurrence," saying he would be glad to "make these suggestions" to his department heads.[13]

So, in the last months of Lincoln's administration, much of the patronage (so far as the President personally could direct it) went to disabled soldiers, to his own relatives and friends, and to deserving politicians. Yet his most frequent and most serious consideration was neither war sacrifice nor friendship and family nor, in the usual uncomplicated sense, political service. As always, he had to consider the needs of factional harmony, the ways of bridging over that neverending dichotomy of his administration, the division between Radicals and Conservatives. Much of the impetus to the new rush for offices came from Radicals who hoped, at last, to control the personnel as well as the policy of the government. Indeed, the quarrel between

---

[11] Brooks to Isaac P. Longworthy, May 10, 1865, published as *The Character and Religion of President Lincoln* (Champlain, N.Y., 1919).

[12] Philadelphia *Public Ledger*, Jan. 10, 1865, p. 2, c. 1; Apr. 1, 1865, p. 2, c. 1; Cincinnati *Daily Gazette*, Apr. 1, 1865, p. 3, c. 7; Apr. 5, 1865, p. 1, c. 8.

[13] *Collected Works*, VIII, 327.

Republican factions arose not only from differences over Reconstruction programs but also from differences over the distribution of the patronage.[14]

In 1864–65 there was a factional quarrel in almost every state, but none so bitter and so demanding of the President's attention as the one in Maryland. There it was the familiar story of the fight, now more fierce than ever, between Henry Winter Davis and Montgomery Blair. The resurgence of Davis's factional bitterness came as a special disappointment to Lincoln. From the beginning, Davis's conduct had seemed "strange" to him, for he had "heard nothing but good" of Davis and had expected nothing but friendliness from the man who was a cousin of his good friend Judge Davis. Then, on election night, Lincoln was inclined to think that Davis's hostility toward him was at last about to disappear. "It has seemed to me recently that Winter Davis was growing more sensible to his own true interests and has ceased wasting his time by attacking me," the President commented. As for himself, he was ready to forgive and forget. "A man has not to spend half his life in quarrels," he said. "If any man ceases to attack me, I never remember the past against him."

The very next day, however, Blair visited the White House and complained bitterly against the "Davis clique." [15] Each side considered the other as the aggressor. The Davisites believed that "little minded men," who had worked against emancipation in the state, were about to "come forward as 'Lincoln men' under the leadership of M. Blair to claim at the President's hands a redistribution of the offices." The Davis group feared that Senator Thomas H. Hicks would be given the Baltimore collectorship, which was both pecuniarily and politically the most valuable job in the state. "Blair is then to be engineered into the U. S. Senate to take Hicks's place. This after his repudiation by the Baltimore Convention and his futile effort to get even meagre support in his application for a seat upon the Supreme Bench!" [16] Lincoln did not have time to show whether, for his second term, he intended to make Senator Hicks the Baltimore collector, for Hicks suddenly died in February. In the Maryland legislature Blair immediately had to fight for Hicks's Senate seat against a Davis man,

[14] Carman and Luthin, *Lincoln and the Patronage*, 321.
[15] Dennett, . . . *Diaries . . . of John Hay*, 234–236.
[16] J. S. Stewart to Simon Cameron, Dec. 27, 1864, Cameron MSS.

Congressman John A. J. Creswell. Though Blair was thought to have Lincoln's favor, Creswell held an advantage in government patronage, since Stanton and the pro-Chase employees of the treasury department were backing him. Blair lost. Davis, as if crowing over Creswell's triumph, which was also his own, promptly challenged the Lincoln policy with a tirade in the House on reconstruction in Louisiana.[17]

Finally Lincoln acted to check the Davis faction and strengthen that of Blair. The latter would have been glad to see Hicks at the head of the Baltimore custom house, and now that Hicks was dead and he himself defeated for the Senate, he was more determined than ever that the President should remove the pro-Davis collector of the port. Lincoln decided to re-deal the Baltimore patronage so as to provide a more even factional balance. He suggested that Blair meet with a representative of the Davisites and draw up a compromise slate of officeholders for the city. On April 14 he received and approved the slate.[18]

From day to day, to the very end, Lincoln thus had to concern himself with the distribution of the spoils. Only by doing so could he hold his party together, and only by holding the party together could he hope to accomplish his program. He did not succeed perfectly but, considering the magnitude and complexity of his tasks, he did extremely well. If his predecessor and his successor had handled the patronage as carefully, they might have been more nearly as successful in the presidency. He accomplished more than James Buchanan or Andrew Johnson partly because he was more of a politician. "In being a competent politician, he became a statesman." [19]

---

17 Welles, *Diary*, II, 243; Carman and Luthin, *Lincoln and the Patronage*, 325–326.
18 *Collected Works*, VIII, 411.
19 Carman and Luthin, *Lincoln and the Patronage*, 336

CHAPTER XIII

THE THIRTEENTH AMENDMENT

THE Radicals of his own party insinuated that Lincoln was willing to see slavery survive the war, and sincere friends of the slave often felt he was too slow and hesitant in striking at the institution. Democrats, on the other hand, portrayed him as a "nigger lover" and fanatical abolitionist.[1] The truth is, he had shared some of the anti-Negro prejudices of the people among whom he lived in Kentucky and southern Indiana and Illinois. But, in the White House, he outgrew his prejudices. He also had possessed anti-slavery feelings which were rather rare among his early neighbors, and these feelings he did not outgrow during his Presidential years. But he doubted whether, as President, he should act upon his personal impulses in disregard of the powers of his office and the demands of statecraft. "I am naturally anti-slavery. If slavery is not wrong, nothing is wrong. I can not remember when I did not so think, and feel." Thus he wrote in April, 1864. "And yet I have never understood that the Presidency conferred upon me an unrestricted right to act officially upon this judgment and feeling." He had moved toward emancipation, he explained, only as it became an "indispensable necessity" for winning the war and saving the Union. "I claim not to have controlled events, but confess plainly that events have controlled me."[2] During the final year of his life, influenced by events and also influencing them, he devoted himself to seeing that slavery, every last remnant of it, should be eliminated from the land, forever.

---

[1] Quarles, *The Negro in the Civil War,* 132–162, 255–257.
[2] Lincoln to A. G. Hodges, Apr. 4, 1864, R. T. L. Coll., 32077–78.

I

Already much had been done toward eliminating it. "When the war commenced, three years ago," Lincoln told the crowd at the Sanitary Fair in Baltimore, April 22, 1864, "no one expected that it would last this long, and no one supposed that the institution of slavery would be modified by it. But here we are. The war is not yet ended, and slavery has been very materially affected or interfered with." [1] It had been and was still being materially affected by acts of Congress, by Presidential decree, and by the actions of several states.

Congress had begun the work less than four months after the firing on Fort Sumter. The first confiscation act, of August 6, 1861, provided that slaveowners should forfeit those of their slaves whom they used in military service against the United States. The second confiscation act, of July 17, 1862, went much beyond that: it declared "forever free" all slaves of owners who committed treason or supported the rebellion. In other acts of 1862 Congress abolished slavery in the District of Columbia, with compensation to the owners, and in the territories, without such compensation. Also in 1862 Congress provided that enemy-owned slaves serving in the Union armies should be free, and their families as well, and in 1864 Congress also gave freedom to slave-soldiers (with their families) belonging to loyal owners. In 1864 Congress finally repealed the fugitive-slave laws of 1793 and 1850 which, up to that time, had continued to provide an indirect sanction for slavery in the Federal statute books.[2]

President Lincoln, with his Emancipation Proclamation of 1863, actually did not go so far as Congress already had gone in the second confiscation act, but he did assert and dramatize the antislavery policy of his own administration. Though in itself the Proclamation did not free a single slave, it appealed to slaves who heard of it and thus brought thousands within the Union lines, where they were freed according to existing laws.[3] How it operated Lincoln was reminded

---

[1] Cincinnati *Daily Gazette*, Apr. 22, 1864, p. 3, c. 8.

[2] Randall, *Civil War and Reconstruction*, 480–481, 481 n.

[3] On the Emancipation Proclamation and its consequences, see *Lincoln the President*, II, 151–203. At the Hampton Roads Conference in February, 1865, Lincoln agreed with Seward's estimate that, up to that time, a total of about 200,000 slaves had gained their freedom under the Proclamation. Alexander H. Stephens, *A Constitutional View of the Late War Between the States*, II, 611.

when, on January 1, 1864, the first anniversary of the Proclamation, General R. H. Milroy wrote to him about the use he had made of it in the Shenandoah Valley. First, Milroy announced it to his men, who cheered and sang "We are coming, Father Abraham" and "John Brown's Body" to the accompaniment of the regimental band. Then he posted and distributed over the countryside a handbill, headed in large type "Freedom to Slaves," which contained a summary of the Proclamation and commanded obedience to it. "That hand-bill order," Milroy now told Lincoln, "gave Freedom to the slaves through and around the region where Old John Brown was hung." [4]

Lincoln himself acted in a manner somewhat reminiscent of John Brown when, in August, 1864, he invited the former slave Frederick Douglass to the White House to discuss ways of encouraging slaves to heed the call to freedom. Lincoln suggested to Douglass that he organize a kind of government-sponsored Underground Railroad.[5] Soon afterward Douglass reported back to Lincoln: " . . . I have freely conversed with several trustworthy and Patriotic colored men concerning your suggestion that something should be speedily done to inform the slaves in the Rebel States of the true state of affairs in relation to them." Douglass outlined a plan according to which Lincoln would appoint a number of Negroes as "agents," with a "general agent" over them, to circulate in the South, talk to slaves, and persuade them to cross the line into Union-held territory.[6] But Lincoln soon lost interest in the plan. He had proposed it in the middle of the dark August when his re-election seemed unlikely. After the clouds lifted, he concentrated on other and more effective ways of extending and confirming the work of emancipation.

He still hoped to see it carried on by the slaveholding states themselves. West Virginia had been admitted to the Union in 1863 with a gradual-emancipation clause in its constitution. In those states being "restored" under Lincoln's ten per cent plan, slavery was duly abolished with the adoption of new constitutions—in Arkansas, March, 1864; in Louisiana, September, 1864; and in Tennessee, February, 1865.[7] He kept watching the border states and encouraging them to act upon his proposal of 1862 for gradual and compensated

[4] R. H. Milroy to Lincoln, Jan. 1, 1864, R. T. L. Coll., 29147-48.

[5] Quarles, *The Negro in the Civil War*, 258-259.

[6] Douglass to Lincoln, Aug. 29, 1864, R. T. L. Coll., 35652-53.

[7] See above, chaps. i and ii.

emancipation, but he ceased to insist upon either compensation or gradualness. "I am very anxious for emancipation to be effected in Maryland in some substantial form," he wrote to Representative A. J. Creswell on March 7, 1864. "I think it probable that my expressions of a preference for *gradual* over *immediate* emancipation, are misunderstood." He had thought "the *gradual*" would produce less confusion and destruction, but if those who knew best preferred "the *immediate*," he would have no objection to it. The important thing was that all favoring emancipation *"in any form"* should co-operate with one another and not delay or jeopardize the movement by bickering among themselves.[8] After the Republican victory of 1864 Maryland did act, merely repealing the slave code, an ordinary law, on which slavery had been based in that state. On January 11, 1865, Missouri also acted, abolishing slavery by means of a special ordinance passed by a state convention. But Delaware, though within its boundaries in 1865 there were about 20,000 free Negroes and fewer than 2,000 slaves, refused to let these people go. And Kentucky also clung to slavery.[9]

For all that the President, the Congress, and the states had done, the great majority of those who had been slaves in early 1861 remained in bondage at the beginning of 1865. Their future status was uncertain and, indeed, so was the future status of those who were already exercising their freedom. The Emancipation Proclamation was based avowedly on the President's war powers; once the war was over, its claim to legality would disappear. The various emancipatory acts of Congress were yet to be tested in the courts; though the anti-slavery champion Salmon P. Chase was now Chief Justice, the constitutional validity of the laws was not absolutely certain. Moreover, these laws conflicted with those of some of the states, and a man claiming freedom under the former might have difficulty in asserting his claim as against the latter. In Kentucky, for example, various state judges held that the Federal law giving freedom to the families of slave-soldiers was unconstitutional, and white employers hiring such persons were prosecuted in the state courts for the offense of harboring slaves. If, when the nation was reunited, slavery were to be permanently and unquestionably abolished everywhere in the United

---

[8] Lincoln to Creswell, Mar. 7, 1864, R. T. L. Coll., 31334–35.

[9] Randall, *Constitutional Problems under Lincoln,* 388–390.

States, abolition would have to be written into the Federal Constitution.[10]

II

When the Thirty-Eighth Congress (1863-65) first met, there seemed little likelihood that a proposal for an antislavery amendment would ever emerge from its sittings. The Republicans, Conservative and Radical, anti-administration and pro-administration, agreed upon the desirability of such a resolution. The Democrats, almost as unanimously, were opposed to it. Its passage would require a two-thirds majority in both chambers. In the Senate the Republicans controlled more than enough votes, but not in the House. When the measure was considered in the first session (1863–64) it met the fate expected of it. When it was reconsidered in the second session (1864–65) it passed, even though the party composition of the House remained essentially unchanged. Its success at that time was due largely to the exertions of the President, acting upon what he considered a mandate from the people in the election of 1864.

Lincoln needed to concern himself little about the action of the Senate, even though rivalries among the Republican leaders seemed at times to jeopardize the party program. Charles Sumner, the antislavery veteran, "whose pride of erudition amounted almost to vanity" (in the words of Nicolay and Hay), threatened at first to divide the majority by insisting upon his own wording for the proposed resolution.[1] A month after John B. Henderson, of Missouri, had introduced a resolution, Sumner (February 8, 1864) introduced another one, to the effect that "everywhere within the limits of the United States, and of each State or Territory thereof, all persons are equal before the law, so that no person can hold another as a slave." He desired this proposal referred to the Committee on Slavery, of which he himself was chairman, but finally consented to let it go to the judiciary committee, to which Henderson's resolution already had gone.[2] Lyman Trumbull, chairman of the judiciary committee, reported back a substitute with wording different from that of either Henderson or Sumner, wording adapted from the Northwest Ordinance of 1787. Sumner now tried to reinsert his "equal before the

---

[10] *Ibid.*, 385–388.   [1] Nicolay and Hay, *Lincoln*, X, 75–76.
[2] *Cong. Globe*, 38 Cong., 1 sess., 521, 1313; New York *Tribune*, Feb. 9, 1864, p. 5, c. 1.

law" phrase, which he had derived from the constitution of revolutionary France. The Senate managed, however, to pass the Trumbull substitute without change: "Neither slavery nor involuntary servitude, except as a punishment for crime whereof the party shall have been duly convicted, shall exist within the United States, or any place subject to their jurisdiction." [3]

Meanwhile Lincoln closely watched the progress of a similar measure in the House, hoping against hope that it might get enough Democratic support to pass. Again and again, consulting with Republican members, he added up the possible votes in its favor, but he could never make a total of two-thirds. After conferring with him, his friend Isaac N. Arnold tested the calculations of Lincoln and the Republicans by introducing a resolution which did not propose an actual amendment but merely declared "that the Constitution should be so amended as to abolish slavery." The vote on this test confirmed Lincoln's apprehensions.[4] When the proposed amendment itself came to a vote (June 15, 1864) only one Democrat supported it with a speech and only four with their ballots. One Republican, James M. Ashley, of Ohio, changed his vote from yea to nay so that, in accordance with the House rules, he could move for a reconsideration of the resolution at the next session of Congress.[5]

III

Though doubtless influencing few votes, the congressional debates on the proposed amendment revealed the kind of case that could be made for or against slavery in the United States in the years 1863–65.

The Republicans denounced the institution on principle, as an evil in itself. Yet in the same breath they urged the amendment as a measure of expediency, as a necessary means for winning the war and making a lasting peace. This argument of expediency was the Lincolnian approach—the President himself stressing the need for the amendment in order to "bring the war to a speedy close" [1]—and it represented the lowest common denominator of Republican thought.

[3] Blaine, *Twenty Years of Congress*, 504 ff., 535 ff.   [4] Arnold, *Lincoln*, 351–352.
[5] Nicolay and Hay, *Lincoln*, X, 77–78; McClure, *Lincoln and Men of War-Times*, 109 ff.
[1] Arnold, *Lincoln*, 358–359.

Senator Henry Wilson, a veteran antislavery man like his Massachusetts colleague, Sumner, made one of the strongest attacks on slavery as a moral wrong. He referred to "its chattelizing, degrading, and bloody codes; its dark, malignant, barbarizing spirit," and the "moral degradation" with which it had "scarred" the face of the nation. But he also stressed the charge that slavery had caused the war, and left the "bosom" of the country "reddened with the blood and strewn with the graves of patriotism." And he neatly combined in one sentence the twin indictment of slavery when he said: "Sir, this gigantic crime against the peace, the unity, and the life of the nation, is to make eternal the hateful domination of man over the souls and bodies of his fellow men." [2] Senator Trumbull made the gravamen of his charge the pragmatic argument: "No superficial observer even of our history, North or South, or of any party, can doubt that slavery lies at the bottom of our present troubles." [3]

Most of the Democrats, on the other hand, made no attempt to justify slavery as an institution, though a few of them did so. Senator Willard Saulsbury, of Delaware, put forth the hoary proslavery argument based on carefully selected passages from the Bible, citing both the Old Testament and the New. He said "the Almighty immediately after the Flood condemned a whole race to servitude," the Negro race presumably being descended from Noah's accursed son Ham. He also said that one of "God's own apostles," Paul himself, had sanctioned slavery in sending the slave Onesimus back to his master.[4]

Occasionally one of the Democrats, such as Representative J. A. McDougall, of California, attempted to refute the Republican's main contention by denying that the amendment would make for victory or peace and insisting that it would only arouse "the fiercer animosity of an already violent foe." [5]

Still others took refuge in Constitution-worship. "Let the Constitution alone. It is good enough," begged Representative Randall, of Pennsylvania. In defense of the good old Constitution, he quoted the sentimental song, popular in that day:

> Woodman, spare that tree!
> Touch not a single bough.

[2] *Cong. Globe*, 38 Cong., 1 sess., 1320, 1323–24.   [3] *Ibid.*, 1313.
[4] Henry Wilson, *Rise and Fall of the Slave Power*, III, 439.   [5] *Ibid.*

> In youth it sheltered me,
> And I'll protect it now.[6]

While the Democrats reiterated their familiar campaign slogan—"The Constitution as it is and the Union as it was"—they urged most strongly and most repetitiously the argument that the abolition of slavery was outside the scope of the Constitution altogether, that an antislavery amendment would be itself unconstitutional. Senator Saulsbury conceded that all the states, when they made the Constitution, could have prohibited slavery in it. He maintained, however, that after all the states had signed the "contract," a mere three-fourths of them could not alter it in such a way as to destroy a domestic institution that antedated the contract.[7] Representative Pendleton, of Ohio, the Democratic vice-presidential candidate in 1864, put the matter this way: "neither three-fourths of the States, nor all the States save one, can abolish slavery in that dissenting State; because it lies within the domain reserved entirely to each State for itself, and upon it the other States cannot enter." [8] Representative John Pruyn, of New York, added: "The Constitution would never have been ratified had it been supposed by the States that, under the power to amend, their reserved rights might one by one be swept away. This is the first time in our history in which an attempt of this kind has been made, and should it be successful it will . . . be an alarming invasion of the principles of the Constitution." Pruyn went on to say that the disposition of slavery ought to be left to the separate states, or else there ought to be passed "a supplementary article to the Constitution, not as an amendment, but as the grant of a new power based on the consent *of all the States, as the Constitution itself is."* [9]

That such objections and counterproposals made sense to their authors is understandable, perhaps, when one remembers that the Constitution had not been amended for some sixty years, not since the Twelfth Amendment was proposed in 1803 and ratified in 1804, and that the proposed Thirteenth Amendment was different in a significant respect from any of the preceding twelve. All the others had dealt with "constitutional" matters in a strict sense, that is, with governmental powers and functions. The new amendment would be

6 Arnold, *Lincoln,* 355.   7 *Cong. Globe,* 38 Cong., 1 sess., 1441.
8 *Ann. Cyc.,* 1865, p. 207.   9 *Cong. Globe,* 38 Cong., 2 sess., 154.

the first to effect a sweeping social reform by means of the amending process. Yet the objecting Democrats, if they truly had been motivated by constitutional considerations, might have concluded that such an amendment dealt as properly with "constitutional" matters as any article of the bill of rights, concerned as it was with the great subject of human freedom. They might also have reflected that the reserved rights of the states, for which Pruyn and others of them were so solicitous, were guaranteed not in the original text of the Constitution but in one of the amendments, the Tenth. They were on weak ground in making any distinction between the Constitution *and the amendments;* they would have been on better ground if they had thought of the Constitution *as amended.*[10] And they should have recognized that (at least after 1808) the Constitution contained no limitations, expressed or implied, on its own amendability.

These are not merely the reflections of a later generation of historians and political scientists. That the Constitution could be amended freely, if the appropriate procedures were followed, was the common-sense view of that time. "After all," observed a Washington newspaper in January, 1865, "the Constitution is but the legally expressed will of the people, susceptible of amendment whenever they choose to exercise the power." [11] As recently as 1861, less than six weeks before the firing on Fort Sumter, Democratic as well as Republican politicians had given indisputable evidence of the general understanding that the Constitution could be amended for any purpose, even for the purpose of abolishing slavery within the states. By a two-thirds vote in the Senate and the House, they proposed for ratification by the states a thirteenth amendment which provided: "No amendment shall be made to the Constitution which will authorize or give to Congress the power to abolish or interfere within any State with the domestic institutions thereof, including that of persons held to labor or service by the laws of said State." [12] If the Senators and Congressmen had not thought that the Constitution, lacking this proposed amendment, could have been amended so as to abolish slavery, there would have been no point in undertaking to add the amendment. Since the amendment failed of adoption, the

---

10 Randall, *Constitutional Problems under Lincoln* (rev. ed.), 394–396.
11 Washington *Daily Chronicle,* Jan. 11, 1865, p. 2, c. 2.
12 *Cong. Globe,* 36 Cong., 2 sess., 350 (Mar. 2, 1861).

Constitution remained as before, with no limit on the ways in which it might be amended. And even if that amendment had been adopted, it of course could have been repealed by another one.

IV

The question was not to be decided by the mere oratory of congressmen but by persuasions of a more powerful kind, by the voice of the people as expressed in the election of 1864 and by the President's efforts to see the popular mandate promptly carried out.

Lincoln had done all he could to make the antislavery amendment a campaign issue. From the outset he intended to run on a platform favoring the proposition. In June of 1864, while the proposition was still before the House of Representatives, he called to the Executive Mansion the chairman of the National Republican Committee, Senator E. D. Morgan, and gave him instructions for his speech opening the Baltimore convention. "Senator Morgan," he is reported to have said, "I want you to mention in your speech when you call the convention to order, as its key note, and to put into the platform as the key-stone, the amendment of the Constitution abolishing and prohibiting slavery forever." [1] At Baltimore Senator Morgan did as the President wished him to do, and the delegates responded in adopting the third plank of the party platform, which stated the prevailing Republican view that slavery was the cause of the rebellion and added that the President's proclamations had aimed "a death blow at this gigantic evil" but that a constitutional amendment was necessary to "terminate and forever prohibit" it. [2] In his statements which were used during the ensuing campaign, Lincoln stressed the indispensability of an antislavery policy as a means of winning the war. On this point, rather than the issue of Union or of peace, he differed most sharply with the rival candidate, McClellan.

When Lincoln was overwhelmingly re-elected, he therefore was justified in feeling that his antislavery program had the sanction of the popular will. When, along with him, so many Republican candidates for Congress also were elected that the party would control more than the needed two-thirds majority in the next House of Representatives, he could look forward confidently to the ultimate con-

---

[1] Arnold, *Lincoln*, 358. [2] Nicolay and Hay, *Lincoln*, X, 78–80.

version of the popular will into a constitutional amendment. But the newly elected Congress, the Thirty-Ninth, would not meet in the usual course of events for over a year, that is, not until December, 1865. The President could call a special session of the new Congress to meet at any time after his own re-inauguration on March 4, and he was prepared to do so if the old Congress, the Thirty-Eighth, should fail to act at its last regular session (1864–65).[3] This Congress contained, in the House, the same sizeable minority of Democrats who previously had blocked the passage of the resolution which the Senate had passed. Many of these Democrats now were lame ducks. Lincoln was eager to get the work done, and he counted on enough lame-duck support to get it done before he finished his first term. He stated his views on the subject in his message to the Thirty-Eighth Congress when it met for its final session in December, 1864:

"At the last session of Congress a proposed amendment of the Constitution abolishing slavery throughout the United States, passed the Senate, but failed for lack of the requisite two-thirds vote in the House of Representatives. Although the present is the same Congress, and nearly the same members, and without questioning the wisdom or patriotism of those who stood in opposition, I venture to recommend the reconsideration and passage of the measure at the present session. Of course the abstract question is not changed; but an intervening election shows, almost certainly, that the next Congress will pass the measure if this does not. Hence there is only a question of *time* as to when the proposed amendment will go to the States for their action. And as it is to so go, at all events, may we not agree that the sooner the better? It is not claimed that the election has imposed a duty on members to change their views or their votes, any further than, as an additional element to be considered, their judgment may be affected by it. It is the voice of the people now, for the first time, heard upon the question. In a great national crisis, like ours, unanimity of action among those seeking a common end is very desirable —almost indispensable. And yet no approach to such unanimity is attainable, unless some deference shall be paid to the will of the majority, simply because it is the will of the majority. In this case

---

[3] Lincoln was reported as saying that if the proposal failed to pass the second session of the Thirty-Eighth Congress he intended immediately to call a special session of the Thirty-Ninth Congress. Philadelphia *Public Ledger,* Jan. 7, 1865, p. 1, c. 4.

the common end is the maintenance of the Union; and, among the means to secure that end, such will, through the election, is most clearly declared in favor of such constitutional amendment." [4]

Here the President was appealing to the Democratic members of the current Congress, and especially to the numerous lame ducks among them. Other Republicans besides the President were thinking of the possibility of winning over some of the opposition and thus passing the proposal soon, during the winter of 1864–65. "The majority against it in the House was I think *eleven*," a correspondent advised Senator Sumner, "& in view of the feeling of the people, as evidenced by the Presidential vote, I think that a sufficient number of Democrats might be brought over without difficulty to carry it thro at once without waiting for the new Congress." [5] Lincoln did not leave it to his party leaders in Congress to persuade these Democrats to change their votes. He invited a number of them individually to the White House for informal interviews in January, 1865.

One of those he interviewed was James S. Rollins, a representative from the strongest slave district in Missouri and himself one of the largest slaveowners in his county, who had voted against the amendment in the previous session but who had not been re-elected to Congress. Lincoln said to him (as Rollins afterward reported the conversation): "You and I were old whigs, both of us followers of that great statesman, Henry Clay, and I tell you I never had an opinion upon the subject of slavery in my life that I did not get from him. I am very anxious that the war should be brought to a close at the earliest possible date, and I don't believe this can be accomplished as long as those fellows down South can rely upon the border states to help them; but if the members from the border states would unite, at least enough of them to pass the thirteenth amendment to the Constitution, they would soon see that they could not expect much help from that quarter, and be willing to give up their opposition and quit their war upon the government; this is my chief hope and main reliance to bring the war to a speedy close, and I have sent for you as an old whig friend to come and see me, that I might make an appeal to you to vote for this amendment." Rollins replied that he already had made up his mind to vote for it. Lincoln then

4 *Collected Works*, VIII, 149.
5 J. Jay to Sumner, Nov. 15, 1864, Sumner MSS., Harvard Coll. Lib.

asked him to see and talk with other members of the Missouri delegation, and Rollins cheerfully agreed to do so.[6]

Possibly, in talking with some of the Democratic holdovers in the
House, Lincoln used the more substantial argument of patronage.
At least one of the Democrats who changed their votes—Moses F.
Odell, of New York—went into a Federal job as navy agent in New
York City after leaving Congress at the end of the session in 1865.[7]
Representative George W. Julian, Republican from Indiana, may
have had patronage deals in mind when he wrote, enigmatically, that
the success of the measure "depended upon certain negotiations the
result of which was not fully assured, and the particulars of which
never reached the public." [8] In any event, Lincoln declined to go as
far as he might have done in "negotiations" with Congressmen. Representative Ashley, in charge of the amendment in the House, urged
upon him a scheme to get the aid of the New Jersey Democrats. A bill
was pending which was intended to curb the monopoly of the Camden
and Amboy Railroad in New Jersey, and the railroad company apparently controlled the congressmen from that state. Senator Sumner
was behind the anti-monopoly bill. If Sumner would postpone it—
so Ashley informed Lincoln—the company "would in return make the
New Jersey Democrats help about the amendment, either by their
votes or absence." But Lincoln felt he could do nothing with Sumner.
He told Ashley that the Senator would become "all the more reso-
lute" if he tried to persuade him to give in.[9]

V

On January 6, 1865, Representative Ashley moved the reconsideration of the resolution for the Thirteenth Amendment and reopened
the debate, which occupied the House off and on until the end of
the month. As before, the Republicans were solidly in favor of the
resolution, but the Democrats were no longer so nearly unanimous
against it. Some of them, moved by Lincoln's persuasions as well as
by the election returns, had come to the conclusion that for political

---

[6] Arnold, *Lincoln,* 358–359.

[7] See the brief sketch of Odell in *A Biographical Congressional Dictionary* . . .
1774–1911.

[8] Julian, *Political Recollections,* 250.

[9] Memorandum of Nicolay, dated Jan. 18, 1865, Nicolay and Hay, *Lincoln,* X, 84–85.

reasons alone, for the salvation and revival of their party, they would
be wise to turn about and support the amendment.

The issue on which many Democrats relied for future success was
the issue of public finance. They generally favored a program of easy
money and continued inflation, and with this program they hoped to
attract not only farmers and wage-earners but also many small businessmen, who feared the deflationary effect to come from the elimina-
tion of state banknotes and the retirement of the greenbacks. Though
these voters, in the North, could be expected to respond to the promise of abundant currency, they could not be expected to rally to a
proslavery party. "You cannot present the issue of the finances till
the slavery question is settled, & that question can be settled but in
one way." So George Bancroft, the historian and prominent party
intellectual, advised Congressman Samuel S. Cox, of Ohio, a few
days before the question came to a final vote. "Do away with slavery
& the democrats will be born[e] into power on the wings of their
sound principles of finance." [1]

Cox himself was not much impressed by Bancroft's advice, not
enough impressed to decide to change his vote. But some of Cox's
Democratic colleagues were influenced by a similar line of argument.
Representative Anson Herrick, a Democrat from New York, addressed
his fellow partisans with a frank appeal to party interest. "It has
been our seeming adherence to slavery, in maintaining the principle
of State rights, that has, year by year, depleted our party ranks," he
said. "Looking at the subject as a party man, from a party point of
view, as one who hopes soon to see the Democratic party in power,
this proposition seems to present a desirable opportunity for the
Democracy to rid itself at once and forever of the incubus of slavery." [2]

Representative Rollins, of Missouri, presented the essence of Lincoln's own argument, as Lincoln had given it to him. "We can never
have an entire peace as long as the institution of slavery remains as
one of the recognized institutions of the country," Rollins declared
in the course of one of the more eloquent speeches of the entire debate. "It occurs to me that the surest way to obtain peace is to dispose
of the institution now." Rollins went on to say that the border states
had missed an opportunity in not accepting Lincoln's suggestion of

[1] Bancroft to Cox, Jan. 28, 1865, Bancroft MSS., Mass. Hist. Soc.

[2] *Cong. Globe,* 38 Cong., 2 sess., 526.

1862. "And, sir, if ever a people made a mistake on earth, it was the men of Kentucky, by whom I was somewhat governed myself, when three years ago they rejected the offer of the President of the United States, who, wiser than we were, seeing the difficulties before us, but seeing the bow of promise set in the sky, and knowing what was to come, proposed to us to sweep the institution of slavery from the border states, offering the assistance of the United States, to aid in compensating the loyal men of those states for their losses in labor and property." [3]

Another Democratic Congressman, however, cited the words of Lincoln to dissuade his fellow Democrats from reversing themselves. "It is not many months since the President of the United States, above his own signature, publicly stated that if he could save the Union he would do so, irrespective of slavery," said Representative Kalbfleisch, of New York. "I am for leaving open to him the opportunity of redeeming the pledge thus given to the country." [4] Like Kalbfleisch, the great majority of the Democrats in the House had no intention of voting for the amendment. Many more of them spoke against it than spoke in favor of it. They tried to postpone or prevent a decision by their stalling tactics.

Thaddeus Stevens got the floor repeatedly to reply to the Democrats and to urge Ashley and the Republicans to press ahead on schedule. Stevens made himself one of the most insistent of the champions of the amendment, saying that he had devoted his whole life to attacking social inequalities wherever he found them. "I will be satisfied," he declared, "if my epitaph shall be written thus: 'Here lies one who never rose to any eminence, and who only courted the low accomplishment to have it said he had striven to ameliorate the condition of the poor, the lonely, the downtrodden of every race and language and color.' " But while he, along with the rest of the Radicals, joined in pushing Lincoln's amendment, he did so in an un-Lincolnian and even an anti-Lincoln spirit. While the President was thinking of peace and reconciliation, the congressman was talking about the "desolation of the South" and the necessity of giving the Southerners "just retribution for their hellish rebellion." [5] The slaveholder Rollins, rather than the self-proclaimed egalitarian Ste-

---

[3] Arnold, *Lincoln*, 360.   [4] *Cong. Globe*, 38 Cong., 2 sess., 528.
[5] Current, *Old Thad Stevens*, 204–207.

vens, was the real spokesman for Lincoln in the House.

On January 31, 1865, the proposal came to a final vote in the House. Stevens had set the hour at three o'clock, but Ashley allowed the Democrats to go on speaking until half past three. A group of angry Republicans gathered around Ashley's seat, Stevens among them. His eyes blazing, he shook his finger at Ashley and read him a lecture for giving way, while Ashley's face, according to a witness, looked "as red as a fresh cut of beef." Though a few minutes behind schedule, the roll call duly began.[6]

As the clerk came to the names of the Democrats who the previous session had voted *nay*, and one after another several of them—Baldwin, Coffroth, McAllister, English, Ganson—now voted *aye*, the crowded galleries burst out with repeated and growing applause, and many of the Republicans on the floor joined in it. All together, thirteen Democrats this day voted in favor of the amendment, besides the four who also had voted for it previously. The resolution carried with more than the necessary two-thirds majority. When Speaker Colfax announced the result, renewed and intensified cheering was heard, and parliamentary order was forgotten. The House quickly adjourned for the day. Outside, cannon boomed.[7]

VI

From Capitol Hill, Representative Arnold with a group of Lincoln's personal friends went at once to the White House to exchange congratulations with the President. "The passage of the resolution filled his heart with joy," Arnold later recalled. "He saw in it the complete consummation of his own work, the emancipation proclamation." [1]

The next day, February 1, 1865, when the resolution was brought to him for his signature, Lincoln signed it, as seemed perfectly natural for him to do. He, along with Speaker Colfax and Vice President Hamlin, had forgotten that the President need not sign a resolution of that kind. On second thought the Senate resolved that "such approval was unnecessary," since the Supreme Court had decided in a case arising in 1798 that the President had "nothing to do" with

6 *Ibid.*, 206. 7 *Cong. Globe*, 38 Cong., 2 sess., 531.
1 Arnold, *Lincoln*, 365-366.

either the proposal or the adoption of constitutional amendments.[2] Only in a technical sense, however, did Lincoln have nothing to do with this one.

The crowd who, on the evening of the day he signed the resolution, marched to the White House to felicitate him, certainly thought that he had had something to do with it. He had done what he could to eradicate slavery by issuing his proclamation, he told the marchers, but the proclamation "did not meet the evil," or so its critics might maintain. "But this amendment is a King's cure for all the evils. It winds the whole thing up." He could not help congratulating everyone in the crowd, himself, the country, and the whole world upon this "great moral victory." [3]

As the news spread, the old abolitionists were among the most enthusiastic of all who rejoiced throughout the North. To them the President long had seemed timid and ineffectual in dealing with slavery. Now, at last, they could give him unstinted and wholehearted praise. "And to whom is the country more immediately indebted for this vital and saving amendment of the Constitution than, perhaps to any other man?" So William Lloyd Garrison asked in the course of a speech to a meeting of celebrators in Boston. "I believe I may confidently answer," he went on, "—to the humble railsplitter of Illinois—to the Presidential chainbreaker for millions of the oppressed—to Abraham Lincoln!" [4]

"The great job is ended," Lincoln himself declared.[5] That is, the first great obstacle had been overcome. "But," as he told the serenaders on February 1, "there is a task yet before us—to go forward and consummate by the votes of the States that which Congress so nobly began yesterday." He was proud to inform the crowd that his own state of Illinois, this very day, had led off by ratifying the amendment. And Maryland was "about half through." [6]

Ratification proceeded apace. After Illinois came Rhode Island and Michigan on February 2, then Maryland, New York, and West Virginia on the next day. Before the end of the month Maine, Kansas, Massachusetts, Pennsylvania, Virginia, Ohio, Missouri, Indiana, Nevada, Louisiana, and Minnesota also acted. By the end of the first

---

[2] *Collected Works*, VIII, 253–254. [3] *Ibid.*, 254–255.
[4] *The Liberator*, Feb. 10, 1865, quoted in Nicolay and Hay, *Lincoln*, X, 79 n.
[5] Arnold, *Lincoln*, 366. [6] *Collected Works*, VIII, 254.

week in April three more states—Wisconsin, Vermont, and Tennessee—had joined the list. Thus a total of twenty ratified while Lincoln was still alive.

Two of the loyal states, Delaware and Kentucky, refused to ratify, and both expressed their refusal in more forceful terms than mere inaction. The General Assembly of Delaware resolved (February 8, 1865) that the proposed amendment was "violative of the reserved rights of the several States," and, if adopted, would "form an insuperable barrier to the restoration of the seceded States to the Federal Union." [7] In Kentucky (also on February 8) Governor Bramlette recommended that the state legislature ratify but provoked more antagonism than support. To the last, a majority of the Kentucky legislators remained sullen and defiant. Like those of Delaware, they declared that the amendment encroached upon the reserved rights of the states, which were "above and superior to the Constitution." They denied that the amendment would be binding upon their state, and they hinted strongly at nullification. [8]

Since Kentucky and Delaware refused to approve it, the amendment would have to have the favorable action of at least four states of the Confederacy, if it was to receive the approval of three-fourths of all the states. In the end, on December 18, 1865, Secretary Seward counted the ratifications of eight ex-Confederate states, in addition to nineteen others, when he proclaimed the Thirteenth Amendment as in full effect. At that time the Radicals in Congress had excluded the Senators and Representatives from the seceding states and had refused to recognize their reconstructed governments. These governments were competent to ratify a constitutional amendment but incompetent, in the eyes of Congress, for anything else. [9]

VII

It would be an oversimplification to say that the Thirteenth Amendment made freemen out of slaves, or even that it was intended to do so. The amendment grew out of a variety of motives, as Henry Wilson said. Some who favored it were motivated by a sense of "re-

---

[7] *Delaware Senate Journal*, 1865, pp. 126, 128; *Delaware House Journal*, 1865, p. 148.
[8] Chicago *Tribune*, Dec. 23, 1865, p. 2.
[9] Randall, *Constitutional Problems under Lincoln*, 396–401.

ligious obligation" or by "humane considerations," but others by "feelings of resentment" against slaveholders, whom they blamed for starting the war. The largest number were moved by "prudential considerations merely," Wilson believed (and, though Wilson did not say so, Lincoln himself was moved by such considerations mainly). "They accepted emancipation not so much from any heartfelt conversion to the doctrine of anti-slavery as from the conviction that the removal of slavery had become a military, if not a political, necessity." The "foul spirit of caste" still "lurked within the hearts of many" who applauded the progress of emancipation.[1] So long as the former slaves suffered from the prejudice of the white community, they would not be free *men* but only free *Negroes*.

The Negroes freed during the war, like those already free when the war began, had to make their way against serious handicaps, whether as soldiers or as civilians and whether as residents of the North or of the South. The plight of the new freedmen was sometimes desperate. Before the end of 1863 fifty thousand of them, mostly women and children, were adrift in the lower Mississippi Valley, with little shelter and practically no food, except occasional army rations of crackers and dried beef. "At present, hundreds of the blacks would gladly return to slavery, to avoid the hardships of freedom," Lincoln was informed.[2] Even the most fortunate of the freedmen faced hardships and dangers to which white men were immune. Negro soldiers ran an added risk (if captured, they could not count upon the usual protection of the laws of war) and Negro laborers in the army were paid, at first, according to their color and not according to their work. Even Negroes born free and living in the so-called free states lacked many of the privileges ordinarily associated with freedom. They could not enter certain occupations, they could not always travel without restriction, and they could not vote or hold office in most of the states, including Illinois.

Before the end of the war the free Negroes and their white friends began a campaign in the state legislatures and in Congress to free the colored population from discriminatory laws. Most of the anti-Negro legislation of Illinois (but not the restriction of suffrage to the

---

[1] Wilson, *Rise and Fall of the Slave Power*, III, 453–454.
[2] Western Sanitary Commission to Lincoln, Nov. 6, 1863, A. A. Lawrence MSS., Mass. Hist. Soc.

whites) was repealed early in 1865. At about the same time Congress passed and the President signed a bill setting up the Freedmen's Bureau to care for refugees. Senator Sumner, who had got Negroes admitted to practice in the Federal courts, tried to obtain for them the privilege of riding on the Washington street cars. Representative Stevens began to talk of confiscating Southern estates and dividing them among the freedmen—"forty acres and a mule" to each family head. The Fourteenth Amendment, presumably designed to protect Negroes in their civil rights, and the Fifteenth Amendment, to guarantee their right to vote, were to be adopted in the early postwar years. These were only the beginning steps in an undertaking which, nearly a century later, was still to fall short of complete success.

The Negro's advancement was hindered less by laws or the absence of laws than by popular attitudes—the "foul spirit of caste," as Henry Wilson called it. Lincoln himself had yielded to this spirit when, in 1862, he urged the resettlement of freed Negroes in foreign lands, with the argument that the white and black races could not be expected to live together in harmony within the United States. While some Negro leaders approved the idea of colonizing their people outside the country, others denounced it, and one wrote impertinently to the President: "Pray tell us is our right to a home in this country less than your own?" [3] Lincoln not only abandoned the colonization idea but also proceeded to give repeated demonstrations that, whether or not Negroes and whites could mingle harmoniously in the country at large, they could certainly do so within his own official home.

He opened the White House to colored visitors as no President had done before, and he received them in a spirit which no President has matched since. At his New Year's Day reception in 1864 "four colored men, of genteel exterior and with the manners of gentlemen, joined in the throng that crowded the Executive Mansion, and were presented to the President of the United States," as the Washington *Morning Chronicle* reported the unprecedented news. There was no scene. "We are neither amalgamationists nor advocates of the leveling of all social distinctions," the *Chronicle* commented; "but we rejoice that we have a President who is a democrat by fact as well as

---

[3] Quarles, *The Negro in the Civil War*, 150.

by nature." [4] On the Fourth of July that same year Lincoln gave permission to the colored schools of the District of Columbia to hold a celebration on the White House grounds, and on August 6 he allowed Negroes to assemble on the grounds in day-long ceremonies observing the national day of humiliation and prayer which he had ordained. [5] In these and other ways he set an example of tolerance for all his fellow countrymen.

Lincoln invited and welcomed prominent individual Negroes. Frederick Douglass met him several times at the Soldiers' Home and paid at least three calls at the White House. He made his last visit as a guest at the reception on the night of the second inauguration. As he approached the door that night he was seized by two policemen and forbidden to enter, but managed to bolt past them. On the inside two other policemen took hold of him. He thought they were going to lead him to the President; instead, they led him out through a window on a plank. At the door again, he appealed to a guest going in to tell Lincoln he was there. In a moment he was invited into the East Room. There, in the presence of an elegant company of ladies and gentlemen, Lincoln said in a voice heard all around: "Here comes my friend Douglass." He shook hands cordially with him and immediately engaged him in conversation. Afterwards Douglass recalled:

"In all my interviews with Mr. Lincoln I was impressed with his entire freedom from popular prejudice against the colored race. He was the first great man that I talked with in the United States freely, who in no single instance reminded me of the difference between himself and myself, of the difference of color, and I thought that all the more remarkable because he came from a state where there were black laws." [6]

Another former slave, the remarkable Sojourner Truth, had a friendly and unstrained conversation with Lincoln when she dropped into see him, October 20, 1864. He obliged her by signing his name in her autograph book, for "Aunty Sojourner Truth," as he wrote. When a delegation of Negro Baptist clergymen sought an appointment with him, he had them shown in and nodded his head in assent

[4] Washington *Morning Chronicle*, Jan. 2, 1864, p. 3, c. 2.
[5] Quarles, *The Negro in the Civil War*, 253–254.
[6] Rice, *Reminiscences of Abraham Lincoln*, 188–193.

as they requested permission to preach to colored soldiers.[7] He gave hearty encouragement to another Negro preacher who wished to send missionaries among the escaping slaves, the "contrabands." [8] Numbers of other colored people also came to him, and all went away gratified at their cordial and respectful treatment.

He did more than send his Negro supplicants away with kind words. When a thousand New Orleans Negroes sent a two-man delegation to Washington (in January, 1864) he responded by assigning James A. McKaye, of the American Freedmen's Inquiry Commission, to look into their needs and wants. McKaye went to New Orleans, attended a colored mass meeting, and learned that they desired public schools, recognition as human beings, and the abolition of the black codes.[9] Lincoln, apparently impressed by the behavior of the Louisiana Negroes, was willing to grant them a little more than they demanded. In March he sent a private letter to Michael Hahn, congratulating him on his inauguration as the first free-State governor of Louisiana, and adding: "Now you are about to have a convention, which, among other things, will probably define the elective franchise. I barely suggest to your private consideration, whether some of the colored people may not be let in—as, for instance, the very intelligent, and especially those who fought gallantly in our ranks. They would probably help, in some trying time to come, to keep the jewel of liberty within the family of freedom." [10]

In the presence of his Negro visitors Lincoln was careful not to use expressions or tell stories which might offend them. In the presence of white men approaching him in the Negro's behalf he was not always so careful, but he was equally responsive to their appeals. "Sometime during the year 1864," according to a memoir left by Henry Samuels, several representatives of the Committee for Recruiting Colored Troops were ushered into the President's private room by Secretary Stanton. "The President was seated at his desk with his long legs on the top of it, his hands on his head and looking exactly like a huge katydid or grass-hopper." He quietly listened until his petitioners had finished, then "turned his head and jocularly said, with one of those peculiar smiles of his": "Well, gentlemen,

---

[7] Quarles, *The Negro in the Civil War*, 252–253.
[8] Cincinnati *Daily Gazette*, June 23, 1863, p. 3, c. 4.
[9] Quarles, *The Negro in the Civil War*, 251.   [10] Nicolay and Hay, *Works*, X, 39.

you wish the pay of 'Cuffie' raised." The youthfully brash and earnest Samuels objected: "Excuse me, Mr. Lincoln, the term 'Cuffie' is not in our vernacular. What we want is that the wages of the American Colored Laborer be equalized with those of the American White Laborer." Lincoln replied: "I stand corrected, young man, but you know I am by birth a Southerner and in our section that term is applied without any idea of an offensive nature. I will, however, at the earliest possible moment do all in my power to accede to your request." About a month later the war department issued an order requiring that Negro teamsters and other laborers employed by the army be paid at the same rate as white men doing the same kinds of work.[11]

Though relatively few Negroes ever saw Lincoln, and still fewer talked with him, Negroes everywhere came to think of him as their friend. They were not backward in expressing their regard for him. The colored people of Baltimore, to show their appreciation of the "distinguished services of President Lincoln in the cause of human freedom," contributed $580.75 to have a copy of the Bible bound in purple velvet, mounted in gold, engraved with a representation of Lincoln striking the shackles from a slave, and enclosed in a walnut case lined with white silk. This imposing volume they presented to the President at the White House in September, 1864. "I can only say now, as I have often said before, it has always been a sentiment with me that all mankind should be free," Lincoln remarked, in thanking the colored delegation. "In regard to the great book, I can only say it is the best gift which God has ever given man." [12] The action of the Baltimore colored people, he told Frank B. Carpenter, gave him more real satisfaction than any other public testimonial he ever received.[13]

In the mail that came to Lincoln from colored correspondents, no letter was more touching than the one signed "don carlous Butler," on St. Helena Island, off the coast of South Carolina, who begged the President to see that his plot of ground, with his improvements on it, was not taken away from him. Don Carlos dictated the letter to Laura Towne, a devoted teacher of the freedmen, and she added a post-script. She said that he had formerly been a confidential servant in

[11] Henry Samuels, "My Interview with Lincoln," typescript dated "3/8/89," Ill. State Hist. Soc.

[12] Baltimore *Sun,* Sept. 8, 1864, p. 1, c. 5.

[13] Quarles, *The Negro in the Civil War,* 254.

the famous Alston family (he had been acquainted with Theodosia Burr Alston before her mysterious disappearance at sea in 1812) and explained that he could read and write but was too old to do it with ease. "He, with others of the Freedmen, often expresses a wish to be able to speak to Massa Linkum, feeling that *he* will listen to their plea for land & do what is best for them." [14]

Lincoln, dead, was nearly deified by many Negroes. "There were no truer mourners, when all were sad, than the poor colored people who crowded the streets, joined the procession, and exhibited their woe, bewailing the loss of him whom they regarded as a benefactor and father." So wrote Secretary Welles, after the funeral ceremonies in Washington.[15] And many years later a Negro historian wrote: "The deep, nation-wide grief of the Negroes was an outward sign that their generation would hold the name of the martyred President in everlasting remembrance. The colored people beheld in Lincoln a father image; he was 'the chieftest of ten thousand, and altogether lovely.' His death burdened every black with a personal sense of loss . . . ." [16]

---

[14] Don Carlos Butler and Laura Towne to Lincoln, May 29, 1864, R. T. L. Coll., 33391.
[15] Welles, *Diary*, II, 293.   [16] Quarles, *The Negro in the Civil War*, 345.

CHAPTER XIV

ANOTHER PEACE BUBBLE

VENTS appeared to be hurrying to a climax as January ended and February began, in 1865. Not only was the Thirteenth Amendment approved by Congress and sent out to the states for ratification. Peace feelers also were being extended from Washington to Richmond, and these culminated in President Lincoln's going to Hampton Roads to meet commissioners from the Confederacy on February 3. Northern newspaper readers assumed for a few days that the war was about to end. Then the peace bubble burst. The Hampton Roads conference left both President and people (with some exceptions) convinced that actual peacemaking must wait upon the final military victory.

I

Victory could not be deferred for long, or so most Northerners believed during the winter of 1864–65. "The people seem to have settled since the election into perfect confidence," a Washington visitor wrote in mid-February, "that the end is sure, that the South must submit and come back, that slavery is dead, & that Grant & Sherman & Thomas are masters of the situation & guarantors of their security." [1]

This confidence was justified by news from the Confederacy. Defeatism was spreading in the ranks of the Confederate armies. Disaffected states, such as North Carolina and Georgia, were threatening to withdraw from the war. President Jefferson Davis was losing more and more of his little popularity among the Southern people, and his critics in high places, including the Vice President himself, Alex-

[1] H. Bellows to his son, Feb. 12, 1865, Bellows MSS., Mass. Hist. Soc.

ander H. Stephens, were becoming increasingly outspoken against him. Some talked merely of impeachment, others of overthrowing the Davis regime and replacing it with a military dictatorship, headed by Robert E. Lee. Lee was finally made, not dictator, but general-in-chief of all the Confederate armies (heretofore he had commanded only the Army of Northern Virginia), giving the Confederacy a unified military command—too late. As a last desperate expedient, Confederate leaders began to take steps toward the recruitment of slave soldiers, which probably would have led to the abolition of slavery itself—if the Confederacy had lasted long enough.[2]

As they looked hopefully ahead to a Confederate collapse, the Northern people (or some of them, at least) began to think about the kind of peace that should be made. How many favored a lenient and how many a vengeful settlement, it was impossible to know. The only poll of public opinion was the one provided by the elections of 1864, and those elections gave no clue to popular preference as between Lincolnian and Radical reconstruction. Lincoln had been triumphantly re-elected, of course, but at the same time the Radical strength in Congress had been increased. Nevertheless, if no cross-section of opinion was available, at least the extremes could be delimited clearly enough.

At one extreme were men like Lieutenant Colonel H. B. Sargent, of Massachusetts. As early as 1862, while on active duty, he had concluded that the South would have to undergo a long period of military occupation after the war. By the end of 1864, as a permanently disabled veteran, he had come to believe, further, that the war should be made "a universal and effective scourge" and should lead to "the precipitation of a new civilization on the South."[3] A similar view was elaborated in an anonymous handbill, circulated in Massachusetts, which listed eight "Conditions of Peace Required of the So-Called Seceded States." These conditions were "unconditional surrender," the hanging of "one hundred of the arch traitors," disfranchisement of all other traitors, confiscation of rebel property, collection from the rebels of the costs of the war, collection of an additional indemnity to compensate the North for its time and trouble in

---

[2] Newspaper clipping, unidentified and undated, in Meigs Diary, 1866, MS., Lib. of Cong.; New York *Herald*, Feb. 1, 1865.

[3] Sargent to John A. Andrew, Apr. 13, 1862, Dec. 10, 1864, Andrew MSS., Mass. Hist. Soc.

having had to fight the war, abolition of slavery, imposition of territorial government upon the seceded states.[4]

At the other extreme were men like Clement L. Vallandigham, Fernando Wood, and other so-called Copperheads, who desired peace without any condition except the return of the seceded states to their old places in the Union.

Probably the majority of Northerners held views which fell somewhere in between the two extremes. The attitude of the moderates was exemplified by the numerous Philadelphians who contributed money for the relief of the citizens of conquered Savannah. The Philadelphia *Public Ledger* approved this generous treatment of the beaten rebels. "All we ask is their submission to the laws," the *Public Ledger* said. "When they are ready to do this they cease to be enemies, and it is our duty to act so as to make them our friends." [5]

There was not only the question of the kind of peace ultimately to be made; there was also the question, very closely related to it, of the procedure for making peace. This was not a case where the President was to negotiate and, with the consent of the Senate, to ratify a treaty, as with a foreign power. What should be the President's role, and what the role of Congress?

The newspapers were full of suggestions for the President after his re-election. Deal with the rebellious states as so many independent nations, beginning with North Carolina, whose legislature seems eager for peace and reunion. Or combine the Union and Confederate armies and send them to the Canadian and Mexican borders, to settle accounts with England and France, thus terminating the Civil War by means of a foreign war, or a couple of foreign wars. Or send a peace embassy to Richmond and promise a liberal amnesty to the rebels and the prompt readmission of Southern senators and representatives to the United States Congress.[6]

Lincoln meanwhile was pondering the peace problem in his own way. On November 25, 1864, he raised the question in cabinet. "He says he cannot treat with Jeff Davis and the Jeff Davis government," Secretary Welles noted, "but whom will he treat with or how commence the work?" Welles had an answer. Though the Confederate

---

4 Handbill, undated, in Mass. Hist. Soc.

5 Philadelphia *Public Ledger*, Jan. 11, 1865, p. 2, c. 1.

6 New York *Herald*, Aug. 27, 1864, p. 4, c. 1; Nov. 9, 1864, p. 4, c. 2; Nov. 17, 1864, p. 4, c. 3; Nov. 18, 1864, p. 4, c. 3; Nov. 20, 1864, p. 4, c. 3.

government itself could not be approached, for it was a "usurpation," and to negotiate with it would be to recognize it, nevertheless the separate states of the Confederacy were "entities" and could be "recognized and treated with." Welles agreed with Stanton's advice that the President should make no offer to any Confederate authority but should approach the Southern people as individuals. He should "hold open the doors of conciliation and invite the people to return to their duty." [7]

In his annual message to Congress, December 6, 1864, Lincoln made a clear statement of his own considered views on peacemaking procedures and peace terms. As for a peace mission to Richmond: "On careful consideration of all the evidence accessible it seems to me that no attempt at negotiation with the insurgent leader could result in any good. He would accept nothing short of severance of the Union—precisely what we will not and cannot give." As for the people of the South: "They can, at any moment, have peace simply by laying down their arms and submitting to the national authority under the Constitution." As for the roles of President and Congress: "Some certain, and other possible, questions are, and would be, beyond the Executive power to adjust; as, for instance, the admission of members into Congress, and whatever might require the appropriation of money. The Executive power itself would be greatly diminished by the cessation of actual war. Pardons and remissions of forfeitures, however, would still be within Executive control."

As for the President's use of his pardoning power: "A year ago general pardon and amnesty, upon specified terms, were offered to all, except certain designated classes; and it was, at the same time, made known that the excepted classes were still within contemplation of special clemency." During the year many had availed themselves of the general provision, and many others had received special pardons. "Thus, practically, the door has been, for a full year, open to all . . . . It is still so open to all. But the time may come—probably will come—when public duty shall demand that it be closed; and that, in lieu, more rigorous measures than heretofore shall be adopted." As for slavery: "I repeat the declaration made a year ago, that 'while I remain in my present position I shall not attempt to retract or modify the emancipation proclamation, nor shall I return

---

[7] Welles, *Diary*, II, 179.

to slavery any person who is free by the terms of that proclamation, or by any of the Acts of Congress.' "

In sum: "In stating a single condition of peace, I mean simply to say that the war will cease on the part of the government, whenever it shall have ceased on the part of those who began it." [8]

To most of the Northern people these terms seemed, on the whole, remarkably lenient. "Taken altogether, no such executive emanation has ever proceeded from the Chief Magistrate of the American Republic," declared the Washington *Chronicle*. "It is an olive branch, a pardon, a welcome to return to the old household, to the penitent." [9] To impenitent Southerners, however, the terms seemed hypocritical, since they actually required complete submission to the authorities of what was to them an enemy power. The Richmond *Enquirer* commented sarcastically: "But 'the good wine is reserved for the last,' and the 'conditions of peace' close the message, and herein the amiability, mercy, and goodness of Mr. Lincoln stick out 'like the ears of an ass.' " [10]

II

Lincoln's message, despite his remark about the futility of his approaching the Confederate authorities, did not put an end to peace rumors or to schemes for opening negotiations. The Peace Democrats continued to insist that peace, with Union, could be had at an early date. Among Republicans, Horace Greeley still made himself the center of peacemaking plans, as he had done the previous summer. Yielding a little to the clamor, Lincoln allowed two separate unofficial peacemakers to cross the Union lines and go to Richmond. The upshot was an abortive peace conference in which the President himself took part.

The first of the unofficial missions was that of Francis P. Blair, Sr., and the impetus to it came from Greeley. On December 15, 1864, he wrote a long letter to Blair in which he suggested that the old man go South and use his talents to play upon the defeatism and disaffection there. If he was "at Raleigh with large powers," he "could pull North Carolina out of the Rebellion in a month." At any rate,

---

[8] *Collected Works*, VIII, 151–152.

[9] Washington *Morning Chronicle*, Dec. 7, 1864, p. 2, c. 2.

[10] Richmond *Enquirer*, Dec. 10, 1864, quoted in *ibid.*, Dec. 14, 1864, p. 1, c. 6.

by offering peace he could weaken the Confederacy. Lincoln ought to let him go. Lincoln ought to learn from the example of Napoleon, who never fought a war "without *seeming* to try hard to avoid it." Lincoln had done this in his first inaugural, but in his more recent public statements there was "no exhibition of the same spirit." His recent management of affairs was "worse on its civil or diplomatic than in its military aspect," and that was "quite bad enough." [1]

Old man Blair needed no urging. He promptly replied to Greeley that he had been thinking of a peace plan for some time and that Greeley's letter tempted him to reveal it to the President very soon.[2] He did hint repeatedly to Lincoln that he wanted to see him, but Lincoln put him off by saying: "Come to me after Savannah falls." [3] On December 28, a few days after Savannah had fallen, Blair got from Lincoln a pass through the Union lines,[4] without telling him what he intended to do. From the Confederate secretary of war he gained permission to enter the Confederate lines on the pretext that he was seeking certain family papers which had been taken from his Silver Springs house at the time of the Early raid.[5]

His destination was Richmond, not Raleigh. Once inside the Confederacy, he sent two letters to Jefferson Davis. One, intended as a cover-up, referred to the lost papers. The other stated his real purpose: to discuss with Davis the "state of the affairs of our country." Blair explained that he was "wholly unaccredited except in so far as I may be by having permission to pass our lines and to offer you my suggestions—suggestions which I have submitted to no one in authority on this side of the lines." [6] Davis, who knew something of the devious language of diplomacy, took these words to mean that Lincoln was, of course, privy to Blair's plans and would espouse them officially in due time. So Davis admitted Blair to a private conference in Richmond on January 12, 1865, to hear his scheme.

And a remarkable scheme it proved to be. It was nothing less than the plan, long familiar in the pages of the New York *Herald,* to end the Civil War by means of a foreign war. Blair talked to Davis about the French in Mexico, about their puppet emperor Maximilian, and about the danger to American republicanism from European mon-

---

[1] Greeley to Blair, Dec. 15, 1864, Blair MSS., Lib. of Cong.
[2] Blair to Greeley, Dec. 20, 1864, Greeley MSS., N. Y. Pub. Lib.
[3] Nicolay and Hay, *Lincoln,* X, 94.   [4] *Collected Works,* VIII, 188.
[5] Seddon to Blair, Dec. 31, 1864, Blair MSS.   [6] Nicolay and Hay, *Lincoln,* X, 94–95.

archy. "Jefferson Davis is the fortunate man who now holds the commanding position to encounter this formidable scheme of conquest," Blair intimated to him, "and whose fiat can at the same time deliver his country from the bloody agony now covering it in mourning." Suppose "secret preliminaries to armistice" should enable Davis to send part of his armies to Mexico to aid in driving out the invader. Then, very likely, "multitudes" from the Union armies would join in the patriotic enterprise. Not only would the Monroe Doctrine be vindicated, but also the United States might be expanded by the annexation of Mexico and most of Central America. Jefferson Davis would thus have credit for completing the work of Thomas Jefferson by "rounding off our possessions on the continent at the Isthmus."

To Davis, this project must have sounded like one of Seward's brainstorms, and he expressed to Blair his suspicions of Seward, whom Confederate leaders generally considered as a crafty and unprincipled schemer. Blair replied that, whatever Seward's failings, Lincoln was trustworthy. "The transaction is a military transaction," he went on, "and depends entirely upon the Commander-in-Chief of our armies." Whatever Davis may really have thought of the Mexican project—he professed to be interested in it—he could see possible gains for the Confederate cause from the appointment of commissioners to a peace conference. He gave Blair a letter, for Lincoln to see, in which he indicated his willingness to appoint such commissioners, "with a view to secure peace to the two countries." [7]

These words, "the two countries," caught Lincoln's eye when, on January 18, Blair brought him Davis's letter and an account of the conversation with Davis. What Lincoln then said about Blair's Mexican project, if he said anything, is not recorded. Doubtless he was more interested in what Blair had to say about the despondency and defeatism of prominent Confederates, with many of whom Blair had talked while in Richmond. Anyhow, Lincoln gave Blair a note to take back to Davis. In it he said he was ready to receive any agent whom Davis might informally send to him "with the view of securing peace to the people of our one common country." [8]

On the day he called on Lincoln, Blair wrote to Greeley that the success of his mission depended upon absolute secrecy, and he did not tell even Greeley what he had in mind, but only that he had

---

[7] *Ibid.*, 95–105.   [8] *Collected Works*, VIII, 275–276.

"*great hopes.*"[9] Greeley kept his *Tribune* fairly free of news on the subject, but other newspapers reported Blair's goings and comings in considerable detail and, with no inhibitions, speculated about the significance of his mission.[10] Many Republicans criticized the President for permitting "the journeyings of Mr. Blair." One of Stanton's correspondents wrote, from Ohio: "The opinion of our thinking men and the masses is, that there should be no negotiation, or discussion or official communication, or understanding with the rebels in regard to peace or a cessation of hostilities, or their condition after peace is established, until there is an unconditional surrender."[11] And one of Washburne's Illinois constituents likewise deplored the rumor of peace. "It does not strike the country favorably here," he wrote. "We think rebels should be made to submit to the government."[12]

Amid wild rumors, South as well as North, Blair reappeared in Richmond and had a second interview with Davis. He tried to explain to Davis that Lincoln, because of Radical opposition, could not approve the Mexican venture. He made a new suggestion—that "political agencies" might be by-passed by the military, Generals Lee and Grant arranging a suspension of hostilities. After returning to Washington, however, Blair sent word to Davis that the idea of a military convention also was unacceptable.[13]

Davis was left with nothing except Lincoln's agreement to an informal discussion of ways to bring peace to "our one common country." He conferred with his cabinet and decided to go ahead with the appointment of commissioners. Alexander H. Stephens thought Davis himself should serve, but Davis appointed Stephens and two other strong peace advocates: the president *pro tem* of the Confederate Senate, R. M. T. Hunter, and the assistant secretary of war (formerly associate justice of the United States Supreme Court), John A. Campbell.[14] The Confederate secretary of state, Judah P. Benjamin, prepared a commission for the three which read: "In com-

9 Smith, *Blair Family*, 311.

10 See, for example, the Cincinnati *Daily Gazette*, Jan. 10, 1865, p. 3, c. 4; Jan. 19, 1865, p. 3, c. 3; Jan. 21, 1865, p. 3, c. 3.

11 James L. Bates to Stanton, Jan. 23, 1865, Stanton MSS.

12 W. Talcott to Washburne, Feb. 4, 1865, Washburne MSS.

13 Davis, *Rise and Fall of the Confederate Government*, II, 616–617.

14 Stephens, *A Constitutional View of the Late War between the States*, II, 594–595.

pliance with the letter of Mr. Lincoln . . . you are hereby requested to proceed to Washington City for conference with him upon
the subject to which it relates . . . ." But Davis changed the commission to read: ". . . for the purpose of securing peace to the two
countries." [15]

After the three commissioners, on the basis of Davis' instructions,
had applied (January 29) for entrance into the Union lines, Lincoln
sent a messenger, Major Thomas T. Eckert, with directions to admit
them only if they would state in writing that they came for the purpose specified in his note of January 18 to Blair. They then addressed a second application to Grant, and in it they referred to
Lincoln's note. Grant accordingly admitted them, and Lincoln sent
Seward to meet them at Fortress Monroe, with instructions to make
clear to them the peace terms (reunion, emancipation, no armistice)
and to hear and report what they had to say, but not to "assume to
definitely consummate anything." As Seward left Washington (February 1) Lincoln repeated to Grant instructions which Stanton already had sent him: to proceed with his military movements and
agree to no armistice.[16] Before Seward arrived, Eckert met the commissioners. When they presented their commission from Davis, Eckert
refused to allow them to proceed to Fortress Monroe. "Thus," as
Lincoln's secretaries have written, "at half-past nine on the night of
February 1 the mission of Stephens, Hunter, and Campbell was practically at an end." [17]

III

In Washington, on the evening of that same February 1, Lincoln
received at the White House a second man who, like Blair, had gone
to Richmond as a self-appointed agent to feel out the chances for
peace. This White House visitor was General James W. Singleton, a
Democratic congressman from Illinois and a member of the Sons of
Liberty.

On January 5, 1865, Lincoln had written out cards authorizing
Singleton "to pass our lines with ordinary baggage, and go South,"
and (on return) "to pass our lines, with any Southern products, and

---

15 Davis, *Rise and Fall*, II, 617.   16 *Collected Works*, VIII, 279–280.
17 Nicolay and Hay, *Lincoln*, X, 116.

to go to any of our trading posts." [1] Before departing, Singleton conferred with Greeley, and after he had gone a friend of his wrote to Greeley that he had "started for Richmond under direction of the President." [2] His mission was supposed to be secret but, along with Blair's, provoked much comment in the Northern press. "The President has given a pass to the notorious Copperhead of Illinois, General J. W. Singleton, to go to Richmond to have a talk with Jeff Davis," one Washington correspondent reported. "It is understood that he has [had] the assurance to tell the President that the rebels would talk freely with him (Singleton) although they will not 'with you Abolitionists.' " [3] Singleton arrived in Richmond (January 13) on the same boat that Blair boarded to return from his first visit. He remained there a couple of weeks and talked with Davis, Lee, and other prominent men of the Confederacy. Then he came back and talked with Lincoln.

Regarding the White House interview on Singleton's return, it was reported: "The President was not carried away by his suggestions as to the best way to restore harmony between the two 'nations.' " [4] Yet, in fact, there was something in the suggestions which must have impressed the President. Singleton's chief conclusions were the following: (1) "The Southern people are all anxious for peace." (2) It is "in the power of the North to reconstruct by an offer of liberal terms—to be considered and acted upon during an armistice of sixty days." (3) "The South will not consent to reconstruction on any other basis than the clearest recognition of the rights of States respectively to determine each for itself all questions of local and domestic government, slavery included." (4) "They will not permit slavery to stand in the way of Independence—to that it would be promptly surrendered, but to nothing else—unless it should be a fair compensation coupled with other liberal terms of reconstruction secured by Constitutional Amendments." [5] This "unless" clause was important. If correct, it meant that there was a possibility of an early peace with reunion and with the abolition of slavery—Lincoln's minimum terms—provided that Lincoln could assure the Southerners that they would be compensated for the loss of their slaves.

---

1 *Collected Works*, VIII, 200.
2 Alexander Long to Greeley, Jan. 11, 1865, Greeley MSS.
3 Cincinnati *Daily Gazette*, Jan. 13, 1865, p. 3, c. 4.
4 *Ibid.*, Feb. 2, 1865, p. 3, c. 5.   5 *Ibid.*, Feb. 8, 1865, p. 3, c. 9.

IV

On the morning after Singleton's visit, Lincoln received a telegram from Seward at Fortress Monroe saying "Richmond party not here," and then a telegram from Eckert at City Point explaining why he was detaining the three commissioners there. Lincoln was about to recall both Eckert and Seward, when another telegram—from Grant to Stanton—was shown to him. ". . . I am convinced, upon conversation with Messrs Stevens & Hunter that their intentions are good and their desire sincere to restore peace and union," Grant said. "I am sorry however that Mr. Lincoln cannot have an interview with the two named in this despatch if not all three now within our lines." This despatch changed Lincoln's mind, and he telegraphed to Grant and Seward that he personally would meet the Richmond "gentle men" at Fortress Monroe as soon as he could get there.[1]

By this decision Lincoln took certain risks, especially the risk of antagonizing Radical opinion in his cabinet, in Congress, and among the Northern people. But he also stood to gain something. At the least, he might silence the Peace Democrats and the Peace Republicans, among the latter the influential journalists Horace Greeley and James Gordon Bennett. At the most, he might actually discover a basis for peace by conceding everything possible except his minimum conditions, Union and emancipation.

The Confederate commissioners themselves might have been satisfied with those conditions, if combined with liberal concessions on collateral points, and if embodied in a formal agreement. Stephens, for one, did not believe that the success of "the Cause" necessarily required independence for the Confederacy or even the permanence of slavery. With him, the Cause depended upon the establishment of a principle, the principle of state rights and constitutional liberties as he viewed them, and this principle might be established regardless of battles won or territory held. He would be satisfied with a peace recognizing his theory and enabling Southern libertarians and Northern Democrats to combine and put it into practice.

Stephens could hope, however, to win more immediate and more concrete gains for the Confederacy. Like Davis, he was convinced

---

[1] *Collected Works,* VIII, 281–282.

that Lincoln was actually behind Blair's suggestion of a truce during which the Confederate armies, with Northern aid, should drive the French out of Mexico. Now, Stephens and his fellow commissioners had no intention of accepting this proposal in the precise form in which Blair had put it forth. They intended to turn it against Lincoln: they would urge a truce during which the *Union* armies, but not the Confederate, might go about enforcing the Monroe Doctrine.[2] At the end of the truce the Lincoln government might or might not be able to resume the war against the South, and the Confederacy would have gained a respite if not final success.

On this point the interests of the Confederate President coincided with those of the Vice President. Davis, too, would have liked to see a truce. But he was not ready to accept a permanent peace that recognized only the theory of secession and state rights; so far as he was concerned, the peace must also embrace the fact of Confederate independence. Not that he expected this kind of peace to come from the mission of his three agents. The most he could hope for was an armistice; the least he could expect was an opportunity to discredit the Confederate peace men—in particular, his agents themselves, who were three of the foremost of Southern peace advocates. He might also get a new argument for appealing to the Southern people to fight on to the last.

The aims of Davis and his three commissioners, considered separately, were realistic enough, but peace did not mean quite the same thing to all these men. The aims of Lincoln and Seward also were realistic, but neither did these two agree precisely on all matters, such as the concessions to be made in regard to slavery. And the Confederates persisted in assuming that Blair's ideas were really Lincoln's. So there developed a curious air of unreality, and the discussion proceeded not only at cross purposes but also on different levels, when Lincoln and Seward met with Stephens, Hunter, and Campbell on board the *River Queen,* anchored off Fortress Monroe in Hampton Roads, for about four hours on the morning of February 3, 1865. It was an informal conference and, as Seward made clear at the outset, no official record was to be kept. Except for the summary reports afterwards made in Washington and in Richmond, the only sources for what was said are the recollections of the Confederate commis-

---

2 Stephens, *Constitutional View,* II, 589, 592.

sioners, and Stephens left much the most circumstantial account. Our knowledge of the Hampton Roads Conference must depend, for most of the details, upon the memory and the veracity of Stephens.[3]

Once acquaintances had been renewed, and old recollections recalled, Stephens set out to commit Lincoln to the truce that was to give the Confederate armies a rest while occupying the Union armies in Mexico. "Well, Mr. President, is there no way of putting an end to the present trouble . . . ?" Stephens began. Lincoln said there was only one way he knew of, and that was for those who were resisting the laws of the United States to cease their resistance. "But," hinted Stephens, is there no other question that might divert the attention of both parties, for a time . . . ?" Lincoln got the hint. He explained that Blair's ideas had not been revealed to him in advance and had never received the least authority from him. "The restoration of the Union is a *sine qua non* with me," he said, "and hence my instructions that no conference was to be held except upon that basis."

Stephens took this to mean merely that the Mexican project was conditional upon a previous pledge that the Union would be restored. He tried to argue that, after the armistice and the vindication of the Monroe Doctrine, reunion was bound to follow, whether or not there was an advance commitment regarding it. "A settlement of the Mexican question in this way," it seemed to Stephens, "would necessarily lead to a peaceful settlement of our own." Lincoln repeated that he could make no treaty or agreement of any kind with the Confederate states, jointly or separately, until the question of reunion had been satisfactorily disposed of. Seward clinched the point by reading the relevant passages of the President's last message to Congress, concluding: "In stating a single condition of peace, I mean simply to say that the war will cease on the part of the Government whenever it shall have ceased on the part of those who began it." [4]

That ended that. There remained, besides the issues of political

---

[3] Stephens' account is in *ibid.*, 599–619; Hunter's and Campbell's are in *So. Hist. Soc. Papers*, n. s., III, 168 ff. and IV, 49 ff. The report of the Confederate commissioners to the Confederate President may be found in Davis, *Rise and Fall*, II, 619–620. Lincoln's report to Congress, with the correspondence relating to both the Blair mission and the Hampton Roads Conference, is given in *Collected Works*, VIII, 274–285.

[4] Stephens, *Constitutional View*, II, 599–602, 608–609.

and property rights for Southerners, the question of slavery. Stephens wanted to know whether, after the war had ended, the Emancipation Proclamation would be held to have freed all the slaves of the South or only those who actually had become free during the war. Lincoln said his own opinion was that it was a war measure and would become inoperative once the war had stopped, but he said the courts might decide otherwise. Seward then broke the news that, only a few days before, Congress had passed the proposal for a constitutional amendment abolishing slavery. He went on to say that this also was a war measure, and he left the commissioners to infer that, if the Confederate states would quit the war, they could defeat the amendment by voting it down as members of the Union.[5]

Lincoln himself did not suggest that they could defeat the amendment, but he did suggest (according to Stephens) that they could postpone its adoption. He advised Stephens to induce Georgia to recall its troops, then to "ratify this Constitutional Amendment *prospectively,* so as to take effect—say in five years," and thus to avoid the evils of immediate emancipation. He added, later, that he thought there was a good chance slaveowners might be compensated. "He believed that the people of the North were as responsible for slavery as the people of the South, and if the war should then cease, with the voluntary abolition of slavery by the States, he should be in favor, individually, of the Government paying a fair indemnity for the loss to the owners. He said he believed this feeling had an extensive existence at the North." But he could not guarantee compensation.[6]

What about confiscated property other than slaves? Would confiscation continue? Lincoln answered that the enforcement of the confiscation acts was up to him, and he gave full assurance that he would exercise his power with the utmost liberality. What about property already confiscated? Would it be returned? Seward explained that this was up to Congress and the courts, and he said they would no doubt make restitution or pay indemnity after the excitement of the times had passed. Would the seceded states be readmitted to representation in Congress if they abandoned the war? Lincoln said he could enter into no stipulations on the subject (Congress being, of course, the judge of its own membership). "His own opinion was, that when the resistance ceased and the National Authority

[5] *Ibid.,* 610–614. [6] *Ibid.,* 614, 617.

was recognized, the States would be immediately restored to their practical relations to the Union." [7]

Such was the kind of peace that Lincoln would have made in February, 1865, if the insurgent leaders and his own Congress and people had permitted him to make it. Let the Southern people lay down their arms and acknowledge the laws of the United States. Let them be represented again in the national Congress. Let them emancipate their slaves—gradually perhaps—and be paid for the loss. Let their other property be restored as soon as possible, and their civic rights at once. These terms, however, were much too generous for the Radical Republicans of the North, and they were much too severe for even the most sincerely peaceminded leaders of the South. "No treaty, no stipulation, no agreement, either with the Confederate States jointly, or with them separately, as to their future position or security!" exclaimed Hunter. "What was this but unconditional submission to the mercy of conquerors?" [8]

V

The American people, both North and South, wanted peace in February, 1865, but peace meant different things to them. In the North it meant reunion at the very least and various degrees of reconstruction besides. In the South it generally meant separation and independence. The popular reactions to the Hampton Roads Conference varied according to the different definitions of peace.

While awaiting the return of the Confederate commissioners, newspapers in Richmond undertook to prepare the Southern people for fighting on. The *Sentinel,* frankly concerned lest the mission should "enfeeble us with injurious expectation," urged its readers to keep in view the aim of independence for which they had drawn the sword, and to consider no peace which would compromise that aim. The *Enquirer* adopted a more positive tone. "We think it likely to do much good for our people to understand in an authoritative manner from men like Vice-President Stephens, Senator Hunter, and Judge Campbell the exact degree of degradation to which the enemy would reduce us by reconstruction," the *Enquirer* said. "We believe that the so-called mission of these gentlemen will teach our people that the

---

[7] *Ibid.,* 610, 617.   [8] *Ibid.,* 616.

A WHITE HOUSE RECEPTION

This lithograph, entitled "Grand Reception of the Notabilities of the Nation at the White House, 1865," and copyrighted by Frank Leslie in 1865, should be viewed as a generalized conception rather than a depiction of a specific event. The artist apparently confused a reception of March 1864, honoring General Grant, with the inaugural reception of March 4, 1865. Andrew Johnson was absent from the first of these occasions and Grant from the second, yet both men are pictured here. The drawing is interesting for its accurate representation of the East Room and its faithful likenesses of many "notabilities" who at one time or another were there. Among them, in the right foreground, the President and the First Lady are greeting Mrs. Grant. Near by are General Grant, Vice President Johnson, Chief Justice Chase, Secretary Stanton, Chase's daughter Kate, and Secretary Seward.

LINCOLN IN RICHMOND

April 4, 1865. The drawing reproduced on the preceding page shows the President riding through Richmond "amid the enthusiastic cheers of the inhabitants." The one on this page shows him entering the "White House of the Confederacy," lately vacated by Jefferson Davis. From sketches drawn by Leslie's special artist on the scene, Joseph Becker, and published in *Frank Leslie's Illustrated Newspaper*, April 22 and 29, 1865.

Courtesy Chicago Hist. Soc.

A WORD TO GRANT

Lincoln's dispatch from City Point, April 7, 1865, admonishing Grant:
"Let the *thing* be pressed." Note Grant's endorsement underneath.

terms of the enemy are nothing less than unconditional surrender." [1]

After the commissioners had returned, Davis appeared to be disappointed at Lincoln's repudiation of the Mexican project, and he attributed it to bad faith on Lincoln's part. Yet he thought something could be salvaged from the results of the conference. "Mr. Davis's position was," according to Stephens, "that inasmuch as it was now settled beyond question, by the decided and pointed declarations of Mr. Lincoln, that there could be no Peace short of *Unconditional Submission* on the part of the People of the Confederate States, with an entire change of their Social Fabric throughout the South, the People ought to be, and could be, more thoroughly aroused by Appeals through the Press and by Public Addresses, to the full consciousness of the necessity of renewed and more desperate efforts, for the preservation of themselves and their Institutions." Davis proceeded to make what propaganda he could. From the commissioners he demanded a written report, despite Stephens's protest that the *"real objects"* of the conference could not properly be disclosed, and he promptly transmitted the report (which was brief and matter-of-fact) to his Congress and to the newspapers. Then he made a fiery speech at a public meeting in Richmond.[2]

As among Southerners, so also among Northerners the news of the conference had some effect in uniting opinions and strengthening the will to fight. Reports from Washington, which gave a fairly accurate overall account of the day-to-day progress of the negotiations, indicated after the conference that it had "resulted in no change of attitude either of the Government or of the rebels. In other words, it was a failure." But the reports also said: "The Administration leaders hold the peace negotiations to have had a highly successful result in this, that they have shown authoritatively and conclusively the baseless character of arguments of opposition against our prosecution of the war. To have obtained from the proper rebel sources an authentic and authorized statement that they are fighting for independence and will consent to nothing less, is in itself a great success." [3] The news undoubtedly had a galvanizing effect upon Peace Democrats. Their leader in the House of Representatives, Fernando Wood, who for

---

[1] Quoted in Cincinnati *Daily Gazette*, Feb. 4, 1865, p. 3, c. 4 and 5.

[2] Stephens, *Constitutional View*, II, 619–623; Davis, *Rise and Fall*, II, 618–620.

[3] Cincinnati *Daily Gazette*, Feb. 6, 1865, p. 3, c. 5.

some time had been urging Lincoln to make overtures to the enemy,[4] said in the House on the day after the Hampton Roads Conference that he was no disunionist and that his complaint against the administration was based on its refusal to accept peace proposals from the rebels. "But," he was now reported as saying, "if the door had now been thrown open by the President, and if the answer to that was that *they would accept recognition and separation, and nothing else, then he desired to say, with his humble efforts, he should aid the conquering efforts of his country to obtain by force what it has been unable to obtain by peace.*" And, with more italics, the Washington *Chronicle* concluded: ". . .   *the action of the President of the United States has united the North.*" [5]

The action of the President was, however, less pleasing to Radical Republicans than to Peace Democrats. A few of the Radicals approved the conference. "I am glad Lincoln was there in person," one of them wrote. "Now we shall have no more talk about commissions. He is shrewd and far seeing, I think." [6] But the Radicals in the cabinet and indeed all the members of the cabinet except Welles and Seward disapproved. "None of the Cabinet were advised of this move," Welles noted, "and without exception, I think, it struck them unfavorably that the Chief Magistrate should have gone on such a mission." [7] The Radicals in Congress also disapproved. "There are ultras among us who do not favor the cessation of hostilities except on terms and conditions which make that event remote," Welles noted further. "They are determined that the States in rebellion shall not resume their position in the Union except on new terms and conditions independent of those in the proposed Constitutional Amendment." [8]

The Radicals in the House called upon the President for information, and he responded by submitting copies of the correspondence relating to Blair's mission and his own. There was no document on the conference itself, and Lincoln's summary of the conversation was extremely brief. "On our part, the whole substance of the instructions to the Secretary of State, herein before recited, was stated and insisted upon, and nothing was said inconsistently therewith," he reported; "while, by the other party it was not said that, in any event, or on any

4 Wood to Lincoln, Nov. 18, 1864, R. T. L. Coll., 38496–97.

5 Washington *Daily Morning Chronicle*, Feb. 6, 1865, p. 2, c. 2; Feb. 7, 1865, p. 2, c. 1.

6 B. F. Prescott to Anna Dickinson, Feb. 13, 1865, Dickinson MSS., Lib. of Cong.

7 Welles, *Diary*, II, 235 (Feb. 2, 1865).   8 *Ibid.*, 239 (Feb. 10, 1865).

condition, they *ever* would consent to re-union, and yet they equally omitted to declare that they *never* would so consent. They seemed to desire a postponement of that question, and the adoption of some other course first, which, as some of them seemed to argue, might, or might not, lead to re-union, but which course, we thought, would amount to an indefinite postponement." [9]

So Lincoln only hinted at the Mexican project, and he said nothing at all about his discussion of slavery. Yet that subject had been much on his mind since his return from Hampton Roads. Apparently Singleton's opinion that the South might accept abolition with compensation, then the reaction of the Confederate commissioners to his own suggestions along that line, had made a deep impression on him. He was also driven to reconsider compensation by demands from Maryland. At Annapolis both the outgoing and the incoming governor, in January, 1865, recalled the pledge which Congress had made in 1862 to give pecuniary aid to those states that should liberate their slaves. In February the Maryland legislature, after resolving that the people of the state had acted in response to the offer of Congress, sent a committee to confer with the President and see whether he could get an appropriation. [10]

On February 5, the day after he arrived home from Hampton Roads, Lincoln presented his ideas on compensation to an evening session of the cabinet. He had prepared a message to Congress, recommending the passage of a joint resolution, and a proclamation to be issued in pursuance of it. The resolution would have empowered him to pay four hundred million dollars in government bonds to the slaveholding states, half of the amount when they ceased their resistance to the national authority, if they did so by April 1, 1865, and the other half after they had ratified the Thirteenth Amendment, if they ratified it in time for it to become law by July 1, 1865. (He had abandoned the idea of a "prospective" ratification, to take effect in five years, if indeed he had proposed that idea at Hampton Roads, as Stephens reported.) The proclamation would have announced "that all political offences will be pardoned; that all property, except slaves, liable to confiscation or forfeiture, will be released therefrom, except in cases of intervening interests of third parties; and that liberality

9 *Collected Works*, VIII, 284–285.
10 Randall. *Constitutional Problems under Lincoln* (rev. ed.), 402.

will be recommended to congress upon all points not lying within executive control." [11]

This was a proposal to buy peace and, with it, the ratification of the Thirteenth Amendment. The way Lincoln presented the plan, it sounded reasonable enough. The war could be expected to last another two hundred days, at least, and the cost of fighting that much longer would amount to four hundred million. Why not spend for peace what the nation was willing to spend for war? But the cabinet unanimously opposed the plan, and Lincoln put it aside. "The earnest desire of the President to conciliate and effect peace was manifest, but there may be such a thing as so overdoing as to cause a distrust or adverse feeling," Welles commented. "In the present temper of Congress the proposed measure, if a wise one, could not be carried through successfully." [12] And even if Congress had been inclined to adopt it, there is no reason to suppose that Jefferson Davis, judged by his reaction to the Hampton Roads Conference, would have been willing to accept it.

[11] *Collected Works*, VIII, 260–261.   [12] Welles, *Diary*, II, 237 (Feb. 6, 1865).

CHAPTER XV

WITH CHARITY FOR ALL

AS OF March 4, 1865, the old Congress had met for the last time, and the new one would not meet for several months (until December) unless the President meanwhile should choose to call it into special session. Lincoln now began his second term, which was not expected necessarily to be his last—gamblers soon were betting that he would be re-elected in 1868.[1] After four years as a war President, he could look ahead to nearly four more, at least, as a peace President. More immediately, with no Congress in session to hinder him, he could look ahead to a few months of peacemaking on his own. He could hope, within that time, to complete the preliminaries of the kind of settlement that he desired.

I

Inauguration day dawned dark and rainy, and rain fell steadily throughout the morning. The streets of Washington, especially Pennsylvania Avenue, were filled with soft mud which oozed up between the bricks even where there was pavement. Before the inaugural ceremonies began, the rain stopped, but most of the spectators, standing in the mud around the east entrance of the Capitol, already were thoroughly bedraggled.[1] The ceremonies themselves were poorly planned, or so they seemed to Secretary Welles, who wrote: "All was confusion and without order,—a jumble." [2] As if the weather and the planning were not bad enough, the new Vice President, Andrew Johnson, made something of a scene when he was inaugurated. Those who heard or read his rambling and maudlin speech wondered whether he was

[1] New York *Herald,* Mar. 19, 1865, p. 4, c. 5.
[1] Cincinnati *Daily Gazette,* Mar. 9, 1865, p. 3, c. 8.   [2] Welles, *Diary,* II, 251.

crazy or only drunk.[3] In fact he was unwell. Having been strongly urged by Lincoln to be present, he had fortified himself with whiskey beforehand, and because of his illness and his temperate habits, the effect was only too noticeable.

Lincoln's own inaugural address was short, the shortest any President had ever made. Its opening lines gave the impression that Lincoln had nothing to say. So many public declarations had been made during the war, he remarked, that "little that is new could be presented." He went on to remind his hearers of the circumstances of his first inaugural, then restated the central issue of the ensuing struggle as he saw it: "Both parties deprecated war; but one of them would *make* war rather than let the nation survive; and the other would *accept* war rather than let it perish. And the war came." Then he elaborated upon the basic issue by speaking of the "peculiar and powerful interest" of slavery. "All knew that this interest was, somehow, the cause of the war." He proceeded to describe the sufferings of the people, both North and South, as divine punishment for the sin of slavery, of which both were guilty. He concluded with the paragraph which made the address forever memorable (except to a later President, who in 1945, in characterizing his own war aims, distorted its spirit by omitting the first two phrases): "With malice toward none; with charity for all; with firmness in the right, as God gives us to see the right, let us strive on to finish the work we are in; to bind up the nation's wounds; to care for him who shall have borne the battle, and for his widow, and his orphan—to do all which may achieve and cherish a just, and a lasting peace, among ourselves, and with all nations." [4]

This second inaugural, like the Gettysburg address, was not hailed unanimously as a classic at its birth. Lincoln himself expected it to "wear as well—perhaps better than" anything he had produced, but he believed it was "not immediately popular." [5] Yet (like the Gettysburg address again) it was not entirely unappreciated by contemporaries.[6] The New York *Herald,* misquoting the phrase "the nation's wounds" and making it read "the nation's *wound,*" found aptness and significance in Lincoln's supposed use of the singular noun. On

---

[3] *Ibid.,* 252; Lincoln to Johnson, Jan. 24, 1865, *Collected Works,* VIII, 235; Philadelphia *Public Ledger,* Mar. 8, 1865, p. 2, c. 1.

[4] *Collected Works,* VIII, 332–333.   [5] Lincoln to Thurlow Weed, *ibid.,* 356.

[6] On the reception of the Gettysburg address, see *Lincoln the President,* II, 311 ff.

the whole, the *Herald* approved the speech while expressing some puzzlement at the personality of its author, "this remarkable rail-splitter." But the *Herald* was disappointed at its brevity and its generality, its failure to spell out peace terms, a failure which might cause the address to be taken as an "unconditional surrender" manifesto in the South.[7] The Washington *Chronicle,* contrasting the second with the first inaugural, thought the second one much superior, for it was "solemnly affirmative" where the other had been "deprecatory, apologetic, explanatory." [8]

At least one American citizen, however, was ashamed of the speech as a literary production. "Lincoln's Inaugural, while the sentiments are noble, is one of the most awkwardly expressed documents I ever read—if it be correctly printed. When he knew it would be read by millions all over the world, why under the heavens did he not make it a little more creditable to American scholarship?" So wrote a Pennsylvanian to Simon Cameron. "Jackson was not too proud to get Van Buren to slick up his state papers. Why could not Mr. Seward have prepared the Inaugural so as to save it from the ridicule of a Sophomore in a British University?" [9] But Cameron's correspondent knew nothing of the actual response in England, and if any British sophomore was inclined to ridicule the address, the Duke of Argyll certainly was not. "I . . . congratulate you both on the good progress of the war, and on the *remarkable speech* of your President," the Duke wrote to his friend Charles Sumner. "It was a noble speech, just and true, and solemn. I think it has produced a great effect in England." [10] The *Times* of London, for all its pro-Southern record, commented favorably on the address, and some of the British reviews gave it superlative praise, the *Spectator* declaring: "No statesman ever uttered words stamped at once with the seal of so deep a wisdom and so true a simplicity." [11] If anything, the second inaugural received even greater immediate acclaim in England than in the United States.

After delivering the address, Lincoln took the oath of his office, kissing the Bible which Chief Justice Chase presented to him. At that

---

7 New York *Herald,* Mar. 4, 1865, p. 4, c. 3; Mar. 5, 1865, p. 1, c. 1–3, and p. 4, c. 2.

8 Washington *Daily Morning Chronicle,* Mar. 6, 1865, p. 2, c. 1.

9 A. B. Bradford to Cameron, Mar. 8, 1865, Cameron MSS., Lib. of Cong.

10 Mass. Hist. Soc. *Proc.,* XLVII, 87.

11 Various English newspaper and magazine reactions to the address are given in *Littell's Living Age,* LXXXV, 86–88 (April 15, 1865).

moment the sun burst forth above the actors and the crowd of spectators. Doubtless many of them, like the Chief Justice himself, looked
for a symbol in the sudden change of weather. Later in the day, sending to Mrs. Lincoln the ceremonial Bible, with the kissed page carefully marked. Chase wrote in a note to her: "I hope the Sacred Book
will be to you an acceptable souvenir of a memorable day; and I most
earnestly pray Him, by whose Inspiration it was given, that the beautiful sunshine which just at the time the oath was taken dispersed the
clouds that had previously darkened the sky may prove an auspicious
omen of the dispersion of the clouds of war and the restoration of the
clear sunlight of prosperous peace under the wise and just administration of him who took it." [12]

II

As Lincoln began his second term, the war was entering upon its
final phase. Sherman's army, having left Savannah, was advancing
northward through the Carolinas but had yet to meet the enemy
under General Joseph E. Johnston, newly restored to command.
Grant's forces were increasing their pressure upon Petersburg and
Richmond. If Lee should escape and join with Johnston against
Sherman, the end of the war might be delayed for some time. If, on
the other hand, Sherman should get past Johnston and combine with
Grant against Lee, the Confederate Capital would be isolated from
the rest of the Confederacy, and Lee would have to surrender fairly
soon.

Lincoln, glad for an opportunity to flee the cares of Washington
and observe the fighting from near at hand, eagerly accepted Grant's
invitation of March 20 to visit the front. With his wife and his son
Tad he left Washington, March 23, on the steamer *River Queen* and
arrived the next day at City Point, on the south side of the James
River, several miles below Richmond. After a week Mrs. Lincoln
went home and brought back a party including Senator Sumner and
Senator and Mrs. Harlan and their daughter, the bride-to-be of Robert
Todd Lincoln, who was on Grant's staff.[1] But Lincoln himself did not
return to Washington for more than two weeks. Making the *River*

---

[12] Chase to Mrs. Lincoln, Mar. 4, 1865, R. T. L. Coll., 41949.

[1] *Collected Works*, VIII, 372–373, Washington *Daily Morning Chronicle*, Apr. 6,
1865, p. 2, c. 3.

Queen his home, he conferred with Grant and other officers—most significantly, with Sherman, who made a quick trip from his new base at Goldsboro, North Carolina. He visited the various camps, chatted with soldiers and was cheered by them. All the while he watched with great interest and with intelligent comprehension the progress of the fighting.

Grant kept him informed by frequent telegrams, which Lincoln forwarded to Stanton at the war department, with his own summaries and comments. But Grant, according to his memoirs, did not confide to Lincoln the fullness of his intentions, which were to capture Richmond and Petersburg and dispose of Lee's army without waiting for Sherman's men to join in the final assault. Grant intended to send Sheridan with his cavalry around to the southwest of Petersburg to take Five Forks and thus cut off Lee's lifeline, the railroad leading to Danville and the south. Lee, in an effort to save his communications and protect his flank and rear, could be expected to weaken his defenses before Petersburg and leave them vulnerable to a breakthrough.[2]

Lincoln, from day to day expecting (and fearing) a great and bloody battle, was not sure just when it would come or what form it would take. On March 30 he telegraphed to Stanton from City Point: "Last night at 10:15, when it was dark as a rainy night without a moon could be, a furious cannonade, soon joined in by a heavy musketry-fire, opened near Petersburg and lasted about two hours. The sound was very distinct here, as also were the flashes of the guns upon the clouds. It seemed to me a great battle, but the other hands here scarcely noticed it, and, sure enough, this morning it was found that very little had been done." On April 1 he learned from Grant that, on this day, something had been done indeed: Sheridan had taken Five Forks. The next day the dispatches came to Lincoln thick and fast. "All going finely," he telegraphed to Stanton. The Union troops had broken through the Petersburg intrenchments at several places, and Sheridan's cavalry was busy tearing up the tracks of the Danville railroad.

"This morning Gen. Grant reports Petersburg evacuated; and he is confident Richmond also is," Lincoln wired again, on the morning of April 3. "He is pushing forward to cut off if possible, the re-

---

[2] Grant, *Memoirs,* II, 440, 459–460.

treating army. I start to him in a few minutes." [3] Lincoln found Grant waiting for him in Petersburg on the piazza of a deserted house. The streets were empty, not a person, not an animal in sight. "I had a sort of sneaking idea all along that you intended to do something like this," Lincoln said, as he shook hands with Grant and thanked him, "but I thought some time ago that you would so maneuver as to have Sherman come up and be near enough to cooperate with you." The tactful General replied: "I had a feeling that it would be better to let Lee's old antagonists give his army the final blow and finish the job." [4] He explained that, if the Western soldiers of Sherman's army should deliver the final blow, Western politicians in after years might taunt the Eastern soldiers of the Army of the Potomac with the charge that the latter had won no important victories in the war, and thus sectional bitterness might arise between the East and the West. Lincoln remarked that, as for himself, he had not cared where aid came from, so long as the work was done. [5]

On his return to City Point he found a telegram from Stanton warning him against visiting Petersburg and exposing his life to rebel assassins. "Thanks for your caution," Lincoln answered; "but I have already been to Petersburg, stayed with Gen. Grant an hour and a half and returned here. I am certain now that Richmond is in our hands, and I think I will go there to-morrow. I will take care of myself." [6]

And to Richmond he went on the following day, by gunboat up the James to where the river was obstructed, then by a boat rowed by twelve sailors to Rockett's wharf. There he landed and, with his son Tad at his side and an escort of army and navy officers around him, proceeded to walk up Main Street a mile or so to the executive mansion of the Confederacy, the house occupied until two days before by Jefferson Davis. On the way the tall President, in his long black overcoat and high silk hat, stood out above those with him. Negroes left the river bank to follow along and crowd around him, many of them singing and shouting their praises. Soldiers white and black cheered as he entered the mansion and took a seat in Davis' chair. [7] His appearance among the people of what had been, until so recently, the enemy capital, deeply moved a Boston newspaper correspondent, who wrote:

[3] *Collected Works*, VIII, 377, 379–380, 382, 384.   [4] Coolidge, *Grant*, 193.
[5] Grant, *Memoirs*, II, 459–460.   [6] *Collected Works*, VIII, 385.
[7] Richmond *Evening Whig*, Apr. 6, 1865, quoted in Washington *Daily Morning Chronicle*, Apr. 8, 1865, p. 1, c. 6.

"He came among them unheralded, without pomp or parade. He walked through the streets as if he were only a private citizen, and not the head of a mighty nation. He came not as a conqueror, not with bitterness in his heart, but with kindness. He came as a friend, to alleviate sorrow and suffering—to rebuild what had been destroyed." [8] In the Davis house he received a number of Union officers and Richmond citizens. He also received and conversed with the only member of the Confederate government who remained in Richmond—John A. Campbell, lately the assistant secretary of war and two months previously one of the Confederate peace emissaries at Hampton Roads. Then he rode about the city in a carriage, to review the troops and to see the sights, especially the extensive ruins left by the great fire which the Confederate authorities accidentally had set at the time of their evacuation.

Back again at City Point, during the next few days he received heartening news of Grant's pursuit of Lee. Grant sent him batches of telegrams, in which the various commanders reported the chase in picturesque detail—"the Road for over 2 miles is strewed with tents baggage cooking utensils some ammunition some material of all kinds"—and in one of which a line of Sheridan's particularly caught the President's eye. "Gen. Sheridan says 'If the thing is pressed I think that Lee will surrender,'" he wired to Grant on April 7. "Let the *thing* be pressed." He would gladly have stayed on for news of the surrender itself, but he decided to go back to Washington because of word from Stanton that Seward had been injured badly in a carriage accident.[9]

He arrived in Washington late in the afternoon of April 9, the day that Lee finally surrendered to Grant near Appomattox Court House, ninety miles west of Richmond. Next morning the news was known to everyone in Washington. The people of the Capital, like those of other towns and cities throughout the North, already had indulged themselves in uproarious celebrations at the tidings of the evacuation of Richmond. Now they outdid themselves. In Washington a crowd, swelled by government employees who had been given a holiday, swarmed into the White House grounds and called for the President, while a band played "Hail to the Chief," "Yankee Doodle," and

---

[8] Boston *Journal*, quoted in *Littell's Living Age*, LXXXV, 137–138 (Apr. 22, 1865).
[9] *Collected Works*, VIII, 390–392.

"America." Lincoln, busy with a cabinet meeting, at first declined to appear but finally yielded to the cries of the crowd. He told the people that he supposed arrangements were being made for a formal celebration either that night or the next. "I shall have nothing to say then," he said, "if I dribble it all out before." Then he suggested that the band play "Dixie." The "adversaries over the way" had tried to appropriate that song, but now the Union forces had captured it, and it was a lawful prize. So the band played "Dixie." [10]

On April 11 Lincoln made, from an upper window of the White House, the speech he had promised. "We meet this evening, not in sorrow, but in gladness of heart," he began. It was to be his last public speech. On the morning of the 14th he held another cabinet meeting —his last. Meanwhile, assuming that the war was over (though Johnston was yet to surrender to Sherman, and Confederate commanders farther south and west were still to lay down their arms), he took several steps signifying the end of hostilities. He issued a proclamation terminating the blockade of Southern ports but closing certain specified ones to foreign commerce. He prepared a memorandum proposing that the size of the regular army be reduced—to a ratio of one soldier for every thousand of the population. After having written a number of passes for individuals desiring to go South, he gave up that chore and noted: "No pass is necessary now to authorize any one to go to and return from Petersburg and Richmond. People go and return just as they did before the war." On that final 14th of April, just four years to the day after the evacuation of Fort Sumter, its former commander, Major Robert Anderson, ran up the Stars and Stripes again over the fort, in ceremonies the President had approved.[11]

The war was over, but peace was yet to be made.

III

During the preceding weeks, while the war was drawing to a close, some people in the North (and some in the South) thought that peace should be made by the military men and not by the politicians. The Peace Democrats clamorously said so, and Greeley and his New York

10 Washington *Daily Morning Chronicle*, Apr. 10, 1865, p. 1, c. 3–5; Cincinnati *Daily Gazette*, Apr. 11, 1865, p. 3, c. 5.

11 *Collected Works*, VIII, 375–376, 396–397, 399, 408, 410, 412.

Tribune agreed with them. Certain generals in both the Union and the Confederate armies took up the idea of ending the war by means of a military convention. Before the beginning of March, 1865, General Longstreet, C. S. A., gathered from a conversation with General Ord, U. S. A., while under a flag of truce for the exchange of prisoners, that Grant would welcome an interview with Lee to discuss peace terms with him. On March 2 Lee proposed such an interview to Grant, and Grant telegraphed to Washington for advice.[1]

When Stanton brought Grant's telegram to the Capitol, where Lincoln was signing bills as Congress finished its work, Lincoln wrote out, word for word, a telegram for Stanton to send back to Grant. "The President directs me to say to you that he wishes you to have no conference with General Lee unless it be for the capitulation of Gen. Lee's army, or on some minor, and purely military matter," Stanton wired. "He instructs me to say that you are not to decide, discuss, or confer upon any political question. Such questions the President holds in his own hands; and will submit them to no military conference or convention." [2] Unfortunately, neither Lincoln nor Stanton nor Grant directed that a copy of this message be sent to Sherman.

The Peace Democrats kept on with their agitation. "We are not little surprised that Seward should stand in the way of peace, and that his organ here, The Times, should now as heretofore, resist any attempt to accomplish this end, save by continued slaughter," two of them in New York wrote to Greeley on March 24. "How can the administration refuse any longer to invest Lt. Gen. Grant with ample powers to meet Gen. Lee in this conference for peace, and here we trust you will stand firm and *drive* the administration, if need be, to accept the opportunity to close if possible, this devastating war." These men trusted that the President was going to the front in order to authorize the conference.[3] Greeley, in his *Tribune,* also interpreted Lincoln's visit to Grant as a sign of possible military negotiations. "The sword in one hand and the olive branch in the other," observed the *Tribune* approvingly, "are always found to work mutually in aid of each other." [4]

Disagreeing with Greeley and the Peace Democrats, Lincoln

[1] Nicolay and Hay, *Lincoln,* X, 157–158.   [2] *Collected Works,* VIII, 347–348.
[3] L. G. Capers and V. W. Kingsley to Greeley, Mar. 24, 1865, Greeley MSS., N. Y. Pub. Lib.
[4] New York *Tribune,* quoted in Philadelphia *Public Ledger,* Mar. 31, 1865, p. 2, c. 2.

thought the generals were likely to make neither an early nor a generous peace. "He had been apprehensive that the military men are not very solicitous to close hostilities," Welles noted, "—fears our generals will exact severe terms." [5] Indeed, he could hardly expect Sherman, in war the scourge of the South, to act as an angel of mercy in peace (though Sherman later was to do just that). He had little reason to think that Grant would be much better, for Grant had a reputation as an unfeeling and unsparing commander. Besides, Grant was inclined to question Lincoln's liberal exercise of the pardoning power.

Lincoln was, of course, a pardoning President. He was human enough that he always found it hard to resist a tearful appeal on behalf of a prisoner or a condemned man. And yet his pardoning proclivities have often been exaggerated and misunderstood. As a rule he was moved by considerations of policy rather than by sentimentality when he granted a pardon. When he refused clemency, he was motivated by similar considerations, and (what is commonly overlooked) he turned down numerous appeals. In the case of John Y. Beall, a Confederate secret agent who had been operating on Lake Erie, Lincoln faced tremendous pressure from influential men desiring to save the prisoner from the gallows. Ninety-one members of Congress, among them Thaddeus Stevens, petitioned for clemency to Beall. Nevertheless, Beall was hanged, late in February, 1865.[6] And, if Lincoln daily released large numbers of captured Confederate soldiers, on condition only that they take an oath of allegiance to the United States, he was responding to the demands of congressmen, mostly from the border states, who requested the release of their constituents and certified to their loyalty.

For military reasons, Grant thought it wrong to free so many prisoners who were willing to take the oath. These men, if they had loyal inclinations, were the very ones to keep and later to exchange for captured Union soldiers. The United States would lose little in exchanging these converted rebels: "They can afterward come into our lines," Grant explained, "if they do not wish to fight." [7]

---

[5] Welles, *Diary*, II, 269.

[6] Dorris, *Pardon and Amnesty under Lincoln and Johnson*, xvii, 77.

[7] *Collected Works*, VIII, 347–348.

At City Point, in conferences aboard the *River Queen* with Grant and Sherman on March 27 and 28, Lincoln went to great lengths to impress the generals with his desire to see the war ended quickly and humanely. "Must more blood be shed! Can not this last bloody Battle be avoided!" So he "more than once exclaimed," as Sherman recalled afterward. He said that "he wanted us to get the deluded men of the Rebel Armies disarmed, and back to their homes, that he contemplated no revenge, no harsh measures, but quite the contrary." [8] More specifically, "he distinctly authorized me to assure Governor Vance and the people of North Carolina that, as soon as the rebel armies laid down their arms, and resumed their civil pursuits, they would at once be guaranteed all their rights as citizens of a common country; and that to avoid anarchy the State governments then in existence, with their civil functionaries, would be recognized by him as the government *de facto* till Congress could provide others." [9] Such, at least, was the impression of the conversation that Sherman took back with him to North Carolina.

About two weeks later Grant presented his terms to Lee at Appomattox. He generously allowed Lee and his officers to keep their horses and their side arms once they had sworn oaths, for themselves and for their men, not to take up arms again against the United States. So far, so good. But Grant added: "This done, each officer and man will be allowed to return to his home, not to be disturbed by U. S. authority so long as they observe their paroles and the laws in force where they may reside." [10] Thus Grant, in effect, extended amnesty to Lee himself and to every officer and man in the Army of Northern Virginia. In doing so, he went beyond Lincoln's amnesty proclamation of December 8, 1863, which excluded officers above the rank of colonel and everyone who had resigned from Congress or the army or the navy to participate in the rebellion. Grant also violated Lincoln's order of March 3, 1865, which prohibited him from deciding upon any political questions, for his amnesty was a political as well as a military matter. But he did not disregard the spirit of Lincoln's recent remarks at City Point. Nor did Lincoln repudiate the terms to Lee. On the contrary, he endorsed them, according to newspaper

---

[8] Sherman to I. N. Arnold, Nov. 28, 1872, MS., Chicago Hist. Soc.
[9] Sherman, *Memoirs*, II, 324–327.   [10] *Offic. Rec.*, 1 ser., XLVI, 58.

reports at the time.[11] Some of the Radical papers denounced Grant for them, but the pro-administration press praised him. Said the Washington *Chronicle,* in publishing his correspondence with Lee, "We cannot omit our almost unutterable gratitude to him for proclaiming this truth to his defeated antagonist, and to all mankind: *'I am equally anxious for Peace with yourself, and the whole North entertain the same feeling.'* "[12]

Sherman, meanwhile, was preparing to put into effect what he thought were Lincoln's policies. If the victors adopted a humane approach, he declared soon after returning to North Carolina, "the State would be the first to wheel into the line of the old Union."[13] He was confirmed in his belief that Lincoln intended to recognize the rebel legislatures, at least temporarily, when he read newspaper reports that on April 6 Lincoln had authorized the reconvening of the Virginia legislature. Grant's terms to Lee on April 9, when Grant informed Sherman of them, seemed to him to be still further evidence that Lincoln intended his generals to exercise broad powers in making a peace of reconciliation.[14]

Lincoln was dead when, on April 18, Sherman finally came to terms with Johnston, at Bennett's farm house, near Durham, North Carolina. Assuming that he was carrying out what had been the President's wishes, Sherman then made with Johnston what amounted virtually to a treaty of peace, subject to the approval of the political authorities in Washington. Sherman not only provided for a general amnesty, as Grant had done. He also guaranteed to the Southern people their political and property rights and, as if that were not enough, he recognized the existing state governments in the South.[15]

It should be emphasized (as Grant emphasized in his memoirs) that Sherman's terms to Johnston were *conditional* upon the approval of the authorities in Washington.[16] Sherman did not pretend to be able to bind the United States by his own say-so. But the authorities in Washington—General Grant, Secretary Stanton, and President Johnson—ruled that Sherman had exceeded his powers. What was worse, Stanton gave to the press a collection of documents and statements

---

11 Philadelphia *Public Ledger,* Apr. 12, 1865, p. 1, c. 5.
12 Washington *Daily Morning Chronicle,* Apr. 10, 1865, p. 2, c. 1.
13 Philadelphia *Public Ledger,* Apr. 3, 1865, p. 1, c. 4.
14 Sherman, *Memoirs,* II, 329; McClure, *Lincoln and Men of War-Times,* 221.
15 Sherman, *Memoirs,* II, 356–357.   16 Grant, *Memoirs,* II, 514–516.

which made it appear that Sherman had deliberately flouted his orders. Throughout the North the Radicals denounced him as no better than a traitor.

Had he really been proceeding according to Lincoln's wishes? Would Lincoln, if alive, have approved the Sherman-Johnston convention? Sherman himself believed so, of course. His brother, Senator John Sherman, agreed with him, as did Admiral Porter.[17] Grant believed that, at least, Sherman *thought* he was doing what Lincoln would have wanted done.[18] Welles conceded that Sherman might have been in error. "But this error, if it be one, had its origins, I apprehend, with President Lincoln, who was for prompt and easy terms with the Rebels," Welles noted. "Sherman's terms were based on a liberal construction of President Lincoln's benevolent wishes and the order to Weitzel concerning the Virginia legislature, the revocation of which S. had not heard [of]." [19]

IV

Whether or not Lincoln made his intentions clear to Sherman, he certainly failed to make them clear to those with whom, on April 4 and 5, he discussed the question of the reassembling of the Virginia legislature. In the executive mansion in Richmond and aboard the gunboat *Malvern* in the James, he then conferred with John A. Campbell, two months previously one of the peace commissioners at Hampton Roads, and with Gustavus Myers, a Richmond attorney and a member of the Confederate Congress. Also present was Major General Godfrey Weitzel, in command of the occupation forces in Richmond. "The result of the conferences cannot be made public," a New York *Herald* correspondent reported from Richmond at the time, "but auspicious results are known to be about to accrue from them." [1] In fact, however, only the most inauspicious results were to accrue— misunderstanding, repudiation, and charges of bad faith which, long afterward, were still to be repeated against Lincoln.[2]

We do not know all that he said to the Virginians, or all that they said to him, at the meetings on April 4 and 5. We do know part of

[17] McClure, *Lincoln and Men of War-Times*, 220 n; Sherman, *Memoirs*, II, 330.
[18] Grant, *Memoirs*, II, 515.   [19] Welles, *Diary*, II, 296 (Apr. 23, 1865).
[1] Quoted in Washington *Daily Morning Chronicle*, Apr. 10, 1865, p. 1, c. 5.
[2] William M. Robinson, Jr., *Justice in Grey* (1941), 592–593, revives the contemporary charge by Southerners that "Lincoln broke faith with the Virginians."

what he said, however, since he presented to them a written statement, copies of which have been preserved. For the rest of the conversation, we must depend mainly on two letters which Campbell wrote, one of them a couple of days afterward and another several months later. We can find confirmation for a portion of Campbell's account in remarks which Weitzel made to Charles A. Dana, Lincoln's assistant secretary of war, and which Dana relayed from Richmond to Washington.

The conferences began with Campbell's requesting terms of peace. In response, Lincoln gave him a paper stating the same indispensable conditions as he had insisted upon at Hampton Roads: "The restoration of the national authority throughout all the States"; "No receding by the Executive of the United States on the slavery question . . ."; "No cessation of hostilities short of an end of the war, and the disbanding of all forces hostile to the government." The paper added that confiscations of property, except for slaves and except where the interests of third parties intervened, would be remitted to the people of any state which promptly should withdraw its troops and other support from resistance to the government.[3]

The conferees also discussed oaths of allegiance, pardon and amnesty, and the calling into session of the Virginia legislature. "The conversation," wrote Campbell in his letter of April 7, "had relation to the establishment of a Government for Virginia, the requirements of oaths of allegiance and the terms of settlement with the United States." Lincoln "assented to the application, not to require oaths of allegiance from the citizens." While he did not offer a general amnesty (as Grant was to do at Appomattox on April 9) he "intimated that there was scarcely any one who might not have a discharge upon the asking." [4] Or, as Weitzel informed Dana, "the President did not promise the amnesty, but told them he had the pardoning power, and would save any repentant sinner from hanging." [5] Campbell also, according to his letter of April 7, "strongly urged" upon Lincoln the "propriety of an armistice." Lincoln "agreed to consider the subject" (though, of course, his written terms had ruled it out). As for the Virginia legislature, Campbell in his nearly contemporary report said

---

[3] *Collected Works*, VIII, 386–387.

[4] Campbell to Joseph A. Anderson and others, Apr. 7, 1865, Stanton MSS., Lib. of Cong.

[5] Dana to Stanton, Apr. 5, 1865, Stanton MSS.

that Lincoln agreed to "send to Genl Weitzel his decision upon the question of a Government for Virginia." [6] On this point Campbell provided additional details in a later account, dated August 31, 1865. Lincoln, according to this account, said he thought he might recall the legislators who had been convening in Richmond and have them vote the return of Virginia into the Union. [7]

On April 6, the day after his last conversation with Campbell, Lincoln sent to Weitzel the following message for him to show to Campbell: "It has been intimated to me that the gentlemen who have acted as the Legislature of Virginia, in support of the rebellion, may now now [sic] desire to assemble at Richmond, and take measures to withdraw the Virginia troops, and other support from resistance to the General government. If they attempt it, give them permission and protection, until, if at all, they attempt some action hostile to the United States . . . ." [8] It should be noted that this message was sent three days before Lee's surrender, at a time when it looked as if Grant might yet have to fight that last great bloody battle which Lincoln so much dreaded. Certainly one of the motives that prompted Lincoln to send the message was the hope that the Virginia legislators might obviate such a battle by simply ordering Lee and his Virginia troops out of the war. The next morning Lincoln remarked to Dana "that Sheridan seemed to be getting Virginia soldiers out of the war, faster than this Legislature could think." [9]

With Virginia confused and distracted in the days following the evacuation of Richmond, it is perhaps surprising that Lincoln should have expected the legislature to think or to act very fast. In fact, considerable time would have to be allowed for the legislators even to assemble. Already, on April 7, Campbell was taking the first, preliminary steps. On that day he met with five of the legislators to consider the President's proposal. He presented them with copies of Lincoln's

---

[6] Campbell to Anderson and others, Apr. 7, 1865.

[7] Campbell to J. S. Speed, Aug. 31, 1865, *So. Hist. Soc. Papers,* new ser., IV, 66–74.

[8] *Collected Works,* VIII, 389.

[9] Dana to Stanton, Apr. 7, 1865, Stanton MSS. On the previous day, in reporting to Grant his arrangement with Campbell, Lincoln had indicated his military motive. "I do not think it very probable that anything will come of this; but I have thought best to notify you, so that if you should see signs, you may understand them," he informed Grant. "From your recent despatches it seems that you are pretty effectually withdrawing the Virginia troops from opposition to the government." *Collected Works,* VIII, 388.

terms and the message to Weitzel and with his own letter in which he gave his version of the recent conversations. He had much more in mind than merely the withdrawal of Virginia troops. "The object of the invitation," he stated to the five, "is for the Government of Virginia to determine, whether they will administer the laws in connection with the authorities of the United States, and under the Constitution of the United States." [10] And on the same day, in a communication to Weitzel, he again asked for an armistice, arguing that peace and the disbandment of the Confederate armies would follow soon. He also suggested to Weitzel that he provide for South Carolina the same facilities as for Virginia, so as to permit the reassembling of the legislature in that state, too. The South Carolinians, like the Virginians, should be "invited to send commissioners to adjust the questions that are supposed to require adjustment." [11] Campbell, obviously, was thinking of a series of peace negotiations between the authorities of the United States and the legislators of the various states of the Confederacy!

In just two days, with Lee's surrender on April 9, Campbell's request for an armistice ceased to have much meaning, and so did Lincoln's plan for the withdrawal of Virginia troops by the action of their own legislature. If Lincoln had known that the surrender would come so soon, he never would have made the arrangement with Campbell. That, at least, was what he told Francis H. Pierpont, the governor of the Restored Government of Virginia, when he summoned him from Alexandria to Washington on April 10 (according to Pierpont's recollection years afterward). Lincoln also told him that Campbell had suggested the idea of the Virginia legislature's meeting in Richmond to take Virginia soldiers out of the army and Virginia itself out of the Confederacy. Lincoln now said he all along had kept in mind the Pierpont government at Alexandria as the rightful government of Virginia and intended eventually to recognize it as such.[12] (According to Campbell, however, Lincoln recently had said that "he had a government in Northern Virginia—the Pierpont government —but it had but a small margin, and he did not desire to enlarge it.") [13]

[10] Campbell to Anderson and others, Apr. 7, 1865, Stanton MSS.

[11] *Collected Works*, VIII, 407–408.   [12] Ambler, *Pierpont*, 255–259.

[13] Campbell to Speed, Aug. 31, 1865, *So. Hist. Soc. Papers*, new ser., IV, 66–74.

In Richmond, on April 11, eight legislators and twenty-five other officeholders and prominent citizens met and issued a request for the governor and the legislature to assemble there on April 25. General Weitzel, General Shepley, and Assistant War Secretary Dana all approved this call before it was published in the Richmond *Whig* and distributed on handbills.[14]

In Washington, on that same April 11, Lincoln met with his cabinet. None of the members liked the idea of the assembling of the Virginia legislature, but Stanton and Speed especially were disturbed by it. They saw Lincoln individually after the cabinet meeting and protested to him. Lincoln then saw Welles, the Conservative stalwart among the secretaries (Seward being still incapacitated by his recent carriage accident), "said Stanton and others were dissatisfied," and asked Welles's frank opinion. Welles confessed that he himself doubted the wisdom of convening rebel legislators, for they might conspire together against the Union, or they might demand terms which would seem reasonable but which would prove unacceptable. Lincoln, however, thought the Southerners were too badly beaten, too exhausted, to make much trouble. "His idea was, that the members of the legislature, comprising the prominent and influential men of their respective counties, had better come together and undo their own work." In the critical transition from war to peace, what was needed was some temporary authority which the Southern people would obey. "Civil government must be reestablished, he said, as soon as possible; there must be courts, and law, and order, or society would be broken up, the disbanded armies would turn into robber bands and guerrillas, which we must strive to prevent. These were the reasons why he wished prominent Virginians who had the confidence of the people to come together and turn themselves and their neighbors into good Union men." But Lincoln said he could not go ahead when all his advisors were opposed to him. He might be wrong, he admitted.[15]

This conversation, as reported by Welles, took place on April 12 and 13—three and four days after the surrender of Lee. In it Lincoln gave no indication that his only purpose, in permitting the as-

14 Robinson, *Justice in Grey*, 592.

15 Welles, *Diary*, II, 279. Welles elaborated somewhat in his article on "Lincoln and Johnson: Their Plan of Reconstruction and the Resumption of National Authority," in *Galaxy*, XIII, 524–525 (April, 1872).

sembling of the Virginia legislature, was to have that legislature withdraw the Virginia troops. So far as Welles's record goes, he did not mention that phase of the subject at all. Indeed, if he had lost interest in the plan because of the surrender, he would have had no issue with the cabinet on April 11 and no occasion for the discussion with Welles on the following two days. Apparently he decided to drop the plan in consequence of the criticisms from his cabinet. He did not avow this opposition as a reason for his change of mind, however, when he informed Weitzel of the change.

At nine o'clock on the morning of April 12 he telegraphed to Weitzel: "Is there any sign of the rebel legislature coming together on the basis of my letter to you? If there is any such sign, inform me what it is; if there is no such sign you may as [well] withdraw the offer." At three in the afternoon of the same day Weitzel wired his reply: "The passports have gone out for the legislature, and it is common talk that they will come together." At six on the evening of the same day Lincoln telegraphed again:

"I have just seen Judge Campbell's letter to you of the 7th. He assumes as appears to me that I have called the insurgent Legislature of Virginia together, as the rightful Legislature of the State, to settle all differences with the United States. I have done no such thing. I spoke of them not as a Legislature, but as 'the gentlemen who have *acted* as the Legislature of Virginia in support of the rebellion.' I did this on purpose to exclude the assumption that I was recognizing them as a *rightful* body. I dealt with them as men having power *de facto* to do a specific thing, to wit, 'to withdraw the Virginia troops, and other support from resistance to the General Government,' for which in the paper handed Judge Campbell I promised a specific equivalent, to wit, a remission to the people of the State, except in certain cases, the confiscation of their property. I meant this and no more. In as much however as Judge Campbell misconstrues this, and is still pressing for an armistice, contrary to the explicit statement of the paper I gave him; and particularly as Gen. Grant has since captured the Virginia troops, so that giving a consideration for their withdrawal is no longer applicable, let my letter to you, and the paper to Judge Campbell both be withdrawn or, countermanded, and he be notified of it. Do not allow them to assemble; but if any have come, allow them safe-return to their homes." [16]

If Lincoln "meant this and no more," and if he had made his intention as clear a week earlier as he did now, neither Campbell nor Weitzel could very well have misunderstood him. If he meant a little more than this, if he intended for the leading Virginians themselves to undo their act of secession and to prevent chaos until some new state government could be established, as Welles's record indicates, then he could have attempted to clarify his purposes instead of cutting Campbell off so peremptorily. But his own purposes seem to have changed somewhat—after his return to Washington and his troubles with his cabinet. [17]

In Richmond, General E. O. C. Ord, Butler's successor and Weitzel's superior, gave the actual notice to Campbell to call off his project, on April 13. [18] The next evening Ord telegraphed to Lincoln that Campbell and his Hampton Roads colleague, R. M. T. Hunter, wished to visit Washington at once with important and urgent communications for the President. The telegram was received in Washington at half past nine. [19] Lincoln already had gone to Ford's Theater.

V

The many-sided problem of reconstruction, of which the question of the Virginia legislature was only one aspect, was a subject of con-

---

[16] *Collected Works*, VIII, 405–407.

[17] Robinson, *Justice in Grey*, 592–593, writes: "In the face of such determined resistance from his advisers, Lincoln renounced his liberal policy and the next day withdrew his permission for the assembling of the State government, attempting to quibble out of his original sanction." Lincoln's reference to Campbell's mere request for an armistice does seem like a rather weak excuse. On the other hand, Campbell was guilty of downright distortion when he said, in his letter to Speed of August 31, 1865, that Lincoln "never for a moment spoke of the Legislature, except as a public corporate body, representing a substantial portion of the State." Also, whether wilfully or not, Campbell certainly had gone beyond Lincoln's original intentions. In giving permission for the Virginia legislature to assemble, Lincoln most likely had two main objectives in mind: one, weakening the military resistance of the enemy; the other, providing a means of governmental transition from war to peace. The first objective lost its importance with Lee's surrender. The second became hopeless both because of the cabinet opposition in Washington and because of Campbell's misunderstanding of the role the Virginia legislature was expected to play. Undoubtedly Lincoln was himself largely at fault in not making himself better understood, but he cannot justly be charged with sanctioning Campbell's plans or with quibbling out of his agreement.

[18] *So. Hist. Soc. Papers*, new ser., IV, 75.

[19] Ord to Lincoln, Apr. 14, 1865, *Offic. Rec.*, ser. 1, XLVI, pt. 3, p. 748.

tinual debate in the North from 1863 on. After reaching a furious pitch in the summer of 1864, the debate had been toned down during the final weeks of the presidential campaign, to be renewed fitfully and shrilly as the final military victory approached. Lee's surrender brought the issue to a climax again. Then, temporarily at least, Lincoln and the Radicals found themselves even farther apart than before. For a while, in early April, 1865, he seemed willing to readmit the Southern states on terms more generous than those he had announced in his ten-per-cent plan and in his amnesty proclamation of December, 1863. But the Radicals were prepared to demand terms even more rigorous than those they had embodied in the Wade-Davis bill, which Lincoln had refused to sign in July, 1864.

With a new sense of urgency the Radicals began to consult with one another and to speak out. On the day after Appomattox, in Washington, General Butler made a speech in which he recommended, on the one hand, that the leaders of the rebellion should be disfranchised and disqualified for public office and, on the other, that the masses including the Negroes should be given immediately all the rights of citizenship.[1] The next evening, in Baltimore on court duty, Chief Justice Chase dined with Henry Winter Davis and other Maryland Radicals, then wrote a letter to the President.[2] "It will be, hereafter, counted equally a crime and a folly," Chase said, "if the colored loyalists of the rebel states shall be left to the control of restored rebels, not likely, in that case, to be either wise or just, until taught both wisdom and justice by new calamities."[3]

That same evening, April 11, Lincoln made his own, last contribution to the public debate when he addressed the crowd gathered on the White House grounds. After a few congratulatory words on Grant's recent victory, he proceeded to defend at some length his own reconstruction view.

The problem, as he saw it, was essentially one of re-establishing the national authority throughout the South. This problem was complicated by the fact that there was, in the South, "no authorized organ" to treat with. "Nor is it a small additional embarrassment that we, the loyal people, differ among ourselves as to the mode, manner, and

---

[1] Philadelphia *Public Ledger*, Apr. 11, 1865, p. 1, c. 7.

[2] David Donald, ed., *Inside Lincoln's Cabinet: the Civil War Diaries of Salmon P. Chase*, 265.

[3] *Collected Works*, VII, 399.

means of reconstruction." He had been criticized, he said, because he did not seem to have a fixed opinion on the question "whether the seceded States, so called," were "in the Union or out of it." He dismissed that question as "a merely pernicious abstraction" and went on to declare: "We all agree that the seceded States, so called, are out of their proper practical relation with the Union; and that the sole object of the government, civil and military, in regard to those States is to again get them into that proper practical relation."

He had been criticized also for setting up and sustaining the new state government of Louisiana, which rested on the support of only ten per cent of the voters and did not give the franchise to the colored man. He confessed that the Louisiana government would be better if it rested on a larger electorate including the votes of Negroes—at least "the very intelligent" and those who had served as soldiers. "Concede that the new government of Louisiana is only to what it should be as the egg is to the fowl, we shall sooner have the fowl by hatching the egg than by smashing it?" The loyalists of the South would be encouraged and the Negroes themselves would be better off, Lincoln argued, if Louisiana were quickly readmitted to the Union. An additional ratification would be gained for the Thirteenth Amendment, the adoption of which would be "unquestioned and unquestionable" only if it were ratified by three fourths of *all* the states.

What Lincoln said of Louisiana, he applied also to the other states of the South. "And yet so great peculiarities pertain to each state; and such important and sudden changes occur in the same state; and, withal, so new and unprecedented is the whole case, that no exclusive, and inflexible plan can safely be prescribed as to details and colatterals." (Virginia was not mentioned.) In concluding, Lincoln said enigmatically that it might become his duty "to make some new announcement to the people of the South. I am considering, and shall not fail to act, when satisfied that action will be proper." [4]

In Washington and throughout the country the speech aroused much speculation about Lincoln's undisclosed intentions, and it provoked mixed feelings about his general approach to reconstruction. The editor of the Philadelphia *Public Ledger* noted that the President had indicated his "feelings and wishes" rather than his "fixed opin-

---

[4] *Ibid.*, 399–405.

ions," then commended him for his lack of "passion or malignancy" toward the late rebels.[5] The Washington correspondent of the Cincinnati *Gazette* believed that Lincoln's position was generally approved except among the Radical Republicans, who were saying that the rebel leaders must be punished and the rebel states subjected to "preliminary training" before being restored to their rights as members of the Union. "The desire of the people for a settlement—speedy and final—upon the easiest possible terms, will, it is believed, sustain the President in his policy foreshadowed in his speech." [6]

Whatever the people might have approved, it was again made clear to Lincoln, when the cabinet met on the morning of April 14 (with General Grant present), that some of his own advisers would not approve a settlement upon easy terms. Secretary Stanton came to the meeting with a project for military occupation as a preliminary step toward the reorganization of the Southern states, Virginia and North Carolina to be combined in a single military district. Secretary Welles objected to this arrangement on the grounds that it would destroy the individuality of the separate states. He said that, in the case of Virginia, there was nothing to do but recognize the Pierpont government, which had been recognized throughout the war, its consent having been necessary for the erection of the new state of West Virginia. The President sustained Welles's objection but did not completely repudiate Stanton's plan. Instead, he suggested that Stanton revise it so as to deal with Virginia and North Carolina separately, and that he provide copies of the revised plan for the members of the cabinet at their next meeting.[7]

Attorney-General Speed got the impression that Lincoln was coming over to the Radicals. "He never seemed so near our views," Speed told Chase the next day. "At the meeting he said he thought [he] had made a mistake at Richmond in sanctioning the assembling of the Virginia Legislature and had perhaps been too fast in his desires for early reconstruction." [8]

Before the cabinet meeting adjourned, Lincoln said he was glad that Congress was not in session. The House and the Senate, he was aware, had the unquestioned right to accept or reject new members

[5] Philadelphia *Public Ledger*, Apr. 13, 1865, p. 2, c. 1.

[6] Cincinnati *Daily Gazette*, Apr. 13, 1865, p. 3, c. 4.

[7] Welles, *Diary*, II, 281; Welles, "Lincoln and Johnson," *Galaxy*, XIII, 526–527.

[8] Donald, *Diaries of Salmon P. Chase*, 268.

from the Southern states; he himself had nothing to do with that. Still, he believed, the President had the power to recognize and deal with the state governments themselves. He could collect taxes in the South, see that the mails were delivered there, and appoint Federal officials (though his appointments would have to be confirmed, of course, by the Senate). He knew that the congressional Radicals did not agree with him, but they were not in session to make official objection, and he could act to establish and recognize the new state governments before Congress met in December. He did not intend to call a special session before that time, as he told the speaker of the House, Schuyler Colfax, later on the day of that final cabinet meeting, as he was entering his carriage to go to Ford's Theater.[9]

When, in December, 1865, the regular session of Congress finally began, Andrew Johnson had been President for nearly eight months. At first, in the days of terror following Lincoln's assassination, Johnson talked like a good Radical. He also acted like one when he ordered the arrest of Jefferson Davis and other Confederate leaders on the charge of complicity in the assassination. But Johnson and the Radicals soon disagreed on reconstruction. During the summer he succeeded in the restoration of state governments according to a plan which required them only to abolish slavery, retract their ordinances of secession, and repudiate their debts accumulated in the Confederate cause. In December the Radicals in Congress refused to seat the senators and representatives from these restored states. After checking Johnson's program, the Radicals proceeded to undo it, while impeaching the President. Eventually they carried through their own program of military occupation, similar to the one Stanton had proposed at the cabinet meeting of April 14, and they undertook to transfer political power from the old master class to the freedmen, as Chase and other Radicals long had advocated.

Whether Lincoln, if he had lived, would have done as Johnson did, is hard to say. Certainly Lincoln would not have hounded Jefferson Davis or other Confederate officials (but, then, the presupposition here is that there would have been no assassination to seem to justify it). At the City Point conversation in March, Lincoln had given Sherman to believe that he would not mind if Davis escaped from the country, "unbeknownst" to him. To his cabinet in April he had

---

9 Welles, *Diary*, II, 281; *Galaxy*, XIII, 526–527.

indicated his hope that there would be no persecution, no bloody work, with respect to any of the late enemy. "None need expect he would take any part in hanging or killing those men, even the worst of them," Welles paraphrased him. "Frighten them out of the country, open the gates, let down the bars, scare them off, said he, throwing up his hands as if scaring sheep."

As for the restoration of state governments, it is impossible to guess confidently what Lincoln would have done or tried to do, since the very essence of his planning was to have no fixed and uniform plan, and since he appeared to be changing his mind on some points shortly before he died. In the states already being reconstructed under his program of December, 1863, he doubtless would have continued to support that program, as he did to the last. In other states he might have tried other expedients, no doubt accepting the Pierpont government (as Johnson did) in Virginia. In no state did he seem inclined, at the very end, to accept the going government as a temporary authority, and the probability is that he would have overruled the Sherman-Johnston convention just as his successor did. In general, Lincolnian reconstruction probably, but not certainly, would have been very similar to Johnsonian reconstruction.

Whether, if Lincoln had lived and had proceeded along Johnson's lines, he would have succeeded any better than Johnson, is another "iffy" question, impossible to answer. It seems likely that, with his superior talent for political management, Lincoln would have avoided the worst of Johnson's clashes with Congress. Yet he could scarcely have escaped the conflict itself, unless he had conceded much more to the Radicals than Johnson did.

Another poser is the question whether Lincoln's approach to peace, if he had lived and had carried it through, would have advanced the Negro toward equal citizenship more surely than did the Radical program, which degenerated into a rather cynical use of the Negro for party advantage. One is entitled to believe that Lincoln's policy would have been better in the long run for Negroes as well as for Southern whites and for the nation as a whole.

CHAPTER XVI

GOD'S MAN

AT FIFTY-SIX Lincoln had not yet arrived at the full development and use of his personal powers. Such was Herndon's
firm belief, and while many of Herndon's judgments must be
discounted, there is little reason for doubting this one.

Certainly, as the President entered upon his second term, he still
possessed a sturdy and resilient physical constitution, one capable of
withstanding the cares of his office and recovering from the shocks of
ordinary disease. A week or so after his re-inauguration he stayed in
bed for a few days, refusing to see visitors, while it was reported on
the one hand that he had "no serious illness" but was "only suffering
from the exhausting attentions of office hunters" [1] and, on the other
hand, that his case had been diagnosed as a "severe attack of influ-
enza." [2] Even after he had improved enough to receive "hosts of
visitors," and then to go out with Mrs. Lincoln to a German opera,
he remained rather feeble for several days. When he left Washington
for his two weeks' stay at City Point, he was seeking to escape the
bothersome jobseekers and to rest and convalesce, as well as to oversee
the closing of the war. He returned to the White House with renewed
vigor and buoyant spirits.[3] At his final cabinet meeting he looked
better than ever, at least to Secretary Speed, who remembered vividly
his "shaved face well brushed clothing and neatly combed hair and
whiskers." [4]

If Lincoln's physical capacity for further accomplishment was great,
his mental and spiritual capacities seemed even more so. Mentally,
he had grown to a remarkable extent since first becoming President.

[1] Cincinnati *Daily Gazettte*, Mar. 15, 1865, p. 3, c. 6.
[2] New York *Herald*, Mar. 15, 1865, p. 4, c. 5.
[3] Washington *Daily Morning Chronicle*, Apr. 18, 1865, p. 1, c. 7.
[4] James Speed to Joseph H. Bennett, Apr. 16, 1885, Barton MSS.

As the London *Spectator* said (March 25, 1865), comparing his debates against Douglas and the second inaugural, to "apprehend truly the character of Mr. Lincoln" one should notice the tremendous "growth of his mind." [5] Spiritually, as Herndon afterwards observed, Lincoln "grandly rose up" year after year.[6] No doubt the circumstances of his untimely death contributed to his later apotheosis, yet his fame might possibly have had an even more substantial foundation in true greatness if he had lived at least another four years.

I

The heroic image of Lincoln, so familiar to later generations, was not entirely a by-product of his martyrdom. While yet alive he became one of the most admired and best loved Americans of all time— a rival of George Washington for the place of first in the hearts of his countrymen, though there was then no such consensus as was afterwards to give him a clear priority over Washington.[1]

The living Lincoln seemed a hero most of all to the Negroes who hailed him as their deliverer and, among the white people of the North, to women and children. Miss Sarah B. Howell, of Trenton, New Jersey, requesting a lock of his hair "to be woven into a bouquet for the 'Sanitary Fair,'" told him in June, 1864, "no other President has come so near our hearts." [2] Other women sent him even more touching letters. "I only wish to thank you for being so good—and to say how sorry we all are that you must have four years more of this terrible toil," Miss Mary A. Dodge wrote him from Hamilton, Massachusetts, on the day of his second inauguration. "You can't tell anything about it in Washington where they make a noise on the slightest provocation. But if you had been in this little speck of a village this morning and heard the soft, sweet music of unseen bells rippling through the morning silence from every quarter of the far-off horizon, you would have better known what your name is to this nation." [3] Doubtless many children shared the aspiration of

---

[5] Quoted in *Littell's Living Age*, LXXXV, 135–137 (Apr. 22, 1865).

[6] Herndon MSS.

[1] The latter-day consensus has been indicated by such polls as that which in 1940 asked six thousand New Yorkers the question, "Who is the greatest American, living or dead?" Lincoln led in the returns, and Washington was second. New York *Times*, Apr. 20, 1940.

[2] Miss Howell to Lincoln, June 6, 1864, R. T. L. Coll., 33565.

[3] Miss Dodge to Lincoln, Mar. 4, 1865, R. T. L. Coll., 41055–56.

Governor Thomas H. Hicks' little son who was "anxious to see" the President and shake hands with him, as Hicks explained in the note he sent along with his servant who, on a May day in 1864, took the boy into the White House.[4]

The living Lincoln seemed a great man also to certain contemporary journalists. Some of these had partisan motives for praising him, no doubt; but others, writing for English publications, viewed him with relative detachment. And, whether English or American, these observers analyzed the elements of greatness in his character as perceptively as any historian or biographer afterwards could do.

An editorial in Henry J. Raymond's New York *Times,* endorsed and reprinted in John W. Forney's Washington *Chronicle,* described Lincoln in the summer of 1863 as resembling Washington in "perfect balance of thoroughly sound faculties," "sure judgment," and "great calmness of temper, great firmness of purpose, supreme moral principle, and intense patriotism."[5] An editorial in the Buffalo *Express,* about a year later, noted Lincoln's "remarkable moderation and freedom from passionate bitterness," then went on to say: "We do not believe Washington himself was less indifferent to the exercise of power for power's sake. Though concentrating in his hands a more despotic authority, in many respects, than had Napoleon, he has never used it for his personal ends, and we believe the verdict of history will be that he has far less frequently abused it than he has failed to use it as terror to evil-doers despite the clamor about arbitrary arrests."[6] The *Spectator* of London, in March, 1865, commented that Lincoln's task was lighter than Washington's but Lincoln had had to meet it without the advantages of Washington's education and experience. Lincoln was great because of his growth to meet his responsibilities. He had outgrown "the rude and illiterate mould of a village lawyer's thought" and had attained "a grasp of principle, a dignity of manner, and a solemnity of purpose, which would have been unworthy neither of Hampden nor of Cromwell," and he had acquired a "gentleness and generosity of feeling toward his foes" which one would hardly have expected from either Cromwell or Hampden.[7] The *Times* of London at about the same time observed

---

[4] Thomas H. Hicks to Lincoln, May 30, 1864, R. T. L. Coll., 33420.

[5] Washington *Daily Morning Chronicle,* Sept. 17, 1863, p. 2, c. 2.

[6] Buffalo *Morning Express,* Aug. 30, 1864, p. 1, c. 1.

[7] *Spectator,* Mar. 25, 1865, quoted in *Littell's Living Age,* LXXXV, 135–137 (Apr. 22, 1865).

that Lincoln, "placed in the most important position to which a statesman can aspire, invested with a power greater than that of most monarchs," fulfilled his duties "with firmness and conscientiousness, but without any feeling of exhiliration." [8]

The Liverpool *Post* (October 1, 1863) believed that, to judge from external appearances, "no leader in a great contest ever stood so little chance of being a subject of hero worship as Abraham Lincoln," with his long legs and long pantaloons, his shambling figure and his general awkwardness, which made him an easy target for caricature and ridicule. "Yet a worshiper of human heroes might possibly travel a great deal farther and fare much worse for an idol than selecting this same lanky American," the Liverpool *Post* continued. His inner traits—his truthfulness, resolution, insight, faithfulness, and courage, together with his equanimity, which was such that none of the bitter personal attacks upon him had ever "drawn from him an explanation of ill humor, or even an impudent rejoinder"—all these qualities would "go a long way to make up a hero," whatever his outward appearance. [9]

II

The concept of Lincoln the hero was inverted in the minds of many of his contemporaries, Northerners as well as Southerners, who thought him no hero but a villain whose death would be a good riddance. A number of them took the trouble to tell him so. One, who signed himself "Joseph," wrote (January 4, 1864): "The same who warned you of a conspiracy, Novr. 18th 1862, is now compelled to inform you, that,—'Your days are numbered,' you have been weighed in the balance & found wanting. You shall be a dead man in six months from date Dec. 31st, 1863." [1] Assassination threats appeared not only in the privacy of crank letters but also in some of the public prints, such as the LaCrosse, Wisconsin, *Democrat*, which avowed during the campaign of 1864: "If Abraham Lincoln should be re-elected for another term of four years of such wretched administration, *we hope that a bold hand will be found to plunge the dagger into*

---

[8] London *Times*, Mar. 17, 1865, quoted in *Littell's Living Age*, LXXXV, 86–88 (Apr. 15, 1865).

[9] Quoted in Washington *Daily Morning Chronicle*, Oct. 19, 1863, p. 1. c. 7.

[1] R. T. L. Coll., 29176.

the Tyrant's heart for the public welfare." [2]

To kidnap or kill the President would be easy, the New York *Tribune* cautioned. A band of rebels or rebel sympathizers might fall upon him at home, on the way to church, on one of his visits to the front.[3] In February, 1865, Stanton was warned: "The President could be seized any reception evening, in the midst of the masses assembled round him, and carried off by fifty determined men armed with bowie knives and revolvers, and once out could be put into a market wagon guarded by a dozen horsemen, and borne off at will,— the conspirators having first set a dozen or twenty hacks in motion to distract attention. Look out for some such dash soon." [4]

No such dash came, but a story of another kind of assassination plot made news a few weeks later. Raving and cursing in the Washington jail, Thomas Clements boasted that he and an accomplice had made the trip from Alexandria to kill the President on inauguration day. Clements said they had arrived just a half hour too late, and his Savior would never forgive him. As for his motive, he explained that the President had robbed him of a large amount of money.[5]

The men around Lincoln, among them Stanton in particular, worried continually about his safety. Seldom was he allowed out of the sight of his personal bodyguard, Ward Hill Lamon, or of other guards, including details of cavalry or infantry and sometimes both.[6] But the President was not inclined to co-operate with the custodians of his welfare, and he frequently disregarded Stanton's advice against exposing his life, as on his visits to Petersburg and Richmond at the end of the war.

His own attitude seemed to vary with his moods. Sometimes he discounted the danger, saying that he did not share his friends' apprehension about his life.[7] On the last day he was alive, when told there had been much uneasiness in the North during his Richmond visit, he cheerfully replied that he would have been alarmed, himself, if someone else had been President and had gone there, but in

2 Quoted, with the italics, in the Buffalo *Commercial Advertiser,* Nov. 5, 1864, p. 2, c. 2.
3 New York *Daily Tribune,* Mar. 19, 1864, p. 1, c. 1.
4 T. Weing to Stanton, Feb. 22, 1865, Ewing MSS., Lib. of Cong.
5 Cincinnati *Daily Gazette,* Mar. 8, 1865, p. 3, c. 6.
6 New York *Herald,* Jan. 3, 1865, p. 1, c. 2.
7 J. D. Defrees to Hugh McCulloch, Apr. 20, 1865, Lincoln National Life Foundation, Ft. Wayne, Ind.

his own case he had not felt any peril whatsoever.[8] In his more gloomy moments he confessed he did not expect to survive the Presidency. One evening, riding from the White House to the Soldiers' Home, he told an Illinois acquaintance that his cavalry escort had been more or less forced upon him by the military men, but he thought such an attempt at protection rather futile. "He said it seemed to him like putting up the gap in only one place when the fence was down all along." [9] On another occasion a representative of the United States Sanitary Commission, who had walked freely through an unguarded door into the White House, ventured to protest to the President about the latter's lack of protection at a time when assassination was openly threatened. "Well," Lincoln answered, "you know that it is as well to have but one trouble of it. Assassination would be one, but continual dread would make two of it!" [10]

No use in worrying. What is to be, must be. If anyone is really determined to kill me, I shall be killed. So Lincoln generally reacted to the thought of personal danger. His reaction was perfectly in keeping with his profoundly fatalistic outlook.

III

Though Lincoln's fatalism grew and developed while he was in the White House, it was in itself nothing new with him, not a product of his Presidential years. It may have derived from the predestinarian doctrines of his parents and of the Kentucky and Indiana communities in which he was reared. Anyhow it was firmly fixed in his mind by the time he ran for Congress in 1846. In that election his opponent, the revivalist Peter Cartwright, "was whispering the charge of infidelity" against him,[1] and he replied with a fairly forthright statement of his personal philosophy. Admitting he was no church member, but denying he was a scoffer, Lincoln said that "in early life" he had been "inclined to believe in" what was called the "Doctrine of Necessity"—the doctrine that the human mind was moved by some power over which it had no control. He added that, in the past, he sometimes had tried to maintain this doctrine by argument, though

---

[8] Washington *Daily Morning Chronicle*, Apr. 17, 1865, p. 2, c. 1, 2.
[9] Gillespie to Herndon, Dec. 8, 1866, Herndon MSS.
[10] Undated memorandum by R. Pearsall Smith, Nicolay-Hay MSS., Ill. St. Hist. Lib.
[1] Lincoln to Allen N. Ford, Aug. 11, 1846, *Collected Works*, I, 383.

not in public, but for more than five years he had "entirely left off" his "habit of arguing." [2] He did not say he had abandoned the belief itself: he only said he had quit arguing it.

The power that controlled the human mind and the human destiny might be called *God*, and Lincoln as a young man sometimes referred to it that way, though he did so apologetically, as when he wrote (in 1842) to his recently married friend Joshua F. Speed: ". . . I was always superstitious; and as part of my superstition, I believe God made me one of the instruments of bringing your Fanny and you together, which union, I have no doubt He had foreordained. Whatever he designs, he will do for *me* yet." [3] Here was an expression of Lincoln's fatalistic philosophy with religious (or, as he said, "superstitious") overtones. God had designs. He foreordained events. He worked through human agents, and Lincoln on occasion was one of them.

Lincoln as President held to the same belief, but he held to it with a far deeper religious assurance and with an appropriately grander conception of his own role in the divine plan. He came to view the war as God's way of removing slavery and punishing the people, both North and South, for the sin that all shared on account of slavery. And he came to look upon himself, humbly, as God's man, God's human agent in the working out of His mysterious providence.

Lincoln's clearest expression of this religious, predestinarian interpretation of the war is found in his second inaugural. "If we shall suppose that American slavery is one of those offences which, in the providence of God, must needs come, but which, having continued through His appointed time, He now wills to remove, and that He gives to both North and South, this terrible war, as the woe due to those by whom the offence came, shall we discern therein any departure from those divine attributes which the believers in a Living God always ascribe to Him?" [4] If Lincoln had said such things only on public occasions, his sincerity might be questioned, but he expressed similar ideas in private letters and conversations, and he did so with the ring of true conviction. "Men are not flattered by being shown that there has been a difference of purpose between the Al-

---

[2] Handbill addressed "To the Voters of the Seventh Congressional District," July 31, 1846, *ibid.*, 382.

[3] Lincoln to Speed, July 4, 1842, *ibid.*, I, 289.   [4] *Ibid.*, VIII, 333.

mighty and them," he wrote to Thurlow Weed in response to the latter's congratulations upon the second inaugural. "To deny it, however, in this case, is to deny that there is a God governing the world. It is a truth which I thought needed to be told; and as whatever of humiliation there is in it, falls most directly on myself, I thought others might afford for me to tell it." [5] Once he wrote to Eliza P. Gurney: "The purposes of the Almighty are perfect, and must prevail, though we erring mortals may fail to accurately perceive them in advance. We hoped for a happy termination of this terrible war before this; but God knows best, and has ruled otherwise." [6] In conversation at the White House he spoke feelingly of God's will and his own submission to it. [7] Thus, before the end of his life, he had substituted the idea of "God's will" for his earlier concept of a "necessity" abstract and mechanistic.

But Lincoln found room within his predestinarian scheme for human will, human choice. He once told Congressman Arnold how, years earlier, he had declined an offer of the governorship of Oregon Territory. "If you had gone to Oregon," Arnold commented, "you might have come back as senator, but you would never have been President." Lincoln agreed, then said with a musing, dreamy look: "I have all my life been a fatalist. What is to be will be, or rather, I have found all my life as Hamlet says:

> There is a divinity that shapes our ends,
> Rough-hew them how we will. [8]

Or, as Lincoln told Mrs. Gurney, we must acknowledge God's wisdom and our own error. "Meanwhile we must work earnestly in the best light He gives us, trusting that so working still conduces to the great ends He ordains." [9]

IV

Since Lincoln's death, more words have been wasted on the question of his religion than on any other aspect of his life. Many preachers in their obituary sermons described him as a true, believing Christian, and one of them obtained from the presumably authorita-

[5] Lincoln to Weed, Mar. 15, 1865, *ibid.*, 356.
[6] Lincoln to Mrs. Gurney, Sept. 4, 1864, R. T. L. Coll., 35907–8.
[7] Carpenter, *Six Months at the White House*, 86.   [8] Arnold, *Lincoln*, 81.
[9] R. T. L. Coll., 35907–8.

tive Noah Brooks an assurance of "Mr. Lincoln's saving knowledge of Christ; he talked always of Christ, his cross, his atonement." [1] Some of the preachers seemed desperately eager to get Lincoln on the side of Christianity, so eager that the Reverend James A. Reed, one of the staunchest defenders of Lincoln's orthodoxy, was constrained to remind the public that "the faith and future of the Christian religion in no wise depends upon the sentiments of Abraham Lincoln." [2] The earliest biographers—Josiah G. Holland, Isaac N. Arnold—pictured their subject as a paragon in every respect, especially in Christian piety. All this was too much for Herndon, the aggressive freethinker of Springfield, and he set out to prove that his former law partner had been an infidel and very nearly an atheist.[3] Lincoln himself had left off arguing religion some thirty years before he died, but afterward countless volunteers took up the argument for him, and they never left it off. Sectarians of all kinds, from spiritualists to biosophers, claimed him as one of them.[4]

In fact, however, Lincoln had never signed any creed, never joined any church. After about 1850 he went to Sunday services regularly, at the First Presbyterian Church in Springfield and then at the New York Avenue Presbyterian Church in Washington. In Springfield he was a friend of the Rev. Dr. James Smith, the Presbyterian minister, and he read with interest Dr. Smith's book designed to lead skeptics to the Christian faith by rational argument. In Washington he was again a friend of his minister, the Rev. Dr. Phineas D. Gurley. But neither Smith nor Gurley won him to the fold.[5]

If Lincoln was no professing Christian, neither was he in any sense an atheist. Indeed, even Herndon did not really think he was. Herndon was driven to overstatement by his zeal against the cant of pious moralizers, yet he sometimes qualified his statements and contradicted

[1] Brooks to the Rev. Isaac P. Langworthy, May 10, 1865, printed as *The Character and Religion of President Lincoln* (Champlain, N.Y., 1919).

[2] Douglas C. McMurtrie, ed., *Lincoln's Religion . . . Addresses . . . by William H. Herndon and Rev. James A. Reed . . .* (Chicago, 1936).

[3] Benjamin P. Thomas, *Portrait for Posterity: Lincoln and His Biographers*, chap. i. See also Albert V. House, Jr., "The Genesis of the Lincoln Religious Controversy," *Proceedings of the Middle States Association of History and Social Science Teachers*, XXXVI (1938), 44–54.

[4] See, for example, Paul Miller, "Was Abraham Lincoln a Spiritualist?" *Psychic Observer*, Feb. 10, 1945, and Arthur E. Briggs, "Lincoln the Biosopher," *Biosophical Review*, Spring-Summer, 1936.

[5] William E. Barton, *The Soul of Abraham Lincoln*, 73–75, 87, 156, 255–256.

himself. "I affirm that Mr. Lincoln died an unbeliever—was not an evangelical Christian," he said in rebuttal against the Rev. James A. Reed.[6] On another occasion Herndon declared that Lincoln *"was in short an infidel*—was a universalist—was a Unitarian—a Theist. He did not believe that Jesus was God nor the son of God etc." [7] Of course, a theist is not an atheist and, except by fundamentalist standards, a universalist or a unitarian is hardly an infidel. Nor is a person necessarily an unbeliever simply because he is not an "evangelical" Christian.

Doubtless Lincoln did share some of the basic Universalist and Unitarian attitudes. Like the Universalists he apparently believed in salvation for all and disbelieved in hell, and like the Unitarians he seems to have rejected the supernatural account of the birth of Christ. While, in private letters and state papers, he referred often to God or the Almighty, he very seldom mentioned Jesus as the Savior, very seldom mentioned Jesus at all (despite Brook's unsupported testimony that he "talked always of Christ, his cross, his atonement").

Lincoln also was inclined toward the Quaker point of view, and he acknowledged that his ancestors had been Quakers. Some of the Friends believed, as his correspondence with Mrs. Gurney reveals, that like them he felt a "true concern" laid upon him by the Heavenly Father.[8] There is no need to look for proof of the as yet unproved story that one of Mrs. Gurney's letters, carefully treasured by him, was found in his breast pocket after the assassination.[9] There is ample evidence, in the correspondence itself, to show that he deeply sympathized with the Quakers and did indeed treasure their good wishes.

In common with the Friends he felt a kind of mysticism, a sense of direct communion with the unseen. He did not carry this so far as to become a spiritualist. True, he permitted a few seances in the White House, after the death of little Willie, but these were Mrs. Lincoln's doing, not his. He commented that the seances reminded him of his cabinet meetings: the voices of the spirits, he said, were as contradictory as was the advice of his secretaries. Nevertheless he had a superstitious belief in various kinds of mysterious signs and

---

[6] McMurtrie, *Lincoln's Religion*, 23.

[7] Herndon to Lamon, Feb. 25, 1870, Herndon MSS.

[8] Mrs. Gurney to Lincoln, Sept. 8, 1864, R. T. L. Coll., 36053–56.

[9] *Friends Intelligencer*, Feb. 12, 1944, p. 102.

portents, especially dreams. Once in 1863, when Mrs. Lincoln with Tad was visiting in Philadelphia, Lincoln thought it important enough to telegraph her: "Think you had better put Tad's pistol away. I had an ugly dream about him." [10] On several occasions the President thought his dreams so significant that he brought them to the attention of his cabinet. On the morning of his final cabinet meeting he related the poignant recurring dream in which he was upon the water and, as Welles recorded, "seemed to be in some singular, indescribable vessel" and "was moving with great rapidity towards an indefinite shore." [11]

A believer in dreams, a mystic with some affinity for the Quakers, a rationalist with Universalist and Unitarian views, a regular participant in Presbyterian services—Lincoln cannot easily be categorized as to religion. Yet it is possible to construct a personal creed from his own statements, as William E. Barton has done.[12] Lincoln believed in God. He believed that God was intimately concerned with human affairs, that nations as well as men were dependent upon Him, that men and nations were punished for their sins, in this world as well as the next. He believed in the Bible as the best gift ever given by God to men. And he believed with all humility that he himself was an instrument in the hands of God.

Indeed, Lincoln was a man of more intense religiosity than any other President the United States has ever had. He had not demonstrated this trait very noticeably during his Illinois years. Reacting perhaps against the backwoods religion of his Baptist father, he had turned to skepticism, read such iconoclastic authors as Volney and Paine, and gained a reputation as a scoffer—a reputation which he felt he must deny when running for Congress in 1846. This early Lincoln was the Lincoln that Herndon knew, or thought he knew, and Herndon insisted that the later Lincoln was exactly the same. For this, Herndon got confirmation from Nicolay. "Mr. Lincoln, did not, to my knowledge, change in any way his religious views, beliefs, or opinions from the time he left Springfield to the day of his death," Nicolay replied to Herndon's query.[13] But Nicolay vitiated his testimony as to Lincoln's unchanging religious beliefs when he added that he did "not know just what they were." And in Lincoln's writings and

---

[10] Barton, *The Soul of Abraham Lincoln,* 232–236.   [11] Welles, *Diary,* II, 282–283.
[12] *The Soul of Abraham Lincoln,* 300.   [13] McMurtrie, *Lincoln's Religion,* 41.

speeches, there is plenty of evidence, whether or not Nicolay could see it and appreciate it, to indicate that Lincoln as President gained a more and more pervasive consciousness of God.

Almost invariably students of Lincoln have noted his spiritual growth, but some have differed in their efforts to account for it. Ruth Painter Randall has explained it as his response to a series of crises both personal and public—the deaths of his sons Eddie and Willie, the awesome responsibilities of his wartime office.[14] Charles W. Ramsdell has suggested that the President's deepening sense of melancholy and charity may have been due in part to a sense of guilt for having contributed to bringing on the war.[15] There may be some truth in Ramsdell's guess—at times Lincoln seemed to make a special point of protesting that not he but God was responsible, as when he wrote: "Surely He intends some great good to follow this mighty convulsion, which no mortal could make, and no mortal could stop."[16] Richard Hofstadter has found a clue to Lincoln's tragic sense of life in an antithesis between Lincoln the ambitious politician and Lincoln the sensitive and humble man of the people. "Lincoln's rage for personal success, his external and worldly ambition, was quieted when he entered the White House, and he was at last left alone to reckon with himself," Hofstadter writes. "To be confronted with the fruits of his victory only to find that it meant choosing between life and death for others was immensely sobering."[17]

Whatever the source of Lincoln's religious feeling, it became a vibrant force in his thought and action as President. It transformed him, even in the view of Herndon, who once wrote: "Do you not see Lincoln's Christ like charity—liberality—toleration loom up & blossom above all."[18] It moved Lincoln's friend Jesse W. Fell to say that, though Lincoln subscribed to no sectarian dogma, "his principles and practices, and the spirit of his whole life, were of the kind we universally agree to call Christian."[19] It led John Hay to call him "the greatest character since Christ."[20] Surely, among successful American

---

[14] Ruth Painter Randall, "Lincoln's Faith was Born of Anguish," *New York Times Magazine*, Feb. 7, 1954, pp. 11, 26–27. See also Harlan Hoyt Horner, *The Growth of Lincoln's Faith* (1939).

[15] Ramsdell, "Lincoln and Fort Sumter," *Journal of Southern History*, III (1937), 288.

[16] Lincoln to Mrs. Gurney, Sept. 4, 1864, R. T. L. Coll., 35907–8.

[17] Hofstadter, *American Political Tradition*, 133.

[18] Herndon MSS.   [19] Fell to Lamon, Sept. 26, 1870, J. S. Black MSS.

[20] Hofstadter, *American Political Tradition*, 92.

politicians, Lincoln is unique in the way he breathed the spirit of Christ while disregarding the letter of Christian doctrine. And the letter killeth, but the spirit giveth life.

V

Lincoln's tastes in literature provide something of a clue to the nature of the inner man. He did not read widely, but he read deeply. He re-read over and over the things he liked, and he liked a rather odd assortment of things. He did not care for philosophical works as such. Though fond of the essays of John Stuart Mill, particularly the famous one on liberty, he considered the tomes of Herbert Spencer and Charles Darwin as "entirely too heavy for an ordinary mind to digest," if Herndon is to be believed. Metaphysical books he considered even worse. "Investigation into first causes, abstruse mental phenomena, the science of being," says Herndon, "he brushed aside as trash—mere scientific absurdities." [1] He liked poetry, including that of Lord Byron and Robert Burns, but his favorite poem was one written by the otherwise undistinguished William Knox, and he often recited it: "Oh! Why should the spirit of mortal be proud?" [2] Among his favorite authors were, at one extreme, the comic writers who went by the names of Petroleum V. Nasby, Orpheus C. Kerr, Artemus Ward, and Joe Miller of the famous jokebook and, at the other extreme, William Shakespeare.[3] Lincoln conformed to the accepted convention of a great man's proper literary tastes in his sincere love of Shakespeare's plays and the Bible.

According to Arnold, he knew the Bible almost by heart. "There was not a clergyman to be found so familiar with it as he." And there is "scarcely a speech or paper prepared by him" from 1834 to 1865 "but contains apt allusions and striking illustrations from the sacred book." [4] According to Brooks, he "would sometimes correct a misquotation of Scripture, giving generally the chapter and verse where it could be found." And, according to Brooks, he much preferred the Old Testament to the New.[5]

Actually, Lincoln did not quote the Bible in his state papers quite so often as Arnold believed, nor in his quotations did he indicate such

---

[1] Daniel K. Dodge, *Abraham Lincoln: The Evolution of His Literary Style*, 17.
[2] *Littell's Living Age*, LXXXV, 239–240 (May 6, 1865).   [3] Dodge, 16–17.
[4] Arnold, *Lincoln*, 45.
[5] Brooks, "Recollections of Abraham Lincoln," *Harper's Magazine*, XXXI (1865), 229.

a preference for the Old Testament as Brooks reported. A sampling of Lincoln's works has shown that, in twenty-five speeches from 1839 to 1865, he alluded to the Bible a total of twenty-two times—to the Old Testament eight times and to the New Testament fourteen. A few of the speeches contain several references each, others contain none at all, and there is a good deal of repetition, as for example of the "house divided against itself" passage.[6] From this it does not necessarily follow that Lincoln was less familiar with the Bible than he has been credited with being or that he preferred the New Testament. Apparently there is no close correlation between, on the one hand, his interest in and familiarity with the Bible, either in whole or in part, and, on the other hand, the frequency of his references to it in public addresses.

The same is true also in regard to Shakespeare's plays. In public addresses Lincoln quoted or paraphrased them even less often than the Bible. In private conversations, however, he not only used a great many Shakespearean allusions but he also discussed problems of interpretation, with remarkable insight, and gave effective performances of his own. Doubtless he would have made a powerful tragic actor as well as a discerning drama critic.

"Unlike you gentlemen of the profession," he wrote to the actor Hackett, "I think the soliloquy in 'Hamlet,' commencing 'O, my offense is rank,' surpasses that commencing, 'To be or not to be.' "[7] The first of these soliloquies—spoken by the King after the murder of Polonius—was a favorite with Lincoln. In the presence of Carpenter he once recited the entire passage from memory, and with more feeling and better understanding than Carpenter had ever heard it done on the stage. Lincoln complained that the passage usually was slurred over by professional actors, and so, he said, was another of his favorites, the opening lines of "King Richard the Third," beginning "Now is the winter of our discontent." This soliloquy, too, Lincoln repeated in Carpenter's presence, "rendering it with a degree of force and power that made it seem like a new creation" to Carpenter. While at Fortress Monroe, in 1862, the President read feelingly from "Hamlet" on the theme of ambition.[8] On shipboard returning from City Point, in 1865, he delighted his fellow passengers, including the

6 Dodge, 18–19.　　　7 Cincinnati *Daily Gazette*, Sept. 30, 1863, p. 1, c. 6.

8 Carpenter, *Six Months at the White House*, 49–52.

Marquis de Chambrun, with Shakespearean readings which lasted for several hours. He was especially moved, and moving, with the verses in "Macbeth" in which Macbeth speaks of Duncan's assassination:

> Duncan is in his grave;
> After life's fitful fever he sleeps well;
> Treason has done his worst: nor steel, nor poison,
> Malice domestic, foreign levy, nothing
> Can touch him further.[9]

With Lincoln, the play was the thing, not the acting, and in the play it was the thought that counted. "It matters not to me whether Shakespeare be well or ill acted," he once remarked; "with him the thought suffices." [10] Unless the acting was unusually good, Lincoln preferred his own reading and interpretation of the play. After seeing Edwin Booth as Shylock he said to Brooks: "It was a good performance, but I had a thousand times rather read it at home, if it were not for Booth's playing. A farce, or a comedy, is best played; a tragedy is best read at home." [11]

At home, in the White House, there was little rest for Lincoln during those tumultuous days and nights of celebration following the surrender at Appomattox. Now, as always, the theater offered him an escape in a physical as well as a psychological sense. It was a place to go to get away from people and be alone while in their midst. Time and again in the past he had sat with an audience and had remained abstracted and unmoved as scene after scene passed.[12] On the evening of April 14, 1865, he planned to seek that accustomed relaxation, this time at Ford's Theater, where a comedy, "Our American Cousin," was playing. At dinner he complained of being worn out from the toils of the day, and he looked forward eagerly to an opportunity to laugh. Mrs. Lincoln, troubled with a headache, suggested that they stay home, but he insisted on their going out; otherwise, he said, he would have to see visitors all evening as usual.[13] And so they went.

---

[9] James Speed to Joseph H. Barrett, Sept. 16, 1885, Barton MSS. The Marquis de Chambrun's account is in *Scribner's Magazine*, XIII (1893), 34.

[10] Carpenter, *Six Months at the White House*, 49–52.

[11] Brooks, "Personal Recollections of Abraham Lincoln," *Scribner's Monthly*, XV (1877–1878), 675.

[12] Forney, *Anecdotes of Public Men*, 272.

[13] A. G. Henry to Mrs. Henry, Apr. 19, 1865, MS., Lib. of Cong. See also Ruth Painter Randall, *Mary Lincoln*, 381.

BIBLIOGRAPHY [1]

Anon., "As Lincoln Knew New Salem." 36 *Life* 79–81 (Feb. 15, 1954).

Abbott, Martin, "Southern Reaction to Lincoln's Assassination." 7 *A. L. Q.* 111–127 (1952).

Adams, George Worthington, *Doctors in Blue: The Medical History of the Union Army in the Civil War.* New York: Henry Schuman, 1952. 253 pp.

Agar, Herbert, *Abraham Lincoln.* New York: The Macmillan Co., 1952. 143 pp. *Brief Lives,* No. 6.

Anderson, Frank Maloy, *The Mystery of "A Public Man:" A Historical Detective Story.* Minneapolis: Univ. of Minnesota Press, 1948. 256 pp. For another version, see Lokken, Roy N.

Anderson, George L., "The South and Problems of Post-Civil War Finance." 9 *Jour. So. Hist.* 181–195 (1943).

Angle, Paul M., "The Changing Lincoln," *The John H. Hauberg Historical Essays,* ed. by O. Fritiof Ander. Rock Island, Ill.: Augustana College, 1954. Pp. 1–17.

———, ed., "The Recollections of William Pitt Kellogg." 3 *A. L. Q.* 319–339 (1945).

———, *A Shelf of Lincoln Books: A Critical, Selective Bibliography of Lincolniana.* New Brunswick: Rutgers Univ. Press, 1946. 142 pp.

———, ed., *The Lincoln Reader.* New Brunswick: Rutgers Univ. Press, 1947. 564 pp.

———, comp., *Abraham Lincoln: His Autobiographical Writings Now Brought Together for the First Time* . . . . Kingsport, Tenn.: Privately printed at Kingsport Press, Inc., 1947. 67 pp.

———, ed., *Herndon's Life of Lincoln.* Cleveland: World Pub. Co., 1949. 511 pp.

———, ed., *Abraham Lincoln by Some Men Who Knew Him* . . . . Chicago: Americana House, 1950. 123 pp.

Arena, Frank C., "Southern Sympathizers in Iowa during the Civil War Period." 30 *Ann. Iowa* (3 ser.) 486–538 (1951).

---

[1] This list is intended to supplement the bibliography in *Lincoln the President,* II, 343–400. Included in the list are, for the most part, items published since that earlier bibliography was prepared. Also included here are certain items of earlier date which are relevant to the subjects treated in volumes III and IV of the biography but not relevant to volumes I and II. This bibliography was prepared by Wayne C. Temple.

Auer, J. Jeffery, "Lincoln's Minister to Mexico." 59 *Ohio Arch. and Hist. Quar.* 115–128 (1950).

Bailey, Thomas A., "The Russian Fleet Myth Re-Examined." 38 *M. V. H. R.* 81–90 (1951).

Ballard, Colin R., *The Military Genius of Abraham Lincoln.* Cleveland: World Pub. Co., 1952. 246 pp.

Banks, N. P. See Harrington, Fred Harvey.

Barbee, David Rankin, "President Lincoln and Doctor Gurley." 5 *A. L. Q.* 3–24 (1948).

———, "The Musical Mr. Lincoln." 5 *A. L. Q.* 435–454 (1949). For the correction of this story, see 6 *A. L. Q.* 37–39 (1950).

Baringer, William E. and Marion D. Bonzi [Pratt], "The Writings of Lincoln." 4 *A. L. Q.* 3–16 (1946).

———, "The Birth of a Reputation." 4 *A. L. Q.* 217–242 (1947).

———, *Lincoln's Vandalia: A Pioneer Portrait.* New Brunswick: Rutgers Univ. Press, 1949. 141 pp.

———, "On Enemy Soil: President Lincoln's Norfolk Campaign." 7 *A. L. Q.* 4–26 (1952).

Barrett, Oliver R., "Lincoln and Retaliation." 49 *Lincoln Herald* 2 ff. (Dec., 1947).

Barton, Robert S., "William E. Barton—Biographer." 4 *A. L. Q.* 80–93 (1946).

———. See also Spears, Zarel C.

Barton, William E., *Lincoln at Gettysburg: What He Intended to Say; What He Said; What He Was Reported to Have Said; What He Wished He Had Said.* New York: Peter Smith, 1950. 263 pp.

Basler, Roy P., *Abraham Lincoln: His Speeches and Writings.* Cleveland: World Pub. Co., 1946. 750 pp.

———, "Lincoln and People Everywhere." 4 *A. L. Q.* 349–355 (1947).

———, "Lincoln in Politics, 1948." 5 *A. L. Q.* 216–233 (1948).

———, "What Did Lincoln Say?" 5 *A. L. Q.* 476–479 (1949).

———, "Isaac Harvey or Samuel Haddam." 6 *A. L. Q.* 353–357 (1951).

———, " 'Beef! Beef! Beef!' Lincoln and Judge Robertson." 6 *A. L. Q.* 400–407 (1951).

———, Marion D. (Bonzi) Pratt, and Lloyd A. Dunlap, eds., *The Collected Works of Abraham Lincoln.* New Brunswick: Rutgers Univ. Press, 1953. 8 vols. Index vol. to follow.

Baxter, Maurice G., "Encouragement of Immigration to the Middle West during the Era of the Civil War." 46 *Ind. Mag. Hist.* 25–38 (1950).

Beale, Howard K., "On Rewriting Reconstruction History." 45 *A. H. R.* 807–827 (1940).

———, "What Historians Have Said about the Causes of the Civil War." In *Theory and Practice in Historical Study* . . . . Ed. by C. A. Beard and others. Social Science Research Council Bulletin No. 54. New York: Social Science Research Council, 1946. Pp. 55–102.

Beck, Warren A., "Lincoln and Negro Colonization in Central America."
6 *A. L. Q.* 162–183 (1950).
Bernard, Kenneth A., "Lincoln and Civil Liberties." 6 *A. L. Q.* 375–399
(1951).
———, "Glimpses of Lincoln in the White House." 7 *A. L. Q.* 161–187
(1952).
Binkley, Wilfred E., *President and Congress.* New York: Alfred A. Knopf,
1947. 312 pp.
Black, Robert C., III, *The Railroads of the Confederacy.* Chapel Hill:
Univ. of North Carolina Press, 1952. 360 pp.
Blum, Virgil C., "The Political and Military Activities of the German
Element in St. Louis, 1859–1861." 42 *Mo. Hist. Rev.* 103–129 (1948).
Bonner, Thomas N., "Horace Greeley and the Secession Movement, 1860–
1861." 38 *N. V. H. R.* 425–444 (1951).
Bonzi, Marion D., "A Sparks Debate Variant." 4 *A. L. Q.* 140–144 (1946).
Briggs, Harold E. and Ernestine B. Briggs, *Nancy Hanks Lincoln: A Fron-
tier Portrait.* New York: Bookman Assoc., 1952. 135 pp.
Brown, Charles Leroy, "Abraham Lincoln and the Illinois Central Rail-
road, 1857–1860." 36 *Jour. Ill. S. H. S.* 121–163 (1943).
Brown, Richard A. See Miers, Earl Schenck.
Brown, Virginia Stuart, *Through Lincoln's Door.* Springfield Li-Co Art
& Letter Service, 1952. 79 pp. Revised edition 1953.
Bullard, F. Lauriston, *Abraham Lincoln & the Widow Bixby.* New Bruns-
wick: Rutgers Univ. Press, 1946. 154 pp.
———, "Lincoln's Copy of Pope's Poems." 4 *A. L. Q.* 30–35 (1946).
———, "Abraham Lincoln and Harriet Beecher Stowe." 48 *Lincoln Her-
ald* 11–14 (June, 1946).
———, "Abraham Lincoln and George Ashmun." 19 *New Eng. Quar.*
184–211 (1946).
———, "Abe Goes down the River." 50 *Lincoln Herald* 2–14 (Feb., 1948).
———, "When—If Ever—Was John Wilkes Booth in Paris?" 50 *Lincoln
Herald* 28–34 (June, 1948).
———, "Anna Ella Carroll and Her 'Modest' Claim." 50 *Lincoln Herald*
2–10 (Oct., 1948).
———, "Church and State in Lincoln's Time." 50–51 *Lincoln Herald* 28 ff.
(Dec., 1948–Feb., 1949).
———, "A Friend in France in '61." 51 *Lincoln Herald* 33–37 (June,
1949).
———, "Garfield and Chase—Their Ideas of Lincoln." 51 *Lincoln Herald*
2 ff. (Dec., 1949).
———, "How Much Did Abraham Lincoln Owe to 'Luck?'" 52 *Lincoln
Herald* 44–45 (Feb., 1950).
———, "A Correction of 'The Musical Mr. Lincoln.'" 6 *A. L. Q.* 37–39
(1950).
———, "Again, the Bixby Letter." 53 *Lincoln Herald* 26 ff. (Summer, 1951).

————, *Lincoln in Marble and Bronze*. New Brunswick: Rutgers Univ. Press, 1952. 353 pp.

Cannon, M. Hamlin, "The United States Christian Commission." 38 *M. V. H. R.* 61–80 (1951).

Carr, R. T. and Hugh Morrow, "We Found Lincoln's Lost Bank Account." 225 *Sat. Eve. Post* 22 ff. (Feb. 14, 1953).

Carruthers, Olive and R. Gerald McMurtry, *Lincoln's Other Mary*. Chicago: Ziff-Davis, 1946. 229 pp.

Catton, Bruce, *Mr. Lincoln's Army*. Garden City: Doubleday & Co., 1951. 372 pp.

————, *Glory Road: The Bloody Route from Fredericksburg to Gettysburg*. Garden City: Doubleday & Co., 1952. 416 pp.

————, *A Stillness at Appomattox*. Garden City: Doubleday & Co., 1953. 438 pp.

Chambrun, Marquis Adolphe de, *Impressions of Lincoln and the Civil War: A Foreigner's Account*. Trans. by Gen. Aldebert de Chambrun. New York: Random House, 1952. 174 pp.

Chase, Salmon Portland. See Donald, David.

Chester, Giraud, *Embattled Maiden: The Life of Anna Dickinson*. New York: G. P. Putnam's Sons, 1951. 307 pp.

Clary, William W., *How Abe Lincoln Went to Oxford*. Claremont, Cal.: Claremont College, 1948. 16 pp.

Claussen, Martin P., "Peace Factors in Anglo-American Relations, 1861–1865." 26 *M. V. H. R.* 511–522 (1940).

Coleman, Charles H., "The Use of the Term 'Copperhead' during the Civil War." 25 *M. V. H. R.* 263–264 (1938).

————, "The Half-Faced Camp in Indiana—Fact or Myth?" 7 *A. L. Q.* 138–146 (1952).

Cramer, J. H., "Lincoln in Cincinnati." 3 *Bulletin Hist. and Philosophical Soc. of Ohio* 11–16 (1945).

————, "The Great and the Small." 49 *Lincoln Herald* 14–20 (Feb., 1947).

————, "A President-elect in Western Pennsylvania." 71 *Pa. Mag. Hist. and Biog.* 206–217 (July, 1947).

————, "Abraham Lincoln Visits with His People." 57 *Ohio Arch. and Hist. Quar.* 66–78 (1948).

————, *Lincoln under Enemy Fire: The Complete Account of His Experiences during Early's Attack on Washington*. Baton Rouge: Louisiana State Univ. Press, 1948. 138 pp.

Craven, Avery O., "The Civil War and the Democratic Process." 4 *A. L. Q.* 269–292 (1947).

————, "The Price of Union." 18 *Jour. So. Hist.* 3–19 (1952).

Cresson, Margaret French, *Journey into Fame: The Life of Daniel Chester French*. Cambridge: Harvard Univ. Press, 1947. 316 pp.

Cross, Jasper W., "The Civil War Comes to 'Egypt.'" 44 *Jour. Ill. S. H. S.* 160–169 (1951).

Current, Richard Nelson, *Old Thad Stevens: A Story of Ambition*. Madison: Univ. of Wisconsin Press, 1942. 344 pp.

Cuthbert, Norma B., ed., *Lincoln and the Baltimore Plot, 1861: From Pinkerton Records and Related Papers*. San Marino: Henry E. Huntington Library, 1949. 161 pp.

Daugherty, James, *Lincoln's Gettysburg Address: A Pictorial Interpretation*. Chicago: Albert Whitman & Co., 1947. 42 pp.

Donald, David, "The Folklore Lincoln." 40 *Jour. Ill. S. H. S.* 377–396 (1947).

————, "The True Story of 'Herndon's Lincoln.'" 1 *The New Colophon* 221–234 (1948).

————, *Lincoln's Herndon*. New York: Alfred A. Knopf, 1948. 392 pp.

————, ed., *Divided We Fought: A Pictorial History of the War 1861–1865*. New York: The Macmillan Co., 1952, 452 pp.

————, "Getting Right with Lincoln." 202 *Harper's Mag.* 74–80 (April, 1851).

————, ed., *Inside Lincoln's Cabinet: The Civil War Diaries of Salmon Portland Chase*. New York: Longmans, Green & Co., 1954. 342 pp.

Donald, Henderson H., *The Negro Freedman: The Life Conditions of the American Negro in the Early Years after Emancipation*. New York: Henry Schuman, 1952. 270 pp.

Dorris, Jonathan Truman, *Pardon and Amnesty under Lincoln and Johnson*. Chapel Hill: Univ. of North Carolina Press, 1953. 459 pp. Introduction by J. G. Randall.

Drake, Julia A., "Lincoln Land Buying." 50–51 *Lincoln Herald* 32–35 (Dec., 1948–Feb., 1949).

Dunlap, Lloyd A., "President Lincoln and Editor Greeley." 5 *A. L. Q.* 94–110 (1948).

————, "Lincoln Saves a Son." 7 *A. L. Q.* 128–137 (1952).

————. See also Basler, Roy P.

East, Ernest E., "Lincoln and the Peoria French Claims." 42 *Jour. Ill. S. H. S.* 41–56 (1949).

Ehrmann, Bess V., *Lincoln and His Neighbors*. Rockport, Ind.: Democrat Pub. Co., 1948. 44 pp.

————, *The Lincoln Pioneer Village: A Lincoln Memorial, Rockport, Indiana*. Rockport, Ind.: Democrat Pub. Co., 1949. 7 pp.

Eisendrath, Joseph L., Jr., "Lincolniana in the Official Records." 4 *A. L. Q.* 201–204 (1946).

————, "Suggestions that Inspired Immortal Words." 5 *A. L. Q.* 212–215 (1948).

Eisenschiml, Otto and Ralph Newman, comps., *The American Iliad: The Epic Story of the Civil War as Narrated by Eyewitnesses and Contemporaries*. Indianapolis: Bobbs-Merrill Co., 1947. 720 pp.

———— and E. B. Long, *As Luck Would Have It: Chance and Coincidence in the Civil War*. Indianapolis: Bobbs-Merrill Co., 1948. 285 pp.

———, "Addenda to Lincoln's Assassination." 43 *Jour. Ill. S. H. S.* 91–99; 204–219 (1950).

———, *The Celebrated Case of Fitz John Porter: An American Dreyfus Affair.* Indianapolis: Bobbs-Merrill Co., 1950. 344 pp.

Elliott, Claude, "Union Sentiment in Texas 1861–1865." 50 *Southwestern Hist. Quar.* 449–477 (1947).

Fatout, Paul, "Mr. Lincoln Goes to Washington." 47 *Ind. Mag. Hist.* 321–332 (1951).

Fehrenbacher, Don E., "The Nomination of Lincoln in 1858." 6 *A. L. Q.* 24–36 (1950).

Fisch, Theodore, "Horace Greeley: A Yankee in Transition." (MS) Ph. D. thesis, Univ. of Ill., Urbana, 1947.

Fischer, LeRoy H., "Lincoln's Gadfly—Adam Gurowski." 36 *M. V. H. R.* 415–434 (1949).

Foster, Genevieve, *Abraham Lincoln: An Initial Biography.* New York: Chas. Scribner's Sons, 1950. 111 pp.

Frank, Seymour J., "The Conspiracy to Implicate the Confederate Leaders in Lincoln's Assassination." 40 *M. V. H. R.* 629–656 (1954).

Freeman, Douglas Southall, *Lee's Lieutenants: A Study in Command.* New York: Chas. Scribner's Sons, 1942–1944. 3 vols.

Freidel, Frank, "General Orders 100." 32 *M. V. H. R.* 541–556 (1946).

———, *Francis Lieber: Nineteenth-Century Liberal.* Baton Rouge: Louisiana State Univ. Press, 1947. 445 pp.

Garraty, John A., "Lincoln and the Diplomats." 46 *Ind. Mag. Hist.* 203–204 (1950).

Geyl, Pieter, "The American Civil War and the Problem of Inevitability." 24 *New Eng. Quar.* 147–168 (1951).

Gillespie, Frances. See Wallace, Sarah A.

Glonek, James F., "Lincoln, Johnson, and the Baltimore Ticket." 6 *A. L. Q.* 255–271 (1951).

Gorgas, Josiah. See Vandiver, Frank E.

Greenbie, Sydney and Marjorie Barstow Greenbie, *Anna Ella Carroll and Abraham Lincoln: A Biography.* Manchester, Me.: Univ. of Tampa Press, 1952. 539 pp. For an evaluation, see Kenneth P. Williams, 54 *Lincoln Herald* 54–56 (Summer, 1952).

Grierson, Francis, *The Valley of Shadows.* Boston: Houghton Mifflin Co., 1948. 278 pp.

Griffith, Albert H., *The Heart of Abraham Lincoln.* Madison: Lincoln Fellowship of Wisconsin, 1948. 16 pp.

Gunderson, Robert Gray, "Lincoln and Governor Morgan: A Financial Footnote." 6 *A. L. Q.* 431–437 (1951).

Hagen, Richard S., "Back-Yard Archaeology at Lincoln's Home." 44 *Jour. Ill. S. H. S.* 340–348 (1951).

Hambrecht, George P., *Abraham Lincoln in Wisconsin.* Madison: Lincoln Fellowship of Wisconsin, 1946. 17 pp.

Hamilton, Holman, "Abraham Lincoln and Zachary Taylor." 53 *Lincoln Herald* 14–19 (Fall, 1951).

Hammand, Lavern Marshall, "Ward Hill Lamon: Lincoln's 'Particular Friend.' " (MS) Ph. D. thesis, Univ. of Ill., Urbana, 1949.

Harkness, David J., "Lincoln and 'The Ship of State.' " 53 *Lincoln Herald* 28–30 (Spring, 1951).

Harnsberger, Caroline Thomas, *The Lincoln Treasury*. Chicago: Wilcox & Follett Co., 1950. 372 pp.

Harper, Robert S., *Lincoln and the Press*. New York: McGraw-Hill Book Co., 1951. 418 pp.

Harrington, Fred Harvey, *Fighting Politician: Major General N. P. Banks*. Philadelphia: Univ. of Penn. Press, 1948. 301 pp.

Harris, Alfred G., "Lincoln and the Question of Slavery in the District of Columbia." 51–53 *Lincoln Herald* 17–21; 2–16; 11–18 (June, 1949–Spring 1951).

Harwell, Richard Barksdale, "Lincoln and 'Dixie:' The Yankee Conversion of Some Southern Songs." 53 *Lincoln Herald* 22–27 (Spring, 1951).

Hawley, Charles Arthur, "Lincoln in Kansas." 42 *Jour. Ill. S. H. S.* 179–192 (1949).

Hays, Roy, "Is the Lincoln Birthplace Cabin Authentic?" 5 *A. L. Q.* 127–163 (1948).

Heathcote, Charles William, "Lincoln's Funeral Train in Pennsylvania." 48 *Lincoln Herald* 13 ff. (Dec., 1946).

———, "Three Pennsylvanians and Lincoln's Nomination—1860." 51 *Lincoln Herald* 38–41 (June, 1949).

———, "The Lincolns of Massachusetts, New Jersey and Pennsylvania." 51 *Lincoln Herald* 17–19 (Dec., 1949).

———, "President Lincoln and John Burns at Gettysburg." 53 *Lincoln Herald* 31–33 (Spring, 1951).

Heintz, Michael G., "Cincinnati Reminiscenses of Lincoln." 9 *Bulletin Hist. and Philosophical Soc. of Ohio* 113–120 (1951).

Hendrick, Burton J., *Lincoln's War Cabinet*. Boston: Little, Brown & Co., 1946. 482 pp.

Hesseltine, William B., "Lincoln's War Governors." 4 *A. L. Q.* 153–200 (1946).

——— and Hazel C. Wolf, "The Cleveland Conference of 1861." 56 *Ohio Arch. and Hist. Quar.* 258–265 (1947).

———, *Lincoln and the War Governors*. New York: Alfred A. Knopf, 1948. 405 pp.

Hewitt, John Hill, *King Linkum the First: A Musical Burletta*. Emory Univ. Library: Higgins-McArthur Co., 1947. 32 pp. Reprint of a play presented at Concert Hall at Augusta, Ga., on Feb. 23, 1863.

Hildner, Ernest G., Jr., "The Mexican Envoy Visits Lincoln." 6 *A. L. Q.* 184–189 (1950).

Hobeika, John E., *The Sage of Lion's Den: An Appreciation of . . . Lyon Gardiner Tyler and of His Writings on Abraham Lincoln . . . .* New York: The Exposition Press, 1948. 64 pp.

Hochmuth, Marie, "Lincoln's First Inaugural." In Wayland Maxfield Parrish and Marie Hochmuth eds., *American Speeches.* New York: Longmans, Green & Co., 1954. pp. 21–71.

Horner, Harlan Hoyt, "Lincoln Replies to Horace Greeley." 53 *Lincoln Herald* 2–10; 14–25 (Spring–September, 1951).

———, "Lincoln Rebukes a Senator." 44 *Jour. Ill. S. H. S.* 103–119 (1951).

———, "Lincoln Scolds a General." 36 *Wis. Mag. Hist.* 90 ff. (1952–1953).

———, *Lincoln and Greeley,* Urbana: Univ. of Illinois Press, 1953. 432 pp.

Howard, Oliver Otis, "Some Reminiscences of Abraham Lincoln." 55 *Lincoln Herald* 20 ff. (Fall, 1953). This sketch was written by Howard on March 1, 1895; MS at Bowdoin College, Brunswick, Me.

Howe, Mark De Wolfe, ed., *Touched with Fire: Civil War Letters and Diary of Oliver Wendell Holmes, Jr. 1861–1864.* Cambridge: Harvard Univ. Press, 1946. 158 pp.

Hubbard, Freeman H., *Vinnie Ream and Mr. Lincoln.* New York: Whittlessey House, 1949, 271 pp.

Hunt, Eugenia Jones, "My Personal Recollections of Abraham and Mary Todd Lincoln." 3 *A. L. Q.* 235–252 (1945).

Isely, Jeter A., *Horace Greeley and the Republican Party, 1853–1861: A Study of the New York Tribune.* Princeton: Princeton Univ. Press, 1947. 368 pp.

James, H. Preston, "Election Time in Illinois, 1860." 49 *Lincoln Herald* 12–21 (June, 1947).

———, "Lincoln and Douglas in Their Home State." 49 *Lincoln Herald* 2–9 (Oct., 1947).

———, "Political Pageantry in the Campaign of 1860 in Illinois." 4 *A. L. Q.* 313–347 (1947).

———, "Lincoln and Douglas in Their Home State: The Election of 1860 in Illinois." 49 *Lincoln Herald* 12–20 (Dec., 1947).

Jillson, Willard Rouse, *Abraham Lincoln in Kentucky Literature.* Frankfort, Ky.: Roberts Printing Co., 1951. 75 pp.

Johannsen, Robert W., "National Issues and Local Politics in Washington Territory, 1857–1861." 42 *Pacific Northwest Quar.* 3–31 (1951).

———, "Spectators of Disunion: The Pacific Northwest and the Civil War." 44 *Pacific Northwest Quar.* 106–114 (1953).

"John, Evan" [Capt. E. J. Simpson], *Atlantic Impact, 1861.* New York: G. P. Putnam's Sons, 1952. 296 pp. This is a history of the *Trent* affair.

Jones, Edgar DeWitt, *The Greatening of Abraham Lincoln*. St. Louis: The Bethany Press, 1946, 38 pp.

———, "Abraham Lincoln Still Walks at Midnight." 48 *Lincoln Herald* 28–31 (Oct., 1946).

———, *Lincoln and the Preachers*. New York: Harper Bros., 1948. 203 pp.

———, "A Preacher at Lincoln's Tomb." 50 *Lincoln Herald* 28–29 (Oct., 1948).

Judson, Clara Ingram, *Abraham Lincoln: Friend of the People*. Chicago: Wilcox & Follett Co., 1950. 205 pp.

Kennedy, Kaywin, "If Lincoln Were Alive Today." 35 *Ill. Bar Jour.* 229–230 (1947).

Kincaid, Robert L., "Kentucky in the Civil War." 49 *Lincoln Herald* 2–12 (June, 1947).

Klement, Frank L., "Jane Grey Swisshelm and Lincoln: A Feminist Fusses and Frets." 6 *A. L. Q.* 227–238 (1950).

———, "Economic Aspects of Middle Western Copperheadism." 14 *The Historian* 27–44 (1951).

———, " 'Brick' Pomeroy: Copperhead and Curmudgeon." 35 *Wis. Mag. Hist.* 106–113 (1951).

———, "Middle Western Copperheadism and Genesis of the Granger Movement." 38 *M. V. H. R.* 679–694 (1952).

Klingberg, Frank Wysor, "James Buchanan and the Crisis of the Union." 9 *Jour. So. Hist.* 455–474 (1943).

———, "The Case of the Minors: A Unionist Family within the Confederacy." 13 *Jour. So. Hist.* 27–45 (1947).

Korn, Bertram W., *American Jewry and the Civil War*. Philadelphia: The Jewish Pub. Soc. of America, 1951. 331 pp.

Korngold, Ralph, *Two Friends of Man: The Story of William Lloyd Garrison and Wendell Phillips and Their Relationship with Abraham Lincoln*. Boston: Little, Brown & Co., 1950. 425 pp.

Kramer, Sidney, "Lincoln at the Fair." 3 *A. L. Q.* 340–358 (1945).

Kunhardt, D. M., "Lincoln's Lost Dog." 36 *Life* 83–86 (Feb. 15, 1954).

Kyle, Otto R., "Mr. Lincoln Steps Out: The Anti-Nebraska Editors' Convention." 5 *A. L. Q.* 25–37 (1948).

Landon, Fred, "Canadian Appreciation of Abraham Lincoln." 3 *A. L. Q.* 159–177 (1944).

Lawson, Elizabeth, *Lincoln's Third Party*. New York: International Pub., 1948. 48 pp.

Lewis, Lloyd, "Lincoln and Pinkerton." 41 *Jour. Ill. S. H. S.* 367–382 (1948).

———, "Lincoln's Legacy to Grant." 5 *A. L. Q.* 75–93 (1948).

Lewis, Montgomery S., *Legends that Libel Lincoln*. New York: Rinehart & Co., 1946. 239 pp.

Lieber, Francis. See Freidel, Frank.

Lincoln, Mary Todd. See Randall, Ruth Painter.

Lincoln, Nancy Hanks. See Briggs, Harold E.

Lockwood, Theodore D., "Garrison and Lincoln the Abolitionist." 6 *A. L. Q.* 199–226 (1950).

Lokken, Roy N., "Has the Mystery of 'A Public Man' Been Solved?" 40 *M. V. H. R.* 419–440 (1953).

Long, E. B. See Eisenschiml, Otto.

Lonn, Ella, *Foreigners in the Union Army and Navy*. Baton Rouge: Louisiana State Univ. Press, 1951. 725 pp.

Lorant, Stefan, *The Life of Abraham Lincoln: A Short, Illustrated Biography*. New York: McGraw-Hill Book Co., 1954. 256 pp.

———, *Lincoln: A Picture Story of His Life*. New York: Harper & Bros., 1952. 256 pp.

Ludwig, Emil, *Abraham Lincoln: The Full Life Story of Our Martyred President*. Trans. by Eden and Cedar Paul. New York: Liveright Pub. Corp., 1949. 505 pp.

Lufkin, Richard Friend, "Mr. Lincoln's Light from under a Bushel—1850." 52 *Lincoln Herald* 2–20 (Dec., 1950).

———, "Mr. Lincoln's Light from under a Bushel—1851." 53 *Lincoln Herald* 2–25 (Winter, [1951]). This issue is misprinted as "Winter 1952."

———, "Mr. Lincoln's Light from under a Bushel—1852." 54 *Lincoln Herald* 2–26 (Winter, 1952).

Luthin, Reinhard H., "Lincoln the Politician." 48 *Lincoln Herald* 2–11 (Feb., 1946).

Macartney, Clarence Edward, *Lincoln and the Bible*. New York: Abingdon-Cokesbury, 1949. 96 pp.

———, *Grant and His Generals*. New York: The McBride Co., 1953. 352 pp.

McClure, Stanley W., *The Lincoln Museum and the House Where Lincoln Died*. Washington: Nat. Park Service, 1949. 42 pp.

McCorison, J. L., Jr., "Mr. Lincoln's Broken Blinds." 50 *Lincoln Herald* 43–46 (June, 1948).

———, "The Great Lincoln Collections and What Became of Them." 50–51 *Lincoln Herald* 2 ff. (Dec., 1948–Feb., 1949).

McGlynn, Frank, *Sidelights on Lincoln*. Los Angeles: Wetzel Pub. Co., 1947. 335 pp.

McMurtry, R. Gerald, *Why Collect Lincolniana?* Chicago: Abraham Lincoln Book Shop, 1948. 19 pp.

———, "The Kentucky Delegation that Attended Lincoln's Funeral, May 3–4, 1865." 53 *Lincoln Herald* 38–40 (Summer, 1951).

———. See also Carruthers, Olive.

Maher, Edward R., Jr., "Sam Houston and Secession." 55 *Southwestern Hist. Quar.* 448–458 (1952).

Malone, Dumas, "Jefferson and Lincoln." 5 *A. L. Q.* 327–347 (1949).

Marsh, Raymond, "Lincoln Patriotics." 52 *Lincoln Herald* 48–53 (Dec., 1950).

Massey, Mary Elizabeth, *Ersatz in the Confederacy.* Columbia: Univ. of South Carolina Press, 1952. 233 pp.

Mayhew, Lewis Baltzell, "The Clay-Thompson Mission into Canada." (MS) A. M. thesis, Univ. of Illinois, Urbana, 1946.

Maynard, Douglas H., "Union Efforts to Prevent the Escape of the *Alabama.*" 41 *M. V. H. R.* 41–60 (1954).

Mearns, David C., "The Lincoln Papers." 4 *A. L. Q.* 369–385 (1947).

——, *The Lincoln Papers.* Garden City: Doubleday & Co., 1948. 2 vols.

——, "Our Reluctant Contemporary: Abraham Lincoln." 6 *A. L. Q.* 73–102 (1950).

Meredith, Roy, *Mr. Lincoln's Camera Man: Mathew B. Brady.* New York: Chas. Scribner's Sons, 1946. 368 pp.

——, *Mr. Lincoln's Contemporaries: An Album of Portraits by Mathew B. Brady.* New York: Chas. Scribner's Sons, 1951. 233 pp.

Merrill, Louis Taylor, "General Benjamin F. Butler in the Presidential Campaign of 1864." 33 *M. V. H. R.* 537–570 (1947).

Miers, Earl Schenck, *The General Who Marched to Hell: William Tecumseh Sherman and His March to Fame and Infamy.* New York: Alfred A. Knopf, 1951. 349 pp.

——, "Lincoln as a Best Seller." 5 *A. L. Q.* 179–190 (1948).

—— and Richard A. Brown, eds., *Gettysburg.* New Brunswick: Rutgers Univ. Press, 1948. 308 pp.

Miller, August C., Jr., "Lincoln's Good-Will Ambassadors." 50 *Lincoln Herald* 17 ff. (June, 1948).

Monaghan, Jay, "Was Abraham Lincoln Really a Spiritualist?" 34 *Jour. Ill. S. H. S.* 209–232 (1941).

——, "Did Abraham Lincoln Receive the Illinois German Vote?" 35 *Jour. Ill. S. H. S.* 133–139 (1942).

——, "The Growth of Abraham Lincoln's Influence in Literature Since His Death." 51 *Lincoln Herald* 2–11 (Oct., 1949).

Moore, Guy W., *The Case of Mrs. Surratt: Her Controversial Trial and Execution for Conspiracy in the Lincoln Assassination.* Norman: Univ. of Oklahoma Press, 1954. 142 pp.

Moran, Benjamin. See Wallace, Sarah A.

Morrow, Hugh. See Carr, R. T.

Nevins, Allan, *Ordeal of the Union.* New York: Chas. Scribner's Sons, 1947–1950. 4 vols.

—— and Milton Halsey Thomas, eds., *The Diary of George Templeton Strong 1835–1875.* New York: The Macmillan Co., 1952. 4 vols.

——, *The Statesmanship of the Civil War.* New York: The Macmillan Co., 1953. 82 pp.

Newman, Ralph. See Eisenschiml, Otto.

Nicolay, Helen, *Lincoln's Secretary: A Biography of John G. Nicolay.* New York: Longmans, Green & Co., 1949. 363 pp.

———, "Lincoln's Cabinet." 5 *A. L. Q.* 255–292 (1949).

Nichols, Roy Franklin, "1461–1861: The American Civil War in Perspective." 16 *Jour. So. Hist.* 143–160 (1950).

Noble, Hollister, *Woman with a Sword.* New York: Doubleday & Co., 1948. 395 pp. A biographical novel about Anna Ella Carroll.

Packard, Roy D., *The Riddle of Lincoln's Religion.* Mansfield, O.: The Midland Rare Book Co., 1946. 12 pp.

———, *The Love Affairs of Abraham Lincoln.* Cleveland: Carpenter Printing Co., 1947. 14 pp.

———, *A. Lincoln: Successful Lawyer.* Cleveland: Carpenter Printing Co., 1948. 14 pp.

———, *The Lincoln of the Thirtieth Congress.* Boston: The Christopher Pub. House, 1950. 52 pp.

Page, Elwin L., "Franklin Pierce and Abraham Lincoln—Parallels and Contrasts." 5 *A. L. Q.* 455–472 (1949).

Parker, Owen W., M. D., "The Assassination and Gunshot Wound of President Abraham Lincoln." 31 *Minnesota Medicine* 147–149 (Feb., 1948).

Parkinson, Robert H., "The Patent Case that Lifted Lincoln into a Presidential Candidate." 4 *A. L. Q* 105–122 (1946).

Pauli, Hertha, *Lincoln's Little Correspondent.* Garden City: Doubleday & Co., 1951. 128 pp.

Peterson, Henry J., "Lincoln at the Wisconsin State Fair as Recalled by John W. Hoyt." 51 *Lincoln Herald* 6–10 (Dec., 1949).

Pollard, James E., *The Presidents and the Press.* New York: The Macmillan Co., 1947. 866 pp.

Pond, Fern Nance, "Two Early Lincoln Surveys." 6 *A. L. Q.* 121–125 (1950).

———, *New Salem Village: Photographic Views and Brief Historical Sketch of New Salem State Park* . . . . Petersburg, Ill.: Ira E. Owen, 1950. 16 pp.

———, "A. L. and David Rutledge." 52 *Lincoln Herald* 18–21 (June, 1950).

———, "New Salem's Miller and Kelso." 52 *Lincoln Herald* 26–41 (Dec., 1950).

Potter, David M., *The Lincoln Theme and American National Historiography.* Oxford: Clarendon Press, 1948. 24 pp.

Pratt, Fletcher, *Stanton: Lincoln's Secretary of War.* New York: W. W. Norton & Co., 1953. 520 pp.

Pratt, Harry E., "Abraham Lincoln in the Black Hawk War," *The John H. Hauberg Historical Essays,* ed. by O. Fritiof Ander. Rock Island, Ill.: Augustana College, 1954. Pp. 18–28.

————, "The Springfield Mechanics Union 1839–1848." 34 *Jour. Ill. S. H. S.* 130–134 (1941).

————, *Lincoln in the Legislature*. Madison: Lincoln Fellowship of Wisconsin, 1947. 16 pp.

————, "A Beginner on the Old Eighth Judicial Circuit." 44 *Jour. Ill. S. H. S.* 241–248 (1951).

————, "Our Growing Knowledge of Lincoln." 39 *Ill. Bar Jour.* 627–629 (1951).

————, "Springfield's Public Square in Lincoln's Day." 40 *Ill. Bar Jour.* 480–488 (1952).

————, "Lincolniana in the Illinois State Historical Library." 46 *Jour. Ill. S. H. S.* 373–400 (1953).

———— and Wayne C. Temple, "James Garfield Randall 1881–1953." 46 *Jour. Ill. S. H. S.* 119–131 (1953). This sketch includes a bibliography of the writings of J. G. Randall.

————, "Lincoln Autographed Debates." 6 *Manuscripts* 194–201 (1954).

Pratt, Marion D. Bonzi. See Basler, Roy P. and Baringer, William E. See also Bonzi, Marion D.

Quarles, Benjamin, *The Negro in the Civil War*. Boston: Little, Brown & Co., 1953. 379 pp.

Randall, J. G., *Lincoln and the South*. Baton Rouge: Louisiana State Univ. Press, 1946. 161 pp.

————, *Lincoln the Liberal Statesman*. New York: Dodd, Mead & Co., 1947. 266 pp.

————, "Lincoln and Thanksgiving." 49 *Lincoln Herald* 10–13 (Oct., 1947).

————, "In Lincoln's Words: Great Issues that Live." *N. Y. Times Mag.*, July 27, 1947, p. 8 ff.

————, "A. Lincoln: A Clearer and Fuller Portrait of Lincoln Is Emerging from a Study of His Papers." *N. Y. Times Mag.*, Aug. 10, 1947, p. 10 ff.

————, "Dear Mr. President." *N. Y. Times Mag.*, Aug. 24, 1947, p. 33.

————, " 'Living with Lincoln'—A New Impression." *N. Y. Times Mag.*, Dec. 14, 1947, p. 13 ff.

————, "The Great Dignity of 'the Rail Splitter.' " *N. Y. Times Mag.*, Feb. 8, 1948, p. 7 ff.

————, *Living with Lincoln and Other Essays*. Decatur, Ill.: Tippett Press, [1949]. 34 pp. The title page is in error, listing the date as "1948."

————, "President Lincoln: Tactician of Human Relations." 28 *Elks Mag.* 10 ff. (1950).

————, *Constitutional Problems under Lincoln*. Urbana: Univ. of Illinois Press, 1951. Revised edition. 596 pp.

————, Lincoln and the Governance of Men." 6 *A. L. Q.* 327–352 (1951).

Randall, Ruth Painter, *Mary Lincoln: Biography of a Marriage*. Boston: Little, Brown & Co., 1953. 555 pp.

Rawley, James A., "Lincoln and Governor Morgan." 6 *A. L. Q.* 272–300 (1951).

Renne, Louis Obed, *Lincoln and the Land of the Sangamon.* Boston: Chapman & Grimes, 1945. 140 pp.

Richardson, Harriet Fyffe, *Quaker Pioneers.* Milwaukee: Privately printed, 1940. 129 pp. Treats Lincoln's friendship with Jesse W. Fell.

Richardson, Robert Dale, *Abraham Lincoln's Autobiography: With an Account of Its Origin and History and Additional Biographical Material.* Boston: The Beacon Press, 1947. 45 pp.

Riddle, Donald W., *Lincoln Runs for Congress.* New Brunswick: Rutgers Univ. Press, 1948. 217 pp.

Ridley, M. R., *Abraham Lincoln.* London: Blackie & Son Limited, 1944. 208 pp.

Roberts, Octavia, "We All Knew Abr'ham." 4 *A. L. Q.* 17–29 (1946).

Robinson, William M., Jr., *Justice in Grey: A History of the Judicial System of the Confederate States of America.* Cambridge: Harvard Univ. Press, 1941. 713 pp.

Roseboom, Eugene H., "Southern Ohio and the Union in 1863." 39 *M. V. H. R.* 29–44 (1952).

Roske, Ralph J., "The Post Civil War Career of Lyman Trumbull." (MS) Ph. D. thesis, Univ. of Ill., Urbana, 1949.

———, "Lincoln's Peace Puff." 6 *A. L. Q.* 239–245 (1950).

Ross, Earle D., "Lincoln and National Security." 22 *Social Science* 80–85 (Jan., 1947).

Russell, Don, "Lincoln Was Tough on Officers." 34 *Jour. Ill. S. H. S.* 344–348 (1941).

———, "Lincoln Raises an Army." 50 *Lincoln Herald* 2–16 (June, 1948).

Sandburg, Carl and J. G. Randall, 'Lincoln Reprimand Becomes a Classic." *Chicago Sun and Times,* Oct. 5, 1947, p. 32.

———, *Lincoln Collector: The Story of Oliver R. Barrett's Great Private Collection.* New York: Harcourt, Brace & Co., 1949. 344 pp.

———, "Abraham Lincoln." 179 *Atl. Mo.* 62–65 (Feb., 1947).

———, *Abraham Lincoln: The Prairie Years and the War Years.* One-volume edition. New York: Harcourt, Brace & Co., 1954. 762 pp.

Santovenia, Emerterio S., *Lincoln in Marti: A Cuban View of Abraham Lincoln.* Trans. by Donald F. Fogelquist. Chapel Hill: Univ. of North Carolina Press, 1953. 75 pp.

Scanlan, V. M., "A Southerner's View of Abraham Lincoln." 43 *Ind. Mag. Hist.* 141–158 (1947).

Schaefer, Carl W., "Lincoln, the Lawyer." 51 *Lincoln Herald* 10–16 (June, 1949).

Schlesinger, Arthur M., Jr., "The Causes of the Civil War: A Note on Historical Sentimentalism." 16 *Partisan Review* 969–981 (1949).

Scott, Kenneth, "Lincoln's Home in 1860." 46 *Jour. Ill. S. H. S.* 7–12 (1953).

Searcy, Earle Benjamin, "A Dead Pig Goes to Court—With Lincoln." 51 *Lincoln Herald* 26–28 (Oct., 1949).

———, "The Lincoln Voice." 51 *Lincoln Herald* 28 (Oct., 1949).

Segal, Charles M., "Lincoln, Benjamin Jonas and the Black Code." 46 *Jour. Ill. S. H. S.* 277–282 (1953).

Seiler, Grace, "Walt Whitman and Abraham Lincoln." 52 *Lincoln Herald* 42 ff. (Dec., 1950).

Shaw, Archer H., ed., *The Lincoln Encyclopedia: The Spoken and Written Words of A. Lincoln* . . . . New York: The Macmillan Co., 1950. 395 pp.

Shutes, Milton H., "Republican Nominating Convention of 1860: A California Report." 27 *Cal. Hist. Soc. Quar.* 97–103 (1948).

———, "The Happy Lincoln." 53 *Lincoln Herald* 19–22 (Spring, 1951).

Sigaud, Louis A., "When Belle Boyd Wrote Lincoln." 50 *Lincoln Herald* 15–22 (Feb., 1948).

Silver, David Mayer, "The Supreme Court during the Civil War." Doctoral dissertation (MS), Univ. of Ill., 1940.

Singmaster, Elsie, *I Speak for Thaddeus Stevens*. Cambridge: Houghton Mifflin Co., 1948. 446 pp.

Simpson, Capt. E. J. See "John, Evan."

Skinner, James G., "Lincoln the Strategist Statesman." 36 *Ill. Bar Jour.* 506 ff. (1948).

Smith, Bethania Meradith, "Civil War Subversives." 45 *Jour. Ill. S. H. S.* 220–240 (1952).

Smith, George Winston, "Some Northern Wartime Attitudes toward the Post-Civil War South." 10 *Jour. So. Hist.* 253–274 (1944).

———, "New England Business Interests in Missouri during the Civil War." 41 *Mo. Hist. Rev.* 1–18 (1946).

———, "The National War Committee of the Citizens of New York." 28 *N. Y. Hist.* 440–458 (1947).

———, "Broadsides for Freedom: Civil War Propaganda in New England." 21 *New Eng. Quar.* 291–312 (1948).

Smith, T. V., *Abraham Lincoln and the Spiritual Life*. Boston: The Beacon Press, 1951. 95 pp.

Smith, Willard H., *Schuyler Colfax: The Changing Fortunes of a Political Idol*. Indianapolis: Indiana Hist. Bureau, 1952. 475 pp.

Snigg, John P., "The Great Prairie Lawyer." 37 *Ill. Bar Jour.* 234–235 (1949).

———, "A Real Lincoln Pilgrimage." 51 *Lincoln Herald* 47–48 (June, 1949).

———, "Edward Dickinson Baker—Lincoln's Forgotten Friend." 53 *Lincoln Herald* 33–37 (Summer, 1951).

Spears, Zarel C. and Robert S. Barton, *Berry and Lincoln, Frontier Merchants: The Store that "Winked Out."* New York: Stratford House, 1947. 140 pp.

Squires, J. Duane, "Some Enduring Achievements of the Lincoln Administration, 1861–1865." 5 *A. L. Q.* 191–211 (1948).

Stampp, Kenneth M., "Lincoln and the Strategy of Defense in the Crisis of 1861." 11 *Jour. So. Hist.* 297–323 (1945).

———, *Indiana Politics during the Civil War.* Indianapolis: Ind. Hist. Bureau, 1949. 300 pp.

———, *And the War Came: The North and the Secession Crisis, 1860–1861.* Baton Rouge: Louisiana State Univ. Press, 1950. 331 pp.

———, "The Historian and Southern Negro Slavery." 57 *A. H. R.* 613–624 (1952).

Stanton, Edward M. See Pratt, Fletcher.

Starr, Thomas I., "The Detroit River and Abraham Lincoln." 3 *Bulletin of Detroit Hist. Soc.* 4–6 (Feb., 1947).

Steen, Ralph W., "Texas Newspapers and Lincoln." 51 *Southwestern Hist. Quar.* 199–212 (1948).

Stoddard, William O., Jr., "Face to Face with Lincoln." 135 *Atl. Mo.* 332–339 (1925).

Strong, George Templeton. See Nevins, Allan.

Stutler, Boyd B., " 'We Are Coming, Father Abra'am.' " 53 *Lincoln Herald* 2–13 (Summer, 1951).

Sumner, G. Lynn, *Meet Abraham Lincoln: Profiles of the Prairie President.* Chicago: Privately printed for Abraham Lincoln Book Shop, 1946. 78 pp.

Taylor, Edgar C., "Lincoln the Internationalist." 4 *A. L. Q.* 59–79 (1946).

Tegeder, Vincent G., "Lincoln and the Territorial Patronage: The Ascendancy of the Radicals in the West." 35 *M. V. H. R.* 77–90 (1948).

Temple, Wayne C., "The Date of the Alschuler Ambrotype of Lincoln." 6 *A. L. Q.* 446–447 (1951).

———, "Lincoln's Fence Rails." 47 *Jour. Ill. S. H. S.* 20–34 (1954).

———. See also Pratt, Harry E.

Thomas, Benjamin P., *Portrait for Posterity: Lincoln and His Biographers.* New Brunswick: Rutgers Univ. Press, 1947. 329 pp.

———, "Our Lincoln Heritage from Ida Tarbell." 6 *A. L. Q.* 3–23 (1950).

———, *Theodore Weld: Crusader for Freedom.* New Brunswick: Rutgers Univ. Press, 1950. 307 pp.

———, *Abraham Lincoln: A Biography.* New York: Alfred A. Knopf, 1952. 548 pp. This is the best one-volume biography of Lincoln.

———, *Lincoln's New Salem.* New York: Alfred A. Knopf, 1954. 166 pp. Revised edition.

———, "Abe Lincoln: Country Lawyer." 193 *Atl. Mo.* 57–61 (1954).

Thomas, Milton Halsey. See Nevins, Allan.

Thornbrough, Emma Lou, "The Race Issue in Indiana Politics during the Civil War." 47 *Ind. Mag. Hist.* 165–188 (1951).

Townsend, William H., *Abraham Lincoln, Defendant: Lincoln's Most Interesting Lawsuit.* Boston: Houghton Mifflin Co., 1923. 40 pp.

——, "Bullard's Bixby Book." 48 *Lincoln Herald* 2–10 (Oct., 1946).

——, " 'The Sage of Lion's Den:' A Review and Rejoinder." 51 *Lincoln Herald* 40–44 (Dec., 1949).

Turner, George Edgar, *Victory Rode the Rails: The Strategic Place of the Railroads in the Civil War*. Indianapolis: Bobbs-Merrill Co., 1953. 419 pp.

Vandiver, Frank E., *Ploughshares into Swords: Josiah Gorgas and Confederate Ordnance*. Austin: Univ. of Texas Press, 1952. 349 pp.

Vasvary, Edmund, *Lincoln's Hungarian Heroes: The Participation of Hungarians in the Civil War, 1861–1865*. Washington: Hungarian Reformed Federation of America, 1939. 171 pp.

Voigt, David Quentin, " 'Too Pitchy to Touch'—President Lincoln and Editor Bennett." 6 *A. L. Q.* 139–161 (1950).

Wagenknecht, Edward, ed., *Abraham Lincoln, His Life, Work, and Character: An Anthology of History and Biography, Fiction, Poetry, Drama, and Belles-Lettres*. New York: Creative Age Press, 1947. 661 pp.

Wallace, Sarah A. and Frances E. Gillespie, eds., *The Journal of Benjamin Moran 1857–1865*. Chicago: Univ. of Chicago Press, 1948–1949. 2 vols.

Warren, Louis A., *Abraham Lincoln's Gettysburg Address: An Evaluation*. Columbus, O.: Charles E. Merrill Co., 1946. 32 pp.

——, *Sifting the Herndon Sources*. Los Angeles: Lincoln Fellowship of Southern California, 1948. 19 pp.

——, "Herndon's Contribution to Lincoln Mythology." 41 *Ind. Mag. Hist.* 221–244 (1945).

——, "The Woman in Lincoln's Life—With Special Emphasis on Her Cultural Attainments." 20 *The Filson Club Hist. Quar.* 207–219 (1946).

Wayland, John W., *The Lincolns in Virginia*. Staunton, Va.: John W. Wayland, 1946. 299 pp.

Weber, Thomas, *The Northern Railroads in the Civil War, 1861–1865*. New York: Columbia Univ. Press, 1952. 318 pp.

Weisberger, Bernard A., *Reporters for the Union*. Boston: Little, Brown & Co., 1953. 316 pp.

Wessen, Ernest J., "Debates of Lincoln and Douglas—A Bibliographical Discussion." 40 *The Papers of the Bibliographical Soc. of America* 91–106 (1946).

Wheare, K. C., *Abraham Lincoln and the United States*. New York: The Macmillan Co., 1949. 286 pp.

Whitton, Mary Ormsbee, *First First Ladies, 1789–1865: A Study of the Early Presidents*. New York: Hastings House, 1948. 341 pp.

Wiel, Samuel C., *Lincoln's Crisis in the Far West*. San Francisco: Privately printed, 1949. 130 pp.

Wiley, Bell Irvin, *The Life of Johnny Reb: The Common Soldier of the Confederacy*. Indianapolis: Bobbs-Merrill Co., 1943. 444 pp.

——, "Billy Yank and Abraham Lincoln." 6 *A. L. Q.* 103–120 (1950).

———, *The Life of Billy Yank: The Common Soldier of the Union.* Indianapolis: Bobbs-Merrill Co., 1952. 454 pp.

Wiley, Earl W., " 'Governor' John Greiner and Chase's Bid for the Presidency in 1860." 58 *Ohio Arch. and Hist. Quar.* 245–273 (1949).

———, "Ohio Pre-Convention Support for Lincoln in 1860." 52 *Lincoln Herald* 13–17 (June, 1950).

———, "Behind Lincoln's Visit to Ohio in 1859." 60 *Ohio Arch. and Hist. Quar.* 28–47 (1951).

Williams, Kenneth P., *Lincoln Finds a General: A Military Study of the Civil War.* New York: The Macmillan Co., 1949–1952. 3 vols.

———, "The Tennessee River Campaign and Anna Ella Carroll." 46 *Ind. Mag. Hist.* 221–248 (1950).

———, Review of *Anna Ella Carroll and Abraham Lincoln.* 54 *Lincoln Herald* 54–56 (Summer, 1952). In this issue, pages 54 and 10 are interchanged in the magazine.

Williams, T. Harry, "The Committee on the Conduct of the War: An Experiment in Civilian Control." 3 *Jour. Am. Military Institute* 139–156 (1939).

———, "The Attack upon West Point during the Civil War." 25 *M. V. H. R.* 491–504 (1939).

———, "Voters in Blue: The Citizen Soldiers of the Civil War." 31 *M. V. H. R.* 187–204 (1944).

———, *Lincoln and His Generals.* New York: Alfred A. Knopf, 1952. 363 pp.

———, "Abraham Lincoln—Principle and Pragmatism in Politics: A Review Article." 40 *M. V. H. R.* 89–106 (1953).

William, Wayne C., *A Rail Splitter for President.* Denver: Univ. of Denver Press, 1951. 242 pp.

Wilson, Rufus Rockwell, "Abraham Lincoln and Ben Montgomery." 48 *Lincoln Herald* 2–5 (Dec., 1946).

———, "Mr. Lincoln's First Appointment to the Supreme Court." 50–51 *Lincoln Herald* 26 ff. (Dec., 1948–Feb., 1949).

———, "President Lincoln and Preacher Luckett." 51 *Lincoln Herald* 42–43 (June, 1949).

———, "President Lincoln and Emancipation." 51 *Lincoln Herald* 43–46 (June, 1949).

———, *Lincoln in Caricature.* New York: Horizon Press, 1953. 327 pp.

Wingfield, Marshall, "The Likeness of Lincoln and Lee." 49 *Lincoln Herald* 21–26 (Feb., 1947).

Woldman, Albert A., *Lincoln and the Russians.* Cleveland: World Pub. Co., 1952. 311 pp.

———, "Lincoln Never Said That." 200 *Harper's Mag.* 70–74 (May, 1950).

Wolf, Hazel Catherine, *On Freedom's Altar: The Martyr Complex in the Abolition Movement.* Madison: Univ. of Wisconsin Press, 1952. 195 pp.

————. See also Hesseltine, William B.

Woodward, William E., *Years of Madness: A Reappraisal of the Civil War.*
New York: G. P. Putnam's Sons, 1951. 311 pp.

Zornow, William Frank, "The Attitude of the Western Reserve Press on
the Re-Election of Lincoln." 50 *Lincoln Herald* 35–39 (June, 1948).

————, "Indiana and the Election of 1864." 45 *Ind. Mag. Hist.* 13–38
(1949).

————, "Treason as a Campaign Issue in the Re-Election of Lincoln." 5
A. L. Q. 348–363 (1949).

————, "Lincoln's Influence in the Election of 1864." 51 *Lincoln Herald*
22–32 (June, 1949).

————, "Lincoln and Chase: Presidential Rivals." 52 *Lincoln Herald* 17–
28; 6–12 (Feb.–June, 1950).

————, "The Missouri Radicals and the Election of 1864." 45 *Mo. Hist.
Rev.* 354–370 (1951).

————, "The Unwanted Mr. Lincoln." 45 *Jour. Ill. S. H. S.* 146–163 (1952).

————, "The Democratic Convention at Chicago in 1864." 54 *Lincoln
Herald* 2–[10] (Summer, 1952).

————, *Lincoln and the Party Divided.* Norman: Univ. of Oklahoma Press,
1954. 264 pp.

INDEX

University of Illinois Press
1325 South Oak Street
Champaign, IL 61820-6903

www.press.uillinois.edu